Science, Strategy

MW00475972

John Boyd is often known exclusively for the so-called 'OODA' loop model he developed. This model refers to a decision-making process and to the idea that military victory goes to the side that can complete the cycle from observation to action the fastest. This book aims to redress this state of affairs and re-examines John Boyd's original contribution to strategic theory. By highlighting diverse sources that shaped Boyd's thinking, and by offering a comprehensive overview of Boyd's work, this volume demonstrates that the common interpretation of the meaning of Boyd's OODA loop concept is incomplete. It also shows that Boyd's work is much more comprehensive, richer and deeper than is generally thought. With his ideas featuring in the literature on Network Centric Warfare, a key element of the US and NATO's so-called 'military transformation' programmes, as well as in the debate on Fourth Generation Warfare, Boyd continues to exert a strong influence on Western military thinking. Dr Osinga demonstrates how Boyd's work can help us to understand the new strategic threats in the post-9/11 world, and establishes why John Boyd should be regarded as one of the most important (post)modern strategic theorists.

Frans P.B. Osinga is a serving officer of the Royal Netherlands Air Force, a former F-16 pilot, and a graduate of the Royal Netherlands Military Academy and the Netherlands Defence College. He completed this study while serving as the Netherlands MoD Senior Research Fellow at the Clingendael Institute of International Relations in The Hague. He is currently stationed at the NATO Headquarters of the Supreme Allied Command Transformation in Norfolk, Virginia.

Series: strategy and history
Edited by Colin Gray and Williamson Murray
ISSN: 1473-6403

This new series will focus on the theory and practice of strategy. Following Clausewitz, strategy has been understood to mean the use made of force, and the threat of the use of force, for the ends of policy. This series is as interested in ideas as in historical cases of grand strategy and military strategy in action. All historical periods, near and past, and even future, are of interest. In addition to original monographs, the series will from time to time publish edited reprints of neglected classics as well as collections of essays.

Science, Strategy and War

The strategic theory of John Boyd

Frans P.B. Osinga

LONDON AND NEW YORK

First published 2007
by Routledge
2 Park Square, Milton Park, Abingdon, Oxon, OX14 4RN

Simultaneously published in the USA and Canada
by Routledge
270 Madison Ave, New York NY 10016

Routledge is an imprint of the Taylor & Francis Group, an informa business

Transferred to Digital Printing 2007

© 2007 Frans P.B. Osinga

Typeset in Times by Wearset Ltd, Boldon, Tyne and Wear

British Library Cataloguing in Publication Data
A catalogue record for this book is available from the British Library

Library of Congress Cataloging in Publication Data
A catalog record for this book has been requested

ISBN10: 0-415-37103-1 (hbk)
ISBN10: 0-415-45952-4 (pbk)
ISBN10: 0-203-08886-7 (ebk)

ISBN13: 978-0-415-37103-2 (hbk)
ISBN13: 978-0-415-45952-5 (pbk)
ISBN13: 978-0-203-08886-9 (ebk)

For Ankie, Timon, Femmeke and Minke.
Who else?

We are survival machines.

Richard Dawkins

Strategy is the mode of survival of a society.

Henry Kissinger

He who can handle the quickest rate of change survives.

John Boyd

Contents

Figures

Boxes

Acknowledgments

This book took off during my stay at the School of Advanced Airpower Studies in 1998–99. Thanks in particular to professor Dennis Drew, my mentor at SAAS who said 'I think you're on to something', thus providing me with the necessary dose of self-confidence for embarking on the academic trail. The Clingendael Institute of International Relations in The Hague has been my home from 2000 till 2005. A special word of appreciation for Professor Alfred van Staden, then director of the Clingendael Institute, for maintaining faith in the project, for his broad perspective, as well as for his patience. From the head of the research department, Professor Jan Rood, I received more latitude to conduct research in a wide variety of topics than I could have wished for. Professor Rob de Wijk, director of the Clingendael Center for Strategic Studies, has assisted me throughout the development of this book with frequent pointed remarks. I have also sincerely benefited from the personal encouragement and support I received from the senior leadership of the Royal Netherlands Air Force in the past decade. I am deeply indebted to LtGen Droste, LtGen Berlijn, LtGen Starink, MGen Hilderink, MGen Melker, and MGen Meulman. I am grateful also to LtCol. Paul Ducheine and Col. Peter Wijninga, who have been brothers in intellectual arms in the past years. I would like to thank Barry Watts, Chet Richards and Dick Safranski for providing me with very valuable comments and suggestions on various drafts of this book, based on their personal acquaintance with John Boyd. Mary Holton-Boyd was very kind in permitting me to incorporate slides from Boyd's work, which greatly help in explaining his ideas. The final word of gratitude goes to professor Grant Hammond, of the Center for Strategy and Technology of the Air War College, and author of the first Boyd biography. He has been the mental and moral driving force in the development of this book since 1999. Indeed, I even owe the title of the book to him.

1   Introduction

> To flourish and grow in a many-sided uncertain and ever changing world that surrounds us, suggests that we have to make intuitive within ourselves those many practices we need to meet the exigencies of that world. The contents that comprise this 'Discourse' unfold observations and ideas that contribute towards achieving or thwarting such an aim or purpose.
>
> John Boyd, *A Discourse*, p. 1

Introducing *A Discourse*

This book aims to provide a better understanding of the strategic thought developed by John Boyd. He has exerted a very substantial influence on recent military thinking in the western world, and continues to do so. On the other hand, his work has invited dismissive critique. Despite this situation, however, there is as of yet no comprehensive study concerning his ideas.

Most people associate Boyd with the so called 'OODA loop', where 'OODA' is generally understood to stand for observation, orientation, decision and action. The idea has gained currency that the OODA loop is the equivalent of a decision cycle. Subsequently, war can be construed of as a collision of organizations going through their respective OODA loops, or decision cycles. In the popularized interpretation, the OODA loop suggests that success in war depends on the ability to out-pace and out-think the opponent, or put differently, on the ability to go through the OODA cycle more rapidly than the opponent. In simplified form, it looks like Figure 1.1.

Few are familiar with the source of the OODA loop: *A Discourse on Winning and Losing. A Discourse* consists of four briefings and an essay. The set has also been labelled as *The Green Book*. It was completed in 1987, although subsequently frequently the specific wording on slides was revised. The essay *Destruction and Creation* was written in 1976. It is a window to Boyd's mind, according to Robert Coram, one of his two biographers.[1] In it Boyd states that uncertainty is a fundamental and irresolvable characteristic of our lives, no matter how good our observations and theories for explanation are.

Patterns of Conflict forms the historical heart of the work. First draft completed in 1977, it has turned into the opus of Boyd's research on conflict and

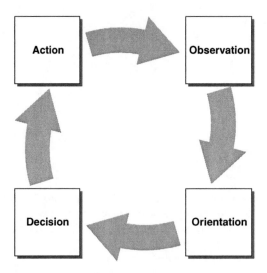

Figure 1.1 Simplified drawing of the OODA loop.

warfare, containing 193 slides. It is a historical analysis of warfare and theories for victory and represents, in Boyd's own words, 'a compendium of ideas and actions for winning and losing in a highly competitive world'.[2] It also contains an introduction to the OODA loop or the 'Boyd Cycle'.

In the presentations *Organic Design for Command and Control* (first draft 1982) and the one intriguingly titled *The Strategic Game of ? and ?* (first draft 1986), he uses insights and conclusions from *Patterns of Conflict* but now in abstract form. He employs these abstractions to develop arguments about leadership and about the essence of strategy, or in Boyd's own description: *Organic Design for Command and Control* 'surfaces the implicit arrangements that permit cooperation in complex, competitive, fast moving situations', while *The Strategic Game of ? and ?* emphasizes 'the mental twists and turns we undertake to surface appropriate schemes or designs for realizing our aims or purposes'.[3] The last very brief presentation, *Revelation* 'makes visible the metaphorical message that flows from this *Discourse*'.

In addition to these briefings he developed three pieces that need to be considered as well for a proper understanding of Boyd's work. While working his essay he also finished a presentation titled *A New Conception of Air to Air Combat*, showing a close relation with the essay and foreshadowing several ideas he was to explore in *Patterns of Conflict*. It is the conceptual bridge between his fighter pilot background and his maturation as a strategic thinker. He also developed two other briefings that are not an integral part of *The Green Book* but are fully in line with, and an elaboration on previous arguments. *The Conceptual Spiral* was completed in 1992. It is a different rendition of arguments, themes and insights he advanced earlier in *Destruction and Creation* now employed to explain how and why innovation occurs in science, engineering and technology. Boyd argues that the dynamics at play here hold universal validity for all types of organizations that strive to survive under conditions of fundamental and unavoidable uncertainty. The final briefing is titled *The Essence of Winning and Losing*, which is a very condensed rendering of Boyd's core ideas. Completed in 1995, only in this short presentation does Boyd offer a picture of the OODA loop, and in a much more elaborated rendition than shown in Figure 1.1.

'A towering figure'

Some regard Boyd as the most important strategist of the twentieth century, or even since Sun Tzu.[4] James Burton claims that '*A Discourse on Winning and Losing* will go down in history as the twentieth century's most original thinking in the military arts. No one, not even Karl von Clausewitz, Henri de Jomini, Sun Tzu, or any of the past masters of military theory, shed as much light on the mental and moral aspects of conflict as Boyd.'[5] Colin Gray has ranked Boyd among the outstanding general theorists of strategy of the twentieth century, along with the likes of Bernard Brodie, Edward Luttwak, Basil Liddell Hart and John Wylie, stating that

> John Boyd deserves at least an honorable mention for his discovery of the 'OODA loop' ... allegedly comprising a universal logic of conflict.... Boyd's loop can apply to the operational, strategic, and political levels of war.... The OODA loop may appear too humble to merit categorization as grand theory, but that is what it is. It has an elegant simplicity, an extensive domain of applicability, and contains a high quality of insight about strategic essentials....[6]

Boyd's influence first became apparent during the late 1970s and 1980s in the development of what later turned out to be the AirLand Battle concept.[7] Later, the US Marine Corps incorporated Boyd's ideas into their new fighting manuals. In the US Joint Chiefs of Staff Publication, JP 3–13.1, Joint doctrine for Command and Control Warfare (C2W) the OODA loop is included in Appendix A (without however mentioning Boyd's name anywhere). Outside the US too, his influence is demonstrable. For instance, the UK military doctrine description of the doctrinally preferred method of war fighting, 'the maneuvrist approach' is also pure Boyd (and fully in line with the US Marines doctrine):

> The maneuvrist approach to operations is one in which shattering the enemy's overall cohesion and will to fight, rather than his materiel is paramount [...] significant features are momentum and tempo, which in combination lead to shock and surprise. Emphasis is on the defeat and disruption of the enemy – by taking the initiative, and applying constant and unacceptable pressure at the times and places the enemy least expects – rather than attempting to seize and hold ground for its own sake. It calls for an attitude

of mind in which doing the unexpected and seeking originality is combined with ruthless determination to succeed. A key characteristic of the maneuvrist approach is to attack the enemy commander's decision process by attempting to get inside his decision making cycle. This involves presenting him with the need to make decisions at a faster rate than he can cope with, so that he takes increasingly inappropriate action or none at all, thereby paralyzing his capability to react. Clearly any degradation of the overall command system which can be achieved by physical or other means will hasten the onset of paralysis.[8]

His influence extends into weapon systems and recent military operations. The 1991 Gulf War air campaign employed F-16, F-18 and F-15 aircraft, fighters that Boyd helped create during the 1960s and 1970s. The war itself is by some considered a validation of the innovation in operational theory and praxis that matured in AirLand Battle.[9] In fact, Boyd has been credited with directly influencing the design of the military ground campaign through his association with Dick Cheney, then US Secretary of Defense, a former member of the so-called Military Reform Group, who was well versed in Boyd's military thinking. In the May 6, 1991 issue of *US News & World Report* Boyd was mentioned, together with two officers who were directly influenced by Boyd, as the persons who determined the tactics employed during the Gulf War.[10]

In the aftermath of the terrorist attacks of September 11 2001, US Secretary of State and former chairman of the US Joint Chiefs of Staff Colin Powell implicitly honored Boyd by talking of a response involving multiple thrusts and getting inside the adversary's decision cycle.[11] In the 1990s his ideas were incorporated in various European military doctrines, while the concept of Network Centric Warfare, a key theme of US and NATO military transformation initiatives ongoing since 2002, surfaces many themes central to Boyd's work. Looking back on the stunning victory of Operation Iraqi Freedom (2003) against substantial Iraqi armed forces, the commander of the coalition troops, General Tommy Franks also referred explicitly to Boyd's idea of getting inside the enemy's decision cycle.[12] This indicates that Boyd's concepts and terminology have become mainstream in the Western militaries, and will also be employed for the security challenges of the twenty-first century.[13]

And his fame has not been confined to military strategy. The OODA Loop has even been discussed in *Forbes* and *Harvard Business Review*.[14] In fact, Figure 1.1 and a discussion of the OODA loop appear in *Competing Against Time*, a book on management.[15] In addition, Tom Peters, author of *Thriving on Chaos*, a book that revolutionized management theories in America, talks of creating and exploiting chaos, of shaping the marketplace and of mutual trust. Peters admitted that his book had been shaped by Boyd's ideas. Since then Boyd's ideas have been applied by consultants and have been taught at business schools, with the active endorsement of Boyd, who considered this an affirmation of the fact that his intellectual legacy encompassed more than war fighting; his ideas were universal, timeless, and could be applied to any form of conflict.[16]

The tribute written two days after Boyd's death by General C.C. Krulak, then Commandant of the US Marine Corps, reflects the view shared by many that Boyd was

> a towering intellect who made unsurpassed contributions to the American art of war. Indeed, he was one of the central architects in the reform of military thought which swept the services, and in particular the Marine Corps, in the 1980's. From John Boyd we learned about the competitive decision making on the battlefield – compressing time, using time as an ally. Thousands of officers in all of the services knew John Boyd by his work on what was to be known as the Boyd Cycle or OODA loop. His writings and his lectures had a fundamental impact on the curriculum of virtually every professional military education program in the United States – and many abroad [. . .] he was the quintessential soldier-scholar – a man whose jovial outgoing exterior belied the vastness of his knowledge and the power of his intellect.[17]

'Deeply flawed'

Controversy and misperception nevertheless surround Boyd's work. Like Clausewitz and Sun Tzu, his work is more heard of than read or understood. Very few people have actually worked their way through the presentations. Instead, the neat graphical depiction of the OODA loop has become the symbol of Boyd's entire work, indeed, it is often regarded as *the* concise representation of his ideas. One expert, for instance, asserts that 'Boyd's theory claims that the key advantage to success in conflict is to operate inside the opponent's decision cycle. Advantages in observation and orientation enable a tempo in decision making and execution that outpaces the ability of the foe to react effectively in time.'[18] And in 1996 this interpretation of the OODA loop was incorporated in, and elevated to, long-term US defense policy when the Joint Chiefs of Staff 1996 document Joint Vision 2010 stated that US Forces will gain 'OODA-loop dominance', being able to 'observe, orient, decide, and act much more quickly than our opponents'.[19]

This particular view on Boyd's work has inspired critique. To be sure, some offer assessments based on a somewhat wider appreciation of Boyd. Colin Gray regards the ideas of Boyd as constituting a general theory of conflict. Others discuss his ideas in particular within the framework of operational level doctrine of warfare, regarding his work as the conceptual foundation of maneuver warfare.[20] Some others dismiss Boyd's ideas on the grounds that they are rather underdeveloped and too theoretical, pointing to the fact that, unlike Baron de Jomini or, more recently, air-power theorist John Warden, Boyd's notions remain too vague to amount to anything other than a moving target of little use in structuring a debate or attempting to educate one's mind on the nature of war before arriving at the battlefield.[21]

But frequently, discussions concerning the merits of Boyd's work focus solely on the merits of the OODA cycle idea, with one school suggesting that cycling through the OODA loop faster than the opponent will result in a decisive advantage.[22] In contrast, in an article that critiques the US dogmatic belief in the value of speed, one author blames the idea that 'quicker decisions often led to victory', attributing this to Boyd's influence. He argues that this idea has permeated US military thinking, in particular the US Marines who hold that 'warfare is necessarily a function of decision making and, whoever can make and implement decisions consistently faster gains a tremendous, often decisive advantage. Decision making in execution thus becomes a time-competitive process, and timeliness of decisions becomes essential to generating tempo.'[23] Alternatively, commentators doubt the relevance of the rapid OODA loop idea for strategic and political level decision making, or for understanding command and control processes.[24] In addition, some point out that the enemy may not be interested in rapid OODA looping, on the contrary, as in the case of guerrilla warfare, prolonging a conflict and stretching out time may be quite rational. One author even denied that anything like an OODA loop exists, pointing the finger at the methodological error Boyd and his associates made in extrapolating from what holds true for fighter operations, from where Boyd derived his insight, to hold also true for command and control in general. As he states:

> The OODA Loop suggests that the process of observation, orientation, decision and action is a circular, iterative process. Military advantage accrues from being able to go around the loop faster than one's opponent. However, the OODA process is not circular. It apparently takes 24 hours to execute a divisional operation. Planning takes a minimum of 12 hours. Thus a divisional OODA loop would have to be at least 36 hours long. Yet the Gulf War and other recent operations show divisions reacting far faster. Military forces do not in practice wait to observe until they have acted. Observation, orientation and action are continuous processes, and decisions are made occasionally in consequences of them. There is no OODA loop. The idea of getting inside the enemy decision cycle is deeply flawed.[25]

Aim and argument

An obvious major factor that contributes to the variety of interpretations is the fact that his ideas have been conveyed through, and contained in, presentations he gave, instead of a coherent book-length study (a state of affairs comparable with the famous work of Sun Tzu). Frequently he changed these presentations when the discussions with the audience, or some new books he had read, had provided him with new or improved insights. Despite the fact that he gave some parts of his briefings about 1,500 times not many people outside the American military community have had the opportunity to attend his lectures, which sometimes lasted 14 to 18 hours.[26] And John Boyd died on 9 March 1997 at the age of seventy. There will be no more Boyd briefings. So if one wants to read Boyd's mind and study his work, this loose collection is all that is left to read. Moreover, his slides exist in different versions, for as recently as the summer of 1995,

Boyd made his last update of his presentations. The stack of slides is not really widely or easily available to the wider public, they have not been officially published, nor are they in themselves self-explanatory throughout. Indeed, his briefings are virtually impenetrable without explanation, Coram asserts.[27]

There is thus a need for a detailed account of his work that stays close to the original and offers a readable version. There are a number of short papers.[28] Most, if not all, deal almost exclusively with the OODA loop concept. Recently, two biographies have appeared, but neither contains an integral rendering of Boyd's work, nor does the educational experience contained within Boyd's slides, his unique use of words and the way he structures his arguments, receive sufficient attention.[29]

In light of the incomplete and contradicting interpretations, and the absence of an accepted authoritive and comprehensive account of Boyd's work, this study aims to develop a comprehensive interpretation of John Boyd's strategic theory. It argues that Boyd's OODA loop concept, as well as his entire work are more comprehensive, deeper and richer than the popular notion of 'rapid OODA looping' his work is generally equated with.

The general perception of what Boyd argues, laid out above, is not so much wrong as it is incomplete. First, the illustration of the OODA-loop included at the beginning of this chapter, which features in a host of publications, is actually a very simplified rendering of a much more complex and informative graphic Boyd developed and included in his work. This simplified version tends towards an exclusive focus on speed of decision making, while obscuring various other themes, theories and arguments that lie behind and are incorporated in it. Simply put, the OODA loop idea as advanced by Boyd says much more than 'just' going through the decision cycle more rapidly than one's opponent, and subsequent critique of Boyd's work should therefore be based not on the simplified model but on the comprehensive picture painted by Boyd himself, as well as on the discussions that preceded the birth of this complex picture.

Second, while acknowledging the relevance and originality of the OODA loop idea, it would be a loss if that were all that was remembered of his ideas, for Boyd's work shows a richness in ideas and a freshness in approach. *A Discourse* is not only about tactical and operational level war fighting. Not only does Boyd address a vision of the proper organizational culture for armed forces, *A Discourse* is also about organizational agility, about the creation of organizations in general, from tactical units, army corps, armed forces, guerrilla bands, businesses, to nation-states and societies, that are adaptive, that can survive and prosper.

Third, the value of Boyd's work lies in great measure in the way he constructs his argument, in the sources that he uses and in the argument he develops concerning the nature of strategic thinking. The value of Boyd's work lies as much in his slides as in the approach he followed in developing it. Ultimately his aim was not to convince people about the validity of this or that doctrine, but instead to create among his audience a way of thinking, a thought process.[30] Boyd would agree with the statement that the message, the relevant part of his ideas, is not only and exclusively in the final product, the OODA loop, but equally resides in his approach to military thought, in the way that he came to those insights that finally led to the OODA loop. Boyd's work thus contains a *strategic theory* but equally the work, its structure, its sources and the thought process that led to the content, constitute an argument about *strategic thinking*. In fact, he states as much on page 2 of *A Discourse*:

> the theme that weaves its way through this 'Discourse on Winning and Losing' is not so much contained within each of the five sections, per se, that make up the 'Discourse'; rather, it is the kind of thinking that both lies behind and makes-up its very essence. For the interested, a careful examination will reveal that the increasingly abstract discussion surfaces a process of reaching across many perspectives; pulling each and everyone apart (analysis), all the while intuitively looking for those parts of the disassembled perspectives which naturally interconnect with one another to form a higher order, more general elaboration (synthesis) of what is taking place. As a result, the process not only creates the 'Discourse' but it also represents the key to evolve the tactics, strategies, goals, unifying themes, etc. that permit us to actively shape and adapt to the unfolding world we are a part of, live-in, and feed-upon.

Thus, any interpretation of Boyd's work must be informed by his methodology. If we are not aware of the background of the theory, the conceptual soil from which his concepts and the abstract theory sprang, it will remain just that, a theory, if it deserves that label, and a set of hypotheses and propositions, a persuasive idea but an abstract and possibly a highly debatable one. And subsequent claims concerning his status as a strategist remain uninformative. A closer look at the material may reveal the logic and the strength of his argument, as well as the extent of consistency and validity of it. A closer examination of the conceptual roots will show the originality of his contribution as well as Boyd's normative view concerning strategic thinking and strategic theory formulation. For a proper understanding one needs to go beyond the OODA loop and go through the same learning process that Boyd wanted his audience to go through when they attended his presentations. We need to follow Boyd through his slides step by step.

A note on strategy

A Discourse on Winning and Losing examines how organizations can 'survive and prosper', and 'improve our ability to shape and adapt to unfolding circumstances, so that we (as individuals or as groups or as a culture or as a nation-state) can survive on our own terms'.[31] Thus terms such as military theory, operational art, doctrine, military strategy, strategic theory and thinking strategically define the content of this study, and need some definition.

Military theory is the aggregate of theories, doctrines, and beliefs belonging to a particular individual, community or period. It refers to the concepts, hypotheses, or principles developed by soldiers and civilians to solve military problems. This term is broad and not in common use, contrary to the term *operational art*, which has found its place in modern doctrine manuals of armed forces across the western world. Operational art is the body of knowledge dealing with the use and behavior of military forces in a military campaign aimed to achieve strategic or operational level military objectives. Campaigns are normally confined in time and geographical scope. *Doctrine* is the aggregate of fundamental methods of fighting, often tacit or implied. Ideally, doctrine provides the foundation for military training and education, as well as force structure and organization.[32]

These terms are here implicitly subsumed in the terms *strategy* and *strategic theory*, which are the preferred terms in this study, because those terms are more common, although not always properly defined in their use, and because using the term 'strategy' allows one a broader scope of activities as well as types and levels of organizations to be studied than war and armed forces. But above all, this choice is inspired by the nature of Boyd's work where strategic behavior is distinctly not confined to the military realm.

Strategy has several meanings, some narrowly defined, some broadly. Several apply to the nature of strategy and strategic theory here under investigation. The first set of interpretations of strategy and strategic theory that pertain to this study concerns the use of military force and war between political communities.[33] In the modern instrumentalist interpretation of strategy, strategy tells one how to conduct a war, or how to achieve political objectives, using the military instrument. Clausewitz famously stated that strategy is the use of engagements for the object of the war.[34] Freely translated, he tells us that strategy is the use of tacit and explicit threats, as well as of actual battles and campaigns, to advance political purposes. However, the strategy may not be (purely) military strategy, instead it may be grand strategy that uses 'engagements', meaning all of the relevant instruments of power as threats or inaction, for the objectives of statecraft.[35]

Strategy thus provides the conceptual link between action and effect and between instrument and objective. It is an idea. Strategy is a plan of action designed in order to achieve some end; a purpose together with a system of measures for its accomplishment.[36] André Beaufre captured the interactive nature, the dueling character of strategic behavior when he states that strategy is the art of the dialectic of two opposing wills using force to resolve their dispute.[37] A recently posited definition emphasizes the dynamic nature of this process, and of strategy, stating that strategy is a process, a constant adaptation to shifting conditions and circumstances in a world where chance, uncertainty and ambiguity dominate, a view that is very much in line with Boyd's idea.[38]

Strategy has also widespread application beyond the military sphere. Since World War II civil institutions – businesses, corporations, non-military government departments, universities – have come to develop strategies, by which they usually mean policy planning of any kind.[39] But here too there are various opinions of what strategy is and does.[40] The following viewpoints enjoy agreement among experts:[41]

- Strategy concerns both organization and environment: the organization uses strategy to deal with changing environments;
- Strategy affects overall welfare of the organization: strategic decisions are considered important enough to affect the overall welfare of the organization;
- Strategy involves issues of both content and process: the study of strategy includes both the actions taken, or the content of strategy, and the processes by which actions are decided and implemented;
- Strategies exist on different levels: firms have corporate strategy (what business shall we be in?) and business strategy (how shall we compete in each business?);
- Strategy involves various thought processes: strategy involves conceptual as well as analytical exercises.

Generally speaking then, in organization and management theory strategy refers to the various ways an organization tries to maintain a strategic fit between an organization's goals, its internal make up and the dynamic environment.

Strategy matters. Strategy has both extrinsic and intrinsic value. The extrinsic merit in strategy lies in its utility for keeping the military assets of a particular security community roughly in balance with the demands and opportunities that flow as stimuli from the outside world, or in organization theoretical terms, in its utility to maintain organizational fitness. The intrinsic merit in strategy resides in its role as conductor of the orchestra of military and other assets so that they can be applied economically to serve political objectives. Strategy transforms tactical performance into strategic effect for strategic performance in the service of policy.[42]

To neglect strategy in defense planning or the conduct of war would be like trying to play chess without kings on the board.[43] Strategy is the essential ingredient for making war either politically effective or morally tenable. Without strategy there is no rationale for how force will achieve purposes worth the price in blood and treasure. Without strategy, power is a loose cannon and war is mindless. Mindless killing can only be criminal. Politicians and soldiers may debate which strategic choice is best, but only pacifists can doubt that strategy is necessary.[44] Flawed strategy will bring the most expert and battle-hardened forces down,[45] while the absence of a strategy does, not means no strategic effects will result from tactical actions. Strategy abhors a vacuum: if the strategic function is lacking, strategic effect will be generated by the casual, if perhaps unguided and unwanted accumulation of tactical and operational outcomes.[46]

A note on strategic theory

The importance of good strategy implies strategic theory to be highly relevant, but like the development of good strategy, developing a good strategic theory is a highly problematic and daunting endeavor, and any study attempting to describe, interpret and appreciate a theory should do so based on an appreciation of the peculiarities of strategic theory. Strategic theory is a strange animal indeed, and as theory it deviates in some important respects from what is generally considered 'proper' scientific theory. Strategic theory concerns thoughts about making effective strategy and about the proper use of force. The strategic theorist speculates about the effect of particular military instruments upon the course of history.[47]

There is no single, all-embracing formula explaining, describing and predicting strategy and its outcome. Instead, it belongs to the domain of social science, in which parsimony is only occasionally appropriate.[48] The phenomena of social science are so complex, with many different influences or 'causes' operating on a particular event, and our knowledge of these complex phenomena is still so imperfect, that few laws have been established. At best the social scientist can give not more than a probability that a particular action will be followed by the desired result.[49] Indeed, Clausewitz pointed out that a positive doctrine for warfare is simply not possible.[50] Theory need not be a positive doctrine, a sort of manual for action,[51] because 'in war everything is uncertain, and calculations have to be made with variable quantities. They direct the inquiry exclusively towards physical quantities, whereas all military action is intertwined with psychological forces and effects. They consider only unilateral action, whereas war consists of a continuous interaction of opposites.'[52] War is too complex. Moreover it is filled with danger, chance, uncertainty, emotions and differential talents of commanders. Subsequently, as Garnett remarks, some of the most useful theories do not in any way meet the strict requirements of 'scientific' theory. If 'scientific' is associated with a predictive capacity of theory, indeed, most strategic theories fail.

But strategic theory is valuable because of its explanatory value. Despite the fact that generalization and hypotheses may enjoy only limited validity, they sometimes throw a good deal of light on strategic behavior in particular conditions and at particular periods of time.[53] If a strategic theory offers better ways of explaining victories and losses it already has much utility for evaluation and policy making; if it can provide some measure of plausible conditional prediction that a certain mode of behavior will result in a higher probability of success, it is extremely useful. Theory assists in deciding whether and how to employ a particular strategy by offering an abstract conceptual model (or a quasi-deductive theory) of each strategy, and general knowledge of the conditions that favor the success of a strategy and conversely, the conditions that make its success unlikely.[54]

Not all strategic theories are equal. Gray distinguishes four levels to categorize strategic theories, and although each level has its merits, a general theory of war provides the most holistic approach and subsequently has the most value for commanders who, in order to shape strategy for a particular war, must understand how war in general, *qua* war, works:[55]

1   A level that transcends time, environment, political and social conditions and technology (for instance Clausewitz and Sun Tzu).
2   A level that explains how the geographical and functional complexities of war and strategy interact and complement each other. (Corbett on naval warfare)
3   A level that explains how a particular kind of use of military power strategically affects the course of conflict as a whole. (Mahan, Douhet, Schelling on the role of maritime power, air power and nuclear power respectively)
4   A level that explains the character of war in a particular period, keyed to explicit assumptions above the capabilities of different kinds of military power and their terms of effective engagement (the use of air power as a coercive tool).

General strategic theory educates politicians and commanders broadly as to the nature, structure, and dynamic workings of the instrument to which they might have to resort. The chief utility of a general theory of war and strategy lies in its ability not to point out lessons, but to isolate things that need thinking about. It must provide insight and questions, not answers.[56] Although quite a few military theorists have aimed to uncover the single principle governing war and who aspired for the scientific capacity to predict and control,[57] the common expectation of military strategic theory today, and the one employed here, is to educate the mind by providing intellectual organization, defining terms, suggesting connections among apparently disparate matters, and offering speculative consequentialist postulates.[58]

Boyd, too, was primarily interested in educating his audience. He attempted not so much to instill verities but to impart a way of thinking about war and strategy, like Mahan who was concerned with the creation of a 'disciplined yet flexible sensibility that would be capable of quick and sound judgment in spite of incomplete or misleading knowledge and risk of serious consequences in the event of error'.[59] Theory, then, is important because it helps to educate and it may shed new light on war. That, and not the aim of developing a general theory which, like the Newtonian laws of physics, holds up for long periods of time, is the purpose of strategic theory.

The educational feature of strategic theory does not imply its value is confined to the academic world. Strategic theory has a nasty feature in that it relates to matters of life and death. 'The strategist's task is to formulate a "theory" explaining how a state can ensure its security and further other interests', Stephen Walt asserted.[60] It therefore needs to perform in practice, just like medical science aims at deriving insights, at understanding the dynamics and interrelationships of the various parts of the human body, in order to achieve success in surgery and treatment.

Strategic theory often has an impact on the formulation of strategy in the real world.[61] Good theories provide relevant and useful conceptual frameworks by means of which to understand the general requirements of a strategy and the general logic associated with its effective employment. Such theoretical-conceptual knowledge is critical for policy making. All policy makers make use of some such theory and conceptual frameworks, whether consciously or not. In employing a strategy they rely on assumptions, often tacit, about the strategy's general requirements and logic.[62] Indeed wherever one looks in modern strategic history one finds testimony to the influence of ideas. There is always a strategic theoretical dimension to the making, execution and doing of strategy.[63] The messy world of defense policy and the use of force provides both the permanent reason why strategic theory is important.[64] The traffic between ideas and behavior in strategic affairs is continuous. As the intellectual history of strategy bears the stamp of particular perceptions and interpretations of strategic experience, so strategic behavior is shaped by the attitudes and ideas that we know as strategic culture. In the practical world of strategy, strategic ideas apply to experience, while strategic experience constitutes ideas in action.[65] Ideas help shape behavior, even as they are shaped in turn by behavior.[66]

Developing a strategic theory is difficult for several reasons. First, strategic theory needs to take into account the complex and multidimensional character of strategy and war. Good strategic theory must be holistic, paying due respect for the interdependency of the various elements and dimensions that give form to strategy.[67] The second problem facing strategic theorists is that the circumstance for which strategic theory is developed will be largely unknown and moreover unknowable much in advance of the moment of testing the strategic theory, though the uncertainty is itself a factor to be reckoned with in one's strategic doctrine.[68]

Moreover, witness the flurry of books on the nature of war since landmark events such as November 9 1989 (end of the Cold War) or '9/11', strategic theory is evolutionary in the sense that theories are developed that take into account novel actors, such as states or terrorist groups, new technologies such as tanks, aircraft or nuclear weapons, or phenomena such as the impact of the industrial revolution or the rise of mass emotions in nationalistically and ideologically inspired wars.[69]

The contemporary social context determines what the actors, weapons, aims, norms, etc. are that are employed in a purposeful manner in war, and as this social context evolves, so does (or should) strategic theory. Strategists have had difficulty abstracting themselves from the features of a given war or period, and identifying the lasting characteristics that would apply to all contexts and all periods.[70] As a result their work generally reflects the war, or factors that affect it, as seen through the eyes of people living in their own time, imparting a contemporary color to their military thinking.

This affects the nature of theory development. The dynamic nature of strategy and war are not conducive to a steady growth of knowledge because the object – war, actors, weapons, rules – alters constantly and in fairly rapid tempo, at least in the past 200 years. Subsequently strategic theory development does not follow a clear cumulative growth path in which new theories built upon former ones, improving the older ones or expanding their range of application. The reader, then, is left with an expanding number of partial theories, each of which has a limited range of applicability, be it bound by geography (continental, maritime, urban, jungle), dimension (air, land, sea), weapon technology and combat method (nuclear, terrorism, counter-insurgency, guerrilla), etc.

The paradoxical nature of strategy and strategic theory reinforces the problematic nature of strategic theory. Strategic theory is not neutral territory, but an arena of competition itself. It needs to account for the fact that it is concerned with people that react, learn and anticipate. Students of social science have recognized that the persons and organizations with which the social sciences deal may be influenced by the scientific generalizations themselves. Thus once such a generalization has been formulated and has become known to the persons whose behavior it attempts to predict, those persons may react in ways different from their past behavior, the observation of which justified the generalization. Such generalizations, therefore, cannot have the scientific character that their truth is independent of human beliefs, and the influence of science on human affairs is thus somewhat paradoxical.[71] Precisely because a strategy worked once, it will likely be emulated or at least learned from, and subsequently strategists must devise new constructs and hypothesis that provide a plausible expectation for success.[72] Strategic theories arise after clashes of old views, in a somewhat Darwinian fashion; when promising ideas and propositions have been tried in battle, they elicit counter ideas negating the validity of formerly successful propositions. For instance, the resort to terrorism by groups such as Hamas and Al Qaeda against nations with high-tech armed forces is explained by some through this dialectic dynamic.[73]

These factors imply strategic theory is dynamic in a fundamental way, and this character affects the potential for making good and lasting theory concerning strategy. Indeed, what the discussion above reveals is that, in matters of war, even if an underlying pattern is discovered and some level of predictability established, the paradoxical nature of strategy guarantees that the pattern will be altered. If social theory differs from the model of theory posited by the natural sciences, strategic theory then may, in the eyes of some, not deserve that label at all, and really these theories are more sets of propositions, hypotheses and models. The activities of a strategic theorist can perhaps be likened to the one who attempts to build a house on the muddy bank of a fast flowing river. The patch of sand constantly changes form, depth, substance and location due to the turbulence of the river. Moreover, it shifts and deforms because of the construction activities. The very fact that one places a stone so as to construct a foundation alters the environment. With war and strategic behavior so fundamentally in flux, strategic theory cannot aspire for high standards of parsimony or general applicability and validity, nor one that holds out for a long period of time. Neither should one necessarily expect an all-embracing theory to develop from the various partial theories, nor a theory with a high level of predictive capability, the standard of 'hard science'.

The formative factors of strategic theory

Understanding the strategist's sources of influence helps understanding his theory. Like social theorists, strategic theorists are influenced by both intellectual and social factors, both internal to the discipline as well as external to the discipline. Internal intellectual factors include the influence of schools and traditions of thought on a theorist, including cognitive paradigms, changes in paradigms, and meta-theoretical tools. External intellectual factors include ideas borrowed from other disciplines. Internal social factors include the influence of social networks on a theorist's work. External social factors include the impact of historical change on the structure and institutions of the society being theorized.[74]

Mintzberg argues that, in addition to fields such as psychology of human cognition, political science of public policy making and military history of strategies in conflict, biology, systems theory, cybernetics, anthropology, economics, quantum mechanics and chaos theory also may provide insight into how organizations change and have indeed informed theories of strategic management.[75] The applied nature of strategic management requires a multidimensional view, incorporating diverse complexities, rationalities and strategies. Quincy Wright stated long ago that the discipline [of the theory of war or the art of war] extends into science, history and philosophy as well as practice. Insights for explanation and the formulation of advice may be sought in sociology, psychology, political science, economics, history and international law. All may assist in 'building of systems of thought which will guide the soldier, general, statesman, or citizen to appreciate the situation and to act so that victory may be won'.[76]

Recent studies into the formative factors of strategic theory suggest that the following factors shape and explain the development of a certain theory of conflict in a particular period, in a particular country or by a specific author.[77]

- the nature of war during successive periods;
- the specific strategic circumstances of the countries involved;
- the personal and professional experience of the particular thinker;
- the intellectual and cultural climate of the period in question.

The nature of war deeply affected the influential writers of the past two centuries. Clausewitz and Jomini where deeply affected by the drift towards total war, a process that had started during the French Revolution and continued during the Napoleonic wars, and their thinking is dominated by the role of the masses in war. The works of Liddell Hart, Fuller, Douhet and Mitchell reflect the trauma of World War I, the mechanization of the battlefield and the increasing and intensifying involvement of society in war, despite the fact that they develop different solutions to the problem of the vast destruction of modern war.[78] The theorists of nuclear war were, of course, influenced by the instantaneous destruction of Hiroshima and Nagasaki.

Specific strategic circumstances of the home country also affect the formation of strategic theory of an author. Clausewitz' work is distinctly continental, reflecting both his experience and the Prussian geo-strategic predicament. Douhet did not conceal the fact that the formulation of his ideas with regard to defeating the enemy through aerial bombing of the civilian population and the industrial infrastructure was influenced by the strategic position of Italy.[79] Even as recently as the 1990s, we can see how specific strategic circumstances can inspire strategic debate. The dilemmas of the ethnic wars in the Balkans during the 1990s produced a new search for the dynamics of coercive diplomacy and military strategies as part of that.

Personal experience is particularly evident in the works of Clausewitz and Jomini, who both took part in battles during the Napoleonic wars, although that by itself does not explain the fundamental insights into the nature of war that Clausewitz in particular developed. The command experiences of Douhet and Mitchell and the didactic responsibilities of Corbett and Mahan have often been noted as important factors for explaining their work. Boyd's work flowed directly from his experience as a fighter pilot.

All of these factors combine in Azar Gat's comparison of Clausewitz and Liddell Hart. Despite differences in character and style, there are striking similarities in their approach to strategy. According to Gat,

> both thinkers reacted to cataclysmic and epoch-making wars which had resulted in a national trauma and profound intellectual transformation. In both, their experiences produced a violent reaction against past military theory and practice, held to be responsible for the disaster. Both advanced a new model of military theory, which they held universally valid and which involved an unhistorical approach to the special conditions that had determined the pattern of the past. Both were not just 'idly theorizing' but developed and preached their ideas out of consuming commitment to their countries' future.[80]

This description could equally be applied to John Boyd. Boyd's work comprises a specific intellectual response to the military problems of the US armed forces in the immediate aftermath of the Vietnam War and his arguments are colored by this predicament in the sense that he aimed to change a specific mindset and a doctrine that, in his view, was dysfunctional.

Dominant scientific currents, too, can, as part of a *Zeitgeist* (here used as a shorthand for the intellectual and cultural environment in a particular period), have a significant impact on the formulation of military theory. For instance, nineteenth-century military thought was dominated by two contending conceptions of the nature of military theory, formulated during the age of Enlightenment and the Romantic period, in the eighteenth and early nineteenth century respectively. Broadly defined, they represent the two fundamental positions towards the study of man and human institutions, which emerged in the wake of the scientific revolution of the seventeenth century. One of these looked to the exact and natural sciences as a model to be adopted and applied. The other, by contrast, maintained that the humanities were different in nature from the sciences and could never be studied by the same methods.[81] The ideal of Newtonian science excited the military thinkers of the enlightenment and gave rise to an ever-present yearning to infuse the study of war with the maximum mathematical precision and certainty possible, maintaining that the art of war was susceptible to systematic formulation, based on rules and principles of universal validity, which had been revealed in the campaigns of the great military leaders of history.[82] Hence it was Jomini who won fame by updating the theoretical outlook of the Enlightenment to produce a striking schematization of Napoleon's aggressive rationale of operations.

In contrast, and in response, the Romantics stressed the complexity and diversity of human reality, which could not be reduced to abstract formulas and which was dominated by emotions, creativity, and the historic conditions of each period. This new outlook on the nature of military theory breached the hitherto absolute hegemony of the military school of the Enlightenment.[83] Clausewitz, for instance, was a 'Social Newtonian' in his methodology in the sense that to Newton 'phenomena are the data of experience',[84] and he deliberately inserted Newtonian, mechanistic metaphors in his work such as the concepts of friction and center of gravity. Yet he recognized that the social world differs from the natural world.[85] Hence Clausewitz' emphasis on the interactive nature of war, the influence of the dialectic of wills, the importance of experience, fear, emotion, intuition, etc.[86]

Thus it is important to look at the broad scientific climate, the prevailing scientific paradigm or the popular perception of new or 'fashionable' scientific insights and concepts of the day, as part of the *Zeitgeist*.[87] These provide metaphors for expression, new ideas and concepts for analysis and explanation, and sometimes novel insights for discovering new patterns of causality. Indeed, military theorists better take heed of their implicit scientific assumptions. For instance, implicit and explicit deterministic reasoning and analysis lay at heart of some of the strategic errors in practice and in theory that occurred in the latter half of the twentieth century, in particular in the field of strategic application of air power and nuclear warfare due to 'Laplacian determinism', construed as a dominant deterministic *Weltanschauung* adopted by physicists in the century following Newton's death.[88] During the planning and execution of the Combined Bomber Offensive (CBO) during World War II, American airmen have tended to be overzealous in their enthusiasm for pet formulas and engineering-type of calculations, ignoring historical contradictory facts and assuming a static opponent. Not only were the CBO plan's predictions concerning bombing effects offered with the quantitative precision of a physical science, they were expressly portrayed as effects that would occur if the requisite bombing forces were made available. The thinking behind the planning was mechanistic in the specific sense of not getting involved in the action–reaction typical of combat between land armies.[89]

Writing in the 1980s, Barry Watts asserted that military theory should instead be based on the assumption that uncertainty is inherent in the physical and social world, and unsolvable. He favored a more organic image of war in which human nature and behavior in war forms the foundation for military theory.[90] The Clausewitzian concept of friction, which is infused with the notion of unpredictability and uncertainty stemming from the interactive nature of strategy and battle, and from the limits of human cognition, should be at the heart of it.[91] He bolsters his argument by referring to Albert Einstein, Werner Heisenberg, Kurt Gödel and Claude Shannon, who laid the physical and mathematical foundation for the philosophical insight that human knowledge is limited by definition.[92] All information is imperfect. There is no absolute knowledge, he quotes Jacob Bronowski, an author whose work Boyd too had studied.[93]

In similar vein, and with direct reference to the work of John Boyd, Pellegrini expects that the shift from the Newtonian framework of cause and effect determinism to the new science concept of probabilities and trends (as embedded in chaos and complexity theory), will change man's concept of the battlefield, emphasizing the capability for rapid observation and action.[94] While Newton's metaphor of the 'Majestic Clockwork' may have influenced military theory during large parts of the past 200 years, work in biology (especially DNA and the workings of the human brain), artificial intelligence and chaos and complexity theory now suggest that the world is composed of complex systems which interact with, and adapt to, each other, making it even more difficult to obtain knowledge about how the universe functions.[95] In that, Pellegrini nicely captured the essence of the scientific *Zeitgeist* during which Boyd developed his ideas.

Organization of this study

Informed by the concept of formative factors, the approach adopted to show what Boyd said and meant, to improve our understanding of Boyd's strategic theory, is in one sense an indirect one. Instead of starting with presenting *A Discourse* right away, Chapters 2, 3 and 4 discuss at some length the formative factors of Boyd's work, thereby providing a conceptual lens to read and interpret his work with. Considering the nature of and method applied in Boyd's work, understanding his work, and appreciating it, will require an examination from a variety of angles, taking insights from a number of disciplines and bodies of knowledge, in particular in light of the fact that one has only his presentations to rely on. In Boyd's case the following four factors can be discerned:

- His professional background;
- The strategic and defense–political context of the US in the period in which Boyd developed his ideas;
- His study of military theory and history;
- His keen and evolving interest in scientific developments and the scientific *Zeitgeist* during which he developed his ideas on military strategy.

Boyd's professional background includes his personal experiences, such as his tour as a fighter pilot during the Korean War and his experimentation in air combat afterwards. A second factor shaping his work lies in his views on the

Vietnam experience and the challenges facing the US military in the aftermath of that war, the time during which Boyd developed his work; and the audience to which he lectured. As is the case with many strategists, Boyd studied military history and strategic theories, and the influence of specific theories and insights permeate and color his work too. Chapter 2 therefore includes a discussion of a number of strategic theorists who exerted an obvious influence on Boyd through his study of strategic theory, such as Sun Tzu, Julian Corbett, T.E Lawrence, J.F.C. Fuller and Basil Liddell Hart. This will introduce ideas that found their place in Boyd's work, thus easing the path for understanding the slides in *A Discourse*. It will also facilitate positioning Boyd in the history of strategic theory as well as provide insights concerning the extent of his contribution to strategic theory.

A very interesting and equally influential formative factor is formed by his avid study of a variety of scientific fields. Chapters 3 and 4 focus on this aspect of Boyd's work. They show the scientific *Zeitgeist* during which Boyd formulated his theory, as well as the way and the extent to which it influenced his work. I argue that Boyd's work is rooted in this scientific *Zeitgeist* and cannot be properly understood without a level of familiarity with the debates and developments that took place in the period Boyd developed his theory.

Against this background, equipped with certain 'conceptual lenses', Chapters 5 and 6 offer a detailed account of Boyd's essay and all of his presentations. This somewhat elaborate examination will give an impression of Boyd's manner of reasoning and of his ideas on how one should think about military strategy. It will show how he constructed his argument and what is behind the popular OODA loop notion. It furthermore substantiates the conclusion laid out in Chapter 7, that his work contains many more arguments and insights concerning successful strategic behavior. Based in particular upon the themes, debates and insights featuring in the scientific *Zeitgeist* that color Boyd's work, and upon the pervasive presence of his ideas in military studies and doctrinal debates in what many analysts have described as the postmodern period of the 1980s and 1990s, I conclude also that Boyd may be considered the first postmodern strategist, in particular considering the conceptual similarities between Boyd and several post-modern social theorists, an argument which, furthermore, underlines the importance of an awareness of the *Zeitgeist* for understanding strategic theory.

2 The seeds of a theory and the fertile soil

There is no such thing as a logical method of having new ideas.
Discovery contains an irrational element or a creative intuition.

Karl Popper[1]

The seed of a theory; Boyd's military life

Flying fighters

A Discourse is the result of a highly creative process, which has its roots in Boyd's early career, his involvement with the design of fighter aircraft and his interest in military history that followed from research projects associated with designing fighters. His ideas flowered because of the fertile soil Boyd found when he developed his thoughts in increasingly coherent form. These three factors will be addressed in this chapter. As is evident from the chronology of key dates and events in Box 2.1, Boyd's ideas materialized over the span of several decades and gained coherent conceptual form only after his retirement in 1975.[2]

Two decades separate his first and last presentation. The years following his retirement were marked by the aftershocks of the Vietnam War, which were felt throughout the US armed forces. But his formative period began with flying fighters in the US Air Force. His military career started in 1945, when at age eighteen he enlisted in the Army and served in the occupation of Japan. Shortly after getting out of the Army, Boyd attended the University of Iowa on the GI Bill and enrolled in Air Force ROTC. In 1952, after graduating from college, Boyd attended Air Force pilot training at Williams Air Force Base in Arizona. There air-to-air combat was an eye-opener and he managed to persuade his commander to change his posting from flying bomber aircraft to fighters. In the winter of 1952–53 he was subsequently assigned to Korea with the 51st Fighter Interceptor Wing, which operated the F-86 Sabre. What Boyd learned and did there constituted the basis for nearly everything he thought and did later, not only in air-to-air tactics, energy maneuverability, and aircraft design but also in his development of OODA loops, his thinking on strategy and maneuver warfare, and ultimately his thought on time and thinking itself.[3]

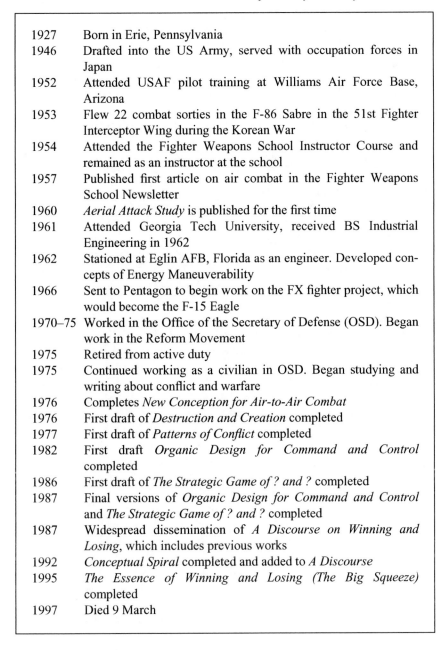

1927	Born in Erie, Pennsylvania
1946	Drafted into the US Army, served with occupation forces in Japan
1952	Attended USAF pilot training at Williams Air Force Base, Arizona
1953	Flew 22 combat sorties in the F-86 Sabre in the 51st Fighter Interceptor Wing during the Korean War
1954	Attended the Fighter Weapons School Instructor Course and remained as an instructor at the school
1957	Published first article on air combat in the Fighter Weapons School Newsletter
1960	*Aerial Attack Study* is published for the first time
1961	Attended Georgia Tech University, received BS Industrial Engineering in 1962
1962	Stationed at Eglin AFB, Florida as an engineer. Developed concepts of Energy Maneuverability
1966	Sent to Pentagon to begin work on the FX fighter project, which would become the F-15 Eagle
1970–75	Worked in the Office of the Secretary of Defense (OSD). Began work in the Reform Movement
1975	Retired from active duty
1975	Continued working as a civilian in OSD. Began studying and writing about conflict and warfare
1976	Completes *New Conception for Air-to-Air Combat*
1976	First draft of *Destruction and Creation* completed
1977	First draft of *Patterns of Conflict* completed
1982	First draft *Organic Design for Command and Control* completed
1986	First draft of *The Strategic Game of ? and ?* completed
1987	Final versions of *Organic Design for Command and Control* and *The Strategic Game of ? and ?* completed
1987	Widespread dissemination of *A Discourse on Winning and Losing*, which includes previous works
1992	*Conceptual Spiral* completed and added to *A Discourse*
1995	*The Essence of Winning and Losing (The Big Squeeze)* completed
1997	Died 9 March

Box 2.1 Chronology of Boyd's life.

What intrigued him was that despite flying in F-86 aircraft with a lower ceiling, a wider turn radius and slower maximum speed than its rival, the Russian Mig-15, the kill ratio was 10:1 in favor of the F-86 during the Korean War. Varying quality of training on both sides affected this ratio, with the US training level far exceeding that of the North Korean pilots. Still, this could not explain all, if for no other anomaly that the North Korean pilots often achieved numerical superiority during air-to-air combat. What also contributed was the bubble canopy of the F-86, which provided a distinct advantage over the constrained view offered by the Mig-15 canopy in visually detecting enemy aircraft. But Boyd was convinced another element was at play as well, a question he took with him to the next position, together with his considerable tactical prowess, 'the guts of his real education'.[4]

Boyd was assigned to the USAF Fighter Weapons School at Nellis Air Force Base near Las Vegas first as a student, and following graduation, as a fighter weapons and tactics instructor. This school focused on air-to-ground and air-to-air gunnery. Air combat tactics was a neglected subject, something Boyd corrected immediately. In the capacity of tactics instructor he acquired the reputation of '40 second Boyd' which amounted to a bet that he could beat any pilot within forty seconds in a 1 versus 1 air combat set-up, a bet he usually won. More importantly, he committed his insights on tactics to paper, publishing several articles in the professional journal of the Fighter Weapons School. In 1960, at the age of thirty-three, he published what is still considered the encyclopedia on air-to-air combat, *Aerial Attack Study*. In 147 pages it details every maneuver possible, in words and graphic illustrations, for a pilot to use in a dogfight. An important feature was that Boyd did not advocate one maneuver over another but presented the options available to the pilot and his opponent in relation to each other. He wanted to show people a variety of moves and countermoves, and the logic of its dynamic. Its content became part of an official Air Force Manual on air-to-air tactics and was disseminated through official and informal channels to other services in time for good use during the Vietnam War. Not one new maneuver has been added since, illustrating the comprehensiveness of Boyd's effort, and subsequently this publication, in various guises, still forms the basis in all jet air forces today.[5] Thus, he changed the nature of the premier air tactics school of the US Air Force.

In the summer of 1960 he moved to Atlanta, Georgia, to get a degree in industrial engineering at Georgia Tech. At Nellis he became aware that, if he wanted to make further headway with the discoveries he had made, he needed to expand his intellectual toolkit with knowledge of mathematics. Industrial engineering would add physics, production lines, thermodynamics and other fields. At Georgia Tech his interest lay not in the mathematical details, but in the underlying concepts. Here he developed a taste for synthesis. And this resulted in another remarkable and very important contribution to air combat, an insight that brought him back to the question concerning the relative excellence of the F-86 in Korea.

At Georgia Tech, Boyd wrestled with the study of thermodynamics. Thermodynamics concerns the study of energy. The Second Law of Thermodynamics is called the law of entropy, and postulates that in a closed system the transfer of heat (energy) goes in one direction, from a high temperature to a low temperature. If two separate volumes of water, one with high and one with low temperature, are mixed, the highly ordered states of the separate volumes disappear and are replaced by a less ordered state. The temperature changes until the temperature across the entire system is uniform. This change is non-reversible. The entropy in the system has increased. The system has moved from order to disorder. In engineering the concept refers to the fact that more usable energy always goes into the system than comes out. No system is 100 percent effective.[6]

Using the insight from thermodynamics, he discovered he could explain air-to-air combat in terms of energy relationships, in which altitude is potential energy to be traded for speed – kinetic energy – and vice versa. Turns became energy-consuming maneuvers, with the rate of consumption depending on the number of g-forces of the turn, and engine power an energy provider for gaining altitude, gaining speed or sustaining a turn, or a combination of these. These relationships could be expressed in calculable equations and the outcomes could be plotted in graphs displaying energy/maneuverability characteristics of a fighter. By overlaying and comparing such graphs of different fighters the speed/altitude areas of relative advantage became immediately obvious. Moreover, it would provide invaluable information for aircraft designers for they could see under what conditions, where, when and how an aircraft could gain an advantage. It was 'as fundamental and as significant to aviation as Newton was to physics', Coram notes.[7]

This was a brilliant and novel insight, if still only in theory. However it required expensive computer time to make calculations and explore this insight. Boyd managed to graduate in 1962 and get a posting to Eglin Air Force Base in Florida, where the USAF Systems Command was located, which housed extensive computing capacity. Thus he could continue his research, albeit covertly, as his project was not endorsed officially by the USAF. This resulted in energy maneuverability theory, or EM theory.

EM theory revolutionized fighter design and caused some stir on the sides when first comparisons of US fighters with latest generation Soviet fighters indicated that the latter (Mig-17, Mig-19 and Mig-21) possessed superior energy-maneuverability characteristics. EM theory provided dynamic rather than static analysis pictures of aircraft performances across a range of altitudes, g-forces and turning radii, and gave a scorecard of its maneuver capabilities. It offered not only a tool for assessment, but also design parameters in the development of tactics and doctrine for air combat engagements. His accomplishments were honored with the Air Force Systems Command Scientific Achievement Award. Not surprisingly this work led to a position at the Pentagon, where people were having problems with the new FX fighter program.[8]

Designing fighters

Boyd left Eglin in the fall of 1966 and was assigned to the Operational Requirements Team in the office of the Deputy for Research and Development at US Air Force Headquarters in the Pentagon. With only a brief interruption for service in Southeast Asia in 1972–73, it would be Boyd's home for the next twenty-two years. At the Pentagon he was assigned to work on the design of the next-generation air superiority fighter for the Air Force, the FX project. The latest dedicated air superiority fighter within the USAF inventory had been the F-86 of Korean War fame. Since then, fighter aircraft had become more complex, more expensive, heavier and less maneuverable. The result was a range of fighters able to conduct offensive air support missions while still possessing some air combat capabilities, but in dogfights these aircraft lost out to latest-generation Soviet dedicated air superiority fighters. While loss ratios over Korea were 10:1, in the skies over Vietnam F-100, F-105 and F-4 aircraft scored dismal ratios of 1:1, sometimes peaking at 2.4:1.

Several factors contributed to this. There were doctrinal faults. North Vietnamese air bases were off limits, violating the doctrinal tenet that air superiority is a *sine qua non* for offensive operations against other targets. Predictable tactics and flying corridors exacerbated the problem. The faith in air-to-air missiles proved premature. Evasive maneuvers to escape from interception by surface-to-air missiles were not taught. US units and technological performance improved over time. Improvements in training, such as the introduction of the Top Gun program, resulted in improved combat performance. However, the structural design problems affecting fighter maneuverability could of course not be solved. This applied also to the backbone of the US air units in the latter phase of the Vietnam War, the F-4. The US Air Force required a new and better air superiority aircraft.

This was to be delivered by the FX project. The FX followed after the F-111 debacle. The F-111 project sprang from the need to marry the operational requirements of the US Navy for a fighter aircraft and the USAF requirement for a replacement for the F-105 long-range strike aircraft. This flawed plan emanated from the office of then Secretary of Defense McNamara, who aimed to achieve economies of scale similar to his experience at the Ford Motor Company. The result was the F-111A attack version with acceptable performances, and a disastrous F-111B fighter, a program that was subsequently canceled. However, the FX too promised to be a heavy fighter with a complex swing-wing layout.

When Boyd entered this project he carried out EM tests and began questioning the swing-wing advantages in light of the structural and weight design penalties. He rejected the FX proposal and, together with technical experts went on the look for options to reduce the weight while increasing its maneuverability. What Boyd and some others around him aimed for was keeping costs down while ensuring maximum relevant performance vis-à-vis current Soviet counterparts. To accomplish this it was necessary to omit all subsystems not absolutely essential to the mission, to resist the temptation to use unproved advanced technology and to eliminate the requirements for complex avionics, high top speeds, and excessive ranges.[9]

Their case was strengthened by the presence of a group of former fighter aces from World War II and the Korean War who had now achieved general officer rank, and who, in 1965, had drafted a paper underscoring the need for an air superiority fighter, not a multi-mission hybrid. This went against the grain of conventional wisdom within the USAF. With high-level backing Boyd and a number of other mid-level military and civilian technical experts within the Pentagon transformed the USAF approach to air superiority between 1966 and 1972.[10] What assisted them also was the rude shock of the 1967 Domodovedo Air Show in Moscow, where the Soviets showcased their latest generation of combat aircraft (the Mig-23, Mig-25 and Mig-27). By 1968 it had become official policy that the USAF needed a first line tactical fighter that was designed primarily for air-to-air combat.

Boyd's continued efforts and his EM concept in no small measure contributed to the subsequent development of the F-15 fighter with excellent performances. However, still unsatisfied with the high costs and still less than optimum performance, due to seemingly unavoidable design compromises resulting in weight increases, Boyd and a few others from within the Pentagon and industry, a group dubbed 'the Fighter Mafia', decided an even lighter and less complex aircraft would give the air superiority capabilities sought after. Central in this effort was the notion of 'agility', a concept later to emerge in Boyd's work on strategy. With EM theory Boyd proved the F-86 advantage in Korea was, in addition to superior US training, in particular due to its ability to transition from one maneuver to another faster than the Mig-15, which in the end would force a Mig-15 to end up in front of the F-86.[11]

The notion of fast transient maneuvering as the key to winning was to remain with Boyd when he developed his thoughts on military success in general. For now, using EM theory he could show that superior maneuvering capability, combined with better training and cockpit design offering an advantage in time and superior 'situational awareness' mitigated the Mig-15 speed and turn advantage. The new lightweight fighter would have unprecedented capability for 'fast transients' in addition to a high thrust-to-weight ratio, which would produce the required energy maneuverability.

Despite USAF reluctance and without official backing the fighter mafia designed an 'austere fighter', the F-XX, and presented their case to various Pentagon officials. Boyd's involvement with fighter development did not end with his short assignment to Thailand from April 1972 to April 1973. The bureaucratic processes behind these programs have been discussed elsewhere in detail.[12] Suffice it here to conclude that the end result was a Light Weight Fighter fly-off competition between the YF-16 and YF-17 (later to develop into the F-18), fighters with unsurpassed maneuverability, excellent visibility, high acceleration and sustained turning capability and relatively low costs. These types have proven their worth in the inventories in most Western air forces.

The last design Boyd had an influence on was the A-10, and, interestingly, his involvement with the A-10 development would influence Boyd, for it was one of two projects that induced him to study military history. The A-10 was designed for Close Air Support (CAS) and killing tanks, an entirely different mission than gaining air superiority. CAS missions are normally flown close to the ground and over the front line. Subsequently, CAS aircraft are exposed to intense ground-to-air threat. When invited to look at the project by a close colleague, Boyd subsequently needed to develop a new set of trade-off studies and design parameters. German World War II experts were interviewed to learn about German tank-killing tactics, the time required to detect and attack ground targets and the maximum time available for aiming and delivering ordnance before air defense systems were cued for effective engagement of the attacking aircraft. This exposed him to the need to look into the history of Close Air Support and air-ground coordination, and German military tactics and strategy of World War II in general.[13] The A-10 too, proved its worth, most notably during Operation Desert Storm, where it demonstrated an awesome capability for taking out tanks, combined with the ability to absorb considerable damage.

From air combat to a general theory of war

From this research Boyd discovered that grasping the essentials of military victory required a thorough reading of military history. In a time when more air force officers could quote Peter Drucker than Clausewitz, Boyd climbed inside the minds of every theoretician from 400 BC to the present.[14] Out of this foray into military history the first sketches of *Patterns of Conflict* emerged, the first draft of which would be ready in 1977. In it he makes a seemingly radical and perhaps unwarranted jump from air combat to operational art. The transition from air combat theory to strategic theory occurred in 1975 when he started working on a presentation titled *A New Conception for Air to Air Combat*, while working on *Patterns of Conflict* and *Destruction and Creation* simultaneously. While *A New Conception for Air to Air Combat* is not included in *A Discourse*, it is the stepping-stone between two periods. In it he combines insights he had already developed in his research for *Destruction and Creation* with his knowledge of air-to-air combat. The suggestions he advances here are directly incorporated in *Patterns of Conflict*, the briefing that was going to form the main body of *A Discourse* together with *Destruction and Creation*.

A New Conception for Air to Air Combat was produced because of a request by NASA. On 4 August 1976 he finished this research. In it he looked again at the issue of maneuverability, due to the fact that in the fly-off competition the YF-16 had unexpectedly dramatically outperformed the YF-17 while EM diagrams had predicted a close contest. Test pilots, however, lauded the YF-16 capability for sudden very tight 'buttonhook turns' (albeit at the cost of airspeed depletion) which brought them inside the turn circle of the YF-17 while still being able to gain energy and maintain high turn rates even at low speeds.

Maneuverability is defined as the 'ability to change altitude, airspeed and direction in any combination'. He developed the insight that in air-to-air combat, one needs 'a fighter that can be used to initiate and control engagement opportunities – yet has a fast transient ('natural hook') that can be used to either force an overshoot by an attacker or to stay inside a hard turning defender'.[15] Expanding this idea, he formulates the suggestion that:

> in order to win or gain superiority – we should operate at a faster tempo than our adversaries or inside our adversaries time scales ... such activity will make us appear ambiguous (non predictable) thereby generate confusion and disorder among our adversaries.

He adds that these suggestions are in accordance with 'Gödel's Proof, The Heisenberg Principle and the Second Law of Thermodynamics', ideas central to *Destruction and Creation*.[16] These ideas posit, according to Boyd, that 'we cannot determine the character and nature of a system within itself and efforts to do so will only generate confusion and disorder'.[17] Thus, he continues, making the giant leap from air-to-air combat to warfare in general:

> Fast transients (faster tempo) together with synthesis associated with Gödel, Heisenberg, and the Second Law suggest a New Conception for Air-to-Air Combat and for Waging War.

Boyd next elaborates this new conception. In one's actions one should:

> exploit operational and technical features to generate a rapidly changing environment (quick/clear observations, fast tempo, fast transients, quick kill).

Containing key themes that appeared also in later presentations, Boyd asserts that furthermore one should:

> inhibit an adversaries capacity to adapt to such an environment (suppress or distort observations).

The goal of such actions is to:

> unstructure adversaries system into a 'hodge podge' of confusion and disorder by causing him to over or under react because of activity that appears uncertain, ambiguous or chaotic.[18]

The last slide contains Boyd's 'message', one that similarly informs his later work:

> he who can handle the quickest rate of change survives.[19]

Boyd's influence on Western fighter design and development thus was tremendous. Starting with his tour in Korea he developed his insights into the essentials of success in air-to-air combat: the ability for fast transient maneuvers coupled to a superior situational awareness. He developed the ability to see air combat as a contest of moves and countermoves in time, a contest in which a repertoire of moves and the agility to transition from one to another quickly and accurately in regard the opponent's options was essential. He managed to develop the intellectual and analytical toolkit to translate his insights from practice into better weapon systems. Because of this insight, and armed with it, he became involved in concept definition, basic engineering and setting performance characteristics of the generation of fighter aircraft that to a large extent defined Western air power and air forces from the 1980s and well into the first decade of the twenty-first century. He changed the art of designing fighters. Boyd's methodology showed trade-off parameters in the design and it brought rationality to the design processes by showing the net contribution of optional technical modifications and equipment. Importantly, his work on fighter design provided also the core of his strategic thinking.

Already the core of Boyd's later ideas appears in the pivotal presentation *A New Conception for Air-to-Air Combat*, albeit in rudimentary form. Those few themes above resurface in subsequent work in expanded and sometimes slightly adjusted form. The ability to adapt, and a strategy aimed at undermining the opponent's ability to do so, feature prominently as key themes in Boyd's theory for winning. At the time, thinking about operating at a quicker tempo, not just faster, than the adversary was a new concept in waging war, as was the expression of military operations within the context of the process of adaptation.

Reading history

One month later, on 3 September 1976, Boyd completed the eleven-page paper *Destruction and Creation*, which manifests his growing interest in various scientific disciplines that would become a distinctive formative factor of his thinking. At about the same time, work on *Patterns of Conflict* resulted in a first draft. *Patterns of Conflict* points clearly to the most obvious and initially also dominant formative factor: military history and existing strategic theories. This presentation slowly evolved through several iterations into a coherent framework that formed the vehicle for arguing doctrinal change within the US military establishment.

Even a casual reading of his main presentation, *Patterns of Conflict*, will suffice to convey the impression that Boyd was influenced directly by various strategic theories and his study of military history and, moreover, that his ideas bear close resemblance to those of a variety of authors. His study covered every known strategist from Sun Tzu, Genghis Kahn and the Mongols, Maurice de Saxe, Pierre de Bourcet, Compte de Guibert, Napoleon, Baron de Jomini and Karl von Clausewitz, Stonewall Jackson, Robert E. Lee, Ulysses S. Grant, Alfred von Schlieffen, Eric von Ludendorff, the British theorist Julian Corbett,

J.F.C. Fuller, T.E. Lawrence and Basil Liddell Hart, the German theorists/
practitioners Heinz Guderian, Eric von Manstein, Hermann Balck and Erwin
Rommel, as well as theorists of revolutionary and guerrilla warfare such as Karl
Marx and Vo Nguyen Giap, to name the most familiar ones.

The bibliography of this presentation also includes books on specific battles
and wars (for instance D-Day, Yom Kippur, Vietnam), biographies of and
autobiographies by soldiers, generals and statesmen (Napoleon, Mao Tse-Tung,
Patton, Rommel). They cover the tactical, technical, psychological, operational,
the strategic, as well as the political dimension. Some deal with deception and
intelligence, others with the Greek art of war, or command and control or tank-
tactics. Nuclear strategy and air power theorists are notably absent from the list.
Interestingly, non-Western approaches (Soviet strategy and guerrilla warfare)
feature prominently. So Boyd deliberately exposed himself to a wealth of perspectives, issues, levels of problems and a variety of theories and analyses. In
addition he read various secondary studies on military history. Interestingly, he
read history backwards; he started with the twentieth century and ended with
Sun Tzu. This approach highlighted continuity and recurring patterns instead of
radical breaks and revolutionary technical developments.

It is neither necessary nor feasible to make a synopsis of all the major works
on strategy that Boyd read and show the extent of their influence on him. The
rationale of the selection of the authors discussed below lies in the close relationship between the ideas contained in their work and those of Boyd.

To a certain extent the argument is valid that Boyd offered merely a synthesis
of existing theories, a contemporary one, important and timely regarding the
context of the 1970s and 1980s, but only a synthesis. Boyd plundered, or alternatively, created a synthesis of military history and strategic theories. He incorporated well-known historical examples and theorists in his presentations. In
Patterns of Conflict he closely followed the historical development J.F.C. Fuller
laid out in *The Conduct of War*, including Fuller's less than positive views on
Clausewitz (which Fuller shared with T.E. Lawrence and Basil Liddell Hart).[20]
Boyd shows how European armed forces lost the art of maneuver warfare in the
Napoleonic era and discusses the rise and disasters of attritional warfare that
occurred in the nineteenth century. In this, of course, Boyd found a similarity
with the situation of US armed forces in the aftermath of the Vietnam War.

Indeed, Boyd's work suggests that when it comes to his views on combat, he
found inspiration in authors who are united in their focus on the mutual
processes of adaptation, on perception, on the mental and moral impact of one's
moves, feints and threats, and on achieving destabilizing effects throughout the
enemy system instead of the more traditional focus on attritting the enemy in a
prolonged head-to-head battle. These authors display a balanced understanding
of the cognitive dimension, in concert with the physical, more than those strategists who focus primarily on the physical aspects of defeating the enemy in
battle.

Discovering fluidity

One such author was the British theorist of naval strategy Julian Corbett, who in 1911 focused on limited war.[21] He developed the idea of sea control not through the wholesale destruction of the enemy fleet, but through the exertion of control over the movement of that fleet by maintaining a fine balance between dispersion and concentration of one's own fleet, by superior knowledge concerning enemy whereabouts, and by a superior capability to concentrate if and where necessary.

A similar idea Boyd recognized in the work of T.E. Lawrence, who compared the sea with the desert, the environment for the operations of the Arab guerrilla fighters he commanded against the Turks during World War I. Lawrence is noteworthy also for the intellectual theme that is hidden within the story. Lawrence's account manifests a deliberately conducted analysis of a dominant conceptualization of war that he was equipped with through his education at Oxford, and to determine the validity of this frame of reference for the environment he found himself in. It depicts strategic theory as a conceptual lens that is relevant and adequate only in a specific context.

As Lawrence noted,

> in military theory I was tolerably read, my Oxford curiosity having taken me past Napoleon to Clausewitz and his school, to Caemmerer and Moltke, and the recent Frenchmen [...] Clausewitz was intellectually so much the master of them, and his book so logical and fascinating, that unconsciously I accepted his finality ... my interest had been abstract, concerned with the theory and philosophy of warfare especially from the metaphysical side. Now, now in the field everything had been concrete ... I began to recall suitable maxims on the conduct of modern scientific war. But they would not fit, and it worried me.[22]

Lawrence could not find a concept suitable to the Arab revolts and the socio-political-military context in any of the works of Jomini, Foch, Moltke and Clausewitz. All these authors had in common a focus on the destruction of the enemy's armed forces by only one method, battle.[23] This would not do for the Arab irregulars fighting the stronger Turks. There were no nations in war and no mass mobilization was possible. Its whole character was different and therefore the concept for victory too should be different. 'Ours seemed unlike the ritual of which Foch was priest', he noted.[24] So Lawrence started to consider the 'whole house of war', going back to the eighteenth-century pre-Napoleonic era of limited war and naval war fighting concepts.

He decided to use the vastness of the desert against the Turks. Constantly guarding every single important object was infeasible for the Turkish army, no matter how vast their number. Lawrence's cards would be speed and time, not hitting power.[25] The Turkish army was like a plant, immobile, firm-rooted, nourished through long stems to the head. In contrast, the Arabs would be an idea, an influence, a thing intangible, invulnerable, without front or back, drifting about like a gas, vapor. He opted for a war of detachment, not of contact. The time, place and object, the decision of what was critical would always be his.[26] According to Lawrence, the character of operations should be like naval war, in mobility, ubiquity, independence of bases and communications, ignoring of ground features, of strategic areas, of fixed directions, of fixed points. Tactics should be 'tip and run', not pushes but strokes. One should never try to improve an advantage. One should use the smallest force in the quickest time at the farthest place.[27] The Arab attacks would focus on destroying the 'minerals' of the Turkish army. The army was dependent on rail transport, so the death of a Turkish bridge or rail, machine gun or charge of high explosive was more profitable than the death of a Turk. At the same time he would 'arrange the mind' of the 'crowd' – the local population – his own troops, and that of the enemy. There might be humiliating material limits, but no moral impossibilities, so the scope of diathetical activities was unbounded, he noted.[28]

Lawrence wrote Liddell Hart that for irregular warfare, as Lawrence had used it, one could as easily write war of movement. Lawrence belonged, with J.F.C. Fuller and Liddell Hart, to those who contributed to the rediscovery of flexibility and maneuver, in other words, those who developed an alternative to the disastrous attritionist mindset that reigned from Napoleon till the trench warfare of 1914–18, theorists Boyd would find much inspiration in, and in their work he discovered much commonality with his own ideas.

Brain-warfare

The influence of Fuller and Liddell Hart on Boyd appears throughout *A Discourse*, both in content as well as in approach. On page 11 of *Patterns of Conflict* Boyd refers to J.F.C. Fuller's book *The Conduct of War* as a good starting point for his investigation. *The Conduct of War, 1789–1961: A Study of the Impact of the French, Industrial and Russian Revolutions on War and Its Conduct*, as the full title runs, was published in 1961, but it was in essence a 'refurbished' and undated version of several earlier books.[29] Boyd found inspiration in Fuller's view on military history, virtually adopting large parts of both the structure and content of Fuller's book in the first half of *Patterns of Conflict* where Boyd tells the story of Napoleon and the effects of the Industrial Revolution on warfare.

Fuller argued that the Great War was based on a gigantic misconception of the true purpose of war, which is to enforce the policy of a nation at the least cost to itself and to the enemy and, consequently to the world, for so intricately are the resources of civilized states interwoven that to destroy any one country is simultaneously to wound all other nations. Militarily, he wrote, since the Prussian victories of 1866 and 1870, the military doctrines of Europe had been founded on the two fallacies that policy is best enforced by destruction and that military perfection is based on numbers of soldiers, and he blames Clausewitz among others for this, as would Lawrence and Liddell Hart.

Fuller claimed that the military had misunderstood the modern nature of war. In the age of the internal combustion engine human masses had become insignificant in comparison with technological advance and perfection. The physical epoch had come to an end; the moral epoch was dawning. There was no longer a need to literally destroy the enemy's armies in the field. Aircraft using gas would disable, demoralize and paralyze unarmored troops, surface ships and civilian populations and infrastructures alike. Armored forces would paralyze, demoralize and cause the disintegration of armies by striking at their rear communications and command system. Paralysis and collapse were central themes.

Boyd incorporated this view on mobile mechanized warfare, the precursor of Blitzkrieg, as the German general Heinz Guderian would later acknowledge, and whose biography (*Panzer Leader*) Boyd would also read while completing *Patterns of Conflict*.[30] In *The Conduct of War* Boyd found reference to the idea that between action and will there exists an intimate connection. As Fuller stated: action without will loses coordination; without a directing brain an army is reduced to a mob. The fighting power of an army lies in its organization, which can be destroyed either by wearing it down or by rendering inoperative its power of command – 'brain warfare'.[31]

Boyd also adopted Fuller's concept of the three spheres of war – the physical, the mental, and the moral dimension, using this idea to structure his argument and develop three modes of conflict. Respectively, these spheres dealt with destruction of the enemy's physical strength (fighting power), disorganization of his mental processes (thinking power), and disintegration of his moral will to resist (staying power). Fuller added that forces operating within these spheres did so in synergistic, not isolated, ways. Thus instead of just focusing on the physical aspects of the enemy, the conduct of modern war should aim at moral and mental objectives and undermine rather than literally destroy the enemy.

Central to his argument is the notion that paralysis should be the aim in war and that the mental and moral dimensions should be the prime target of a military operation. Fuller insisted that 'brain warfare' was the most effective and efficient way to destroy the enemy's military organization and hence its military strength. To economize the application of military force, one needed to produce the instantaneous effects of a 'shot through the head', rather than the slow bleed of successive, slight body wounds.[32]

Fuller realized, however, explicitly, that the tank would produce its own counter measures and he foresaw the anti-tank gun and anti-armor mine, which would, in a new cycle of evolution, limit the advantage of the tank.[33] War and its tools develop in an evolutionary scheme. In Fuller's positivist, evolutionary and dialectical interpretation history shows a progression from rural to urbanized and industrialized civilization. Embedded within this transformation lay an evolutionary pendulum of weapon power, slowly or rapidly swinging from the offensive to the protective and back again in harmony with the speed of civil progress. Every measure enjoys a period of success following its introduction, but thereby provokes countermeasures to redress the balance. In this light his deliberate and extensive inclusion of Marxist and Leninist theories of revolutionary war also can be seen as part of the dialectic cycle of one form of warfare leading to another mode of warfare. This view permeates *The Conduct of War* as well as Boyd's *Patterns of Conflict*, which contains various sections in which a specific style of warfare is contrasted with its logical counter, including the Marxist, Leninist and Maoist versions of revolutionary warfare.[34]

The Indirect Approach

The foregoing authors found their ideas incorporated in the influential arguments put forward by Basil Liddell Hart,[35] and Boyd's work in turn bears close resemblance to the ideas of Liddell Hart, not surprising, considering the fact that Boyd had read if not all, at least most of his work.[36] His most popular and well-known book is *Strategy*,[37] which introduces the idea of the 'Indirect Approach'.

Boyd also resembles Liddell Hart in his didactic method. Liddell Hart had a message and was not out to make good history.[38] The search for a stratagem that would avoid the massacres of World War I was to occupy Liddell Hart during the Interbellum and, like Fuller, Liddell Hart criticized the political and military leadership of World War I. Liddell Hart, and Boyd in his wake, used the ideas of the French Neo-Napoleonic School of the late nineteenth and the early twentieth centuries to attack the strategies of the major powers in the nineteenth century and World War I that were based on Clausewitz's faulty or incomplete analysis. In dissecting Napoleon's campaigns, the school emphasized Napoleon's clear determination of the decisive point and line of advance, the resolute and carefully coordinated marches and rapid concentration of all forces to overwhelm the enemy. Equally they highlighted the flexibility of his operational formation, the 'battalion carré', loosely dispersed until the last moment and maintaining its freedom of action to operate and strike in all directions.

These principles, already proposed by De Bourcet in the eighteenth century, had helped to leave the opponent in the dark and guessing regarding Napoleon's intentions and ultimate line of attack. The pattern had been *dispersion and only then concentration* (*vide* Corbett here), with each of Napoleon's operational plan having many branches or alternative options. The school also highlighted the use of deception, feints and diversions to create surprise, disorientation and miscalculation on the enemy's part. They countered Clausewitz's claim that Napoleon had never engaged in strategic envelopment by citing the many instances of Napoleon's maneuvers against the enemy's rear, one of the most fundamental patterns of Napoleonic strategy.[39]

Liddell Hart's criticism of Clausewitz centers on what he considered the three dominant theories in *On War*: the theory of absolute warfare, with its corollary of the nation in arms; the theory that one must concentrate fire against the main enemy; and the theory that the true objective in war is the enemy's armed forces, so that everything is subject to the supreme law of battle.[40] Clausewitz had been the 'mahdi of mass' and mutual massacre and Foch in the pre-war era had been the amplifier for Clausewitz's more extreme notes.[41] Boyd would agree, noting in the margins of *Strategy*, that Clausewitz' proposals were exactly contrary to those of Sun Tzu, and devote five pages for critique on Clausewitz (but also criticizing Liddell Hart for failing to acknowledge the valuable concept of friction).

Proposing an alternative, in *Strategy: The Indirect Approach* Liddell Hart strives to show that the achievements of the great captains of all ages had rarely been brought about by the direct clash of forces but all usually involved the prior psychological and physical dislocation of the enemy. He argued that 'the most decisive victory is of no value if a nation be bled white while gaining it'.[42] Thus, following Fuller, he states that a strategist should think in terms of paralyzing, not of killing. A man unnerved is a highly infectious carrier of fear, capable of spreading an epidemic of panic. On a higher plane of warfare, the impression made on the mind of the opposing commander can nullify the whole fighting power his troops possess, and on a still higher plane, psychological pressure on the government of a country may suffice to cancel all the resources at its command – so that the sword drops from a paralyzed hand.[43]

The role of Grand Strategy is to coordinate and direct all the resources of a nation or band of nations towards the attainment of the political object of the war. It should both calculate and develop the economic resources and manpower of nations in order to sustain the fighting services. Also the moral forces of the people should be mobilized, their spirit and motivation raised. A good cause is a sword as well as armor.[44] In *Patterns of Conflict* Boyd includes the idea of a good cause as a strategic asset in his own advise concerning grand strategy, an idea he would expand upon in *The Strategic Game of ? and ?* in a section titled 'A Moral Design for Grand Strategy'.

Next comes strategy, which has as its purpose not to overcome resistance but to diminish the possibility of enemy resistance, and it seeks to fulfill this purpose by exploiting the elements of movement and surprise[45] in order to reduce fighting to the slenderest possible proportions.[46] The aim of a strategist is not so much to seek battle as to seek a strategic situation so advantageous that if it does not of itself produce the decision, its continuation by a battle is sure to achieve this.

In other words, dislocation is the aim of strategy, its sequel may be either the enemy's dissolution or his easier disruption in battle.[47] Dissolution may involve some partial measure of fighting, but this has not the character of a battle. In the psychological sphere, dislocation is the result of the impression on the commander's mind of the physical effects just listed. The impression is strongly accentuated if his realization of his being at a disadvantage is sudden and if he feels that he is unable to counter the enemy's move. Psychological dislocation fundamentally springs from this sense of being trapped.[48] Thus, Liddell Hart argues, a move around the enemy's front against his rear has the aim not only of avoiding resistance on its way but in its issue. In the profoundest sense, it takes the line of least resistance.

However, as this is known to any enemy that is worth his mettle, this move needs to be combined with the equivalent in the psychological sphere; an attack along the line of least expectation.[49] Tempo also comes into play here. Movement generates surprise and surprise gives impetus to movement, for a movement which is accelerated or changes its direction inevitably carries with it a degree of surprise, while surprise smoothes the path of movement by hindering the enemy's counter measures and counter movements.[50] The move against the enemy's rear or the threat of it has the purpose of distraction in the sense that it is meant to deprive the enemy of his freedom of action, a theme Boyd would harp upon. It should cause a distention of his forces or their diversion to unprofitable ends, so that they are too widely distributed and too committed elsewhere to have the power of interfering with one's own decisively intended move.

In the psychological sphere the same effect is sought by playing upon the fears of and by deceiving the opposing command. To mystify and mislead constitutes distraction, while surprise is the essential cause of dislocation. As Liddell Hart posits: 'It is through the distraction of the commander's mind that the distraction of his forces follows. The loss of his freedom of action is the sequel to the loss of his freedom of conception'.[51]

Corbett's ideas surface when Liddell Hart explains that an army should always be so distributed that its parts can aid each other and combine to produce the maximum possible concentration of force at one place, while the minimum force necessary is used elsewhere to prepare the success of the concentration. Effective concentration can only be obtained when the opposing forces are dispersed, and, usually, in order to ensure this, one's own forces must be widely distributed. Thus, Liddell Hart asserts, true concentration is the product of dispersion.[52]

Related to this is the principle of having alternative objectives in addition to the prime objective. If you take a line that threatens alternative objectives, you distract the enemy's mind and forces, an idea Boyd was to come to refer to as the use of *Nebenpunkte*, next to *Schwerpunkte*, or 'Centers of Gravity'. This, moreover, is the most economic method of distraction, for it allows you to keep the largest proportion of your force available on your real line of operation, thus reconciling the greatest possible concentration with the necessity of dispersion.[53] Underlying this is Liddell Hart's conviction, one shared by Boyd, that 'adaptability is the law which governs survival in war as in life – war being but a concentrated form of the human struggle against environment'.[54]

To keep such adaptability, while still keeping the initiative, the best way is to operate along the line which offers alternative objectives. These notions apply equally well to tactics as they do to strategy and their underlying essential truth is that for success two major problems must be solved: dislocation and exploitation.[55]

All these ideas would find their place in Boyd's work, most clearly in 'Patterns of War'. Subsequently, Boyd's work can be easily understood as standing in a direct theoretical line with that of Liddell Hart.

Boyd's conceptual father: Sun Tzu

The final strategist surveyed is Sun Tzu, who must be considered the true conceptual, albeit ancient, father of Boyd's work. In a 1981 article on the Military

Reform Movement, Michael Gordon already noted that '*Patterns of Conflict* draws on the writings of Chinese philosopher Sun Tzu'.[56] Indeed, this presentation in various places presents ideas of Sun Tzu, and Sun Tzu's ideas form one of the starting points of the briefing, while reappearing in the concluding part. Sun Tzu's book encapsulates many elements of theories developed by Fuller and Liddell Hart, who paid tribute to Sun Tzu by incorporating sections from *The Art of War* in the introductory pages to *Strategy*. Boyd was to adopt Sun Tzu's philosophy of war, so a somewhat elaborate discussion on Sun Tzu's ideas is therefore warranted.[57]

The first important idea is preservation. War is the most important issue a state should concern itself with, according to Sun Tzu; it is a matter of life and death and it will determine the fate of a state. War is to be avoided as much and as long as possible because inherent in war is the chance of catastrophe. War was only justifiable when all possible alternatives have been exhausted and must be entertained with the utmost seriousness and restraint. The commander must therefore be in pursuit of a quick termination and preservation of life and resources, not only one's own but also those of the opponent, while the ability to resume normal life and relations after hostilities must be kept in mind. Whenever possible, 'victory' should be achieved through diplomatic coercion, thwarting the enemy's plans and alliances and frustrating his strategy. Only when a state is threatened by an enemy with military action or refuses to give in to demands otherwise, should the government resort to armed conflict. And even then, a clash of arms is not preferred.

A crucial activity for a ruler is to keep a constant eye on one's relative power position or what we would perhaps call the state of national security, or *shih*. An ambiguous concept, it is used at all levels, not just the grand strategic level, and has a cluster of meanings such as situation, outward shape, force, influence, authority, latent energy, tactical power, positional advantage and strategic advantage.[58] The *shih* constantly shifts according to what is happening in the internal and external environment of the state. At any one time the *shih* is formed by intangible factors such as morale, opportunity, timing, psychology and logistics.

For a correct estimate of one's *shih* a ruler needs 'foreknowledge' about the environment. Sun Tzu's work implies it is possible to have complete knowledge, but it emanates not from the attainment of absolute certainty, but from the formation of a correct interpretation of the situation, a very important theme in Boyd's work. Foreknowledge springs from the ability to discern patterns and relations, implying that it derives from a holistic view of an object. Even if one has perfect information it is of no value if it is not coupled to a penetrating understanding of its meaning, if one does not see the patterns. Judgment is key. Without judgment, data mean nothing. It is not necessarily the one with more information who will come out victorious, it is the one with better judgment, the one who is better at discerning patterns. Moreover, it is a judgment of highly dynamic situation. Sun Tzu only claims that one who excels at warfare can tell when a situation will offer chances for victory or defeat, realizing that this particular impression of *shih* is a snapshot from a distance at a particular time. The closer war and battle approach in time and space, the finer becomes the detail of Sun Tzu's investigations, all the way down to indicators of the actions of an army setting up camp and the order of flags in tactical formations.

Sun Tzu's stratagems

Once the estimate of *shih* has indicated that it is both necessary and feasible to embark on war, Sun Tzu argues for adhering to several stratagems that would become very much Boyd's own:

> Warfare is the Tao of deception. Thus although you are capable, display incapability to them. When committed to employing your forces, feign inactivity. When your objective is nearby, make it appear as if distant; when far away, create the illusion of being nearby. Display profits to entice him. Create disorder (in their forces) and take them. If they are substantial, prepare for them; if they are strong, avoid them. If they are angry, perturb them; be deferential to foster their arrogance. If they are rested, force them to exert themselves. If they are united, cause them to be separated. Attack where they are unprepared. Go forth where they will not expect it. These are the ways military strategists are victorious. They cannot be spoken of in advance.[59]

Several related concepts are later further developed. These derive from the idea that strategy is about getting the enemy off balance, about creating disharmony and chaos. Sun Tzu offers a myriad of strategic and tactical factors which span the mental, the moral and the physical dimensions, that, together with the grand strategic factors such as the quality of the alliances of the opponent, combine to get the enemy off balance. The aim is to get the opponent in a position or situation against which all the potential energy of one's army can be released with the maximum effect, that is, against a disorganized and locally inferior force. The basic idea is to go forth where they do not expect it and attack where they are not prepared.[60] Battle must be avoided until one is certain that a favorable balance of power (and that means not just in number) has been created. This is what is really behind the familiar statements:

> One who knows when he can fight, and when he cannot fight, will be victorious.[61]

> One who knows the enemy and knows himself will not be endangered in a hundred engagements.[62]

> Subjugating the enemy's army without fighting is the true pinnacle of excellence.[63]

These must be understood within a logical context of the aim for preservation and the aim of fighting an enemy who is completely off balance and about to collapse. The chances of getting the enemy off balance are magnified by adhering to the concepts laid out in Box 2.2. These can be considered as modes of behavior, or effects one wants to accomplish. All these elements surface in Boyd's work.

His mechanism starts with the assumption that one can shape an opponent through the principle of 'according with the enemy', which requires (battlefield-level) foreknowledge and cohesion. These three concepts combined gird the scheme of getting the opponent off balance by the use of surprise through deception and deceit, and the methods Sun Tzu proposes to achieve surprise: the idea of formlessness and being unfathomable, maintaining a high tempo, ensuring variety and flexibility in actions, the idea of using the unorthodox and orthodox, and finally of knowing how to discern the vacuous and substantial.

According with the enemy contains the assumption that one can shape the opponent, and for that one should act in accord with the opponent's actions. This is an essential idea in Chinese philosophy and it is expressed as *yin*. Every situation has its give and take and can be turned into an opportunity. *Yin* involves responsiveness to one's context, to adapt oneself to a situation in such a manner as to take full advantage of the defining circumstances, and to avail oneself of the possibilities of the situation in achieving one's own purposes: 'Do not fix any time for battle, assess and react to the enemy in order to determine the strategy for battle'.[64]

Yin requires sensitivity and adaptability. Sensitivity is necessary to register the full range of forces that define one's situation, and on the basis of this awareness, to anticipate the various possibilities that can ensue. Adaptability refers to the conscious fluidity of one's own disposition. One can only turn prevailing circumstances to account if one maintains an attitude of readiness and flexibility. One must adapt oneself to the enemy's changing posture as naturally and as effortlessly as flowing water winding down a hillside.[65] The concept of fluidity is one that is also embedded within Boyd's work.[66] *Yin* means shifting your posi-

---

According with the enemy
Foreknowledge
Cohesion
Surprise
Deception and deceit
Formlessness and being unfathomable
High tempo
Variety and flexibility
Orthodox and unorthodox
Vacuous and substantial

Box 2.2 Sun Tzu's stratagems.

tion so adroitly and imperceptibly that, from the enemy's perspective, you are inscrutable.[67] To accord with the opponent one needs to know the opponent's aims, plans and position of forces as well as the character of the commander. And this leads us to a second look at 'foreknowledge', this time more specific for the strategic and tactical level, as opposed to the grand strategic level we have dealt with before.

Foreknowledge is essential for the grand strategic level, but it permeates the whole body of thought. It means something different at each level of war. Sun Tzu specifies the different answers a commander would want to know at a certain level. Each level has different issues to address in different levels of detail. At the tactical levels a general needs to know the number of campfires in the enemy camp and the sounds that emanate from it, etc. Foreknowledge makes possible the other concepts such as deception, being fathomless and formless, attacking the vacuous, the use of orthodox and the unorthodox.

Maintaining cohesion is another important prerequisite for creating and exploiting disorder. Morale is one aspect: one should attack when the *ch'i*, or spirit, of the enemy troops is low but only if and when one's own *ch'i* is high. Trust, fairness, integrity, leadership, esprit de corps and discipline are other (modern) terms relating to this, ones Boyd would also incorporate. Thus, a commander should be able to direct his troops as though commanding one man[68] and 'one whose upper and lower ranks have the same desires' (and will thus be victorious)[69] so he can 'in order await the disordered'.[70]

Surprise, deception and deceit. Without surprise at some stage it will be difficult to mass superior force at a certain point. Surprise is achieved through the interaction, the reinforcing effect of several methods applied simultaneously.[71] It involves the employment of deception and deceit. For instance, it is achieved by moving separated and keeping the opponent guessing where one will unite. If one is united, one can disperse again in the hope that the opponent has united and thereby committed his forces. Troop deployments, or the image thereof, used together with disinformation from (expendable) spies, as well as feigning certain activities that serve as indicators of upcoming operations to the trained eye of the opposing commander, all serve the end of deceiving the opponent. Of course all efforts to deceive must be matched by making sure one's real intentions and movements are shrouded in secrecy and with this we arrive at the concept of being *unfathomable* and *formless*.

Being unfathomable and formless. Sun Tzu stresses the need for a commander to be unfathomable and obscure, never revealing his plans or intentions even to his own troops. Being unfathomable through deception and deceit will cause the opposing commander to be confused or forced to respond in a way that is not according to his initial plan. He is forced to react especially when he suddenly discovers that his opponent is moving to an object that he needs to defend. Thus he is shaped. These ideas surface in the statement: 'One who excels at moving the enemy deploys in a configuration to which the enemy must respond. He offers something that the enemy must seize. With profit he moves them, with the foundation he awaits them.'[72]

Related to deception and being unfathomable is the idea of being *formless*. Whenever the army deploys onto the battlefield, its configuration, being immediately apparent, will evoke a reaction. Whether the enemy will then modify his original anticipations, vary his tactics or view the events as confirming a preconceived battle plan, depends upon his evaluation of the unfolding situation. By being formless – without having a recognizable configuration – this evaluation becomes difficult. Thus being formless also implies being unfathomable. False appearances kept secret in turn help being unfathomable. Formless can also mean that one lacks an identifiable mass and the enemy cannot discern a pattern or a main body, again perhaps due to the true physical dispersion of our forces or through being unfathomable and employing deceit and being successful in deception activities. Not knowing our position, and in order to defend what he treasures or to cover the possible routes we can go, he must disperse his forces. These tactics aim at getting the opponent dislocated and confused.

Speed, rapidity. To enhance the creation of confusion, and being unfathomable, one should also use superior speed and rapidity. Speed, rapidity of movement and attacks help in shaping the opponent and wear him down.[73] The same holds true for the concepts of *variety and flexibility*. This is reflected in: 'Men all know the disposition by which we attain victory, but no one knows the configuration through which we control the victory. Thus a victorious battle (strategy) is not repeated, the configurations of response to the enemy are inexhaustible.'[74]

A particular kind of this is captured in the concept of *the orthodox (cheng) and the unorthodox (ch'i)*. It is an important set of polar opposites and one Boyd would frequently refer to. It can be translated as the 'straightforward method and the crafty method' or 'the direct method and the indirect method'. *Ch'i* and *cheng* must be understood in the widest sense as meaning energy, strategy, ideas or forces (moral, mental and physical). The point is that one can use force (and not forces as in specific types of units) in conventional–traditional as well as in imaginative–unconventional ways in dealing with an opponent. Nothing in itself is either straightforward or crafty, direct or indirect: characteristic of the concept is the fact that the unorthodox can become the orthodox. Whether it is one or the other depends on what one thinks one's opponent will expect in the particular circumstances of the battle.

The concept of *ch'i* and *cheng* is about conceptualizing, characterizing, manipulating forces within – and by exploiting an enemy's expectation. When a frontal attack is expected, a conclusion derived from one's previous strategy and tactics and one's disposition of forces at that particular moment, then that is the orthodox, and an enveloping movement will be the unorthodox. The concept also refers to the functions of forces; to fix the opponent is the orthodox but the *coup de grâce* will be delivered by the unorthodox in a flanking attack.[75] The extraordinary forces are used to take the enemy by surprise. Indeed, what is unorthodox and orthodox, expected or strange, direct or indirect, regular or irregular, extraordinary or normal (to name a few meanings of *cheng* and *ch'i*) is dependent on the opponent, so the actions of both sides are again mutually influenced. Thus, using the expectations of the opponent's commander and employing forces in ways, times, places, movements and formations he does not expect it, we can get the opponent off balance.

Sun Tzu does not advocate one above the other, the indirect nor the direct, but stresses the novel combination of both.[76] It is from the interaction of the unorthodox and the orthodox that the enemy is confused, demoralized, disorganized, dislocated, looking at the wrong direction, etc. Variation and novel combinations of types of forces, of maneuvers and methods of deception and deceit are important.

However, understanding the enemy's dispositions (*hsing*) and his potential power (*shih*) and knowing how to apply the concept of the orthodox and unorthodox is not enough. It is incomplete unless one knows how to target one's forces against the enemy's disposition and power. The commander must have an appreciation for the concept of the polar opposites *emptiness (hsu)* and *fullness, or solidness (shih)*, or the *vacuous* and *substantial*. *Hsu* means empty or weak in a sense that goes beyond the physical. To be empty in the *hsu* sense can indicate a poorly defended position or a well defended position, but with troops imbued with a weak morale, lack of legitimate purpose or feeble leadership. *Hsu* indicates the crevices in an opponent's defenses, which allow penetration. Conversely, *shih* can be a strongly defended position or a capable force that has every positive quality. It has high morale, strong leadership and its actions are in accord with its moral code. The problem is that no position of force is permanently solid (nor empty for that matter) and Sun Tzu sees this as a way of providing the opponent with the dilemma we already stumbled upon: what to defend and what to attack.[77]

Boyd's work resembles *The Art of War*. There are similarities in the prime role of information accorded to strategy, to the role of perception, to the attention for pattern recognition, to the importance of tempo, surprise, novelty and mismatches, and the use of *cheng/ch'i*. Boyd follows Sun Tzu when the latter argues that any favorable outcome of a conflict is the result of multiple methods applied simultaneously at several levels, and reinforcing one another and shaping conditions for others to be effective. War is not only the affair of armies. In formulating strategy one should address the entire enemy system. At the grand strategic level this is manifest in the list of strategies available, including diplomatic, economic and military methods. At the military strategic level, operational and tactical level we see it in the interactions of the supporting concepts which all, at the different levels, aim to get the enemy off balance, to isolate sections of the opponent at different aggregation levels of his system.

Actions are not exclusively aimed at one particular domain, be it the physical or mental or moral, instead they aim to impact at least two at the same time. They aim at disrupting connections (moral, informational, spatial, ideational, logistical) between the ruler and his people, between the commander and his troops, and between units, by physically separating them, isolating them, dislocating them, by morally disrupting cohesion through creating distrust and decreasing support for the ruler by thwarting his plans and taking away his army, spreading false information, bribing officials and diplomatic pressure, disrupting his alliances and generally chipping away at the power-base of a ruler and the legitimacy and integrity of his actions. Through the combination of unanticipated physical movement, actions aim to confuse (mental sphere) and work on the moral fiber of the enemy. Through the use of secrecy, rapid movements and attacks, by attacking where not expected, by combined use of orthodox and unorthodox methods, the enemy is dislocated and confused and numerically inferior, which works on the morale of the troops. The simultaneous use of multiple methods affects moral, mental and physical aspects of the enemy's system through all its levels.

These themes surface at various places in Boyd's work, in particular in *Patterns of Conflict*. Indeed, if there is one strategic author Boyd must conceptually be related to, and compared with, it is Sun Tzu. And the ideas of Sun Tzu were far from common knowledge in the US military that faced severe problems in the aftermath of the Vietnam War. These problems shaped the content of his work, while they also translated into a receptive background for novel ideas, and a stimulating and fertile environment for translating ideas into practice.

Fertile soil: the US Military after Vietnam

Turbulent environment

Upon his return in 1973 from Thailand, were he worked on a classified intelligence operation,[78] Boyd became part, even the nucleus, of the 'Military Reform Movement'. This amorphous group consisted of the fighter mafia, serving and retired military officers, journalists such as James Fallows and academics such as Edward Luttwak,[79] experts from industry as well as influential politicians such as Newt Gingrich, Gary Hart, Sam Nunn and Dick Cheney. After his retirement on 1 September 1975, Boyd remained active as a (deliberately) non-paid consultant to the Office of the Secretary of Defense[80] and continued his involvement with this group with zeal. In many respects Boyd became the intellectual leader of the group, which was glued together by Boyd's reputation and his ideas that slowly matured in the initial *Patterns of Conflict* briefing.[81]

The reform movement steadily expanded in numbers of followers, visibility and in influence, exposing an increasing number of people in various offices and from all services and political parties to Boyd's ideas, while Boyd in turn kept on expanding *Patterns of Conflict* and briefed the evolving content to the growing number and variety of people he gained access to. It brought him in touch with people who were looking for valuable ideas to change the prevailing approach in US defense planning and the prevailing military doctrine, so as to incorporate the lessons of the Vietnam War. Their efforts and arguments were certainly not beyond dispute and were often polemical, categorical and confrontational, but the critics admitted that the group performed a valuable service in driving the debate even if they did so by functioning as one pole in a dialectic.[82]

Boyd's work bears the marks of the agenda of the military reform movement. From 1976 to 1986 the group rallied against the ever-upward-spiraling complexity and costs of military equipment. Weapon development was not necessarily driven by sound operational requirements so much as by industrial interests and a faith in technology on the part of Pentagon officials. Such rising costs would moreover be budgetarily unsustainable. The reform movement revolted against the managerial approach and the 'culture of procurement', which was characterized by an emphasis on the tangibles of war, such as the state of military technology and the quantity of fighter aircraft, tanks and naval vessels, and the firepower potential on the battlefield. Defense planning was considered a rather straightforward and rational exercise in calculation, based on the assumption that indeed it was possible to make some pretty accurate predictions concerning the nature of combat engagements with future foes. There was a distinct overvaluation of systems analysis in strategic debate and defense policy, one analyst observed in 1973.[83] The dominant school of strategic theory followed an ahistorical, apolitical method of calculating purportedly correct 'answers' to defense problems. A tendency existed to seek refuge in technology from hard problems of strategy and policy. Defense preparation as well as war were characterized by an emphasis on the technical and logistical rather than the well-informed and operationally agile, noted another one.[84] Writing in 1981, James Fallows warned that this approach manifested a neglect of the 'intangibles' of war, such as leadership, doctrine, morale, personal skills, combat experience, tactical ingenuity, information and strategy. It ignored or dismissed the fundamentally uncertain nature of war.

In addition, the strategic discourse during the Vietnam War was dominated by nuclear strategy, reflecting prevailing US international security concerns.[85] Nuclear missions were emphasized and conventional weapons and training minimized. Strategic nuclear forces were considered up to well in the 1960s as an instrument to prevent war at all levels.[86] Although there was a constant debate concerning the right balance of conventional and nuclear capabilities, conventional forces were discussed within the context of deterrence. The debates were mostly focusing on the European theatre, and the dominant mode in strategy was one of annihilation of the enemy.[87] Limited wars had only a very limited influence on the orientation of the US armed services when choices had to be made concerning system development, acquisitions and doctrine.[88]

The Vietnam War was in that respect a defining experience, revealing the consequences of the nation's previous fixation on nuclear strategy at the expense of adequate preparations for conventional war. It provided a wake-up call regarding the kinds of defenses the United States and members of NATO would have to contend with in configuring themselves for a possible future counteroffensive against Soviet and Warsaw Pact forces in Central Europe, as well as the need of attention for the operational level of war, which had been neglected since World War II.[89]

The period from Jimmy Carter's presidency to Ronald Reagan's second term was one of intense soul-searching and turmoil within the US defense establishment. There was confusion about national security strategy, national military strategy, the transition from conscription to an all-volunteer force, militarily relevant technologies, arms control, and conflict among the services on individual weapons systems and just why the war had been lost. The military had to reinvent itself after military defeat and steel itself for challenges at both ends of the spectrum.[90] While most military professionals believed that the Vietnam War had been ineptly conceived and badly run, disillusionment with political and military leadership inculcated an attitude of mistrust that manifested itself in bitterness toward senior military and civilian leadership. It also drove a zealous desire for internal reform.[91]

The Israeli experience during 1973, despite considerable differences with the Vietnam experience, only reinforced the impression among US military that conventional war-fighting capabilities needed to be addressed and that operational-level doctrine needed serious attention.[92] With Egypt armed with the latest Soviet equipment, in particular SAM systems, the United States and its NATO allies got an arresting preview of what an all-out showdown with the newly expanded Soviet conventional force posture might entail. It demonstrated the extent of the Soviet military buildup from 1965 to 1972. Not only did the Soviets achieve acknowledged parity with the US in both number and quality in the crucial realm of intercontinental and submarine-launched ballistic missiles, they also upgraded their forward-deployed conventional forces.[93] The 1979 Soviet invasion in Afghanistan provided a midcourse reminder of the US armed service's need to reshape and recast themselves.

This was neither a simple process nor one that led to immediate changes in military effectiveness. Instead, numerous changes had to occur before planners could be confident that the services had the kind of forces, body of thought and doctrine, and weapons to confront various levels of warfare, ranging from support to client states in Third World conflict to actual large-scale commitment of American forces in, for example, a NATO–Warsaw Pact war. This was a bottom-up driven process. While the Reagan era defense build-up after 1980 greatly accelerated, expanded and encouraged this get-well process, progress (in particular during the latter half of the 1970s) was mostly the result of programs, initiatives and experiments undertaken by the services, spurred on by mid-level managers and combat veterans who wanted to redress the procedural, organizational, doctrinal and equipment shortcomings of the Vietnam era,[94] a process in which Boyd was closely involved.

Indeed, Boyd's work must be seen and explained as an answer to these challenges. Boyd's work focused exactly on the intangibles of war, on non-attritionist doctrine, and on critical thinking, innovation and experimentation as essential parts of organizational culture, critiquing the managerial mindset, which he equated with the attritional style of warfare that employed predictable linear tactics and numerical superiority to bleed the enemy to death.[95] Boyd, in a series of profound briefings, began to remind everyone: 'Machines don't fight wars. Terrain doesn't fight wars. Humans fight wars. You must get into the minds of humans. That's where the battles are won.' This aspect had been totally missing from the debates in the Pentagon, according to one analyst who sided with the reform group.[96]

Brodie's remark that the military profession provides some of the most barren soil for the nurture of independence of thinking may be correct in principle;[97] in this period after – and because of – the Vietnam War an environment nevertheless emerged in which new ideas on doctrine and strategy would find fertile soil, and indeed, Boyd's ideas evolved in symbiotic fashion with efforts of different services to develop new and appropriate doctrinal frameworks.[98]

Adaptive Marines

Reform within the US military occurred along various axes and was an arduous process. Hardware improvements were one axis of transformation. The US Navy registered significant gains in terms of hardware, including the addition of Aegis-class highly advanced air-defense ships and cruise missiles, but its basic orientation was not altered and consisted mainly of hunting down Soviet submarines and protecting the sea lanes connecting the US and Europe, and neutralizing any Soviet air or naval force that might contest American control of the high seas worldwide. The US Army modernized its equipment inventory by the introduction of the M1 Abrams tank, the M2 Bradley armored vehicle, the AH-64 Apache attack helicopter, the UH-60 Blackhawk utility helicopter. In the decade from 1975 to 1985 the US Air Force improved its inventory of precision weapons, electronic warfare assets, its capability to suppress enemy air defenses, the ability to operate at low level during night and adverse weather conditions. Finally, stealth technology was developed. These technological advances were coupled to improvements in training, with the creation of large complexes from where large formations of fighters, bombers and supporting aircraft could exercise in a highly realistic environment against air and SAM systems mimicking Soviet assets and tactics.[99]

But Boyd must be credited for providing the conceptual heart of the dominant and perhaps most relevant theme characterizing the transformation within the US armed services. Boyd drew different conclusions than the historian Russell Weighly, who, in his study of *The American Way of War* of 1973, concurred with admiral Wylie's remarks that conventional military force and any form of military strategy had lost its utility in light of the experience of Vietnam and the ever-threatening specter of nuclear war.[100]

Instead, Boyd found alternatives to the attrition style of warfare, which is merely a matter of sacrificing men and treasure to win battles. It does not require superior mental capacity, strategy or great generalship as long as one side has the firepower and manpower to overwhelm the enemy. Boyd argued for non-linear tactics, avoiding and bypassing enemy positions, venturing deep into enemy territory without too much concern for one's own flanks. The prize was not territory but time, surprise and shock. Such tactics would force the enemy to react. They would create the impression US troops were everywhere and could strike anytime anyplace.

Feeding upon technological progress in the field of precision munitions, armor and surveillance equipment, and in turn inspiring technological developments,[101] both the US Army and US Marines abandoned the prevailing defensive orientation and attrition mentality, and turned towards a new concept of maneuver warfare aimed at engaging attacking enemy forces both close and deep simultaneously, and with heavy reliance on air support. This implied a move away from a focus on linear operations, a reliance on overwhelming force and massive firepower, toward a style of operation consisting of multiple thrusts, surprise, deception, non-linear fluid actions aimed at uncovering enemy weaknesses and an emphasis on achieving disintegration, shattering the cohesion among enemy units and their action, rather than destruction by a continuous and predictable battering of enemy strong-points. Integral with this shift was a rediscovery of the operational – or theater – level of war.

The US Marines adopted the maneuvrist approach for a number of reasons. The Vietnam experience had convinced them that the American way of attrition warfare was not effective. Moreover they realized they had neither the numbers nor the equipment to survive in the European environment, where large-scale armored and mechanized units were supposed to clash. Within NATO they were subsequently assigned the mission to guard NATO's northern front in Norway. Still, here too they faced the prospect of a big battle. With concurrent debates on the actual relevance of large amphibious operations, many in the Corps deemed it necessary to think about changing the way they thought it should prepare and fight in future wars. Boyd played a very active part in this process and was closely associated with leading advocates of doctrinal change within the US Marines. In particular, from 1979 onwards several Marine Corps officers later to achieve high ranks were exposed to Boyd's ideas through lectures and discussions Boyd had with them, on their invitation.

This association also explains the format of his work. Slides were a flexible and appropriate tool, in particular with his primary audience, the military, which has a visually oriented culture in which overhead slides feature prominently as a mode of communication. As one author who walked the halls of the Pentagon stated, 'Boyd was a tireless briefer [. . .] and indeed made a major contribution to an entirely new Pentagon *Zeitgeist* on the use of force'.[102] Using his slides as an educational tool, he guided his audiences through his ideas, spreading the philosophy of the [reform] movement. He made them go through the step-by-step process of analysis and synthesis. To understand Boyd nowadays, one needs to regard his slides as the manifestation of this learning process. But it was also a discourse, a two-way process. As Coram remarked, Boyd needed the dialectic of debate.[103] And while Hammond rightly observed that 'there is little doubt that Boyd's hundreds of *Patterns of Conflict* briefings around the Pentagon and throughout the US military had prepared the ground for a different approach to war fighting for the American military',[104] equally, this interaction and the background of the interaction produced *A Discourse*; they stimulated the growth of ideas and conceptual innovation. Boyd refined and polished his ideas in response to discussions and the expanding list of literature he devoured.[105]

His maturing ideas were incorporated in experiments ongoing in the Amphibious Warfare School in discussions within the Marine Corps Development Center (which is the doctrine development organization). Boyd emphasized speed, tempo, variety, surprise, trust, initiative, movement, and that his view the moral and mental dimensions came before technology, superiority in numbers and massed firepower, items the Corps was short of, was obviously appealing. Instead of focusing on terrain and the amphibious landing, Boyd taught them to focus on the enemy. While not a new concept of course, the way Boyd presented maneuver warfare was.[106]

Boyd's ideas were translated after a decade of lectures, briefings and debates in Marine Corps doctrine.[107] Chapter 1 of the US Marine Corps prime war-fighting manual, MCDP-1, which was published in the mid 1990s captures the US Marines' vision of the nature of war by employing Boydian concepts such as the pervasiveness of non-linearity, uncertainty, risk, fluidity and disorder, the view that war is a meeting of complex systems, and that war is the emergence of collective behavior of these complex systems in conflict with each other. Chapter 4, 'The Conduct of War', contains the Marines' interpretation of maneuver warfare, which bears in particular Boyd's influence. It states that

> the essence of maneuver is taking action to generate and exploit some kind of advantage over the enemy [...] That advantage may be psychological, technological, or temporal as well as spatial. Especially important is maneuver in time – we generate a faster operating tempo than the enemy to gain a temporal advantage. Maneuver warfare is a war fighting philosophy that seeks to shatter the enemy's cohesion through a variety of rapid, focused and unexpected actions which create a turbulent and rapidly deteriorating situation with which the enemy cannot cope.[108]

Further on it describes the Marines' command philosophy, and again Boyd's advice permeates directly into the doctrine: 'in order to generate the tempo of operations we desire and to best cope with the uncertainty, disorder, and fluidity of combat, command and control must be decentralized'.[109] One of the authors later described war as 'an organic exchange of energy, matter, and information between open, linked hierarchies according to the laws of far-from-equilibrium thermodynamics'.[110]

Indeed, it was in this novel conceptualization that the new US Marine Corps doctrine constituted a major breakthrough, as David Alberts and Thomas Czerwinski assert.[111] The relevance of Boyd's contribution can be judged by the fact that he was bestowed the distinguished title of 'honorable Marine' and that the US Marine Corps University houses Boyd's collection of papers by specific request of the commandant of the US Marine Corps.

Boyd and tanks

The US Army chose to reorient itself on the main challenge: countering a surprise Warsaw Pact armored assault against NATO.[112] It considered the involvement in counterinsurgency in Vietnam as an aberration and a mistake to be avoided, while the 1973 war in the Middle East provided sufficient rationale for focusing on conventional warfare. Moreover, Europe was the undisputed core of US foreign policy aimed at the containment of the Soviet Union and its defense the central role for US troops, a position only reinforced under the tenure of then Secretary of Defense James Schlesinger, who aimed to re-establish European confidence in the American commitment to the defense of Europe.[113]

This reorientation constituted also an organizational need, as the Army was in critical decline. The Army was so utterly run-down in the aftermath of, and due to, the Vietnam War, that it had to focus first on its principal mission. In 1972 only four of the Army's thirteen active divisions were rated as ready for combat. Moreover, development of doctrine, equipment, training and education had stood still for nearly a decade. Additionally, Army units in Europe had been used as a rotation base for short tours in Vietnam, resulting in an inability to maintain military proficiency there. On top of these problems, the Army faced the challenge of transitioning from a force based on mobilization and conscription towards a fully professional Army.[114]

US Army leadership thought the solution to the superior numbers and offensive doctrine lay in a synergistic marshalling of the alliance's air and ground assets against identifiable weak spots in the Warsaw Pact's concept of operations. This led to several doctrinal experiments, publications and debates. In 1976 the US Army Active Defense Field Manual 100–5 was published. It aroused a debate within the US Army and within the Military Reform Movement which Boyd aired in his lectures for US Army officers. Critics said it placed too much emphasis on the defense and 'winning the first battle', ignoring the psychological dimension of warfare, and focused too narrowly on Europe.[115] Indeed, US Army leadership focused not on the most likely conflict but on the one with the largest consequences and on the belief that the battle in Central Europe would be the most demanding mission the US Army could be assigned. Whatever its flaws, the manual did succeed in making the officer corps care about doctrine and it led to a renaissance of professional discourse on how the army should fight.[116] In 1981 one junior officer noted with some sense of understatement that 'the sobering perception that our historic firepower-attrition method of warfare offers a recipe of defeat has begun to surface in military journals'.[117]

Boyd was closely associated with the leading reformers in the US Army (such as Huba Wass de Czege) and like-minded policy advisers (such as Senator Gary Hart's aide for military affairs Bill Lind, who authored a book titled *Maneuver Warfare*, which was based on Boyd's ideas). Several army officers noted the positive reaction of the Marines to Boyd's presentation.[118] Subsequently, following the publication of FM 100–5, topics such as *Blitzkrieg, Auftragstaktik, Schwerpunkt*, and new leadership principles, the ideas of Sun Tzu, J.F.C. Fuller and B.H. Liddell Hart, the merits of maneuver warfare versus attrition-type warfare, the concept of the operational level of war, the determinants of successful change in armies, Soviet Operational Art, and even Genghis Khan, frequently appeared in articles, all themes present in Boyd's work that evolved during that time.[119]

A young captain's explanation of Boyd's message at the time sheds light on the measure of Boyd's influence as well as on the state of development of his thinking in 1979–81. He explains that Boyd rediscovered the philosophers and practitioners of maneuver warfare such as Alexander, Genghis Khan, Maurice de Saxe, de Bourcet, Guibert, J.F.C. Fuller and Heinz Guderian. Next he offers Boyd's ideas to lay out the alternative to the attrition method. As he states:

> Colonel Boyd observed that in any conflict all combatants go through repeated cycles of an observation – orientation – decision – action (OODA) loop [. . .] The potentially victorious combatant is the one with the OODA loop which is consistently quicker than his opponent (including the time required to transition from one cycle to another). As this opponent repeatedly cycles faster than his opponent, the opponent finds he is losing control of the situation [. . .] his countermeasures are overcome by the rapidly unfolding events and become ineffective in coping with each other. He finds himself increasingly unable to react. Suddenly, he realizes there is nothing else he can do to control the situation or turn it to his advantage. At this point he has lost. In essence his command circuits have been overloaded, thereby making his decisions too slow for the developing situation [. . .] all that remain are uncoordinated smaller units incapable of coordinated action. The enemy's defeat in detail is the eventual outcome.[120]

This method would require, he asserted, continuous high-tempo operations, a focus on creating and exposing flanks and rears, and on weaknesses instead of enemy's strengths. Firepower would be used primarily for disrupting the enemy and not solely for its attrition effect. It would require, furthermore, mission tactics or *Auftragstaktik*, for the party which can consistently operate the longest without new orders will inevitably have the greater advantage over an opponent awaiting orders after every action. Such a command style requires mutual trust and a reliance on small-unit initiative.[121]

The debate resulted via the improved 1986 FM 100–5 edition in the AirLand Battle concept and the Follow On Forces Attack plan.[122] It involved a refocusing of attention toward the moral and human dimensions of battle, introducing into the US doctrine the clarifying notion of the operational level of war and a return to the fundamental principles of attaining victory and appreciation of immeasurables of combat such as leadership, initiative and the commander's intuitive sense of time and maneuver.[123] At its heart lay an approach to war that was based on intellectual innovation rather than sheer material superiority,[124] the result of a cognitive crisis the civilian reformers had ignited and the professional debate of the late 1970s that this inspired.

Boyd's influence was not only due to the merits of his arguments alone. Boyd had no objection to airing his views and critique, if necessary through the national media. In the spring of 1981, his theories burst into the national scene with articles in for instance the *Washington Post* and *Atlanta Constitution* running titles such as 'New War Theory Shoots Down Old War Ideas'. Not surprisingly this gained his ideas attention but also gained him enemies. He deliberately embarrassed the leadership of the US military, in particularly that of the US Army, by asserting that there were no real military theorists practicing their craft in the US. They had been replaced by scientist and technologists, people who had no idea about a concept such as Sun Tzu's *cheng/ch'i*. But the US Army did take notice, or rather, plagiarized his work.[125] As in the case of Boyd's involvement with the US Marine Corps, in the US Army too, Boyd's ideas were in particular readily accepted by the relatively young field-grade officers, whereas more senior leaders tended to hang on to established ideas.[126]

Five years after Boyd had begun lecturing *Patterns of Conflict*, the US Army formally changed its doctrinal course. Boyd's ideas were interpreted almost literally into four basic tenets comprising the conceptual skeleton of the AirLand Battle doctrine: initiative, agility, depth and synchronization.[127] Initiative meant maintaining an offensive spirit, not in the foolish sense of the French army in the first years of World War I, but, rather, in the constant effort to seize or retain independence of action. It emphasized that subordinates must be able to act independently within the framework of an overall plan. Depth meant combining elements of time, distance and resources across the entire spread of a battlefield to prevent an enemy from concentrating his firepower and maneuvering freely. Agility emphasized being more responsive, anticipatory, and flexible in decision making and movement than an enemy to avoid enemy strength and exploit vulnerabilities. Finally, synchronization emphasized coordinated action and an all-pervading unity of effort.[128]

In the course of its new conceptual enterprise, resulting from the post-Vietnam professional perplexity, American military mentality moved from an addiction to attrition based on tactical parochialism and technology to the adoption of the operational maneuver.[129] However, the true significance of this period for the US Army was not the crafting of AirLand Battle, but the inculcation of a tradition of creativity and introspection. It institutionalized creativity and conceptual thinking in the US Army.[130]

Experience, curiosity and challenges

This chapter has shed light on three formative factors of *A Discourse*: Boyd's personal experience as a fighter pilot, his study of military history, and the state of the US military in the aftermath of the Vietnam War. It has shown the initial source of the OODA loop idea and the way his curious mind attempted to discover the dynamics behind success in air-to-air combat. It has indicated his contribution to fighter development, and it has shown how Boyd made the leap from fighter design and air-to-air tactics to strategic theory. The chapter has also shed light on Boyd's intellectual predecessors, such as Corbett, Lawrence, Fuller, Liddell Hart and Sun Tzu. This discussion hinted at Boyd's other role, that of *reconceptualizing* maneuver warfare and, by extension, other schools of strategic thought, with the employment of the OODA loop model. It suggested that an important role of Boyd lay in *rediscovering* and *synthesizing* existing theories and insights and offering them in a very digestible and convincing format to his audience.

Like Clausewitz, Fuller and Liddell Hart in their times, Boyd's ideas evolved and matured at a time when the US military was searching for novel ideas to solve concrete strategic and operational problems. While reflecting his experience as a fighter pilot, his involvement in fighter design, as well as his study of military history, his work also strongly reflects an explicit institutional requirement, and matured by virtue of the interaction with a receptive audience. It is no coincidence Boyd harped on the intangibles of war, on the fundamental uncertainty of war and strategy, and on the alternatives to the attritional style of warfare. The reform effort inspired his work and his insistence on maneuver warfare as an alternative for the alleged flawed attritional war fighting style. He developed his arguments and ideas with the purpose of inducing change and an innovative organizational culture. Considering the dominant strategic and military culture, it is all the more remarkable and equally impressive that someone was able first of all to develop a new, distinctive and coherent military theory in such an environment, and second, to gain the wide influence Boyd achieved with his non-conformist ideas.

Indeed, in time perhaps he became as much a formative factor of the military *Zeitgeist* as the military *Zeitgeist* was a formative factor of his ideas. As Burton posits, Boyd's mindset was infused with a measure of frustration concerning the sorry state of strategic thinking in the US military establishment: 'Boyd would change that and would force the military to scramble like mad to catch up with him as he produced theory after theory that was unique and revolutionary in the art of war'.[131] And the next chapter will show that some of these theories came from unsuspected sources.

3 Science

Boyd's fountain

Knowledge is an unending adventure at the edge of uncertainty.

Jacob Bronowski

Boyd and science

Introduction

The scientific *Zeitgeist* has exerted a defining influence on Boyd's work. The following two chapters present a panorama of the scientific *Zeitgeist* of Boyd's lifetime, in no small measure based on the same books Boyd read during the sixties, seventies, eighties up to the mid-nineties. Chapter 3 describes the scientific developments that occurred during the early decades of the twentieth century that Boyd incorporated in his work, and which had a tremendous influence beyond physics, from which these developments originated. In addition, the epistemological debates of the sixties will be discussed that in part arose from these developments, as well as systems theory (including the cognitive revolution), all of which have left their mark on Boyd's work. Chapter 4 completes the study of the influence of the scientific *Zeitgeist* by taking a look at the development of chaos and complexity theory that took place during the late seventies, eighties and nineties, developments which Boyd closely followed and incorporated in his work (in particular in his last three presentations). It finishes with an assessment of the implications of the findings for understanding Boyd.

Hidden fountain

Destruction and Creation is the first part of Boyd's strategic opus and also the first indication of the way and extent to which science influenced his thinking. It is the conceptual heart of his subsequent work as well as his most impressive intellectual achievement and 'the culmination of a quest to find scientific, mathematical, and logical verification for principles Boyd knew intuitively to be true'.[1] The attention Boyd paid to developments in and insights from science was fundamental and essential. It can be argued that:

1   Boyd's scientific education followed the scientific *Zeitgeist*, not unconsciously, but deliberately;
2   Boyd thought the study of war required an interdisciplinary study of science;
3   His education matured while the scientific *Zeitgeist* shifted;
4   Boyd was aware of this shift;
5   He made this new paradigm central in his work;
6   He considered this paradigm as the appropriate way to approach the study of war.

Indeed, the scientific *Zeitgeist* can be considered his hidden fountain. While his study in Georgia Tech University and his work on fighter design primed him, another factor making him study various fields of science was more of an introvert nature. Already before he started working on *Destruction and Creation* in 1972 he had been pondering about the working of the brain and the nature of creativity. His path-breaking work on EM theory made him aware that apparently his thought process somehow worked differently than others', how else could such a simple theory as EM theory not have been conceived by someone else before his discovery? On 15 October 1972 he wrote from his base in Thailand to his wife that 'I may be on the trail of a *theory of learning* quite different and – it appears now more powerful than methods or theories currently in use'. Learning for him was synonymous for the process of creativity. Without any premeditated overall design or goal, he read every available book in the base library on philosophy and physics and math and economics and science and Taoism and half a dozen other disciplines, according to Coram.[2] It laid the foundation for what would become the major focus of his life.

From there on, during the latter twenty years of his life, the period in which *A Discourse* was developed, Boyd delved deeper and probed more widely and connected more completely insights from a variety of disciplines. He would call his friends and disciples, sometimes in the middle of the night, to discuss the latest piece he had read, which could be the work of the German philosopher Hegel, Gödel, Piaget, Skinner, Polanyi, a book on quantum physics, history or social science.[3] This impression is reinforced by the list of books read by Boyd, according to the archive that the US Marine Corps University maintains on him. Exceeding twenty pages, the list includes annotated works that describe developments marking the scientific *Zeitgeist*, such as

John Briggs and F. David Peat, *Looking Glass Universe: The Emerging Science of Wholeness* (1984)
John Briggs and F. David Peat, *Turbulent Mirror, An Illustrated Guide to Chaos Theory and the Sciences to Wholeness* (1989)
Jacob Bronowski, *The Ascent of Man* (1973)
James Gleick, *Chaos: Making of a New Science* (1987)
Brian Goodwin, *How the Leopard Changed its Spots* (1994)
Nick Herbert, *Quantum Reality, Beyond the New Physics* (1985)

Michio Kaku and Jennifer Trainer, *Beyond Einstein, The Cosmic Quest for the Theory of the Universe* (1987)

Ernst Mayr, *The Growth of Biological Thought* (1982)

Heinz Pagels, *The Cosmic Code: Quantum Physics as the Language of Nature* (1982)

Heinz Pagels, *The Dreams of Reason: The Computer and the Rise of the Sciences of Complexity* (1988)

Jeremy Rifkin, *Entropy: A New World View* (1980)

Ian Stewart, *Does God Play Dice? The Mathematics of Chaos* (1989)

Alexander Woodcock and Monte Davis, *Catastrophe Theory* (1980)

Fred Alan Wolf, *Star Wave, Mind, Consciousness and Quantum Physics* (1984)

Gary Zukav, *The Dancing Wu Li Masters: An Overview of the New Physics* (1979)

Indeed, science played an increasing role in Boyd's thinking on conflict and strategy. And whereas his study of military history went from the contemporary to the past, a travel back in time, his study of science progressed in reverse order. From epistemology, cybernetics and systems theory of the 1960s he ventured into evolution theory, cognitive sciences, chaos and complexity theory, which were popularized in a growing number of very accessible books during the late 1970s, 1980s and early 1990s. In incorporating insights from science in his work he deliberately introduced concepts from the scientific *Zeitgeist* into the military *Zeitgeist*. And his audience became aware of this aspect of his work. As Faber recalled: 'Boyd introduced the language of the New Physics, Chaos Theory, and Complexity Theory.'[4]

Relying in large part on books Boyd read, the following detailed description of the scientific *Zeitgeist*, or rather, the sweeping changing taking place in and coloring this *Zeitgeist*, will provide themes, theories, concepts and models that Boyd employed in his own work, either directly and explicitly, or implicitly.

Shifting foundations

A new sensibility

Boyd's intellectual education occurred in the period of roughly the three decades of 1960–90. This has been an important period for science, philosophy and culture, for in this period a 'paradigm shift' occurred in the natural sciences, and by extension, also in the social sciences and culture. It was a tumultuous period. In the sixties and seventies, a 'new sensibility' arose.[5] Others would call it a cultural revolution, the great disruption or the crisis decades.[6] The student revolts of May 1968, the sexual revolution, the rise of pop-art and pop culture, race and gender issues dominating politics, competed with the landing of the first man on the moon in 1968. Individualism was on the rise, reinforcing the sense that culture in modern society was waning or already absent. The novelist Thomas Wolfe had published *The Me Decades* in 1976 and three years later Christopher

Lasch wrote *The Culture of Narcissism*. For Theodore Roszak this meant instead that culture was shifting and showing *The Making of a Counter Culture*, which he published in 1970. He posited that this was a youth revolt and, as much as anything, was opposed to the reductionism of science and technology. Everything was called into question: family, urbanism, science, technology, progress, the meaning of wealth, love and life, and who decides what is knowledge or reason.[7]

In 1973 the oil crisis and the attack by Egypt and Syria on Israel fuelled doubts about the viability of the modern western capitalist industrialized societies. Modernism was becoming suspect with, for instance, the publication of the Club of Rome Report on *The Limits to Growth* in 1969, a report Boyd was aware of.[8] Indeed, Boyd had read the somber opening question, 'Is there hope for man?' in Robert Heilbroner's book *An Inquiry into The Human Prospect*, as well as the sobering answer, 'no there is no such hope'. It told him about threats to humanity arising from environmental degradation, resource shortages due to industrialization and population growth, about scarcity and poverty, social tensions, and the inevitability of wars of redistribution and pre-emptive seizure. Nicholas Georgescu-Roegen and Jeremy Rifkin painted a future characterized by increasing disorder due to the force of the Second Law of Thermodynamics, which pointed to the equally inescapable depletion of the earth's resources.[9] This spurred on the development of the evolutionary approach to economic theory and inspired the 'green' worldwide political movement exemplified by Greenpeace.

These studies came on top of French works by Raymond Aron and Herbert Marcuse who both believed the 1960s to have been a critical decade, since they had revealed science and technology as real threats to freedom, not just in the form of weapons and weapon research, which had tied so many universities to the military, but also because the civil revolution in general had been underpinned by a psychological transformation of the individual, who had discovered new ways of freedom and manners to express it. In similar vein, Boyd read Robert Persig's 1974 bestseller *Zen and the Art of Motorcycle Maintenance*, which rallies against the 'Church of Reason' and moves between Eastern mystics, Zen Buddhism and the classical Greek philosophers, offering an alternative to the rational scientific mindset of modernity.[10] This cultural wave cohered in postmodernism.

Scientific waves were equally unsettling. The Big Bang Theory was widely discussed when Steven Weinberg published *The First Three Minutes* in 1977. Genetic engineering became a feasible option after new discoveries from 1972 to 1978 in microbiology, which made cloning and sequencing of DNA possible. E.O. Wilson, a Harvard zoologist, made the link between genes, social organization and human nature when he published *Sociobiology: The New Synthesis* in 1975 and argued that social behavior is governed by biology, by genes.[11] One year later, Richard Dawkins advanced the idea, in *The Selfish Gene*, that we must think of the central unit of evolution and natural selection as the gene; 'the gene, the replicating unit, is "concerned" to see itself survive and thrive'.[12]

These books were foreshadowed by Jacques Monod's *Chance and Necessity* (1971). Monod felt that ideas, culture and language are survival devices.[13] Importantly for the study of Boyd, they also sparked a highly publicized resurgence of Darwinian thinking that characterized the last quarter of the century.[14] Fred Hoyle for instance suggested to Boyd how Darwinian principles were also at play at an organizational and societal level, explaining the somewhat Hobbesian and social-Darwinist slant to his work.[15]

Changes in the philosophy of science were an integral part and stimulant of the tumultuous period, for they involved a re-evaluation of the nature of knowledge itself. With the publication of Thomas Kuhn's *The Structure of Scientific Revolutions* in 1962, at a stroke the issue of scientific change had been placed at the center of debate for historians and philosophers of science alike, soon to be joined by radical sociologists who quickly saw within the Kuhnian legacy the seeds of a new and more cogent relativism, from which not even science could remain exempt,[16] because, as one of those radicals, Paul Lyotard (one of the premier postmodernists) asserted, 'the status of knowledge is altered as societies enter what is known as the postindustrial age and cultures enter what is known as the postmodern age'.[17]

Towards 'A theory of intellectual evolution'

Fully aware of these changes in the scientific *Zeitgeist*, Boyd starts his opus with an investigation into the way man develops mental patterns or concepts of meaning, or rather, how he learns and adapts his mindset to an ever-changing environment amid unavoidable uncertainty. This investigation was thoroughly and explicitly inspired and influenced by Kuhn, and by Michael Polanyi's work *Knowing and Being* (1969). Judging by the notes he made in his books, it likely started with his study of Jean Piaget, *Structuralism* (1971 edition), and of James Bryant Conant, *Two Modes of Thought* (1970 edition) while these in turn seem to have been preceded by Werner Heisenberg's *Physics and Philosophy* (1958) and *Gödel's Proof* (1958) by Ernest Nagel and James Newman, both works that told Boyd there are limits to what we can know. Entropy, too, probably through the work of Georgescu-Roegen and Rifkin, was a concept from early onward. The bibliography of *Destruction and Creation* (see annex A) also includes works on creative thinking by Edward DeBono and Joseph Chilton Spearce,[18] and works on cybernetics, psychoanalysis and cognitive science. Later this list would grow to include Karl Popper's seminal works *The Logic of Scientific Discovery* (1968) and *Conjecture and Refutations: The Growth of Scientific Knowledge* (1965) and Michael Polanyi's work *The Tacit Dimension* (1967).

So Boyd starts his strategic theory with forming his own ideas about learning. In fact, in notes in several of the books mentioned above, he refers to the ideas he laid out in *Destruction and Creation* as his 'theory for intellectual evolution',[19] or alternatively as a 'meta-paradigm of mind and universe', as 'an inductive-deductive engine of progress', a 'dialectic engine' or 'cybernetic engine'.[20] The picture of the comprehensive OODA loop he developed in 1995 still deeply reflects this early interest in the epistemological debate. Indeed, in a sense, the OODA loop seems a cybernetic rendering of the 'normal model' of scientific research developed by Karl Popper. However, a look at the more comprehensive drawing of the loop suggests it was Polanyi's work, and in particular Kuhn's reaction to Popper on the way science advances, how scientists learn and how knowledge grows, that perhaps more deeply informed Boyd's ideas. A discussion of Popper, Polanyi and Kuhn is thus essential for a proper understanding of Boyd's ideas concerning strategic behavior, and the function of strategic theories and military doctrines.

Popper's evolutionary epistemology

Karl Popper advanced the idea that science made progress through falsification. Popper had become disenchanted with the idea that science is special because it can be derived from facts, the more facts the better. He denied the positivist assertion that scientists can 'prove' a theory through induction, or repeated empirical tests or observations. One never knows if one's observations have been sufficient; the next observation might contradict all that preceded it.[21]

Therefore, according to Popper, a claim to truth by a theory is only possible if it can be shown to be false. What sets the scientific enterprise apart from everything else is that it only entertains knowledge or experience that is capable of falsification. This is what distinguishes science from religion or metaphysics. Science is regarded as a neatly self-correcting process. It is never finished in the sense that anything is knowable as true for all time. It increases incrementally through constant but piecemeal efforts of falsification so that each new element introduced could be tested to see whether it was an improvement on the earlier arrangement.[22]

As observation is guided by and presupposes theory, theories cannot be established as true or probably true in the light of observational evidence. Theories are construed as speculative and tentative conjectures or guesses freely created by the human intellect in an attempt to overcome problems encountered by previous theories to give an adequate account of some aspects of the world or universe. Once proposed, speculative theories are to be rigorously and ruthlessly tested by observation and experiment. Theories that fail to stand up to observational and experimental tests must be eliminated and replaced by further speculative conjectures.[23] Science progresses by trial and error, by conjecture and refutations, a dynamic captured by Boyd in *The Conceptual Spiral* in his definition of science as 'a self-correcting process of observation, hypothesis, and test'.[24]

Not surprisingly, and quite relevant for understanding the importance of Popper for Boyd and for Boyd's take on the function of military doctrine and strategic theory, Popper named his theory an 'evolutionary epistemology'. In 1961 Popper claimed that growth of our knowledge is the result of a process closely resembling what Darwin called 'natural selection', that is, the natural selection of hypotheses: our knowledge consists, at every moment, of those hypotheses which have shown their (comparative) fitness by surviving so far in their struggle for existence; a competitive struggle which eliminates those hypotheses which are unfit. In this Popper sees strong similarities between the processes of adaptation at play in genes, science and human behavior (for which Popper regards culture and genetic heritage as prime determining factors driving the process of adaptation, factors also included in Boyd's drawing of the OODA loop).[25] All theories are being subjected to variation and selection, according to criteria that are themselves subject to variation and selection. The whole process resembles biological evolution. A problem is like an ecological niche, and a theory is like a gene or a species, which is being tested for viability in that niche. Variants of theories, like genetic mutations, are continually being created, and less successful variants become extinct when more successful variants take over. 'Success' is the ability to survive repeatedly under selective pressures – criticism – brought to bear in that niche. As David Deutsch explains, both in science and in biological evolution, evolutionary success depends on the creation and survival of *objective knowledge*. The ability of a theory or gene to survive in a niche is not a haphazard function of its structure but depends on whether enough true and useful information about the niche is implicitly or explicitly encoded there.[26]

Here Boyd found reinforcement, and additional insight, in Dawkins' work. Boyd owned two copies of *The Selfish Gene*, in addition to Dawkins' other famous books *The Extended Phenotype* and *The Blind Watchmaker*. Dawkins introduced the term 'meme' as the cultural replicator. Memes are the vehicle for cultural evolution, just as much as the genes are the vehicles for genetic evolution. Memes should be regarded as living structures, not just metaphorically but technically. Ideas, including strategic ones, replicate like genes and survive, mutate or become ignored and extinct. They are entities that are capable of being transmitted from one brain to another and can be considered a virus of the brain. Popper in particular, according to Dawkins, illuminated the analogy between scientific progress and genetic evolution by natural selection.[27]

Polanyi and the tacit dimension

Some disagreed with this representation and within the OODA loop graphic, in *Destruction and Creation* and in *The Conceptual Spiral*, Boyd explicitly incorporated essential insights from two such authors: Michael Polanyi and Thomas Kuhn. Polanyi's book that Boyd read, *Knowing and Being*, is a collection of short essays. It deals with Kant, Hegel, Piaget, Nagel and many other social theorists and philosophers. It includes themes from *The Tacit Dimension* and *Personal Knowledge*, Polanyi's *magnum opus* of 1958, which pertain to the practice of science and the way scientific knowledge grows. It addresses the structure of consciousness and even includes the role of DNA as a factor in shaping consciousness. A noteworthy feature too is that the editor states in her lengthy introduction that 'all knowing is orientation'.[28]

A first important idea Polanyi advances is that there are two levels of aware-ness, and human beings employ both,[29] an idea that is closely related to Boyd's insistence that understanding requires analysis as well as synthesis, a central theme of *Destruction and Creation*. In fact, Boyd points to Polanyi as one of two sources for this idea.[30]

Knowing is action oriented and a process. Polanyi regards the process of knowing as fragmentary clues, senso-motoric or from memory, which are integ-rated under categories. We make sense of reality by categorizing it. This is the lower level of awareness: it observes separate clues. However, this process of logical disintegration has reduced a comprehensive entity to its relatively mean-ingless fragments. The higher form of awareness recreates the comprehensive entity of which the disparate clues are a part and he emphasizes that 'the higher principles which characterize a comprehensive entity cannot be defined in terms of the laws that apply to its parts in themselves', a theme which will reappear later when systems thinking is discussed, to which Polanyi sometimes refers.

This 'integrating power of the mind' is what Polanyi terms 'tacit knowing'. And tacit knowing is implicit. It is the patterns of categories that contain theo-ries, methods, feelings, values and skill that can be used in a fashion that the tra-dition judges valid. This integration of knowledge is a personal skill in itself, it cannot be known by others. This tacit dimension is essential. The knowledge that underlies the explicit knowledge is more fundamental. All knowledge is either tacit or rooted in tacit knowledge. New experiences are always assimilated through the concepts that the individual disposes and which the individual has inherited from other users of the language. Those concepts are tacitly based, and important for understanding Boyd's OODA loop, Polanyi asserts that the indi-vidual changes, 'adapts', the concepts in the light of experiences and reinterprets the language used. When new words or concepts are brought into an older system of language, both affect each other. The system itself enriches what the individual has brought into it.

A second relevant element in Polanyi's work is based on the correlate of the former ideas, which is that knowledge is social. Subsequently Polanyi criticized the ideal of objectivity,[31] asserting that much of science stems from guesswork and intuition and that although, in theory, science is continually modifiable, in practice it doesn't work like that. 'The part played by new observations and experiment in the process of discovery is usually over-estimated', he noted. It is not so much new facts that advance science but new interpretations of known facts, or the discovery of new mechanisms or systems that account for known facts. Moreover, advances often have the character of 'gestalt', as when people suddenly 'see' something that had been meaningless before. His point was that scientists actually behave far more intuitively than they think, and that, rather than being absolutely neutral or disengaged in their research, they start with a conscience, a scientific conscience. This conscience operates in more than one way. It guides the scientist in choosing the path of discovery, but also guides him in accepting which results are 'true' and which not, or need further study.[32]

Indeed, intuition, a tacit element, plays an underestimated role in the growth of science, Polanyi repeatedly asserts. As he explains, science grows through the discovery of interesting problems: 'problems are the goad and the guide of all intellectual effort, which harass and beguile us into the search for ever-deeper understanding of things'.[33] All true scientific research starts with hitting on a deep and promising problem, and this is half the discovery'.[34] Boyd was to incorporate this insight using the term 'mismatch' instead of problem, tension or 'logical gap'. 'Illumination' was Polyani's term for the leap by which the logical problem was crossed, a word Boyd was to use quite frequently.[35]

Science thus starts with the act of perception and proceeds through intuition and creativity. Intuition is a skill, rooted in our natural sensibility to hidden patterns and developed to effectiveness by a process of learning. Great powers of scientific intuition are called originality, for they discover things that are most surprising and make men see the world in a new way'.[36] 'We have here the paradigm of all progress in science: discoveries are made by pursuing unsuspected possibilities suggested by existing knowledge',[37] an idea Boyd would makes his own, in particular in *The Conceptual Spiral*, and one that contrasts with Popper's idea of hypothesis and test.

Still, even the highest degree of intuitive originality can operate only by relying to a considerable extent on the hitherto accepted interpretative framework of science, Polanyi acknowledges.[38] Science can only be pursued and transmitted to succeeding generations within an elaborate system of traditional beliefs and values.[39] This social and consensual character of scientific knowledge comes to the fore when Polanyi notes that 'the first thing to make clear is that scientists, freely making their own choice of problems and pursuing them in the light of their own personal judgment, are in fact cooperating as members of a closely knit group'.[40]

The practice of science therefore contains an 'internal tension'. On the one hand, acceptance of the results of research depends on the level of plausibility of the result and the scientific value of the research conducted in terms of the accuracy, its systematic importance, and the intrinsic interest of its subject-matter. These elements translate into a social constraint in the sense that they tend to enforce conformity. On the other hand, the element of originality, also a prime criterion for judging scientific merit, encourages dissent. This internal tension, Polanyi asserts, is essential in guiding and motivating scientific work.[41] The authority of scientific opinion enforces the teachings of science in general, for the very purpose of fostering their subversion in particular points. Scientific opinion imposes an immense range of authoritative pronouncements on the student of science, but at the same time it grants the highest encouragement to dissent from them in some particular.[42]

This feature leads to an additional relevant assertion: knowledge grows out of the 'network' that scientists form together; which forms 'consensual chains'. No single scientist has a sound understanding of more than a tiny fraction of the total domain of science. Polanyi asserts that a joint opinion of what constitutes reality emerges due to the fact that each scientist can usually judge an area adjoining their own special studies that is broad enough to include some fields on which other scientists have specialized. As there is considerable overlap between fields, the whole of science will be covered by chains and networks of overlapping neighborhoods. This network is the seat of scientific opinion; it is split into thousands of fragments, held by a multitude of individuals, each of whom endorses the others' opinion at second hand, by relying on the consensual chains which link him to all the others through a sequence of overlapping neighborhoods.[43]

Interestingly, Polanyi extends these practices of science to apply also to society if one strives for an open and free society, thus transferring the principles governing science and the growth of knowledge to the wider social realm and into the dynamic of organizational survival. The essay 'The Republic of Science', Polanyi noted, shows us an association of independent initiatives, combined towards an indeterminate achievement. It is disciplined and motivated by serving a traditional authority, but this authority is dynamic; its continued existence depends on its constant self-renewal through the originality of its followers.[44] Such an attitude was deliberately destroyed in the Soviet Union. Stalinism was a closed system, he asserts. The political realm had subverted the scientific realm, and this would have disastrous effects on societal cohesion throughout the communist world the moment people came to realize this.[45] 'Stalin's regime virtually ceased to exist when its basic conceptions of intellectual and moral reality lost their hold on thought', he proclaimed.[46]

A free society, on the other hand, may be seen to be bent in its entirety on exploring self-improvement, suggesting a generalization of the principles governing the 'Republic of Science'. A society bent on discovery must advance by supporting independent initiatives, coordinating themselves mutually to each other. Such adjustments may include rivalries and opposing responses, which, in society as a whole, will be far more frequent than they are within science. Even so, all these independent initiatives must accept for their guidance a traditional authority, enforcing its own self-renewal by cultivating originality among its followers.

Several of these themes resurface in his essay, but also in the presentations *Organic Design for Command and Control, The Strategic Game of ? and ?* as well as *The Conceptual Spiral*. Boyd would stress the importance of the tacit dimension, an organizational culture marked by trust and open communications, a tolerance for failure and an encouragement for innovation and experimentation and a comfort with a variety of views, even conflicting ones, and dissent, as long as the entities would be bound by a common, overarching goal, a shared view or belief.

Kuhn's revolution

Thomas Kuhn developed another alternative view of scientific progress, the occurrence of revolutions in science, one that includes Polanyi's sensitivity for the social aspect of the activities of scientists. Kuhn noted that falsification was to some extent a flawed concept.[47] If everyone is constantly questioning the fundamentals of a discipline, as characterized in Popper's method of 'conjectures and refutations', it is unlikely to make significant progress simply because principles do not remain unchallenged long enough for esoteric work to be done. Moreover, an embarrassing historical fact for falsificationists is that if their methodology had been strictly adhered to by scientists, then those theories generally regarded as being among the best examples of scientific theories, such as Niels Bohr's theory of the atom or the Copernican revolution, would have been rejected in their infancy.[48]

He advanced the idea that a better way to explain the work of scientists and describe how science advances was through shifts in paradigms. He defined a paradigm as 'a constellation of achievements – concepts, values, techniques, etc. – shared by a scientific community and used by that community to define legitimate problems and solutions'.[49] It also refers to a set of fundamental assumptions on the basis of which theories and models are developed.[50] It embodies a particular conceptual framework through which the world is viewed and in which it is described, and a particular set of experimental and theoretical techniques for matching the paradigm with nature. However, there is no a priori reason to expect any one paradigm is perfect or even the best available. There are no inductive procedures for arriving at perfectly adequate paradigms.[51]

A paradigm defines what is construed as 'normal science' by a scientific community. Scientists are educated and trained to conduct scientific research using tools, concepts, fundamental laws and theoretical assumptions, to such an extent that most of the 'rules of the scientific game' have become internalized, exerting a controlling influence on what is observed, which problems to focus on and how reality is explained. They will articulate and develop the paradigm in their attempt to account for and accommodate the behavior of some relevant aspects of the real world as revealed through the results of experimentation.[52]

Science progresses not via a neat gradual accumulation of knowledge[53] but through discontinuous, revolutionary breaks called 'paradigm shifts'. In Kuhn's view the transformation of a paradigm appears as a crisis.[54] Such a revolution is defined by the appearance of new conceptual schemes. Before a paradigm shift, scientists practicing normal science within the reigning paradigm encounter anomalies. Initially, these are not considered to undermine the basic assumptions of the paradigm. However, over time the number of anomalies produced by research within a paradigm accumulates and they manifest a persistent character. The potential of a new paradigm brings to the fore aspects which previously were not seen or perceived, or even suppressed in 'normal' science. The basic assumptions of the reigning paradigm are actually questioned by the member of the scientific community. They challenge the legitimacy of their methods. Thus the community diversifies. Different points of view, cultural experiences and philosophical convictions are now expressed and often play a decisive role in discovery of a new paradigm. The rival paradigms are put to the test until the academic world determines the victor, which becomes the new 'norm science'. Hence there is a shift in the problems noticed and investigated and a change of the rules of scientific practice.[55] A scientific revolution corresponds to the abandonment of one paradigm and the adoption of a new one, not by an individual scientist only but by the relevant scientific community as a whole. While Popper looked at scientific progress within a paradigm, Kuhn thus looked at scientific progress as a succession of paradigms.

These paradigms are 'incommensurable'. Different paradigms have no common standard for comparison. Each paradigm will regard the world as being made up of different kinds of things. Rival paradigms will regard different kinds of questions as legitimate or meaningful, and because of the fundamental different set of standards and metaphysical principles, there will be no purely logical argument that demonstrates the superiority of one paradigm over another and that thereby compels a rational scientist to make the change.[56]

Kuhn does not dismiss the value of normal science. Periods of normal science provide the opportunity for scientists to develop the esoteric details of a theory, thereby improving the match between the paradigm and nature to an ever-greater degree. However, as there is no way to tell in advance which theory will hold up to scrutiny, science should contain within it a means of breaking out of one paradigm into a better one. And this is the function of revolutions. Chalmers explains Kuhn in terms that could have been taken directly from Boyd's presentations *Destruction and Creation* and *The Conceptual Spiral* when he asserts that, according to Kuhn, all paradigms will be inadequate to some extent as far as their match with nature is concerned. When the mismatch becomes serious, that is, when a crisis develops, the revolutionary step of replacing the entire paradigm with another becomes essential for the effective progress of science.[57] Thus, progress – as improved understanding of real-world phenomena – depends on the Popperian notion of problem solving within a paradigm as well as on the Kuhnian emphasis on discovering mismatches between a paradigm and reality.

In Boyd's work these notions are already apparent in *Destruction and Creation*. Directly referring to Kuhn's 1970 edition of *The Structure of Scientific Revolutions* Boyd includes a rendering of the Popperian dynamics of science within a paradigm:

> the effort is turned inward towards fine tuning the ideas and interactions in order to improve generality and produce a more precise match of the conceptual pattern with reality. Toward this end, the concept – and its internal workings – is tested and compared against observed phenomena over and over again in many different and subtle ways.

But at some point, Boyd asserts, following Kuhn, 'anomalies, ambiguities, uncertainties, or apparent inconsistencies may emerge'.[58] In subsequent presentations he refers often to the idea that a paradigm, a closed system of logic, cannot be falsified from within. One needs to look across various systems to ascertain the nature of reality and one needs to evolve one's orientation patterns. Indeed, in several sections in *The Conceptual Spiral* Boyd manifests a 'Polanyiist/Kuhnian' inspiration:

Novelty is produced by a mental/physical feedback process of analyses and synthesis that permit us to interact with the world so that we can comprehend, cope with, and shape that world as well as be shaped by it.[59]

The presence and production of mismatches are what sustain and nourish the enterprise of science, engineering and technology, hence keep it alive and ongoing.[60]

The practice of science/engineering and the pursuit of technology permit us to continually rematch our mental/physical orientation with that of the changing world so that we can continue to thrive and grow in it.

The enterprise of science, engineering, and technology affects us personally as individuals, as groups, or as societies by changing our orientation to match with a changing world that we, in fact help change.[61]

Very simply, review of *Destruction and Creation*, this presentation, and our own experiences reveal that the various theories, systems, processes, etc., that we employ to make sense of that world contain features that generate mismatches that, in turn, keep such a world uncertain, ever-changing, and unpredictable.[62]

Strategic activities thus are similar to the Kuhnian scientific endeavor. Indeed, Boyd asserts, *The Conceptual Spiral* also represents 'A *Paradigm* for Survival and Growth'. And,

Since survival and growth are directly connected with the uncertain, ever-changing, unpredictable world of winning and losing we will exploit this whirling (conceptual) spiral of orientation, mismatches, analysis/synthesis, reorientation, mismatches, analysis/synthesis ... so that we can comprehend, cope with, and shape, as well as be shaped by that world and the novelty that arises out of it.[63]

Paradigm shift

Beyond Newton

In the past four decades such a Kuhnian scientific paradigm shift has occurred, according to various authors, or at least a novel conceptual framework has evolved to complement the reigning one in important ways, and Boyd was intimately aware of these views. This shift was highly visible in a much-discussed and bestselling work such as Douglas Hofstadter's *Gödel, Escher, Bach* (1979), an influential book Boyd was familiar with, but Polanyi and Heisenberg also explicitly alluded to the end of the Newtonian paradigm, as well as a host of other authors featuring in the bibliography of *Patterns of Conflict*, who were among the first to discuss the contemporary scientific changes in popular scientific works, such as Fritjof Capra's *The Tao of Physics* (1976), Richard Dawkins' *The Selfish Gene* (1976), E.O. Wilson's *On Human Nature* (1978) and Ilya Prigogine's widely acclaimed book *Order out of Chaos* (1984). Together with other bestselling works like Capra's *The Turning Point: Science, Society and the Rising Culture* (1982), Stephen Hawking's *A Brief History of Time* (1988), Dawkins' *The Blind Watchmaker*, James Gleick's *Chaos* (1987) and Mitchell Waldrop's *Complexity, The Emerging Science at the Edge of Order and Chaos*, these books marked the popular acceptance of science.[64]

The shift can be described as a movement away from a scientific worldview entirely based on what are often and variously labeled Cartesian, Newtonian, linear, analytical, objectivistic, reductionist, deterministic or mechanical concepts, towards a focus on change, diversity, evolution, unpredictability, complexity, uncertainty, non-equilibrium and non-linearity.

The Newtonian paradigm rests firmly upon linear principles. A linear system has two defining mathematical characteristics. First, it displays proportionality. The second characteristic of linear systems is that the whole is equal to the sum of its parts. Given a set of linear equations and initial conditions, we can calculate the future values of the variables. Consequently, if we can describe a system by a linear mathematical model, we can determine its future states exactly from its given initial state.

Reductionism is an important consequence of the Newtonian paradigm; the analyst breaks the problem into its constituent pieces, solves each piece separately, then sums the results from the pieces to obtain the overall solution to the problem. It also leads to the principle of replication, which means that the same action or experiment under the same conditions will come out the same way, that results are repeatable and therefore independently verifiable. Finally, cause and effect are demonstrable.

Therefore the nature of linear systems is that if you know a little about their behavior, you know a lot. You can extrapolate, change scales and make projections with confidence. A consequence of the Newtonian paradigm is the view of systems as closed entities, isolated from their environments. Outside events do not influence such a system; the only dynamics are those arising from its internal workings. The analyst thus has an inward focus. This leads to the deterministic character of the Newtonian view. The 'cosmic machine', once in motion, was seen as being completely causal and determinate. All that happened had a definite cause and gave rise to a definite effect, and the future of any part could – in principle – be predicted with absolute certainty if its state at any time was known in detail.

Thus, it was also believed that the world could be described objectively, i.e. without ever mentioning the human observer.[65] Laplace hypothesized that a sufficiently intelligent being (or 'demon') could grasp any future event from an adequate comprehension of the present. The perceiving subject is a neutral observer and the object a pure datum of perception. Defined as a 'mirror of nature', the mind was thought capable of representing the world through objective knowledge that was stable, certain, and accurate.[66]

From the seventeenth to the twentieth centuries this modern Newtonian paradigm emerged and reigned, organized around the logic of determinism, and rooted in the objectifying, mechanistic, abstract, and a temporal mode of thought stemming from the natural sciences. Scientism became a modern faith, promoting the belief that the scientific method alone provided the royal road to truth, that there was one legitimate logic and one reliable methodology, and that eventually all sciences and fields of intellectual endeavor could be unified within the same framework.[67]

However, the assumptions of classical physics upon which we have confidently erected our entire way of organizing life turn out to be largely fallacious, Rifkin, Prigogine and Gell-Mann told Boyd.[68] The classic paradigm has proven incapable of solving certain phenomena. Or, as Capra informed Boyd,

> modern science has come to realize that all scientific theories are approximations to the true nature of reality; and that each theory is valid for a certain range of phenomenon. Beyond this range it no longer gives a satisfactory description of nature, and new theories have to be found to replace the old one, or, rather, to extend it by improving the approximations.[69]

The end of certainty

The new paradigm developed from changes of concepts and ideas that occurred in physics during the first three decades of the twentieth century, changes that feature prominently in Boyd's work: thermodynamics, evolution theory, relativity theory, quantum mechanics and the uncertainty principle. The first blow to the Laplacian school dominating science was delivered by thermodynamics. The Second Law of Thermodynamics, which Boyd alludes to in *Destruction and Creation* and *A New Conception for Air-to-Air Combat*, deals with dissipation of energy.[70] While the total energy involved in a process is always constant, the amount of useful energy is diminishing, dissipating into heat, friction, and so on. The broader philosophical significance was that it introduced into physics the idea of irreversible processes, of an 'arrow of time'.

According to the Second Law, there is a certain trend in physical phenomena. Mechanical energy is dissipated into heat and cannot be completely recovered, as when hot and cold water are brought together. What such processes have in common is that they proceed in a certain direction – from order to disorder. Any isolated physical system will proceed spontaneously in the direction of ever increasing disorder. This unidirectional process was described in a new quantity called 'entropy'. Entropy is a quantity that measures a degree of evolution of a physical system.

Entropy in an isolated physical system will keep increasing and because this evolution is accompanied by increasing disorder, entropy can also be seen as a measure of disorder. This process will continue until an equilibrium has been reached called 'heat death'. Then all activity has ceased, all material is evenly distributed and at the same temperature. According to classical physics the universe as a whole evolves toward such a state of maximum entropy; it is running down and will eventually grind to a halt,[71] which was the message of books by Nicholas Georgescu-Roegen and Jeremy Rifkin that Boyd read and a prospect Boyd included as a warning for members of closed strategic entities.

Darwinism also forced scientists to abandon the Cartesian conception of the world as a machine. Instead the universe had to be pictured as an evolving and ever-changing system in which complex structures developed from simpler forms. Whereas in biology evolution meant a movement toward increasing order and complexity, in physics (thermodynamics) it came to mean just the opposite – a movement toward increasing disorder. This grim picture of cosmic evolution is in sharp contrast to the ideas of biologists and the emergence of evolution in physics thus brought to light a limitation of the Newtonian theory. The mechanistic conception of the universe as a system of billiard balls in random motion is far too simplistic to deal with the evolution of life.[72]

Relativity theory and atomic physics shattered all the principal concepts of the Newtonian worldview: the notion of absolute space and time, the elementary solid particles, the strictly causal nature of physical phenomena, and the ideal of an objective description of nature.[73] The philosophical implication of the theory was that time can change and depends on the circumstances, and the position of the observer is essential for the measurement of time, a theme that was to become one of the characteristics of the new physics of the first three decades of the twentieth century. The universe is experienced as a dynamic inseparable whole, which always includes the observer in an essential way, as Capra noted.[74]

Quantum theory delivered a further blow. Where relativity theory is valid on the very large cosmological scale and replaces Newtonian physics, in the realm of elementary particles, atoms, and molecules, quantum theory replaces classical physics. Ever since Newton physicists had believed that all physical phenomena could be reduced to the properties of hard and solid material particles. Quantum theory forces them to accept the fact that the solid material objects of classical physics dissolve at the subatomic level into wavelike patterns of probabilities. There is wave-particle duality. Subatomic particles have no meaning as isolated entities but can be understood only as interconnections, or correlations, among various processes of observation and measurement. In other words, subatomic particles are not things but interconnections among things. Shifting the attention from macroscopic objects to atoms and subatomic particles, nature does not show us any isolated building blocks, but rather appears as a complex web of relationships among the various parts of a unified whole. These relationships are expressed in quantum theory in probabilities, which are determined by the dynamics of the whole system. Whereas in classical mechanics the properties and behavior of the parts determine those of the whole, the situation is reversed in quantum mechanics. It is the whole that determines the parts.[75]

The duality feature also led Werner Heisenberg in 1927 to formulate his famous 'uncertainty (or indeterminacy) principle', which Boyd incorporated in *Destruction and Creation* and *A New Conception for Air-to-Air Combat*, and referred to in most other presentations. Heisenberg noted that it is possible to determine the coordinate of a subatomic particle, but the moment we do so, the momentum of the particle will acquire an arbitrary value, and vice versa. We can measure coordinates or movements, but not both. It meant that the more precisely we know the measured value of one quantity, the greater the uncertainty in another 'conjugate' quantity.[76] Quantum mechanics obliged us to speak less absolutely about the location of an object.

This was a fundamental observation with far reaching-consequences, for again, as with relativity theory, it meant that the act of observation heavily shaped reality. No single theoretical language articulating the variables to which a well-defined value can be attributed can exhaust the physical content of a system. Various possible languages and points of view about the system may be complementary. They all deal with the same reality, but it is impossible to reduce them to one single description. The irreducible plurality of perspectives on the same reality expresses the impossibility of a divine point of view from which the whole of reality is visible.

It implied that reality studied by physics is a mental construct. Heisenberg noted that 'what we observe is not nature itself, but nature exposed to our method of questioning'.[77] For Prigogine the real lesson to be learned from the principle of complementarity consists in emphasizing the wealth of reality, which overflows any single language, and single logical structure. Each language can only express a part of reality.[78] For Boyd it implied another variation of the same theme of uncertainty, along with Kuhn's thesis of the workings of paradigms. Inspired, among other works, by Heisenberg's own book *Physics and Philosophy*, Boyd literally includes Heisenberg's indeterminacy principle as formulated above, and adds to this that the uncertainties involved in observing phenomena 'hide or mask phenomena behavior'. Under these circumstances, 'the uncertainty values represent the inability to determine the character or nature (consistency) of a system within itself'.[79]

Boyd also came across another source of uncertainty. As Jean Piaget asserted in the book Boyd read for his essay, 'In 1931 Kurt Gödel made a discovery which created a tremendous stir, because it undermined the then prevailing formalism, according to which mathematics was reducible to logic and logic could be exhaustively formalized. Gödel established definitely that the formalist program cannot be executed'.[80] Gödel thus added another theory that describes limits to knowledge, one Boyd also includes in *Destruction and Creation* and *A New Conception for Air-to-Air Combat*. He tells no less firmly than Heisenberg's uncertainty principle that there are things we cannot know. Gödel stated that within any consistent formal system, there will be a sentence that can neither be proved true nor be proved false. In addition, he states that the consistency of a formal system of arithmetic cannot be proved within that system. Thus he established that there are limits to math and logic. It was a form of mathematical uncertainty principle.[81]

Destruction and Creation includes two typed pages devoted to Gödel. According to Boyd, Gödel showed that 'any consistent system is incomplete' and that 'even though such a system is consistent its consistency cannot be demonstrated within the system'. Boyd also noted that Gödel showed

> that a consistency proof of arithmetic can be found by appealing to systems outside that arithmetic. Thus Gödel's proof indirectly shows that in order to determine the consistency of any new system we must construct or uncover another system beyond it. Over and over this cycle must be repeated to determine the consistency of more and more elaborate systems.[82]

Whereas Kuhn, Popper and others wrote about the process of scientific, or intellectual growth and creativity, these three ideas/authors – the Second Law of Thermodynamics, Heisenberg and Gödel – showed the fountains of uncertainty, and frequently Boyd would make a note in a book that a section resembled the insights offered by the combination of these three.[83] Various authors did point out the fundamental changes and the similarities of the philosophical and epistemological implications.[84] Capra, for instance, noted in 1975 that we were forced now to 'adopt a much more subtle, holistic, and "organic" view of nature'.[85] Connecting the three concepts, however, was a genuine creative original act, most certainly in the realm of military thought.

The emerging systems view of the world

Wholes, not parts

The link between thermodynamics and Heisenberg/Gödel may well have been inspired by Jean Piaget's work *Structuralism*, to which Boyd frequently explicitly refers in this essay. The book contains a broad overview of disciplines that deal with structures. Translated from French, it not only deals with Gödel but also includes explanations of the work of systems theoretician Ludwig von Bertalanffy, the linguist Noam Chomsky, the sociologists Talcott Parsons and Michel Foucault, anthropologist Claude Lévy-Strauss, Charles Darwin, Thomas Kuhn, Karl Popper, Ernest Nagel and a host of others. According to Piaget, they all explain their subject in terms of systems or structures and in terms of processes of transformations that sustain these structures or systems; structure *is* a system of transformations; a structure is a systematic whole of self-regulating transformations;[86] there is no structure apart from construction,[87] views entirely congruent with Boyd's comprehensive OODA loop model. These books capture the nexus between the epistemological issues discussed above and the next characterizing feature of Boyd's scientific *Zeitgeist*: the systems view of the world.[88]

The new complementary paradigm that emerged carries various labels. The contours are described by various authors in various ways, depending in part on the moment of publication and their own discipline. Yet several similarities appear throughout. Capra noted in 1982 that

Out of the revolutionary changes in our concept of reality that were brought about by modern physics, a consistent world view is now emerging. In contrast to the mechanistic Cartesian view of the world, the world view emerging from modern physics can be characterized by words like organic, holistic, and ecological. It might also be called a *systems view*, in the sense of *general systems theory*. The universe is no longer seen as a machine, made up of a multitude of objects, but has to be pictured as one indivisible dynamic whole whose parts are essentially interrelated.[89]

The essence of the new paradigm is alternatively captured in words such as the 'Organismic Revolution',[90] the 'Evolutionary Paradigm'[91] and 'Prigoginianism'.[92] Watson asserts that we are now in an era of 'universal Darwinism'.[93] Capra notes that this paradigm shift transcends the boundaries of the physical sciences: 'today, twenty-five years after Kuhn's analysis, we recognize the paradigm shift in physics is an integral part of a much larger cultural transformation', while Ilya Prigogine, contends that there is a 'radical change in our vision of nature towards the multiple, the temporal and the complex',[94] and 'this development clearly reflects both the internal logic of science and the cultural and social context of our time'.[95]

Heisenberg had recognized the shift from the parts to the whole as a central aspect of the conceptual revolution occurring in the 1920s.[96] At the same time, in biology organismic biologists took up the problem of biological form and explored the concept of organization. This involved a shift away from function to organization and implicitly also from mechanistic to systemic thinking. Organization was determined by configuration, relationships which formed patterns as a configuration of ordered relationships.

What early systems thinkers recognized very clearly is the existence of different levels of complexity with different kinds of laws operating at each level. The term 'organized complexity' was introduced as the subject of study. At each level of complexity the observed phenomena exhibit properties that do not exist at the lower level. The new science of ecology in the 1930s added to the movement. Ecologists study 'communities' of organisms, or super-organisms, which for all intent and purposes act as an entity. Ecology also introduced the concept of 'network' to describe the fact that organisms and communities of organisms are integral wholes whose essential properties arise from the interaction and interdependence of their parts.

The word 'system' was coined to denote both living organisms and social systems and from that moment on a system had come to mean an integrated whole whose essential properties arise from the relationships between its parts, and systems thinking, the understanding of a phenomenon within the context of a larger whole.[97] According to the systems view, the essential properties of an organism, or living system, are properties of the whole, which none of the parts have. Systemic properties are properties of a pattern. These properties are destroyed when the system is dissected, either physically or theoretically, into isolated elements.

As Ludwig Bertalanffy noted, the great shock of twentieth century science has been that systems cannot be understood by analysis, for the application of the analytical procedure depends on two conditions. First, the interaction between parts is non-existent or very weak, second; the relationships describing behavior of parts is linear. These conditions are not fulfilled in the entities called systems, i.e. consisting of parts 'in interaction'.[98] The properties of the parts are not intrinsic properties but can only be understood within the context of the larger whole. Instead of focusing on the parts, systems thinking concentrated on basic principles of organization. Analysis means taking something apart to understand it; systems thinking means putting it into the context of the larger whole.

Not surprisingly Boyd recommends both analysis and synthesis to comprehend the world, and an opponent's system. One of the early works Boyd had read for *Destruction and Creation* actually centered on this dichotomy. In *Two Modes of Thought* James Bryant Conant, one time President of Harvard and under whose auspices Thomas Kuhn wrote *The Structure of Scientific Revolutions*, discussed the benefits and dangers of the theoretical-deductive and empirical-inductive approach respectively. He asserts that 'the great scientists can and have used both modes of thought', without a combination science does not progress.[99] Indeed, he continues, the reconciliation of both types is essential for the continuation of a free society in an age of science and technology.[100]

Already in *Destruction and Creation* Boyd devotes a considerable section towards this systems-theoretical theme. He notes how deduction, analysis and differentiation are related and can be referred to as unstructuring or destruction, hence *destructive deduction*. But applying this to a 'comprehensive whole' will result in parts but also in loss of order and meaning. He contrasts this approach with induction, synthesis and integration, which can be labeled as creative or *constructive induction*. Both are required:

> the crucial step that permits creative induction is the separation of the particulars from their previous domains by destructive deduction. Without this unstructuring the creation of a new structure cannot proceed – since the bits and pieces are still tied together as meaning within unchallenged domains or concepts.[101]

Elsewhere, in order to make a point in his discourse on the essence of strategy, he notes that: 'We will use this scheme of pulling things apart (analysis) and putting them back again (synthesis) in new combinations to find how apparently unrelated ideas and actions can be related to one another.'[102] Indeed, this mode of thinking, which is in line with the ideas of Polanyi, became a key insight Boyd wanted to get across as an essential element of proper strategic thinking. Both *Destruction and Creation* and *The Conceptual Spiral* revolve around this theme. The combination of destruction of mind sets, ideas, concepts, observations, doctrines, etc., and construction of the separate elements into novel combinations, the combination of analysis and synthesis, the combination of

induction and deduction, these were 'the engines for matching observed phenomena or physical patterns with mental models or mental patterns', he noted on
pages 63 and 64 of his copy of Kuhn's *The Structure of Scientific Revolutions*,
while on page 155 in Polanyi's *Knowing and Being* he labels the dynamic of
destructive deduction and constructive induction as 'the cybernetic engine'.

Cybernetics

Cybernetics was the next important stepping stone in the development in
systems thinking, another important theory for understanding Boyd.[103] In 1948
Norbert Wiener published a book called *Cybernetics*. Cybernetics focuses on
how systems function, regardless of what the system is – living, mechanical or
social. Wiener proposed that the same general principles that controlled the thermostat may also be seen in economic systems, market regulation and political
decision-making systems. Cybernetics encapsulated the multidisciplinary
insights from meetings of, e.g., biologists, anthropologists, mathematicians,
engineers and evolutionary theorists in the 1940s. Their intention from the
beginning was to create an exact science of the mind. Their investigations led
them to the concepts of feedback, *self-regulation*, and later to self-organization,
concepts that Boyd incorporated in his work. Figure 3.1 depicts a simple
feedback loop, which immediately shows the parallels with the OODA loop.[104]

Self-regulation of systems by feedback became an engineering principle in
particular in cars, aircraft, missiles and air defense systems.[105] A feedback loop
is a circular arrangement of causally connected elements, in which an initial
cause propagates around the links of the loop, so that each element has an effect
on the next, until the last 'feeds back' into the first element of the cycle. The
consequence is that the first link ('input') is affected by the last ('output'), which
results in self-regulation of the entire system. Feedback is the control of a
machine on the basis of its actual performance rather than its expected performance. In a broader sense feedback has come to mean the conveying of information about the outcome of any process or activity to its source.

The cyberneticists distinguished between this type of *negative* or *balancing*
feedback, which dampens the effects of change and leads to less of the action

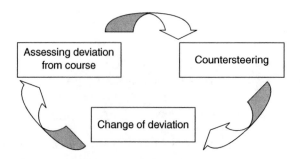

Figure 3.1 Example of a simple feedback loop.

that is creating it, and *positive* or *reinforcing* feedback, in which changes return to the system and amplify a change in the same direction.[106] It was recognized as the essential mechanism of *homeostasis*, the self-regulation that allows living organisms to maintain themselves in a state of dynamic balance.

From the beginning cybernetic theorists were aware that feedback is an important concept for modeling not only living organisms but also social systems. Like an individual, a social system is an organization that is bound together by a system of communication and it displays dynamics in which circular processes of a feedback nature play an important role. They recognized the similarity between the concept of feedback, the interplay of thesis and antithesis in the dialectic of Hegel and Marx and, for instance, the economic theory of Adam Smith that argues for the self-regulation of markets. All of these ideas implied circular patterns of causality that can be represented by feedback loops. It was the major achievement of cybernetics and informed investigations in other fields, such as biology and psychiatry.

Systems thinking matured with the integration of several scientific fields, including cybernetics, into *General Systems Theory* in the 1960s, which was also the title of the seminal work by Ludwig von Bertalanffy which Boyd had read. Bertalanffy is commonly credited with the first formulation of a comprehensive theoretical framework describing the principles of organization of living systems.[107] He was convinced that understanding systems behavior required a profoundly interdisciplinary approach.[108]

Bertalanffy pinpointed a dilemma that had puzzled scientists since the nineteenth century, when the novel idea of evolution entered into scientific thinking. Evolutionary thinking – thinking in terms of change, growth and development – required a new science of complexity. Focusing on the Second Law of dissipating energy, as described above, that operated in closed systems, Bertalanffy recognized that living systems are *open systems* that cannot be described by classical thermodynamics;[109] 'open' because they need to feed on a continual flux of matter and energy from their environment to stay alive. As Bertalanffy describes it:

> We express this by saying that living systems are basically open systems. An open system is defined as a system in exchange of matter with its environment, presenting import and export, building up and breaking down of its material components ... Closed systems are systems which are considered to be isolated from their environment.[110]

Unlike closed systems, which settle into a state of thermal equilibrium, *open systems maintain themselves far from equilibrium* in this 'steady state' characterized by continual flow and change.

This ability depends on the availability of a *requisite variety*, as cyberneticist W. Ross Ashby noted. It states that the internal regulatory mechanisms of a system must be as diverse as the environment with which it is trying to deal. The greater the number of sets and elements comprising the system, the greater the variety a system has, and importantly, the greater the number of states a system can achieve. Variety is an extremely valuable commodity for a system to possess because a system is 'constrained' if it does not have sufficient elements and arrangements of elements to deal with variety imposed upon the system by the environment or other systems. Ashby noted that the severity of constraint is shown by the reduction it causes in the number of arrangements a system can take to counteract opposing elements and that, when a constraint exists, a system can be taken advantage of because it is predictable.[111] Thus only by incorporating required variety into internal controls can a system deal with the variety and challenge posed by its environment. Any system that insulates itself from diversity in the environment tends to atrophy and lose its complexity and distinctive nature, an insight Boyd was to adopt.

The basis of the open-system model is the dynamic interaction of its components (and not the feedback cycle as in cybernetics). In cybernetics the goal and function of feedback is the maintenance of a desired value. The theory of open systems is thermodynamics, but in open systems order can increase and entropy can decrease. In contrast, in closed feedback mechanisms entropy increases (which is information of the measure of order), therefore information never increases. Information can be transformed into noise but not vice versa. An open system can 'actively' tend toward a state of higher organization, i.e., it may pass from a lower to a higher state of order. Notably, according to Bertalanffy, a feedback mechanism in open systems can reactively reach a state of higher organization owing to 'learning', i.e., information fed into the system.[112] These insights were later on refined and mathematically under-girded by Ilya Prigogine and form the basis for chaos and complexity theory.[113]

Systems everywhere

The structure of the brain

Cybernetics and systems thinking had a large impact on cognitive science, biology and psychology, psychiatry, the concept of mind and organization theory. B.F. Skinner based his model of 'stimulus–response' on it, which forms the heart of the behaviorist school of psychology. Skinner asserted that in order to understand human behavior we must take into account what the environment does to an organism before and after it responds. Behavior is shaped and maintained by its consequences. In the 1960s and 1970s his theories enjoyed a vogue and in many clinics 'behavior therapy' was adopted. Although criticized for an alleged under-appreciation of the influence of experience and thought (and free will), behaviorists are generally credited with discovering much that we know about learning, conditioning and the proper use of reward and punishment.[114]

In his book *Beyond Freedom and Dignity*, which Boyd studied for his first essay, Skinner extends this idea to the problem of equality and freedom. Skinner saw human nature as the product of evolution and as an adaptation to the environment. The environment exerts a confining influence, a measure of control, on man. For Skinner, freedom is merely the state in which man does not feel the control that is exerted over him. Freedom is, moreover, the lack of adverse stimuli in the environment. Manipulating and shaping the environment to effectuate a decrease in adverse stimuli thus becomes the obvious method for people to enhance freedom.[115] While difficult to assign direct linkage, the echo of Skinner cannot be ignored in Boyd's often repeated statement concerning the strategic goal of an organism: 'to diminish adversary's freedom-of-action while improving our freedom-of-action so that our adversary cannot cope while we can cope with events/efforts as they unfold.'[116]

Wiener, von Neumann and others such as Alan Turing and Marvin Minksy developed the 'computational theory of mind'. This fueled the cognitive view in psychology. The central idea is that much human behavior can be understood in terms of the mental processing of information through mental modules, and patterns of connections and patterns of activity among the neurons of the brain.[117] The idea was that the mind is like a program, and the brain is the hardware on which the program runs. The mind resembled a computer to the extent that cognition, the process of knowing, can be defined as information processing, a feature included in Boyd's OODA loop. [118] It led to functionalism, i.e. a focus on the functional organization of matter and on the input–output operations of the mind. The computer model of mental activity became the prevalent view of cognitive sciences and dominated all brain research for the next thirty years. Figure 3.2 shows a typical model that illustrates this school of thought.[119]

The cybernetic loop was also employed to explain learning. Learning is defined as a process in which one changes due to experience.[120] This process is generally represented as a simplified reinforcing cybernetic loop as shown below (Figure 3.3), that also includes the element of goal-orientation.[121]

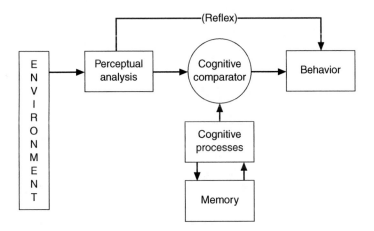

Figure 3.2 Example of a cybernetic model of the brain. From *Human Information Processing*, 2nd edition, by LINDSAY © 1977. Reprinted with permission of Wadsworth, a division of Thomson Learning: www.thomson-rights.com. Fax 001 800 730-2215.

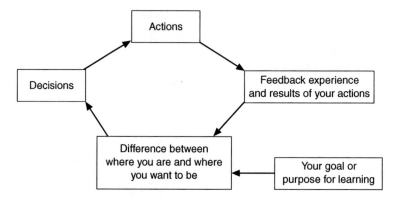

Figure 3.3 Model of a double loop learning process. From *The Art of Systems Thinking* by Joseph O'Connor and Ian McDermott. Reprinted by permission of HarperCollins Publishers Ltd © O'Connor 1997.

Boyd delved deeply into the literature mapping this cognitive revolution that started at the end of the 1950s and took off fully in the 1960s and 1970s, showing the influence and relevance of cybernetics for understanding human thought processes.[122] Indeed, Boyd's model may in part be retraced to cyberneticists such as Gregory Bateson, who developed a model of mind based upon systems-theoretical principles.[123] Bateson made the connection between evolution theory and mental processes, asserting that 'if you want to understand mental process, look at biological evolution and conversely if you want to understand biological evolution, go look at mental process'.[124] In similar vein, from Monod, Boyd learned that the prime functions of the nervous system could be defined in the following way:[125]

1   To control and coordinate neuromotor activity, notably in accord with sensory inputs;
2   To contain, in the form of genetically determined elements of circuitry, more or less complex programs of action, and to set them in motion in response to particular stimuli;
3   To analyze, sift, and integrate sensory inputs so as to obtain a representation of the outside world geared to specific performances [of an organism];
4   To register events which are significant in light of those specific performances;
5   To group them into classes according to their analogies;
6   To enrich, refine, and diversify the innate programs by incorporating these experiences into them;
7   To imagine – represent and simulate – external events and programs of action for the organism itself.

Monod asserts that we observe and respond through a genetically determined program, which is the result of 'experience accumulated by the entire ancestry of the species over the course of its evolution', which in turn shapes action and current experience after analysis of the effect of the action.[126]

Boyd's model, in line with Monod's description, also reflects the criticism of purely cybernetic models: human intelligence is utterly different from a machine.[127] As Grush observed, the cognitive revolution that occurred during the 1960s and 1970s in essence was the realization that any adequate theory of human and animal mentality would need to posit representational states between sensory stimulus and behavioral response – at least for a great many domains of behavior. The cognitive revolution brought about a renewed legitimacy of talk and theorizing about some types of mental or cognitive states, specifically, content-bearing states such as beliefs and desires. Functionalism, too, received criticism for the same reason. Genuine understanding is not just a matter of our mental implementation of the right program. The mind is not just a functional organization of matter.[128]

The human nervous system interacts with the environment by continually modulating its structure, and emotions and experience play a large role in human intelligence, human memory and decisions. Moreover, conceptualizing the brain as an information-processing devise is flawed, for the human mind thinks with ideas, not with information. Ideas create information, they are the integrating patterns that derive not from information but from experience.

Also, in the computer model of cognition, knowledge is seen as context and value free, based on abstract data. But all meaningful knowledge is contextual knowledge, and much of it is tacit and experiential. As Boyd was aware, the psychologist Jean Piaget and later neo-Darwinists Monod, Dawkins and Wilson all talked about mental structures. Dawkins and Wilson advanced the idea that genetics and culture (in that order) play a substantial role.[129] Culture became a prime area of interest, reinforcing these insights. In his landmark book of 1973 *The Interpretation of Cultures*, Clifford Geertz offered the view that, due to culture, all knowledge is 'local'. In it Boyd read that subjectivity is *the* phenomenon for anthropologists (and others in the human sciences) to tackle,[130] while in Edward Hall's book *Beyond Culture* from 1977 Boyd learned that 'everything man does is modified by learning and is therefore malleable. But once learned, these behavior patterns, these habitual responses, these ways of interacting gradually sink below the surface of the mind and, like the admiral of a submerged submarine fleet, control from the depths', a sentence Boyd was to incorporate in 'The Strategic Game'.[131] Thus, the cognitive revolution made common currency of the view that complex behavior is, in large part at least, controlled by inner representational states.[132] As Piaget stated, 'all learning and remembering depend upon antecedent structures'.[133] This did not invalidate cybernetics, merely the unwarranted metaphor of the mind as a computer.[134]

In systems thinking, and in Boyd's model, these insights are partly incorporated by introducing the concept of 'generative learning' – or 'double loop learning' – and the notions of 'mental models', or 'cognitive maps'. A cognitive map is an internal image or other mental representation of spatial relationships (or other kinds of knowledge), which allows one to choose alternative paths towards one's goals. Mental models consist of general ideas that shape one's thoughts and actions and lead one to expect certain results. They are theories in use, based mostly on observation and experience. They form belief systems, give meaning to events, and we interpret our experience in light of them. They are formed through socialization, culture and experience, elements Boyd would include in the Orientation element of his OODA model as well.[135]

In generative learning we allow our mental models to be influenced, perhaps changed, by the feedback. It provides one with a wider number of choices, new strategies and decision rules to apply. It leads to questioning one's assumptions and seeing a situation in a different way. When a person becomes exposed to a new perception or an experience, which challenges existing schemas, a process of reorganization and adaptation occurs, leading to new schemas, a process captured in the following model from 1984 (Figure 3.4), which, incidentally, shows the element of application and testing, a feature Boyd refers to in *The Conceptual Spiral*:[136]

Creativity

Systems thinking recognizes the limits mental models can and will put on one's viewpoints. It recognizes that the world is always richer than any perspective we have of it. Therefore the more perspectives we can gain the better. Piaget had informed Boyd that 'a fundamental trait of science today is the multiplicity of their interactions, which tend to form a system closed upon itself with many cross-linkings', words Boyd would almost literally include in his own work.[137] An additional relevant point of systems thinking is the awareness that this requires a certain level of curiosity, i.e. a deliberate and continuous search for novelty and new insights. This process, according to systems theory, is what generates new, varied, enriched and improved mental models. As McDermott

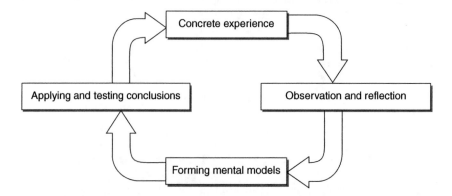

Figure 3.4 Refined model of generative learning. From Edward Borodzicz and Kees van Haperen, 'Individual and Group Learning in Crisis Simulations', *Journal of Contingencies and Crisis Management*, Vol. 10, No. 3 (September 2002). Reprinted with permission from Blackwell Publishing.

and O'Connor state, 'creativity and different sorts of intelligence all involve taking different viewpoints, and therefore getting different sorts of feedback'.[138] Peter Senge referred to this as *creative tension* and regarded it as a necessity for organizational as well as for individual learning; 'the gap is the source of creativity', words that sound very much like Boyd's own and echo those of Polanyi.[139] Senge informed Boyd too that the ability to grow under acknowledged uncertainty is part and parcel of creative people and organizations.[140]

Boyd's interest in the nature of creativity, and cognitive processes in general, surfaces in his bibliography, which includes Chilton Pearce's works, Edward De Bono with *New Think: The Use of Lateral Thinking in the Generation of New Ideas* (1971) and *Lateral Thinking: Creativity Step by Step* (1973), Henri Bergson's *The Creative Mind* (1975), J. Bronowski, *The Origins of Knowledge and Imagination* (1978) and P.E. Vernon, *Creativity* (1970). *Destruction and Creation* includes the notion that 'creativity is related to induction, synthesis and integration'.[141] According to Coon, creative thinking for solving problems involves what Boyd actually proposed: inductive, deductive, logical, illogical modes of thinking, as well as fluency (the total number of suggestions you are able to make), flexibility (the number of times you shift from one class of possible uses to another) and originality (how novel or unusual your suggestions are). Box 3.1 offers an overview of characteristics of creative persons, incidentally showing not only what Boyd practiced in reality (and indeed describing his character rather accurately), but also his normative view concerning strategic thinking.[142]

Organizational learning

From the 1960s onwards systems thinking became a popular concept also outside of the scientific community. In the 1950s and 1960s it had a strong influence on engineering and management, resulting in concepts such as

Thinking abilities	Personality characteristics	Thinking styles
Use metaphors in thinking	Willing to take intellectual risk	Challenges assumptions
Flexible decision maker	Curiosity and inquisitiveness	Looks for novelty and gaps in knowledge
Uses broad categories	Openness to new experiences	Draws new ideas out of existing knowledge
Uses mental images	Tolerates ambiguity	
Can cope with novelty	Broad range of interests	
Can break mental sets	Playful with ideas	
Finds order in chaos	Intuitive	

Box 3.1 Characteristics of creative people.

'system-oriented management', 'system dynamics' and 'management cybernetics' featuring in titles. Boyd for instance studied several works on systems thinking such as F.E. Emery, *Systems Thinking* (1976), John Gall, *Systemantics: How Systems Work and Especially How They Fail* (1977), Marvin Kasner and Lewis Andrews, *Biofeedback: Turning on the Power of Your Mind* (1973), C.T. Landes, *Control and Dynamic Systems: Advances in Theory and Applications* (1973). The cybernetic and systems view was applied in the reports to the Club of Rome.

The metaphor of the organization as an organism and as a learning brain proved fruitful correctives for the prevalent view of the organization as a machine, which had dominated management theory up until the 1960s. Both metaphors were based on open systems theory.[143] This spawned the 'Organic School' of management theory. The idea that organizations are more like organisms guided the attention toward the more general issues of survival, organization–environment relations and organizational effectiveness, and away from goals, structures and efficiency, which were key themes in the machine metaphor. It also induced a focus on information flows and learning processes. Organization theory became a kind of biology in which the distinctions and relations among molecules, cells, complex organisms, species and ecology are paralleled in those between individuals, groups, organizations, populations (species) of organizations and their social ecology.

The dynamic of organizational learning resembles the process described by Boyd. Included in Boyd's notion of orientation is the idea of institutional memory in the form of doctrine, practices, values and shared experiences, that guide action and that inform newcomers in the organization. He found such ideas too in Japanese business practices of 'just in time management' and 'total quality management'. There is some evidence that Boyd found confirmation of his simple OODA loop model in the Deming cycle, which is a simple cybernetic planning cycle of Plan–Do–Check–Action, which became famous during the 1980s in studies on Japanese management practices.[144]

Other traits too, betray the organizational learning character of the OODA loop. The OODA loop model includes double feedback loops that allow an individual or organization to monitor the continued relevance of its goals, its repertoire of responses and the adequacy of the lens of its institutional memory. Box 3.2 gives an impression of definitions of organizational learning in which both the cybernetic as well as the evolution-theoretical elements are evident.[145]

The organizational capacity to learn is considered essential for professional-type organizations that operate in highly complex environments, where the knowledge required to create strategy is widely diffused, or that face truly novel situations, and/or that operate in dynamic and unpredictable environments.[146] Adaptability and flexibility, for which learning is essential, is the defining parameter for corporate success, i.e. long-term survival.[147]

Recognizing the value for military organizations, in *Organic Design for Command and Control*, Boyd argues for a permissive and loosely structured organization, a view in accordance with, for instance, Chris Argyris and Donald

- Organizational learning means the process of improving actions through better knowledge and understanding.
- Organizational learning is defined as increasing an organization's capacity to take effective action.
- An entity learns if, through its processing of information, the range of potential behaviors is increased.
- Organizational learning is a process of detecting and correcting error.
- Organizational learning is defined as the process by which knowledge about action-outcome relationships between the organization and the environment is developed.
- Organizations are seen as learning by encoding inferences from history into routines that guide behavior.
- Organizational learning occurs through shared insights, knowledge, and mental models [and] builds on past knowledge and experience – that is, on memory.

Box 3.2 Definitions of organizational learning.

Schon, who suggested in 1978 that a loosely structured organization, unfettered by rigid internal hierarchies and overspecialization, would be more amenable to a free internal debate that would facilitate organizational learning and so facilitate change.[148] Facilitators for learning include a broad base of contributors and data sources; a process for sharing diverse perspectives and points of view and a willingness to embrace contradictory and unexpected findings; quick feedback; and forums for brainstorming in which new ideas are generated and creative thinking should be stimulated. When organizations interpret acquired information, they should adopt a dialectic mode in which various views are debated and tested. When information is transformed into action, new approaches must be tried, even when they result in some mistakes and failures.[149] Other facilitators are listed in the left column of Box 3.3.[150] Boyd's view on the optimum military organization in both peacetime and war mirrors these insights. In particular *Organic Design* and *The Conceptual Spiral* bear the markings of this school of thought.

Boyd and the first stage of the paradigm shift

Boyd and the systems view of life

In 1975 Capra told Boyd about the five criteria of the new-paradigm thinking in science. The *first* criterion, according to Capra, concerns the relationship between the part and the whole [...] the properties of the parts certainly contribute to our understanding of the whole, at the same time the properties of the parts can only be fully understood through the dynamics of the whole.

Positive indicators	Negative indicators
Operating characteristics	
Anticipatory	Reactive
Long-term focus	Short-term focus
Change = opportunity	Change = threat
Adapts to change	Static organization
Culture	
Simple structure	Complex and bureaucratic
Participative management style	Directive/autocratic
Strong networking	Lack of sharing/disconnected functions
Open flow of information	Information used as power base
External scanning encouraged	Insular/lacking external contacts
Encourage questioning and review	Closed mind-set/tunnel vision
Innovation/experimentation encouraged	Non-risk-taking

Box 3.3 Positive and negative indicators of learning organizations.

The *second* criterion of new-paradigm thinking in science concerns a shift from thinking in terms of structure to thinking in terms of process. Process is primary and every structure is a manifestation of an underlying process. The *third* criterion is the shift from objective science to epistemic science. Whereas in the old paradigm scientific descriptions were believed to be objective, that is, independent of the human observer and the process of knowledge, in the new paradigm epistemology – the understanding of the process of knowledge – has to be included explicitly in the description of natural phenomena. The *fourth* criterion is a shift towards networks as the metaphor for knowledge. Things exist by virtue of their mutually consistent relationships. There is no hierarchy of fundamental laws or principles as the widely held metaphor of knowledge as a building suggests. The *last* criterion involves the shift from truth to approximate description. The Cartesian paradigm was based on a belief in the certainty of scientific knowledge. Instead, the paradigm shift described by Capra advances the idea that all scientific concepts and theories are limited and approximate.[151] Or, as Piaget had suggested to Boyd, 'Rather than envisaging human knowledge as a pyramid or building of some sort, we should think of it as a spiral the radius of whose turns increases as the spiral rises.'[152]

Boyd was profoundly influenced by central themes of these developments such as pervading uncertainty, the combination of analysis and synthesis, deduction and induction, feedback, open systems versus closed systems, etc. In his strategic theory this becomes evident not only through his bibliographies, but also in various sections in different presentations, as already alluded above. First of all,

Boyd adopted the key insight that living systems are essentially open systems, and need to be if they aspire to exist and grow. He often employs the term 'organic whole'. In *Patterns of Conflict*, for instance, when he summarizes the 'theme for vitality and growth', he states that the aim is to 'improve fitness as an organic whole to shape and expand influence or power over the course of events in the world'.[153] In fact, this idea informed Boyd's thoughts concerning the essence of strategy, which he expressed in systems theoretical terms. In his presentation 'The Strategic Game of ? & ?', in which he distills the abstract essence of strategy, he includes what he termed an 'essential element' the idea that:

> Living systems are open systems; closed systems are non-living systems. Point: if we don't communicate with outside world – to gain information for knowledge and understanding as well as matter and energy for sustenance – we die out to become non-discerning and uninteresting part of that world.[154]

Indeed, when we do not maintain communication with the outside world, Boyd asserts, both Gödel and the Second Law will 'kick in':

> One cannot determine the character or nature of a system within itself.

> Moreover, attempts to do so lead to confusion and disorder.[155]

In *Patterns of Conflict* he also employs the Second Law by stating that one of the key elements of victory consists of:

> 'Diminish own friction (or entropy) and magnify adversary friction (or entropy).'[156]

Boyd thus regarded the Second Law as another 'producer' of uncertainty on a par with the principles described by Gödel and Heisenberg. In *Destruction and Creation* he asserts that

> Confusion and disorder are also related to the notion of Entropy and the Second Law of Thermodynamics ... Accordingly, whenever we attempt to do work or take action inside such a system – a concept and its match-up with reality – we should anticipate an increase in entropy hence an increase in confusion and disorder. Naturally, this means we cannot determine the character or nature (consistency) of such a system within itself, since the system is moving irreversibly toward a higher, yet unknown, state of confusion and disorder.[157]

Strategy, creativity, doctrines and mental modules

A second obvious influence lies in the importance Boyd attaches to creativity, the availability of a multitude of mental modules and the necessity to constantly improve existing mental modules. Devising strategy as an act of creativity and the ideas armed forces operate on – doctrine – or in Boyd's words, orientation patterns, are like mental modules. Boyd's very starting point of *Destruction and Creation* is a search for ways we form – create – mental models or 'mental concepts', as Boyd labels them. His investigation begins with the question 'how do we generate or create the mental concepts to support [this] decision making?'[158] In 1987, Boyd elaborated on the element of Orientation of the OODA loop by asserting that 'Orientation, seen as a result, represents images, views, or impressions of the world shaped by genetic heritage, cultural traditions, previous experiences, and unfolding circumstances'.[159] In *Destruction and Creation* he advances the notion that for creating relevant mental concepts, we need to heed the warnings of Polanyi, Kuhn, Gödel, Heisenberg and the dynamics of the Second Law. The following examples, again from Boyd's presentation *Organic Design for Command and Control* also reflect this concept:

> Orientation is the Schwerpunkt. It shapes the way we interact with the environment – hence orientation shapes the way we observe, the way we decide, the way we act.

> Orientation shapes the character of present observation-orientation-decision-action loops – while these present loops shape the character of future orientation.

These insights implied to him that 'We need to create mental images, views, or impressions, hence patterns that match with activity of world.' And they gain a strategic character when Boyd advances the idea that 'We need to deny adversary the possibility of uncovering or discerning patterns that match our activity, or other aspects of reality in the world.'[160] The necessity of applying a multitude of perspectives comes to the fore when Boyd asserts in 'Organic Design':

> Orientation is an interactive process of many sided implicit cross-referencing projections, empathies, correlations and rejections. . . .[161]

> expose individuals, with different skills and abilities, against a variety of situations – whereby each individual can observe and orient himself simultaneously to the others and to the variety of changing situations.[162]

In 'The Strategic Game of ? & ?', which he finished one month after completing 'Organic Design', he includes several statements referring to this theme, exemplifying the fact that indeed this issue is of an essential nature for Boyd:

> To discern what is going on we must interact in a variety of ways with our environment.
> We must be able to examine the world from a number of perspectives so that we can generate mental images or impressions that correspond to that world.[163]

We can't just look at our own personal experiences or use the same mental recipes over and over again; we've got to look at other disciplines and activities and relate or connect them to what we know from our experiences and the strategic world we live in.[164]

When he discusses the ways to maintain interaction with the ever-changing world so as to ensure one's ability to adapt, he asserts that this is accomplished:

By an instinctive see-saw of analysis and synthesis across a variety of domains, or across competing/independent channels of information, in order to spontaneously generate new mental images or impressions that match up with an unfolding world of uncertainty and change.[165]

Conclusion

The changes in the scientific *Zeitgeist* thus directly informed Boyd's thinking, and awareness of the works Boyd studied and the themes he was interested in helps explain his work. As science progressed, and developed a new language to address and explain the dynamics of living systems, so Boyd actively developed his mental concepts accordingly. The epistemological debates he read about informed him about the pervasiveness of uncertainty and about the ways science progresses. Reading Conant, Polanyi, Kuhn, Popper and others brought him the themes of analysis and synthesis, the central role of the observer and the influence of existing theories and paradigms on the act of observation. Cybernetics and systems-theory, including the cognitive revolution, informed him about the concepts of entropy, feed back, interdependency, adaptation, and about the role of experience and genetics and their role in shaping mental modules. His study of a wide range of scientific topics suggested a multi-spectral, multidisciplinary and holistic approach and offered him a new frame of reference and a new lexicon for understanding war and strategy. At the end of the 1970s new concepts emerged that would cohere later into chaos theory and complexity theory – a development Boyd followed from its beginning to the end of his life – and the subject of the next chapter.

4 Completing the shift

Physicists, mathematicians, biologists, and astronomers have created an alternative set of ideas. Simple systems give rise to complex behavior. Complex systems give rise to simple behavior. And most importantly, the laws of complexity hold universally, caring not at all for the details of a system's constituent atoms.[1]

James Gleick

Riding the wave

Neo-Darwinism and the new worldview

This chapter continues the survey of Boyd's scientific *Zeitgeist* by looking at chaos and complexity theory and the concept of *Complex Adaptive Systems*, or CAS, ideas that emerged in what is often labeled as the postmodern era. It will also discuss the implications of Boyd's study of scientific sources for the interpretation of his work. It takes off with the rise of neo-Darwinism. The neo-Darwinist perspective dominated the wave of popular scientific literature from the late 1970s onward with the cognitive process often playing a central role. As Jeremy Rifkin noted in 1987, 'the old Darwinian view of "survival of the fittest" is now being cast aside in some quarters in favor of a new view of "survival of the best informed" '. Whereas standard neo-Darwinian orthodoxy held that each species up the evolutionary line is better able to utilize scarce resources more efficiently, the emergent theory characterized each species up the evolutionary chain as better adept at processing greater stores of information in shorter time spans.[2] Boyd's very first presentation carries the marks of this perspective, indeed, his ideas about war and strategy are pregnant with Darwinian notions. In the opening remarks in the essay *Destruction and Creation*, one reads that 'studies of human behavior reveal that the actions we undertake as individuals are closely related to survival'. Hence Boyd's statement that the goal of an individual is 'to improve our capacity for independent action'. In the opening slides of *Patterns of Conflict* this surfaces again when he discusses human nature. The goal, again, is to survive, and to survive on one's own terms, or improve one's capacity for independent action. Due to forced competition for limited resources to satisfy these desires, one is probably compelled to diminish adversary's capacity for independent action, or deny him the opportunity to survive on his own terms, or make it impossible to survive at all.

Life is conflict, survival and conquest.

And he actually notes explicitly that in studying war: 'one is naturally led to the Theory of Evolution by Natural Selection and The Conduct of War'. Also in *Organic Design for Command and Control*, again he refers to Darwin, stating that 'we observe from Darwin that the environment selects [and] the ability or inability to interact and adapt to exigencies of environment select in or out'.[3]

This was not a coincidence, considering that the various works discussed in the previous chapters had referred to this theme. Now this perspective was gaining profile among popular scientific books he devoured. The works he was reading and re-reading at the time of his death (Box 4.1) are almost exclusively concerned with the 'new sciences', as they are sometimes referred to. It includes Brian Goodwin's *How the Leopard Changed Its Spots*, which deals with the evolution of complexity, and is marked with a post-it note reading 'Dad's favorite'.[4] Box 4.2 lists some keywords for an impression of the worldviews contained in these works.[5]

Dissipative structures

One key concept is the notion of self-organization, which propelled further research into system dynamics. Early models of self-organization developed by

---

John Barrow, *The Artful Universe*
John Barrow, *Pi in the Sky*
John Barrow, *Theories of Everything*
Richard Brodie, *Virus of the Mind*
Fritjof Capra, *The Web of Life*
Jack Cohen and Ian Stewart, *The Collapse of Chaos*
Peter Coveney and Roger Highfield, *Frontiers of Complexity*
Peter Coveney and Roger Highfield, *The Arrow of Time*
Richard Dawkins, *The Blind Watchmaker*
Richard Dawkins, *The Selfish Gene*
Stephen Gellert, *In the Wake of Chaos*

Murray Gell-Mann, *The Quark and the Jaguar*
John Horgan, *The End of Science*
Konrad Lorenz, *Behind the Mirror*
Marvin Minsky, *Society of the Mind*
Robert Ornstein, *The Evolution of Consciousness*
Roger Penrose, *Shadows of the Mind*
Roger Penrose, *The Emperor's New Mind*
Ilya Prigogine and Isabelle Stenger, *Order out of Chaos*
Stephen Rose, *The Making of Memory*
David Ruelle, *Chance and Chaos*
Mitchell Waldrop, *Complexity*

Box 4.1 Boyd's reading list at the time of his death.

Traditional	Emerging
Reductionism	Holism
Linear causality	Mutual causality
Objective reality	Perspective reality
Determinism	Indeterminism
Survival of the fittest	Adaptive self-organization
Focus on discrete entities	Focus on relationships between entities
Linear relationships	Non-linear relationships
Newtonian physics perspectives	Quantum physics perspectives
World is predictable	World is novel and probabilistic
Modern	Postmodern
Focus on hierarchy	Focus on heterarchy (within levels)
Prediction	Understanding
Based on nineteenth-century physics	Based on biology
Equilibrium/stability/deterministic dynamics	Structure/pattern/self-organization/ life cycles
Focus on averages	Focus on variation

Box 4.2 Traditional versus emerging worldview

cyberneticists asserted that structural changes take place within a given 'variety pool' of structures, and the survival chances of the system depend on the rich-ness, or 'requisite variety' of that pool, as noted above. There is, however, no creativity, no development, no evolution. The later models include the creation of novel structures and modes of behavior in the processes of development, learning and evolution. Two features characterize this process:[6]

- self-organization occurring when the open system is operating *far-from-equilibrium;*
- *non-linear interconnectedness* of the system's components.

   In 1967 Ilya Prigogine, one of the fathers of chaos and complexity theory, presented his theory of 'dissipative structures', for which he was awarded the Nobel prize in 1977. He discovered that classical thermodynamics lead to the concept of 'equilibrium structures' such as crystals.[7] Here the dissipation of energy in heat was always associated with waste. In contrast, Prigogine's concept of a dissipative structure introduced a radical change in this view by showing that in open systems dissipation becomes a source of order. This idea emphasizes the close association between structure and order on the one side and dissipation of energy on the other. In certain chemical reactions he noted that, as the system moved farther away from equilibrium (that is from a state with uniform temperature throughout the liquid), it reached a critical point of instability, at which certain ordered patterns in the fluid emerged, such as hexagonal patterns. This was a spectacular example of spontaneous self-organization.

He had found that when systems are driven far-from-equilibrium entirely new things can happen. This non-equilibrium is maintained by the continual flow of heat through the system. Dissipative structures not only maintain themselves in a stable state far-from-equilibrium, but may even evolve. When the flow of energy and matter through them increases, they may go through new instabilities and transform themselves into new structures of increased complexity.

While dissipative structures receive their energy outside, the instabilities and jumps to new forms of organization are the result of fluctuations amplified by positive feedback loops. Thus, amplifying feedback, which had always been regarded as destructive in cybernetics, appeared as a source of new order and complexity in the theory of dissipative structures. As Prigogine noted in 1984, 'non-equilibrium is the source of order, non-equilibrium brings order out of chaos'.[8] This concept goes much further than that of an open system (as developed by Bertalanffy) as it also includes the idea of points of instability at which new structures and forms of order emerge. Prigogine's theory implied a radical reconceptualization of many fundamental ideas associated with structure – a shift of perception from stability to instability, from order to disorder, from equilibrium to non-equilibrium, from being to becoming.[9]

In his presentation 'Strategic Game' Boyd included a telling section from *Order out of Chaos* in which Prigogine marks the inadequacy of equilibrium thermodynamics to explain nature, making a cautious jump to social systems in the process:[10]

> Equilibrium thermodynamics provides a satisfactory explanation for a vast number of physicochemical phenomena. Yet it may be asked whether the concept of equilibrium structures encompasses the different structures we encounter in nature. Obviously the answer is no.
>
> Equilibrium structures can be seen as the result of statistical compensation for the activity of microscopic elements (molecules, atoms). By definition they are inert at the global level. . . . Once they have been formed they may be isolated and maintained indefinitely without further interaction with their environment. When we examine a biological cell or a city, however, the situation is quite different: not only are these systems open, but also they exist only because they are open. They feed on the flux of matter and energy coming to them from the outside world. We can isolate a crystal, but cities and cells die when cut off from their environment. They form an integral part of the world from which they can draw sustenance, and they cannot be separated from the fluxes that they incessantly transform.

The non-linearity of nature

Boyd's ideas on the essence of strategic encounters would revolve around this notion, as well as around the idea that this involved highly non-linear processes.

Far-from-equilibrium, the system's flow processes are interlinked through multiple feedback loops and the corresponding mathematical equations are non-linear. The farther a dissipative structure is from equilibrium, the greater its complexity and the higher is the degree of non-linearity in the mathematical equations describing it.[11] Out of these developments chaos theory emerged in the 1980s, which focuses on thoroughly unstable regions and on non-linearity of systems behavior. It reflects the recognition that non-linear phenomena dominate much more of the inanimate world than we had thought, and that they are an essential aspect of the network patterns of living systems.

In the Newtonian paradigm the discovery of non-linear relationships would be immediately 'linearized', in other words, replaced by linear approximations. In the world of linear equations we thought we knew that systems described by simple equations behaved in simple ways, while those described by complicated equations behaved in complicated ways. In the non-linear world, simple deterministic equations may produce an unsuspected richness and variety of behavior. On the other hand, complex and seemingly chaotic behavior can give rise to ordered structures, to subtle and beautiful patterns.[12] Small inputs in a closed system may produce large, unpredictable consequences, and these systems may jump from ordered states to chaotic states, based on those small inputs. This feature is the consequence of the frequent occurrence of self-reinforcing feedback processes.

The point of chaos theory is that the fate of the system is determined by small factors, which become magnified over time. It is the fact that these factors are too many and too small to know that causes the system to be unpredictable. The behavior of chaotic systems is not merely random but shows a deeper level of patterned order. Advances in computer technology as well as new mathematical techniques appearing in the 1970s and 1980s enabled scientists to make these underlying patterns visible in distinct shape.

The philosophical thrust of chaos theory is that uncertainty can be caused by small changes, which, even if these changes are anticipated, result in an unpredictable system. This does not mean that the behavior of the system is totally unpredictable. Long-term trends can be distilled with a certain level of probability. The range of change can to some extent be estimated. However, the 'Sensitivity to Initial Conditions' (SIC) of many systems does force one to shift from a quantitative towards a qualitative analysis[13] as long-term predictions are meaningless. Interestingly for understanding Boyd, this condition of SIC offers yet another dimension of fundamental uncertainty. As Gell-Mann notes, 'chaos gives rise to effective indeterminacy at the classical level over and above the indeterminacy in principle of quantum mechanics'.[14]

Phase space and forks in the road

To describe non-linear behavior of systems the idea of 'phase space' was coined, which describes the range of positions a system can occupy.[15] The problem with chaotic systems is that, unlike a clock's pendulum (which will slowly return to a standstill), they never pass through the same point, i.e. the system never repeats itself, so that each cycle of a pendulum (to continue the example) covers a new region of phase space. It will not be possible to predict which point in phase space the system will pass through at a certain time but it will be possible to map the phase space, for in spite of the seemingly erratic motion, the points in phase space are not randomly distributed. Together they form a complex, highly organized pattern (aptly named *attractor*) which computers are able to visualize.

When energy is added to the system, the system moves further away from equilibrium and moves to the edges of the phase space. In the absence of significant perturbations, a dissipative system will usually follow a 'normal' linear trajectory. There will be the usual boundary testing, but in the absence of any sustained increase in environmental energy, the system will return to its original point of reference. At some point such movement may be due to internal micro-fluctuations or due to external perturbations from the environment. This may give rise to a self-amplifying cycle. At the boundary zone, far-from-equilibrium, systems may *bifurcate*.

The bifurcation point is a crisis point of a system, where the variables of parameters fluctuate constantly. The system first fluctuates between two or more new points, and as the oscillations continue it will abandon the original path and 'chooses' between two possible new trajectories on the basis of very small differences in the values of the controlling parameter(s) at the point of change. Figure 4.1 depicts a bifurcation diagram for chemical reactions far-from-equilibrium.[16]

Change is the result of perturbation beyond a boundary. This perturbation may be very small, but due to the non-linearity of complex systems, the outcome can be a radical regime change. It signifies the transition of a system from the dynamic regime of one set of attractors, generally more stable and simpler ones, to the dynamic regime of a set of more complex and chaotic attractors. Alternatively, the system may find a new area of stability. Dissipative structures thus evolve. They make a transformation from the apparently chaotic to increasingly

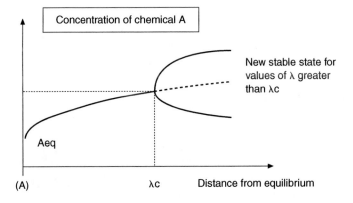

Figure 4.1 Bifurcation diagram.

ordered state on the other side of the bifurcation point. Dissipative structures thus manifest the process of self-organizing. They arise spontaneously and may evolve towards greater complexity and a higher degree of the system's order. However, the move into the chaotic regime, to the bifurcation point, may also lead to a fatal perturbation that causes the system to disintegrate. Thus bifurcation also denotes a critical state in which the system either evolves or becomes extinct.[17] This obviously has implications for strategic theory.

Which path it will take will depend on the system's history, and on various external conditions and can never be predicted. The existence of bifurcations at which the system may take several different paths therefore implies also that indeterminacy is another characteristic of Prigogine's theory, adding another 'producer' of fundamental uncertainty of dissipative systems to the indeterminacy due to non-linearity caused by the SIC property.[18] It means, in the words of Nicolis, that 'we therefore give up the idea of obtaining exact results of a global character and limit our attention to the local behavior of the solutions in the vicinity of the bifurcation point'.[19]

From chemistry to life: autopoiesis

Subsequently a multitude of such processes were discovered in physical and biological systems. In biochemical systems, such as enzymes, when exposed to energy flows, different catalytic reactions were found to combine to form complex networks that sometimes contain closed loops, in which the enzymes produced in one cycle act as catalysts in the subsequent cycle. These cycles turned out to be not only remarkably stable, but also capable of self-replicating and of correcting replication errors, which meant that they can conserve and transmit complex information. A striking lifelike property of such cycles is their ability to evolve by passing through instabilities and creating successively higher levels of organization that are characterized by increasing diversity and richness of components and structures.[20]

In the early 1970s Maturana and Varela made the step from non-living to living systems. They asserted that the nervous system operates as a closed network of interactions, in which every change of the interactive relations between certain components always results in a change of the interactive relations of the same or of other components. The circular organization of the nervous system is the basic organization of all living systems. Living systems are organized in a closed causal circular process that allows for evolutionary change in the way the circularity is maintained, but not for the loss of the circularity itself. This also implied that the components that specify the circular organization must also be produced and maintained by it.

They coined the term 'autopoietic system' for such a network of production processes, in which the function of each component is to participate in the production or transformation of other components in the network. The product of the system's operation is its own organization. This is the 'self-generating' property. This production includes the creation of a boundary – for instance the membrane of a cell – that specifies the domain of the network's operations and defines the system as a unit.[21] Autopoietic systems are 'self-bounded', and the boundary is an integral part of the network. The final property is 'self-perpetuation': all components are continually replaced by the system's processes of transformation.

Autopoietic systems are 'organizationally closed' in the sense that their order and behavior are not imposed by the environment but are established by the system itself. In other words, living systems are autonomous. This does not mean they are isolated from their environment. On the contrary, they interact with the environment through a continual exchange of energy and matter. Here the dissipative feature of open systems is applicable. Living systems are 'structurally open' for matter and energy, which flow continually through the system, but the system maintains a stable form, and it does so autonomously through self-organization.[22] It preserves the web-like pattern of organization but undergoes continual structural changes.

It accomplishes this through a developmental process of 'structural coupling' with the environment. New connections in the autopoietic network are created either through environmental influences or as a result of the system's internal dynamics. Structural coupling refers to recurrent interactions with the environment, each of which triggers structural changes in the system. For instance, an organism's nervous system changes its connectivity with every sense perception.[23]

However, in keeping with the autonomous character of autopoietic systems, the environment only triggers the structural changes, it does not specify or direct them. Not all disturbances cause structural changes. It is the living system that specifies which perturbations from the environment trigger them.[24] There are many disturbances that do not cause structural changes because they are 'foreign' to the system. In this way each living system builds up its own distinctive world according to its own distinctive structure. As it keeps interacting with its environment, a living organism will undergo a sequence of structural changes, and over time it will form its own, individual pathway of structural coupling.

At any point on this pathway, the structure of the organism is a record of previous structural changes and thus of previous interactions, i.e. history. The organism's structure conditions the course of its interactions and restricts the structural changes that the interactions may trigger in it. The implication is that the structural changes in the system constitute acts of cognition.[25] Rather than suggesting that the system adapts to an environment or that the environment selects the system configuration that survives, autopoiesis places principal emphasis on the way the total system of interactions shapes its own future.[26]

Influenced in the 1960s by cybernetics, Maturana postulated that the nervous system is not only self-organizing but also constantly self-referring. This implied that perception cannot be viewed as the representation of an external reality but must be understood as the continual creation of new relationships within the neural network. Perception, and more generally, cognition, do not represent an external reality, but rather specify one through the nervous system's process of circular organization. Thus Maturana hypothesized that the process of circular organization itself (with or without a nervous system) is identical to the process of cognition.

From that he drew the conclusion that living systems are cognitive systems, and living as a process is a process of cognition. The living system is a multiple interconnected network whose components are constantly changing. There is great fluidity in this network, which allows the system to respond to disturbances from the environment. The range of interactions a living system can have with its environment is defined as its 'cognitive domain' and as the complexity of a living organism increases, so does its cognitive domain.[27]

The link with Boyd's work is obvious, as is the link with Polanyi's notion of tacit knowing. Structural coupling, for instance, is evident in Boyd's assertion shown earlier that:[28]

> Orientation is the schwerpunkt. It shapes the way we interact with the environment [...].

In this sense

> Orientation shapes the character of <u>present</u> observations-orientation-decision-action loops – while these present loops shape the character of <u>future</u> orientation.

Indeed, Boyd followed developments in the fields of cognitive sciences and neurophysiology closely.[29] In fact, he explicitly included three sections in his briefing *The Strategic Game of ? and ?*[30] in which Maturana's concept of structural coupling clearly comes to the fore:[31]

> [...]a neuron's fibers can change significantly in a few days or weeks, presumably in response to changing demands on the nervous system ... research has shown neurons continually rewire their own circuitry, sprouting new fibers that reach out to make contact with new groups of other neurons and withdrawing old fibers from previous contacts.... This rewiring process may account for how the brain improves one's abilities such as becoming proficient in a sport or learning to play a musical instrument. Some scientists have suggested that the brain may use this method to store facts.[...]
> [...]the complexity of the human brain is dependent upon a vast number of synapses (connections) between brain cells ... these synaptic connections are established or fall by the wayside according to how frequent they're used. Those synapses which are in frequent use tend to endure ('are stabilized') while others are eliminated ... In other words, ... interaction with the environment ... [exerts] ... tremendous influence on the way the human brain works and how it has evolved.

Some pages later Boyd combined dissipative structures, autopoiesis, Gödel, Heisenberg and the Second Law of Thermodynamics to take the audience slowly towards the essence of strategy. Like Goodwin, who had told him that 'deprivation produces disorder', Boyd notes that:[32]

> Physical as well as electrical and chemical connections in the brain are shaped by interacting with the environment. Point: without these interactions we do not have the mental wherewithal to deal or cope with that environment.
>
> Gödel's Incompleteness Theorems, Heisenberg's Uncertainty Principle, and the Second Law of Thermodynamics, all taken together, show that we cannot determine the character or nature of a system within itself. Moreover, attempts to do so lead to confusion and disorder – mental as well as physical. Point: We need an external environment, or outside world, to define ourselves and maintain organic integrity, otherwise we experience dissolution/disintegration – i.e., we come unglued.
>
> Living systems are open systems; closed systems are non-living systems. Point: If we don't communicate with the outside world – to gain information for knowledge and understanding as well as matter and energy for sustenance – we die out to become a non-discerning and uninteresting part of that world.

Beyond open and chaotic systems: complexity theory

Complex adaptive systems

These concepts return in complexity theory. Complexity theory and chaos theory are now mostly mentioned interchangeably. Indeed, the term 'chaoplexity' has been coined. It is not so much an organized, rigorous theory as a collection of ideas that have in common the notion that within dynamic patterns there may be underlying simplicity. In 1987 the publication of James Gleick's *Chaos: Making a New Science* and Mitchell Waldrop's *Complexity: The Emerging Science at the Edge of Order and Chaos*, introduced this new area of intellectual activity.[33]

Briefly stated, complexity theory examines emergent order in large, interactive, adaptive networks such as neural networks or ecosystems.[34] These *Complex adaptive systems* (CAS) co-evolve with the environment through self-organizing non-linear behavior of agents navigating 'the fitness landscapes'. Under selective pressure they exhibit hierarchical self-organization.[35] They also exhibit emergence: the interactions of agents may lead to emerging global properties that are strikingly different from the behaviors of individual agents. These properties cannot be predicted from prior knowledge of the agents. The global properties in turn affect the environment that each agent 'sees', influencing the agents' behaviors. A synergistic feedback loop is thus created; interactions between agents determine emerging global properties, which in turn influence the agents. Self-organization arises as the system reacts and adapts to its externally imposed environment. Such order occurs in a wide variety of systems, including for example convective fluids, chemical reactions, certain animal species, and societies.

Complexity theory deals with behavior at 'the edge of chaos', where spontaneous organization, life and consciousness can occur. Complex systems have acquired the ability to bring order and chaos into a special balance (i.e. the edge of chaos), they never quite lock into place, yet never quite dissolve into turbulence either. The edge of chaos is where life has enough stability to sustain itself and enough creativity to deserve the name of life, it is where new ideas and innovative genotypes are forever nibbling away at the edges of the status quo.[36]

There is no optimum in system fitness. Dynamic systems can occupy a 'universe' composed of three regions.[37]

- The first is an ordered, stable region. Perturbations to the systems tend to die out rapidly, creating only local damage or changes to the system. Information does not flow readily between the agents.
- In the second region, chaotic behavior is the rule. Disturbances propagate rapidly throughout the system, often leading to destructive effects.
- The final region is the boundary between the stable and chaotic zones. Known as the complex region or the 'edge of chaos', it is a phase transition zone between the stable and chaotic regions.

Deep in the ordered regime, perturbations cannot propagate through the system. Deep in the chaotic regime, the system would be too sensitive to small perturbations to maintain its organization.[38] Thus, complex behavior is on the border between predictability and non-predictability. Complex systems possess characteristics of both stable and chaotic systems. On the one hand they exhibit sufficiently stable behavior to allow retention of information, to transfer information across different systems and across time, and to reproduce themselves, on the other hand, they are sufficiently chaotic to permit the creative use of information and to allow change.

Complex Systems, for short, are quite different from most systems that have been studied scientifically. A remarkable finding is that different non-linear systems have inherently identical structures. Whether it refers to biological evolution, the behavior of organisms in ecological systems, the operation of the mammalian immune system, learning and thinking in animals, the behavior of investors in financial markets, political parties, ant colonies, etc., the systems feature common processes.[39] It teaches modesty too, for it points to fundamental limits in our ability to understand, control and manage the world, and the need for us to accept unpredictability and change.[40]

Several other brief observations can be made about the make up and behavior of complex adaptive systems (Box 4.3).[41]

- They are systems that are networks of 'agents' acting in parallel. In a brain the agents are nerve cells, in ecologies the agents are species, in an economy the agents are firms and individuals or even nations.
- Each agent finds itself in an environment produced by its interactions with the other agents in the system.
- It is constantly acting and reacting to what the other agents are doing.
- And because of that essentially nothing is fixed in its environment.
- The control of complex systems is highly dispersed. There is not, for example, a master neuron in the brain.
- Organization within these systems is created by both competition and cooperation with other systems.
- A complex adaptive system has many levels of organization, with agents at any one level serving as the 'building blocks' for agents at a higher level. Cells will form a tissue, a collection of tissues will form an organ, organisms will form an ecosystem.
- Complex adaptive systems typically also have many niches, each one of which can be exploited by an agent adapted to fill that niche.
- There are intercommunicating layers within the hierarchy. Agents exchange information in given levels of the hierarchy, and different levels pass information between themselves as well.
- Correspondingly, the complex system has a number of disparate time and space scales.
- Complex systems are constantly revising and rearranging their building blocks as they gain experience.
- Complex adaptive systems anticipate the future.
- They exhibit coherence under change, via conditional action and anticipation. For this they employ internal models of the world (as in systems theory).
- They are characterized by rich patterns of tight, moderate and loosely coupled linkages. Chains of interdependency branch in complicated patterns among actors. This protects the system against environmental shock by providing multiple paths for action. If one pattern of interdependency in a network is disrupted, the dynamic performed by that subsystem can usually be rerouted to other areas of the network. This makes it difficult to damage or destroy the complex system, for complex interaction leads to amazing resilience.
- Complex systems are robust (or fit). They resist perturbation or invasion by other systems.
- Importantly, all operate in accordance with the Second Law of Thermodynamics, exhibiting entropy and winding down over time unless replenished with energy.

Box 4.3 Features of complex adaptive systems.

Schemata

A key behavior of complex systems is their ability to process information and use of schemas.[42] This is similar to the idea of mental modules of systems theory. Systems sense their environments and collect information about surrounding conditions. They then respond to this information via a set of internal models that guide their actions. In the data stream a system identifies particular regularities and compresses them in concise schemas or internal models (in psychology schemas refer to a pattern used by the mind to grasp an aspect of reality). This schema is used to sift through data in subsequent stages, to describe the environment and make predictions of events. The descriptions can be more or less accurate and the prescriptions can lead to more or less favorable outcomes. All these consequences are then fed back to exert 'selection pressures' on the competition among various schemata. A schema has several functions: a description of an observed system, a prediction of events, or a prescription for behavior of the complex adaptive system itself. Whether complex systems adapt to change depends in part on their capability to process information, to form and select adequate models and to anticipate. Thus variants of the model are subject to selection and progressive adaptation.[43]

'Maladaptive schemata' exist too. In a section that offers direct associations with Boyd's work, Gell-Mann notes that one of the most common reasons for the existence of maladaptive schemata is that they were once adaptive, but under conditions that no longer prevail. The environment has changed at a faster rate than the evolutionary process can accommodate. Moreover, a system's mechanisms for varying and selecting schemata may lag behind.[44] Compare this with Boyd when he asserts in the more recently developed presentation *The Conceptual Spiral* that:

> People using theories or systems evolved from a variety of information will find it increasingly difficult and ultimately impossible to interact with and comprehend phenomena or systems that move increasingly beyond and away from that variety – that is, they will become more and more isolated from that which they are trying to observe or deal with, unless they exploit the new variety to modify their theories/systems or create new theories/systems.[45]

Figure 4.2 shows Gell-Mann's graphic illustration of the way a complex adaptive system works through the functioning of schemata, showing close parallels with Boyd's OODA loop graphic and Boyd's view on the function of doctrine, shared experience, culture and other factors included in his notion of orientation pattern.[46]

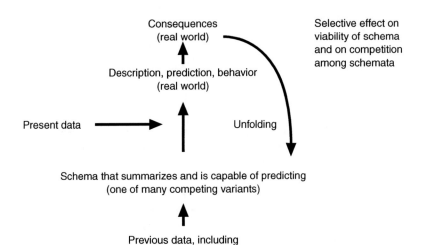

Figure 4.2 Functioning of schemata according to Murray Gell-Mann. From *The Quark and the Jaguar* by Murray Gell-Mann. Copyright 1994 by Murray Gell-Mann. Reprinted by permission of Henry Holt and Company, LLC.

Levels of adaptation

This naturally leads to the key theme of adaptation and evolution. Adaptation takes place on at least four different levels:[47]

1   *Direct adaptation* takes place as a result of the operation of a schema that is dominant at a particular time (as in a thermostat or cybernetic device). None of the behavior requires any change in the prevailing schema.
2   The next level involves *changes in the schema*, competition among various schemata, and the promotion or demotion depending on the action of selection pressures in the real world.[48]
3   The third level of adaptation is the Darwinian *survival of the fittest*. A society may simply cease to exist as a consequence of the failure of its schemata to cope with events.
4   The fourth level is directed evolution, which is caused by selection pressures exerted by individual human beings.

The first three modes of adaptation are characterized by increasing flexibility and decreasing reversibility. Successive modes of adaptation restore as much as possible the flexibility that the organism has lost under environmental stress. The flexibility of an individual will depend on how many of its variables are kept fluctuating within their tolerance limits; the more fluctuations, the greater the stability of the organism. For populations of organisms the criterion corresponding to flexibility is variability. Maximum genetic variation within a population provides the maximum number of possibilities for evolutionary adaptation.[49]

The three levels of adaptation take place, generally speaking, on different time scales. An existing dominant schema can be translated into action right away; within days or months. A revolution in the hierarchy of schemata is generally associated with a longer time scale, although the culminating events may come swiftly. Extinctions of societies usually take place at still longer intervals of time. Obviously, the question whether adaptation is successful at any one level is in large part a function of the measure of the rate of change of the environment in relation to the rate of adaptation an organism is capable of, a theme close to Boyd's heart.

He included this notion of different hierarchies and time-horizons in *Patterns of Conflict*. The pattern of success in war consists of a combination of activities to disrupt the adaptability of the opponent at the tactical, the grand tactical, the strategic and grand strategic level. And although conceptually the activities at the different levels are similar, Boyd recognized that in practice adaptation at each level required a specific type of action and involved a specific time horizon. At the highest level, Boyd formulates the 'national goal' and 'grand strategy' as: 'Improve our fitness, as an organic whole, to shape and cope with an ever-changing environment.'[50] This requires a grand strategy that creates the favorable conditions. At this level this implies, according to Boyd, that

> For success over the long haul [. . .] one needs some unifying vision that can be used to attract the uncommitted as well as pump-up friendly resolve and drive and drain-away or subvert adversary resolve and drive. [. . .] what is needed is a vision rooted in human nature so noble, so attractive that it not only attracts the uncommitted and magnifies the spirit and strength of its adherent, but also undermines the dedication and determination of any competitors or adversaries.[51]

This unifying vision is

> A grand ideal, overarching theme, or noble philosophy that represents a coherent paradigm within which individuals as well as societies can shape and adapt to unfolding circumstances – yet offers a way to expose flaws of competing or adversary systems.[52]

Thus, at the grand strategic level, Boyd addresses the societal level and does not talk of rapid OODA looping but of an attractive and agreeable ideology which fosters internal unity and offers a 'moral high ground' which is conducive to creating alliances. It favors cooperation, or at least does not unnecessarily arouse animosity. It must act as 'a catalyst or beacon around which to evolve those qualities that permit a collective entity or organic whole to improve its stature in the scheme of things'.[53] One level down, he formulates his view of the general 'strategic aim' in purely neo-Darwinian terms as: 'Diminish adversary's capacity while improving our capacity to adapt as an organic whole, so that our adversary cannot cope while we can cope with events/efforts as they unfold.' His advice for strategy is geared more specifically towards the military organization. As at the grand-strategic level, it is not the temporal dimension which is the prime focus, but the set of factors (or in Boyd's words 'connections') that glue the enemy system together at the strategic level. Boyd's view on strategy makes it comparable to 'level-two' adaptation in which the emphasis lies on schemata, for the 'strategy' should:

> Penetrate adversary's moral-mental-physical being to dissolve his moral fiber, disorient his mental images, disrupt his operations, and overload his system, as well as subvert, shatter, seize or otherwise subdue those moral-mental-physical bastions, connections, or activities that he depends upon [. . .][54]

At the 'grand-tactical level' Boyd shifts his attention towards the enemy command system and the connections between units that hold them together so they operate coherently at the operational level. Together with the 'tactical level' it can be compared with direct adaptation, in which time pressure is more prominently a factor than in the former two levels. The pattern for success at the grand-tactical level is to:

> Operate inside adversary's OODA loops [. . .] to create tangles of threatening and/or non-threatening events/efforts as well as repeatedly generate mismatches between those events/efforts adversary observes, or imagines and those he must react to, to survive;

thereby

> Enmesh adversary in an amorphous, menacing, and unpredictable world of uncertainty, doubt, mistrust, confusion, disorder, fear, panic, chaos [. . .];

thereby

> maneuver adversary beyond his moral-mental-physical capacity to adapt or endure so that he can neither divine our intentions nor focus his efforts to cope with the unfolding strategic design [. . .][55]

At the 'tactical level' units should:

> OODA more inconspicuously, more quickly, and with more irregularity as basis to keep or gain initiative as well as shape and shift main effort: to repeatedly and unexpectedly penetrate vulnerabilities and weaknesses exposed by that effort [. . .][56]

Ecosystems and fitness landscapes

Capra noted in 1982 that one of the key insights of research in the 1970s and 1980s had been that the tendency to associate, establish links, live inside one another and cooperate is an essential characteristic of living organisms. Larger networks of organisms form ecosystems, together with various inanimate components linked to the animals, plants, and microorganisms through an intricate web of relations involving the exchange of matter and energy in continual cycles. Like individual organisms, ecosystems are self-organizing and self-regulating systems in which particular populations of organisms undergo periodic fluctuations.

Ecological communities are not likely to reach or even closely approach an ultimate steady state, as each species evolves in the presence of constantly changing congeries of other species. Such changes offer *niches* organisms can fill in. In both economics and ecology, the advent of a new business or a new organism (or of a new type of behavior) will alter the 'fitness landscape' for the other members of the community.

Fitness is a biological concept that describes the relative success of a species in relation to others in its environment and can be seen as a measure of how well an agent is adapted to its niche in the landscape. Competition can be said to occur on a fitness landscape. That landscape is not fixed but changes in response to the effects of the actions of all other actors. Indeed, always exploring, seeking out opportunities, experimenting with novelty, the complex adaptive system tries out increases in complexity and occasionally discovers solutions that open up the possibility of whole new structures, including new kinds of complex adaptive systems. This is emergent order through self-organization.

There are several key elements determining the strength of an ecosystem, which can also be found in Boyd's work, in particular in his arguments concerning command and control. Boydian elements such as variety, harmony, trust, flexibility, the OODA loop, shared experience, organization in semi-autonomous units mirror the descriptors of an ecosystem:

- Interdependence
- Feedback (and cyclical flow of resources)
- Cooperation
- Partnership
- Flexibility
- Diversity

The flexibility of an ecosystem is a consequence of its multiple feedback loops, which tend to bring the system back into balance whenever there is a deviation from the norm due to changing environmental conditions. Disturbances are ever-present because things in the environment change all the time. The net result is continual fluctuation. All the variables we can observe in an ecosystem – population densities, available nutrients, weather patterns and so forth – always fluctuate. The more variables are kept fluctuating, the more dynamic is the system, the greater is its flexibility, and the greater is its ability to adapt to changing conditions. Lack of flexibility manifests itself as stress in the system. This will occur when one or more variables of the system are pushed to their extreme values, which induces increased rigidity throughout the system.

The role of diversity is closely connected with the network's structure. A diverse ecosystem will also be resilient, because it contains many species with overlapping ecological functions that can partially replace one another. A diverse community will be able to survive and reorganize itself because a damaged link in the network can at least partially be compensated for by other links. In other words, the more complex the network is, the more complex its pattern of interconnections, the more resilient it will be. Repeating earlier observations from systems theory, diversity means many different relationships, many different approaches to the same problem.[57]

Perpetual novelty

Indeed, change, novelty and mismatches are what keep the evolutionary process going. If the discovery of uncertainty was the start of the paradigm shift, the discovery of the essence of perpetual novelty may be considered one of the key themes of the Prigoginian era. And instead of chance and random mutations driving evolution, as classical Darwinist theory asserts, it is the capacity to learn, to propagate successful traits and schemata, and to recombine in novel relationships, that leads to the emergence of adaptation and evolution. As Prigogine observes, 'nature is indeed related to the creation of unpredictable novelty',[58] while Holland asserts that complex adaptive systems are characterized by 'perpetual novelty'.[59]

Boyd would make this reveling in novelty, combined with the pervasive presence of uncertainty, key themes. If uncertainty is indeed pervasive, it is imperative for organizations to create the ability to operate comfortably in this condition; in fact, they need to embrace it and turn the capacity to their advantage by introducing uncertainty and novelty into the environment themselves. *Destruction and Creation*, and in particular his last major presentation – *The Conceptual Spiral* – revolve around this very theme. Indeed, the major works Boyd studied early on, such as those of Popper, Polanyi, Kuhn and Piaget are pregnant with this theme. Moreover, the bibliography attached to *Patterns of Conflict* includes many books on the role of uncertainty, surprise and the value of deception.[60] In *The Conceptual Spiral*, Boyd lists nine 'producers' of uncertainty, features that are contained within the theories, systems, processes, etc. that we employ to make sense of the world (Box 4.4).[61]

The last mentioned feature implies that novelty is not only an endemic property of our environment, it is also a fundamental characteristic of social systems and activities. Our own schemata and the interaction among schemata of people

- Uncertainty associated with the unconfinement, undecidability, incompleteness theorems of mathematics and logic.
- Numerical imprecision associated with using the rational and irrational numbers in the calculation and measurement processes.
- Quantum uncertainty associated with Planck's Constant and Heisenberg's Uncertainty Principle.
- Entropy increase associated with the Second Law of Thermodynamics.
- Irregular and erratic behavior associated with far-from-equilibrium open non-linear processes or systems with feedback.
- Incomprehensibility associated with the inability to completely screen, filter, or otherwise consider the spaghetti-like influences from a plethora of ever-changing, erratic, or unknown outside events.
- Mutations associated with environmental pressure, replication errors, or unknown influences in molecular and evolutionary biology.
- Ambiguity associated with natural languages as they are used and interact with one another.
- Novelty generated by the thinking and actions of unique individuals and their many-sided interactions with each other.

Box 4.4 Boyd's list of sources of uncertainty.

produce mismatches. The OODA loop is both the way we make sense of the world as well as the source of further uncertainty: 'Novelty is produced by a mental/physical feedback process of analysis and synthesis that permits us to interact with the world so that we can comprehend, cope with, and shape that world as well as be shaped by it.'[62] Boyd further highlights how novelty is the one feature that social systems need to take into account:

> The presence and production of <u>mismatches</u> are what sustain and nourish the enterprise of science, engineering, and technology, hence keep it alive and ongoing – otherwise there would be no basis for it to continue.[63]

> The practice of science/engineering and the pursuit of technology not only change the physical world we interact with – via new systems, new processes, new etc. – but they also change the mental/physical ways by which we think about and act upon that world.

In this sense

> The practice of science/engineering and the pursuit of technology permit us to continually <u>rematch our mental/physical orientation</u> with that changing world so that we can continue to thrive and grow in it.

Put simply

> The practice of science/engineering and the pursuit of technology affects us personally as individuals, as groups, or as societies by <u>changing our orientation to match</u> with a changing world that we, in fact, help change.[64]

In a lengthy section he explains how this relates to his investigation on winning and losing. In a passage that seems to marry ideas ranging from Polanyi to those of Gell-Mann, Boyd states that

> Novelty is produced continuously, if somewhat erratically or haphazardly. In order to thrive and grow in such a world we must match our thinking and doing, hence our orientation, with that emerging novelty. Yet, any orientation constrained by experiences before that novelty emerges introduces mismatches that confuse or disorient us. However, the analytical/synthetic process permits us to address these mismatches so that we can rematch thereby reorient our thinking and action with that novelty. Over and over this continuing whirl of <u>re-orientation, mismatches, analysis/synthesis</u> enables us to comprehend, cope with, and shape as well as be shaped by <u>novelty</u> that literally flows around and over us.[65]

Novelty enters strategy when Boyd concludes that winning and losing revolves around the capability to deal with uncertainty and to exploit this feature of novelty in the contest with opponents:

> Since survival and growth are directly connected with the uncertain, ever-changing, unpredictable world of winning and losing we will exploit this whirling (conceptual) spiral of orientation, mismatches, analysis/synthesis, reorientation, mismatches, analysis/synthesis.[66]

It seems, then, that in *Conceptual Spiral* of 1992 Boyd comes full circle when we compare this statement with the following of Piaget: 'Dialectic over and over again substitute "spirals" for the linear or "tree" models with which we start, and these famous spirals or non-vicious circles are very much like the genetic circles or interactions characteristic of growth.'[67]

Science obviously influenced the content of his slides and the themes of his thinking. Boyd's work is rooted in a fundamental philosophical debate, and Boyd derived specific insights from this debate on the nature of knowledge and the process of knowing. Both revolve around the pervasive presence of uncertainty. This theme would become the starting point, and the foundation, of his work. The cognitive process, which through various strategies constantly exerts itself to minimize the effects of uncertainty, in both individuals and organizations, would become the second point of gravitation of his work. The third, and closely related, process Boyd was constantly focusing on concerned the dynamics of open non-linear systems, and more precisely, the myriad processes of adaptation at the various levels of a system and its subsystems.

In that respect Boyd may be considered the first 'postmodern strategist', for he did for strategic thinking what others did in other fields of social studies, when they were confronted with these developments in physics and the natural sciences.

The postmodern turn

Boyd developed his ideas while postmodernism arose to prominence in cultural and scientific life, when key figures such as Lyotard, Derrida, Habermas, Foucault, Baudrillard, Bauman and Giddens published widely discussed studies on the 'postmodern condition',[68] in response to the scientific breakthroughs of the previous decades and the social and cultural revolution of the 1960s. Major sources of influence were evolutionary biology and ecology, quantum mechanics and relativity theory, cybernetics and information theory, and chaos and complexity theory.[69] These key figures of postmodernism claimed that the modern mechanistic, reductionist and determinist worldview of Newtonian physics was giving way in the twentieth century to a new mode of scientific thinking based on concepts such as entropy, evolution, organism, indeterminacy, probability, relativity, complementarity, interpretation, multispectrality, chaos, complexity and self-organization. It became a leading school of thought in Europe,[70] permeating virtually all facets of contemporary life in the West.

Postmodernism has gained several meanings[71] and has left few disciplines untouched.[72] It is a 'periodizing' category in which the pre-modern leads via the modern to the late- or postmodern era and the 'information society'.[73] In the social and ethical dimension one can also discern a nihilist or extreme relativist position, that claims that anything goes in terms of truth and values, that there is no progress, and that certainly the modern Western society is not the exponent of progress. It points at a failing of the 'Enlightenment project' and features an absolute relativism towards claims or paradigms for understanding reality.[74] A more moderate view – critical postmodernists[75] – considers the positivistic method, with its claims of objectivity or limited subjectivity, as invalid, opposing that phenomena can constitute themselves as objects of knowledge independently of discursive practices. What counts as a socially meaningful object or event is always the result of an interpretive construction of the world out there, based on a shared system of codes and symbols, of languages, life worlds and social practices. Reality and knowledge about it are subjective and contextual.[76] But not all views are equal, some are more privileged by offering a better, more plausible, more explanatory narrative.

A short look at this development will illustrate the extent of the validity of Boyd's synthesis and application of scientific developments, as well as improve our understanding of Boyd's ideas; for his concern with, and take on, epistemology, and the centrality in Boyd's work of the factor of uncertainty, his insistence on exploiting a multitude of ideas and perspectives for understanding and shaping action, and his deconstructive method of pulling perspectives apart and look for new possible connections and meaning, is shared with postmodern notions such as deconstructionism and structuration theory. A description of three dominant strands of thought of postmodernism will paint this part of the canvas of Boyd's *Zeitgeist*.

Lyotard and Boyd

As in Boyd's work, knowledge production is at the heart of what many consider the core text of postmodernism: Lyotard's book *The Postmodern Condition, a Report on Knowledge*, published in French in 1979 and in English in 1984. Influenced in part by Heisenberg and Gödel,[77] Lyotard's aim is to study the condition or status of knowledge about society in the postmodern age.[78] Like Boyd's opening essay, Lyotard is concerned with the basic conceptual frameworks that we adopt in order to understand modern life. He argues that the Enlightenment model of science does not apply to current social life, because the main feature of the Enlightenment approach to knowledge is its concern to be scientifically legitimate, which in this sense implies objective and impartial knowledge of the world. He introduces the term 'narrative' to explain that knowledge is in fact the outcome of a multiplicity of discourses, of narratives that are locally determined (*vide* Geertz), not legitimated externally. Different institutions and different contexts produce different narratives, which are not reducible to each other. He argues for a narrative understanding of knowledge, portraying it as a plurality of smaller stories that function well within the particular contexts where they apply.

Lyotard asserts that the Enlightenment picture of pure knowledge itself is just such a narrative and even a myth, because it derives its legitimacy by reference to a higher level storyline, which he terms 'meta-narratives'. Such meta-narratives contain hidden value statements and particular worldviews. And if the objective grandeur of science actually always turns out to rest upon some sort of meta-narrative or other – none of which can be objectively proven or refuted, but each acting as the philosophical rationalization of human ideologies – then the very claim of objectivity and value-neutrality is spurious, deceitful and self-canceling. Subsequently, no meta-narrative is inherently privileged over any other, indeed, we need to be very skeptical about the ultimate truth-claims of all meta-narratives.[79]

This does not indicate that every individual can stake a claim for truth, nor that knowledge is an illusion. Knowledge and meaning are constituted through the networked nature of individuals: a person is always located at 'nodal point' of specific communication circuits. The self is understood in terms of a 'fabric of relations', a node in a network. There is 'local determinism'. There are 'interpretative communities'. Institutions such as universities, prisons, but obviously also armed forces, form such interpretative communities. Such communities are made up of both producers and consumers of particular kinds of knowledge, of texts. Individuals and groups are held to control mutually within these domains what they consider to be valid knowledge.[80]

Through relationships different local narratives interact, and produce knowledge. And within specific audiences, each having its own criterion of accreditation, the reality of knowledge is a huge array of 'moves' within pragmatic 'discourses' or 'language games'.[81] Cilliers explains Lyotard's view on the functioning of the network in producing meaning in words that could be taken directly out of Boyd's briefing *The Conceptual Spiral:*

No discourse is fixed or stabilized by itself. Different discourses – clusters in a network – may grow, shrink, break up, coalesce, absorb others or be absorbed. It is a self-organizing process in which meaning is generated through a dynamic process, and not through the passive reflection of an autonomous agent that can make 'anything go'. Instead of being self-sufficient and isolated, discourses are in constant interaction, battling with each other for territory.

This dynamic of discourse also leads Lyotard, like Polanyi, to observe that scientific progress is made through the meeting of dissension and destabilizing forces with dominant views. Whereas paradigms aim to fix knowledge in a permanent grid, Lyotard's view is that we discard the idea of consensus. To proliferate knowledge, we have to proliferate discourses without trying to fix them into a permanent grid.[82] Thus, Boyd's discussion on Gödel and Heisenberg could as easily have included Lyotard.

Structuration Theory

Another idea central to social theory from the late 1970s onwards is the concept of reflexivity of knowledge.[83] It forms a core element of Structuration Theory, a leading theory concerning social change developed by sociologist Anthony Giddens.[84] Social change can be explained by focusing either on contextual, structural factors or on the actions of agents. Giddens explains instead that both need to be examined and that both are mutually constituted. Agents act according to the structural factors that constrain them and they form structures by abiding by them, but also by changing them. The individual both initiates change and participates in it. Structures – rules, ideas, institution and resources recursively implicated in social reproduction – can be changed by action.[85] The structure–agency debate is relevant for strategy, for

> structures do not determine outcomes, but define the potential range of alternative strategies. Agents have the opportunity of choosing from several strategies within the structure. Strategic action is the dialectical interplay of intentional and knowledgeable, yet structurally-embedded actors and the pre-constituted contexts they inhabit. Eventually, structure may also be transformed by agency over time.[86]

From a military perspective this sounds like the doctrine development, or force structuring processes in which previous experience, established practices and organizational traditions and structures not only shape a military response but also compete with new conceptual insights, more recent experiences, and opportunities for improving organizational fitness.

At the heart of this theory is the individual as a conscious strategic actor, making decisions based on experience and knowledge and amid uncertainty. Indeed, in Giddens' conception of postmodernity,[87] uncertainty is dominant, as no pre-existing foundations of epistemology have been shown to be reliable. We are living in a world of multiple authorities.[88] The twentieth century proved that all claims to knowledge are corrigible (including meta-statements made about them) and this has become the existential condition in modern societies. Although many forms of scientific knowledge are relatively secure, all must be in principle regarded as open to question and at every juncture a puzzling diversity of rival theoretical and practical claims are to be found in the 'moving' areas of knowledge.[89]

Furthermore, knowledge is a factor for change. Modern man's assumption that an increase in knowledge concerning the social and natural world would lead to greater certainty about the conditions under which we lead our lives, and would thereby subject to human dominance what was once the domain of other influences have proven false. The connections between the development of human knowledge and human self-understanding have proved more complex.[90] Giddens labels this connection 'the reflexive appropriation of knowledge'. Mirroring Boyd's views on military innovation, Giddens states that:

> The reflexive nature of modern social life consists in the fact that social practices are constantly examined and reformed in the light of incoming information about those very practices, thus constitutively altering their character'.[91]

> The production of systematic knowledge about social life becomes integral to system reproduction ... knowledge applied to the conditions of system reproduction intrinsically alters the circumstances to which it originally referred.[92]

If an actor notices that his knowledge does not produce desired result in action, he will seek to improve the accuracy of his knowledge. At the same time the environment is constituted because of knowledge about it and that knowledge allows us to control it at the same time, and alter it. Knowing about the economic behavior of people and nations allows us not only to observe and understand, but also to design economic policy, thereby altering the economic behavior and perhaps even altering the rules for economic behavior, and thereby invalidating previous knowledge about economic behavior. Knowledge is thus reflexive. Knowledge and observation lead simultaneously to understanding and to uncertainty. This is what Giddens the 'double hermeneutic' of social life.[93] The double hermeneutics problematizes exactly the relationship between self-interpretations and second order interpretations. For not only do observers rely on first-hand interpretations, their interpretations, in turn, can have a feedback on the former.[94]

For Giddens, the growing awareness of inherent uncertainty of social life and the conscious and deliberate embedding of reflexivity of knowledge in institutions marks the nature of the postmodern condition. Boyd's views on knowledge, his views on the function of orientation patterns, and the evolutionary nature of the development of strategic theory and military doctrine, are entirely consistent with Giddens' conceptualization of postmodernity.

Deconstructionism

In the same period that Boyd developed *A Discourse* out of his survey of a wide variety of sources, pulling ideas apart and forming new syntheses, Derrida became famous for his idea of deconstructionism. Originating from text analysis, it holds that texts have no exact and final meaning and can be read in a number of ways instead. Deconstructionism acknowledges that the observer of social events and artifacts cannot possibly be objective, because he himself is entangled in a history, with particular prejudices, language with specific meanings, rituals and symbols etc., that color his perception. Deconstruction is a journey fuelled by historical evidence, implicit and explicit assumptions, the analyst's worldview, etc., that yields different interpretations of particular texts, in other words, an activity heavily influenced by what Boyd calls orientation. Though none of the different interpretations can possibly equate to the author's understanding, a richer appreciation of the text is developed.[95]

Thus Lyotard, Giddens and the deconstructionists offer the view that reality – facts, actors and behaviour – is in large part a social construction. Through dialogue, exploration, criticism and using various perspectives a picture can be painted that gives us enough confidence to momentarily base our decisions on, a view that closely correspond with the ideas Boyd put in his graphic of the OODA loop.

It is tempting to compare the deconstructive method with the way Boyd constructs his argument; the way he makes sudden connections between seemingly disconnected insights, the way he frequently tears texts apart only to recombine them in a slightly different order than before, and his deliberate refusal to 'finish' a briefing. Indeed, it goes to the heart of Boyd's argument that the way to survive and prosper is

> by an instinctive see-saw of analysis and synthesis across a variety of domains, or across competing/independent channels of information, in order to spontaneously generate new mental images or impressions that match-up with an unfolding world of uncertainty and change.[96]

It seems that he attempts to solve the problems posed by the characteristics of the socially constructed world listed in Box 4.5.[97]

Combined, these schools thus agree on a multi-theoretical perspectivism. And this eclecticism in theoretical approaches and ideas itself constitutes a postmodern sensibility: 'The postmodern world is now understood to be composed of interpenetrating and multiple realities [...] these realities discount the utility of mono-theoretical accounts. Instead, it suggests the need for multiple theoretical analysis', Jarvis notes.[98]

In the past two decades various authors have applied postmodern or critical theory in studying war and security.[99] Constructivists focus on the normative

1   We know the world only as we perceive it;

2   Our perceptions are based on learned interpretations;

3   This learning is social: we learn from and among persons in social interactions.

4   The main vehicles which convey meaning are:

    a   symbols, including language

    b   cultural myths

    c   the structure and practice of our institutions

    d   our rules for congruent action.

5   These vehicles of meaning together construct:

    a   our world view: how the world works, causality in it, what is valuable

    b   our sense of ourselves, our identity and purpose

    c   our ideologies.

6   Our selves, our societies and institutions change continually through interaction.

Box 4.5 A deconstructionist's view on reality and cognition.

character of ideas, language, identities, images, belief systems and institutions as sources of change, behavior and power.[100] Meanwhile the very idea of security is debated, involving a shift in focus from abstract individualism and contractual sovereignty to a stress on culture, civilization and identity; the role of ideas, norms and values in the constitution of that which is to be secured; and the historical context within which this process takes place. Epistemologically, this involves moving away from the objectivist, rationalist approach to a more interpretive mode of analysis'.[101] A state is not only an actor, but also a social construct that has been given meaning and role; it is socially constituted and presumes a state culture.[102]

These schools point towards the impact of practice, institutional traditions, repertoires of responses, language, perceptions of behavior of actors in the international arena in matters of national and international security.[103] Ideas are not merely rules, or 'road maps for action', but rather ideas operate 'all the way down' to actually shape actors and action in world politics.[104] When ideas are norms, they not only constrain actors, but also constitute actors and enable action.[105] Others point at strategic and organizational culture to explain the differences in doctrines, military power or method of control of military forces.[106]

Boyd's ideas thus mirror contemporary notions, arguments and concepts in postmodern social science, including security studies, suggesting that in incorporating these ideas, Boyd was doing for the military realm what others were doing for philosophy, sociology and the arts at the end of the 1970s and in the early 1980s.

Chaos everywhere

Early expectations

Boyd's application of scientific developments in strategic thought was warranted also because of another development. It was not long after non-linear dynamics gained legitimacy in the late 1970s and early 1980s that sometimes cautious, sometimes bold forays were made into applications of chaos theory to human history. Prigogine, for instance, cautiously suggested that:

> We know now that societies are immensely complex systems involving a potentially enormous number of bifurcations exemplified by the variety of cultures that have evolved in the relatively short span of human history. We know that such systems are highly sensitive to fluctuations.[107]

In particular, after the publication of James Gleick's book *Chaos: Making a New Science*, did the field of chaoplexity emerge as a full-blown pop-culture phenomenon.[108] Filled with illustrations of chaotic behavior in natural and human life, it states that:

> Now that science is looking, chaos seems to be everywhere [. . .] That realization has begun to change the way business executives make decision about insurance, the way astronomers look at the solar system, the way political theorists talk about the stresses leading to armed conflict.

Mitchell Waldrop would echo that view in his 1992 bestseller on complexity theory. The number of studies in various fields suggesting common concepts underlying the dynamics of the phenomena under investigation since the early 1980s had become overwhelming in the early 1990s. We live in a highly non-linear world, one social scientist therefore concluded.[109] In economics, for instance, it was noted that, instead of equilibrium-seeking, markets are distinctly non-linear and always in disequilibrium.[110] Instability was also noted in the financial system: sudden fluctuations in one region can ripple through the entire tightly connected global financial system. The disciplines of history and international relations, the rise of societies and social structures of ever-growing complexity too have been exposed to the new paradigm.[111] The New Sciences have also been widely applied to organizational behavior, both from an intra-organizational perspective (the dynamics within an organization) as well as from the inter-organizational perspective (competition, market dynamics, war).

Non-linearity and organizational life

Concerning the intra-organizational perspective, Perrow introduced the idea that organizations can be categorized as either simple or complex systems, and they consist of processes that are either linear or non-linear. Linear interactions are those in expected and familiar production or maintenance sequence, and those that are quite visible even if unplanned, whereas non-linear interactions are those of unfamiliar sequences, or unplanned and unexpected sequence, and either not visible or not immediately comprehensible.

Complex as well as simple systems can have *tight* and/or *loose coupling* among subsystems and subprocesses. In a loosely coupled system there is slack or a buffer. Subsequently, what happens in the one item may not affect the other, until the buffer has been exceeded. Unexpected demands, or lack of resources can be handled. In tightly coupled systems, on the other hand, there is no slack or buffer between two items. Quantities must be precise; resources cannot be substituted for one another. Additionally, in tightly coupled systems, not only are the specific sequences invariant, but the overall design of the process and the number of specialized personnel and other essential, non-substitutionable production resources allow only one way to reach the production goal.[112]

Generally, tightly coupled systems will respond more quickly to perturbations. However, due to the rapid onset of non-foreseeable non-linear effects they may also react more violently and in more directions, with several layered effects, than loosely coupled systems.[113] Failure may not only be rapid, it may also manifest itself in various dimensions, at various moments and in various parts of the system and probably in totally unexpected places. The chance of incidents turning into accidents and systemwide catastrophe is larger in complex tightly coupled systems due to these factors, and the demands made on failure prevention and recovery measures are very high. In contrast, loosely coupled systems can incorporate shocks and failures and pressures for change without destabilization. Loosely coupled systems tend to have ambiguous or perhaps flexible performance. Processes are not necessarily optimized for efficiency. It is possible to allow some parts latitude. In loosely coupled systems there is generally more time for recovery.[114]

The required type of control is a function of the level of complexity of a system, the level of coupling of subsystems and processes and of the risks involved. When a system is linear and tightly coupled, centralization is required, for failures will result in predictable and visible effects, and responses can be pre-programmed, rehearsed by all concerned, and subsequently initiated and controlled from the central authority. Top-level detailed control and monitoring, and lower-level meticulous obedience, are required because response times need to be minimal and the response precise. Subsequently there is hardly room for lower-level deviation/adjustment. Linear and loosely coupled systems can operate on either control set-up. Centralization is possible because of linearity, decentralization is feasible because of the loose coupling.

A special problem is the class of complex and tightly coupled systems, which also pose the most risk for incidents getting out of hand. The demands on a control system are inconsistent and neither set-up is optimal. Complexity would suggest decentralization, but tight coupling suggests centralization to ensure rapid recovery from failure before tightly coupled processes push the system over the brink. Suggestions that lower levels can be allowed latitude by setting decision premises by higher levels are invalid because, due to the unforeseeable nature of failures throughout the system, it is impossible to set correct decision premises. In fact, those premises, according to Perrow, may actually be counter-productive.[115] So, decision-making elites will need to balance both requirements.

Concerning loosely coupled complex systems, Perrow argues that complexity requires that those at the point of disturbance are free to interpret the situation and take corrective measures, because that is where the incident is first noted. They should be allowed to diagnose the situation and take steps to contain the problem before the effects spread to other parts of the system. Because the inter-actions are loosely tight, there is time to develop a coherent picture and appro-priate responses. Together with non-directive modes of synchronization and coordination, such as informal processes, shared culture, shared professional ethos, stable interaction patterns, slack and buffers, decentralization will allow a sufficient degree of control and sufficient failure recovery potential. These ele-ments appear in Boyd's work on command and control.

Various authors argue that models of organization that are based on living systems are naturally organic and adaptive.[116] For organizations to survive, they need to co-evolve with their environment while maintaining internal stability. This requires variety, creativity and learning communities. An organization must embody enough diversity to provoke learning but not enough to overwhelm the legitimate system and cause anarchy. These studies maintain that, like ecosys-tems, organizations thrive when equipped with variety. Practically speaking, organizations (should) possess a range of coupling patterns, from tight to loose. Loosely coupled structures allow an organization to adjust to environmental drift, and when environmental shocks are particularly severe, loose structures react sluggishly, thus buying time to recover. Moderately and tightly coupled structures prevent an organization from over-responding to environmental per-turbation. Coupling patterns, then, allow organizations to maintain relative stability in most environments and protect the system even against severe shocks.[117]

'Robust' systems are characterized by 'rich patterns of tight, moderate and loosely coupled linkages; chains of interdependency branch in complicated pat-terns across nearly every actor in a broad network of interaction. Such complex patterns of interaction protect the organization against environmental shock by providing multiple paths for action. If one pattern of interdependency in a network is disrupted, the dynamic performed by that subsystem can usually be rerouted to other areas of the network. Such robustness makes it difficult to damage or destroy the complex system, for complex interaction lends it amazing resilience'.[118]

Structurally, the key theme is self-organization.[119] The optimal organizational form for adaptation in turbulent environments is seen as the 'cellular' form oper-ating in a network, an idea included in Boyd's views on command and control. Small teams operating relatively autonomously pursue entrepreneurial opportun-ities and share know-how among each other.[120] Meanwhile, the shared values of corporate culture in belief systems provide tight but internal, and perhaps even 'tacit', control as a form of protocol. At the same time, loose control comes from interaction between supervisor and employees that encourages information-sharing, trust and learning. The key to loose control is management's trust in employees to act according to shared values, therefore setting them free to search for opportunities, learn, and apply accumulating knowledge to innovative efforts.[121] Successful leaders of complex organizations allow experimentation, mistakes, contradictions, uncertainty and paradox, so the organization can evolve. Managing an organization as a complex system means letting go of control and a focus instead on the power of the interconnected world of relationships and the feedback loops.

Strategy and planning do not escape from the application of insights from complexity theory. Due to quantum mechanical uncertainty, and sensitivity to initial conditions, it is frequently impossible to find a best strategy. Instead, robustness doesn't consist so much in having a particular pattern of response as in having an enormous set of possible responses.[122] Box 4.6 shows the array of possible implications of complexity theory for strategic management of commercial organizations by contrasting the holistic approach required for managing complex organizations to the mechanistic view of earlier management theorists such as Taylor.

Several of these ideas surface in Boyd's vision on command and control, which hinges on trust, implicit communication, open flow of information, and a shared view on the organizational purpose. Boyd argues for a relaxed approach on command, allowing units and commanders sufficient latitude to respond to and shape their rapidly changing environment. He advocates lateral relations among subordinate units, which will encourage self-organization. Boyd allows uncertainty to exist and he wants commanders not to impose a certain course of action but to set the boundaries of behavior, the overall direction, and to develop relevant organizational orientation patterns (schemata).

The non-linearity of war

The leap from chaoplexity theory to the study of war and the formulation of military strategy has also been made.[123] In a wide-ranging study that focuses on policy making, and includes many references to military strategy, Robert Jervis noted that within non-linear complex systems:[124]

- It is impossible to do merely one thing;
- Results cannot be predicted from the separate actions;
- Strategies depend on the strategies of others;
- Behavior changes the environment.

Echoing Perrow, he notes that connections, interactions and interdependencies are the all-important and problematic features of complex systems. In a system the chains of consequences extend over time and many areas. The effects of action are always multiple. Some call it that actions have side effects, but

From	To
Linear	Non-linear
Static, cause-effect view of individual factors	Dynamic, constantly changing field of interactions
Microscopic, local	Wide angle, global
Separateness	Relatedness
Marketplace	Environment
Reductionist	Non-reductionist
Component thinking	Seeing and thinking in wholes
Time cards, task analysis	Complex Adaptive Systems
Problem solving	Butterfly Effect, system feedback
Brainstorming	Self-organization, adaptation
Polarization	Environmental scanning plus mapping
Structure creates process	Underlying processes and interactions of a system's variables create self-organizing patterns, shapes and structures
Pays attention to policies and procedures that are usually fixed and inflexible	Pays attention to initial conditions, perking information, emerging events, and strange attractors
Standing committees	Ad hoc working groups, networks
Politics	Learning
Planning as discrete event	Planning as continuous process
Planning by elite specialist group	Planning requires whole system input
Implementation of plan	Implementation flexible and constantly evolving in response to emerging conditions
Forecasting through data analysis	Foresight through synthesis
Quantitative	Qualitative
Controlling, stabilizing or managing change	Responding to and influencing change as it emerges
Dinosaur behavior	Entrepreneurial behavior
Change as threat	Change as opportunity
Leads to stagnation and extinction	Leads to renewal and growth

Source: adapted from T. Irene Sanders, *Strategic Thinking and the New Sciences, Planning in the Midst of Chaos, Complexity and Change* (New York, 1998), pp. 146–50.

Box 4.6 The new planning paradigm as defined by the new sciences.

besides being mostly undesired there is nothing that distinguishes one effect from another. Basically it is impossible to do merely one thing.[125] When the interconnections are dense, it may be difficult to trace the impact of any change even after the fact, let alone predict it ahead of time, making the system complex and hard to control.[126]

Interconnections can defeat purposive behavior. Not only can actions call up counteractions, but multiple parties and stages permit many paths to unanticipated consequences.[127] And because most systems either have been designed to cope with adversity or have evolved in the face of it, breakage or overload at one point rarely destroys them. Systems have ways to compensate, they are flexible and may have redundancy built in. So actions against interconnected systems may not lead to direct results, but they will produce disturbances at other points.[128] Jervis concludes his book with three suggestions for strategies that may overcome or take into account the problems we have discussed:

- Constraining the opponent's options;
- Understanding the non-linearity of the environment;
- Aim for indirect effects and apply multiple strategies.

First, people can *constrain* other actors and reduce if not eliminate the extent to which their environment is highly systemic and characterized by unintended consequences. Constraints can be induced by foreclosing options and by severing interconnections. It limits the decision space of an opponent.[129] It reduces the number of alternatives one needs to take into account in devising counterstrategies. It makes the system more predictable.

Second, *understanding* of the fact that one is operating within and against a system, both within an environment, may enable one to compensate for the result that would otherwise occur.[130] If one knows that something might happen one can anticipate it, prepare for it, thereby reducing the chance of it occurring if only by making the other believe that that particular option has been covered.

A third strategy is *aiming for indirect effects and applying multiple policies*, both in the expectation that the cumulative effect will lead to the other having problems to adapt.[131] If one measure fails, another one may succeed, or the interaction of them may be too much to cope with. A form of this is manipulating the environment in which the systems operate, for example widening or narrowing the number of allies. A final suggestion Jervis makes is to leave yourself some slack, some flexibility and room to respond if their anticipations are incorrect.[132]

Besides the work by Barry Watts on non-linearity and strategy that appeared in the 1980s, Boyd's list of personal papers includes three other papers on war and chaoplexity that appeared in the early 1990s. In 1992 Steven Mann published a paper on chaos theory and strategy listing four factors of the environment of a strategic entity which shape the criticality of a system of which it is part: (1) initial shape of the system, (2) underlying structure of the system, (3) cohesion among the actors, (4) conflict energy of the individual actors. These factors, he states, should be examined before we can begin with creating strategies.[133]

The second article is a study by Alan Beyerchen, titled *Clausewitz, Non-linearity, and the Unpredictability of War*. It emphasizes the relevance of the new sciences for the study of war, arguing that core themes of chaoplexity have implicitly always been incorporated in the cornerstone of Western military thought: Clausewitz' *On War*.[134] Beyerchen asserts that Clausewitz understood that war is inherently a non-linear phenomenon, and perceived the nature of war as an energy-consuming phenomenon involving competing and interactive factors. He regarded war as a system driven by psychological forces and characterized by positive feedback, leading 'in theory' to limitless extremes of mutual exertion by the adversaries and efforts to get the better of one another. But he contends that an actual war never occurs without a context; that it always takes time to conduct, in a series of interactive steps; and that its results are never absolutely final – all of which imposes restrictions on the analytically simple 'pure theory' of war. Any specific war is subject to historical contingencies. Wars, therefore, are not only characterized by feedback (a process distinctly involving non-linearities), but inseparable from their contexts.

Clausewitz's grasp of the non-linear character of war is also manifest in his claim that war is 'a remarkable trinity' composed of (a) the blind, natural force of violence, hatred, and enmity among the masses of people; (b) chance and probability, faced or generated by the commander and his army; and (c) war's rational subordination to the policy of the government. Thus the strategist's task is to develop a theory that maintains a balance between these three tendencies, 'like an object suspended between three magnets'. This metaphor confronts us with the chaos inherent in a non-linear system sensitive to initial conditions, for the probability is vanishingly small that the pattern formed by the track of a pendulum is the same each time it is released over three equidistant and equally powerful magnets. Contrary to Newtonian assumptions in the pure theory of war, in the real world it is not possible to measure the relevant initial conditions accurately enough to replicate them in order to get the same pattern a second time, because all physical measurements are approximations limited by the instrument and standard of measurement. Nor is it possible to isolate the system from all possible influences around it, and that environment will have changed since the measurements were taken. Anticipation of the overall kind of pattern is possible, but quantitative predictability of the actual trajectory is lost.

Consideration of the political environment leads Clausewitz to generate his famous second definition of war as 'merely the continuation of policy by other means', claiming that war is never autonomous, for it is always an instrument of policy. Yet the relationship is not static, nor does it imply the instrument is unchanging, nor that the political goal or policy itself is immune to feedback effects. The ends–means relationship clearly does not work in a linear fashion.

Clausewitz's emphasis on unpredictability is another key manifestation of the role that non-linearity plays in his work. Unpredictability is caused by interaction, friction and chance. A military action produces not a single reaction, but dynamic interactions and anticipations that pose a fundamental problem for any theory. Such patterns can be theorized only in qualitative and general terms, not in the specific detail needed for prediction. Moreover, friction as used by Clausewitz entails two different but related notions that demonstrate the depth of his powers of observation and intuition (and both surface in Boyd's work). One is the physical sense of resistance embodied in the word itself, which in Clausewitz's time was being related to heat in ways that would lead ultimately to the Second Law of Thermodynamics and the concept of entropy. Friction is a nonlinear feedback effect that leads to the heat dissipation of energy in a system and an increase of entropy. Military friction is counteracted by training, discipline, inspections, regulations, orders and, not the least, the 'iron will' of the commander. New energy and effort are sucked into the open system, yet things still never go as planned; dissipation is endemic due to the interactive nature of the parts of the system.

The second meaning of 'friction' is the information-theoretical idea of 'noise'. Plans and commands are signals that inevitably get garbled amid noise in the process of communicating them down and through the ranks, even in peacetime, and increasingly so, due to the effects of physical exertion and danger in combat. From this perspective, his famous metaphor of the 'fog' of war is not so much about a dearth of information as about how distortion and overload of information produce uncertainty as to the actual state of affairs. Training, regulations, procedures and so on are redundancies that enhance the probability of signal recognition through the noise. Friction conveys Clausewitz's sense of how unnoticeably small causes can become amplified in war until they produce macro-effects, and that one can never anticipate those effects.

Chance is the final one of the trinity. Comparing war to a game of cards, Clausewitz not only suggests the inability to calculate probabilities, but also hints at the limits of knowledge of human psychology in 'reading' the other players, sensing when to take risks, and so on. The precise knowledge needed to anticipate the effects of interaction is thus unattainable. Another type of chance is a result of our inability to see the universe as an interconnected whole. The drive to comprehend the world through analysis, the effort to partition off pieces of the universe to make them amenable to study, opens the possibility of being blindsided by the very artificiality of the partitioning practice. This form of chance is a particularly acute problem when our intuition is guided by linear concepts.

The third paper included in Boyd's list is the study of Pat Pentland, *Center of Gravity Analysis and Chaos Theory*.[135] His main argument is that, considering the insights provided by the paradigm shift, the key to the analysis of enemy centers of gravity is to incorporate the real and dynamic complexities of the natural world explained by chaos theory. He disaggregates an adversary's system in elements of power (Box 4.7).[136] Each element exists in three dimensions: a source, a linkage and a manifestation. The linkage assists in transforming the source into a force, and it provides connectivity within and between the elements of power. Each element of power is a center of gravity as well as a strange attractor. Power is determined by the mass of the source, the intensity of the force, interconnectivity within the system, and the rate of exchange flow within the linkages.[137]

Source	Linkage	Force
Armed forces	Command and Control, Logistics, Training	Military
Government bureaucracy	Leadership and Communication	Political and Diplomatic
Industry and Natural resources	Transportation and Technology	Economic
Society and Culture	Family, Education, Socialization	Social-Cultural
Value system	Religion and Philosophy, Indoctrination	Ideological

Box 4.7 Pentland's set of potential centers of gravity.

Chaos theory comes into play in this construct as it describes what can happen when additional external force is introduced into open systems, or what happens when the linkages of power are severed.[138] He constructs an analytical approach for selecting centers of gravity as focus for military planning based upon the description of the dynamics of non-linear systems listed in Box 4.8.[139]

Based on the model of the adversary and on the dynamics of chaotic systems, Pentland asserts that crisis points can be precipitated by:

- closing a system off from its environment and propelling it into equilibrium;
- eliminating feedback within the system;
- driving any of the dimensional dynamics to singularity by overloading or destroying it;
- applying quantum amounts of broad external energy to the entire system.

Only if massive force disparities exist is the latter option available. A chaotic system tends to be very resilient, able to maintain its structure and even organize into higher levels of organization as long as energy can be drawn from their environment. This also applies to disturbances to the system. If targeted, an element of power adjusts from within to compensate, and draws upon resources from the other elements of power through interconnected linkage mechanisms. In the economic sphere, for instance, an opponent can opt for economic slack, substitution, reallocation, reengineering, reconstitution, stockpiling, rationing, importing and dispersing. And while a society may be defeated militarily, deep cultural and political powers are almost immune to military force, short of pro- longed occupation. Alternatively, different sorts of military power may be sought after, for instance by responding to a conventional attack with a long, low-intensity, irregular campaign. This feature forces one to acknowledge that war is a process of appraisal, innovation and adaptation. The opponent's society

- Chaos theory predictions are general in nature, and describe system interactions rather than specific end states;
- Initial conditions and the dynamic factors that govern system dynamics can seldom be absolutely known or defined;
- It is possible to anticipate certain processes and functions;
- Long-term prediction is, however, impossible, you cannot predict specifically what will happen next after an event or when an event will occur;
- They are often self-repeating, exhibiting scaled structures;
- Minute differences over time can produce surprisingly diverse results;
- Patterns within a dynamic system will form around functions ('strange attractors'); these patterns will resemble each other by exhibiting similar properties, but will never exactly repeat themselves;
- Systems open to their environment will self-organize into similar patterns in accordance with their fundamental structures;
- Non-linearity can stabilize systems as well as destabilize them;
- Open systems can be driven to crisis points where they will either bifurcate and self-organize again, or go into a period of stochastic chaos (exhibiting erratic randomness).

Box 4.8 Pentland's description of non-linear systems dynamics.

will constantly appraise, innovate, and adopt new combinations of power to achieve different results.[140]

This overview, although far from exhaustive, offers a representative description of studies in which authors of varying backgrounds have attempted to apply insights of chaos and complexity theory to the social realm, in the belief that these developments were indeed relevant for understanding social phenomena and could improve upon the reductionist mode of analysis.[141] It suggests that Boyd's application of insights from dynamic processes in chemical and biological systems to the social arena was not only very fruitful, offering him important insights, but was also warranted.

A Discourse and the scientific *Zeitgeist*

Science, strategic theory and thinking strategically

Boyd's work is thus clearly a product of his *Zeitgeist* and the survey of the scientific *Zeitgeist* thus far has not only offered a window into the literature Boyd studied, it has also introduced ideas, themes and insights that Boyd thought relevant for military strategy and strategic thinking. The study of science was essential to the development of his arguments. As Hammond states 'his study of chemistry, physics, and biology, his investigations about how the brain works, the nature of memory, how one learns, thinks, and questions, were central to his worldview'.[142] Indeed, in various ways science plays a more distinct role as formative factor in Boyd's work than in that of other strategic theorists.

First, Boyd's contribution to strategic theory lies in part in his use of the insights of the new sciences. Boyd deliberately made science an essential element in his work. It starts with an essay which is firmly grounded in the epistemological debates of the 1960s. The influence of science increased over the years. Even *Patterns of Conflict*, which is at heart a survey of military history and for which he studied works on military history and strategy, the list of sources he consulted includes several books from other scientific disciplines. To wit, a 1981 version of *Patterns of Conflict* lists Dawkins, E.O. Wilson and Gregory Bateson as the few notable studies not directly related to military history and strategy, while in the final 1986 edition the number of non-military works in the bibliography grew to thirty. Not surprisingly Burton describes *Patterns of Conflict* as the product of Boyd's analysis of historical patterns of conflict and his synthesis of scientific theories for successful operations.[143] In briefings developed after *Patterns of Conflict* the number of references to scientific insights, the number of scientific works included in the bibliography, and use of scientific illustrations increases significantly, while the number of references to, and illustrations from military history decreases markedly. The briefing 'Strategic Game of ? & ?' is almost devoid of references to military history. In *The Conceptual Spiral* there is no military history at all; science and engineering dominate the slides, showing how both evolve and shape our lives.

On a somewhat different level science played a different role too. The effort itself of reading, studying, analyzing, taking ideas apart, making connections by analogy with other books and articles he had analyzed, and creating a new synthesis would become as much an integral part of his ideas on strategy as the content. It represents Boyd's didactic approach. Boyd finds fault with the separation of inductive and deductive approaches. One needs both and must mix and match analysis and synthesis. It is not a matter of choosing between cumulative inductive processes; rather, their combination enriches the cumulative inductive and deductive achievements and provides what Boyd refers to as many-sided, implicit cross-references.

His research on cognition, on learning, on creativity inspired his idea that making strategy, devising military plans, *works like* these mental processes. Strategic theory development is like the scientific enterprise, which is like the way organisms develop, modify or discard schemata. And as the literature he read manifested a thorough interdisciplinary approach, strategic theory, like cognitive sciences, systems theory, complexity and chaos theory, should incorporate and follow from a thoroughly interdisciplinary approach. Boyd specifically included a list of 'disciplines or activities to be examined' when going to the heart of strategy. This list mentions mathematical logic, physics, thermodynamics, biology, psychology, anthropology and conflict studies.[144] The point of this is that innovation in ideas came not from only thinking inductively. The real advances are the breakouts of creative thinking beyond the limits of the then known. He therefore actively and purposefully oriented himself in a variety of disciplines in order to acquire new insights, a better understanding of the complex phenomenon of war and strategic behavior. Contrary to Jomini, for instance, and later J.F.C. Fuller, who both aimed to formulate a theory that could hold up to the way physics developed theory, in order to gain an aura of universality (and a good measure of scientific acceptability), Boyd deliberately did not favor one scientific model or discipline over the other, for each discipline could provide insights into the behavior of human organizations in violent conflict, and metaphors for seeing new things in familiar objects. Hammond describes Boyd's Way as 'a sort of Western Zen':

> It is a state of mind, a learning of the oneness of things, an appreciation for fundamental insights known in Eastern philosophy and religion as simply the Way [or Tao]. For Boyd, the Way is not an end but a process, a journey [. . .] The connections, the insights that flow from examining the world in different ways, from different perspectives, from routinely examining the opposite proposition, were what were important. The key is mental agility.[145]

His multi-disciplinary approach was thus both part of his efforts to improve his own 'orientation' as well as part of his message. He emphasized the importance of using different theories and disciplines to look for connections and new lines of causality that might explain and illuminate familiar processes and events, all the while looking for connections that might lead to a more general elaboration of what is taking place. This aspect of *A Discourse*, he noted in his introduction,

> represents the key to evolve tactics, strategies, goals, unifying themes, etc., that permit us to actively shape and adapt to the unfolding world we are part of, live in and feed upon . . . it is the kind of thinking that both lies behind and makes up its very essence.[146]

Finally, *A Discourse* emerged in its final form, after numerous changes, from just such a dialectic process of destruction and creation. In fact, it evolved through the application of the OODA loop. It is the result of a discourse with history, science and the audience, inspired by an insight from his experience as a fighter pilot.

For Boyd then, this deliberate search for novel insights by studying various fields of knowledge, a deliberate maintenance of an open attitude towards various disciplines had a normative character. It is the way strategy and war should be studied. Studying scientific literature in an interdisciplinary way, and gaining an understanding how scientific knowledge develops was as normative as the study of military history if one wanted to gain a proper understanding of conflict, winning and losing. The metaphors, analogies and illustrations Boyd employed were deliberately chosen. Moreover, they were, and are, also part of the scientific and cultural *Zeitgeist*. Boyd was riding a wave in science and translating it and applying it to the military realm.

Boyd was most likely the first military theorist to note the significance of the emerging paradigm for understanding war and strategy. Contradicting those who assert that Boyd was only implicitly and retrospectively a 'non-linearist',[147] these chapters have indicated that, based on the literature Boyd studied from the early 1970s till the time of his death, on the examples he included in his work, on the remarks by several experts who knew Boyd on a personal basis and on Boyd's own assertion, the conclusion is warranted that Boyd explicitly employed the Prigoginian or postmodern perspective when he developed his work, in particular in the presentations he developed after *Patterns of Conflict*.

Boyd's metaphors

The second implication of Boyd's avid and varied reading frenzy lies in the metaphors these works provided. Boyd hints at this in the assertion that: 'the key statements of these presentations, the OODA Loop Sketch and related insights represent an evolving, open-ended, far-from-equilibrium process of self-organization, emergence and natural selection'.[148] Science provided him with novel metaphors, analogies and illustrations, in other words, novel conceptual lenses, to approach and explain military conflict. He could interpolate among and between these bits of information and create sweeping insights into hidden dynamics.[149]

In general we can discern two metaphors in Boyd's work.[150] First, he employs the *organic metaphor*: armed forces are and behave *like* organisms. The OODA loop and Boyd's theory for success, explain what is necessary to survive. The OODA loop can be compared with the genetic reproduction cycle of organic species. Instead of genes, an organization passes on ideas, orientation and action repertoires from one to the next cycle, discarding those orientation patterns and actions that appeared to be dysfunctional. Like organisms, according to Boyd, armed forces compete, learn, evolve, survive, or not. Military doctrine and strategic theory also are seen in this evolution theoretical light. The ones that 'work' survive and will be retained (up to a point when it leads to dogma and specific effective counter-doctrines). Boyd adopts the idea that, like science, strategic theory develops according to a self-correcting mechanism. He wants armed forces to operate as learning organizations.

The second metaphor lies in considering *armed forces as open systems*. Throughout the work Boyd emphasizes connections, tendons, relationships between various interdependent subsystems laterally and among hierarchical levels of organization, and the need for continuous interaction with the environment. Extending this metaphor, Boyd also regarded *armed forces as Complex Adaptive Systems*, such as ecosystems. Here the themes of non-linearity, novelty, variety, levels of organized complexity and different ways, modes and timescales of adaptation and evolution are at play. War is like the non-linear clash of two Complex Adaptive Systems. Units are filling niches in the ecosystem and should be able to operate with a sufficient level of autonomy, yet in an interdependent way, with other systems. Doctrines, procedures, tactics, organizational culture are *like* the strange attractors of chaos theory, explaining the overall behavior of a system. They are also *like* schemata that need to evolve. Armed forces are *like* autopoietic systems, continually making efforts to maintain their distinctive character despite the turbulent environment. Defeat, demoralization and a disorganized retreat can be seen as symptoms of a system disintegrating after the bifurcation point, unable to cope in the available time with the radical changes imposed on it by the environment, unable to adjust the schemata or to speed up the rate of adjustment.

Conceptualizing military strategies of complex adaptive systems

This has implications for the interpretation of his work. As will become evident from reading his work and following logically from the panorama of the scientific *Zeitgeist*, his work revolves around the themes of organizational survival and its solution – adaptability. Boyd focuses on the factors that can impair an opponent's capability to adapt and those that preserve one's own capacity to do so.

The system for which the strategic theory is designed will be the armed force and its environment. An armed force is by design a fairly robust system. It is designed to cause change within an opponent's system and oppose the need to do so itself. It will equip itself with redundant connections, ample units of diverse nature, good sensors, relevant schema and a supportive environment. It will do anything to ensure a modicum of coherence of its actions. The aim is therefore to push a system away from its ordered, disciplined state towards one where indeed the several subsystems need to self-organize because of lack of higher direction, and then towards a state of randomness, but not necessarily in such a time-sequenced order. Randomness, the loss of cohesion, is the opposite of the capability to adapt. The units may still exist but not as part of a higher complex system. This mechanism of decreasing cohesion and fading capability to adapt can be applied to any system and subsystem to the lowest level that can be described as a system; in armed forces this is the individual soldier. But it is not necessary to have the system completely disintegrate in one massive blow. Because an error in response or a slower response will magnify in impact over time through the feedback loops, it is basically only necessary to create an initial advantage and prevent the opponent from compensating for it.

The nature of a system can change from less complex to complex, or alternatively, to the point where there is hardly any connection any more, where information is not shared and where cohesion of action ceases to exist. Then the different elements of a system act at random and do not constitute a part of a system. Applied to armed forces, we can envision an army at the beginning of a conflict executing a plan in a well-ordered fashion with a high degree of cohesion, but after setback, degradation of capabilities, the loss of connections and units, cohesion of the system degrades. Initially the central directing body can issue new orders to maintain cohesion, thus providing part of new schemas (what is expected of units, how to behave) and how the environment should look (by providing intelligence). When the capability to communicate degrades, units need to look after themselves for longer periods of time and through doctrine and training will be able to self-organize for some time. After longer periods the outdated schemas will not match reality any more and, without connections and inputs, the units will fail to react properly, and the more units do so the more the system as a whole will fail to adapt correctly to unfolding circumstances. This explains the importance of the cognitive factor in Boyd's work.

Building on the insights of this and the previous chapters, several interrelated methods can be distilled from the dynamics of open, complex, non-linear adaptive systems that can be translated into strategic moves – albeit abstract – to accomplish the basic aim of social systems in conflict (Box 4.9). Most, if not all, are present in Boyd's work.

- Ensure a large variety of conceptual lenses;
- Organize in semi-autonomous cells, avoid rigid hierarchical structures/ culture;
- Use multiple strategies/avenues;
- Affect the accuracy of the cognitive/feedback process. If comprehension helps to achieve cohesion, and maintain purposeful behavior, the corollary is that confusion helps to create collapse;
- Overload cognitive capacity;
- Eliminate (and/or threaten) particular crucial (real or imaginary) subsystems;
- Diminish the variety of subsystems (affecting the capability to respond to a variety of threats, and diminishing the decision or adaptation space) alternatively achieving and maintaining a relative and relevant advantage in variety;
- Disrupt the moral, physical and/or informational vertical and horizontal relations (i.e. cohesion) among subsystems;
- Close the enemy off from his physical/social environment;
- Shape the environment of a system faster than the opponent's capability to cope with it;
- Disrupt the information flow between the environment and the system, and
- Ensure the irrelevance of the schemata of the opponent, or the inability to validate those while ensuring sufficient accuracy of one's own schemata;
- Change the nature of war: waging a form of warfare that does not correspond to the opponent's doctrine and strategic preference (schemata);
- Change the environment in terms of alliances, location and/or stakes involved.

Box 4.9 List of CAS informed stratagems.

It is this conceptualization of war and strategic behavior that underlies Boyd's thinking, as will become evident from the description of *A Discourse* that follows in the next chapters.

Concluding words

Boyd developed his work while fully aware of the significant scientific developments of his era. The scientific *Zeitgeist* provided him with metaphors and new insights that connected to patterns he discerned in military history and strategic theory, as well in his own military experience. Like the postmodern social scientists and authors who exploited the new sciences to explain familiar social phenomena from new angles, providing new insights along the way, Boyd may be considered the first strategist to incorporate the paradigm shift in science of the twentieth century into strategic theory, deliberately and normatively, and to construct a theory based on the insights the paradigm shift spawned. When it comes to interpreting his work, these chapters strongly suggest that Boyd argues much more than 'merely' the rapid OODA loop idea and that within the OODA loop idea a wealth of concepts and insights add levels of meaning to the simple graphic.

5 Core arguments

> *Patterns of Conflict* represents a compendium of ideas and actions for winning and losing in a highly competitive world.
>
> John Boyd

A Discourse in prose

Introduction

The previous chapters have provided a conceptual lens through which we can examine Boyd's presentations. The following chapters lay out in full prose what Boyd sketched out in his slides. They demonstrate that, although the idea of 'rapid OODA looping' is indeed an important theme in Boyd's work and significant in its own right, in fact his work is much broader and more complex than 'merely' this insight suggests. In addition to developing an approach for fighting conventional war, with the rapid OODA loop notion as its conceptual heart, Boyd distills distinct 'categories of conflict', each with its own particular logic. They will also demonstrate that Boyd did not stop at the tactical and operational levels of war; on the contrary, he addressed the strategic and grand strategic levels as well and in considerable detail. Indeed, he is at pains to reconceptualize the meaning of these terms by putting them in the context of adaptability, as levels in the game of survival.

Furthermore, in his discussion on these issues, he departs from the rapid OODA loop idea in recognition of the fact that other factors come into play at the higher levels of war. In particular, in his last two presentations Boyd takes his arguments towards higher levels of abstraction, turning his military theory into a general theory of strategy, or rather, a general theory of organizational survival. Finally, these chapters will illustrate Boyd's view on the proper approach for strategic thinking, for *A Discourse* is both an argument on a specific approach for winning in conflict, a reconceptualization of the term 'strategy', as well as an argument for how one should think strategically.

Preceded by an introduction to each presentation, the chapters stay close to Boyd's slides and the structure of his argument. This does not allow for much analysis, commentary or explanation. The intent is to provide the content of his slides in readable prose. As much as possible Boyd's own language and terminology is adhered to. Moreover, the original structure of each presentation is kept clearly visible.

Structure

However, the description of the separate parts of Boyd's work does not follow the sequence as presented in *A Discourse*. Instead a chronological order is followed in order to show the way he builds his arguments and to understand how he developed his ideas. The essay is so central to both the content and the development of his entire work that proper comprehension of Boyd's work is not served by discussing it last. Just to underline this, it is worth mentioning here that in his last two briefings he returns to his earliest insights and themes from the essay and elaborates on them even further.

The sections are divided in two chapters for organizational purposes and for the qualitative distinction between the essay and *Patterns of Conflict* (this chapter) on the one hand, and the shorter presentations on the other hand, that can be considered elaborations of specific themes introduced in the essay and *Patterns*. This chapter starts with the essay *Destruction and Creation*, written in 1976, which Boyd put almost at the end of *A Discourse*, followed by *Patterns of Conflict*. Both contain the complete array of themes, insights and arguments Boyd wanted to get across, and together they initially formed *Patterns of Conflict*. Chapter 6 consists of the presentations *Organic Design for Command and Control, The Strategic Game of ? and ?*, and the very brief *Revelation*. Moreover, although *Conceptual Spiral* and *The Essence of Winning and Losing* do not form an integral part of *A Discourse*, they do constitute two more key elements of his work, so they have been included as well. These presentations build upon the foundation laid by the essay and *Patterns*, elaborating, exploring and refining specific themes and arguments, taking the audience to new levels of abstraction.

This structure emphasizes how Boyd expands upon impressions and themes formulated in *A New Conception in Air-to-Air Combat*, the essay and *Patterns of Conflict*. Early on he discovered a pattern, a core process and his presentations build upon and reinforce the idea. Furthermore, through the use of newspaper articles and book sections, these presentations explain in layman's language and in practical terms quite abstract concepts of the essay, in addition to providing fresh substantiation of it.

Despite these modifications, by sticking rather closely to the actual wording of his slides, but armed with the conceptual lenses provided by the previous chapters, we can develop a good feel of the message and the structure of Boyd's argument and the unique Boydian way for peeling new insights from familiar matter and his unique strategic lexicon. We can at least see his mind at work. This starts with the 'Abstract' he offers, in which he clearly alludes to the overarching themes embedded in this work that he considered important. *It is here offered verbatim.*

Boyd's 'Abstract' of *A Discourse*

To flourish and grow in a many-sided uncertain and ever changing world that surrounds us, suggests that we have to make intuitive within ourselves those many practices we need to meet the exigencies of that world. The contents, hence the five sections, that comprise this *Discourse* unfold observations and ideas that contribute toward achieving or thwarting such an aim or purpose. Specifically:

- *Patterns of Conflict* represents a compendium of ideas and actions for winning and losing in a highly competitive world;
- *Organic Design for Command and Control* surfaces the implicit arrangements that permit cooperation in complex, competitive, fast moving situations;
- *The Strategic Game of ? and ?* emphasizes the mental twists and turns we undertake to surface appropriate schemes or designs for realizing our aims or purposes;
- *Destruction and Creation* lays out in abstract but graphic fashion the ways by which we evolve mental concepts to comprehend and cope with our environment;
- *Revelation* makes visible the metaphorical message that flows from this *Discourse*.

As one proceeds from *Patterns* through *Organic Design, Strategic Game,* and *Destruction and Creation* to *Revelation* he or she will notice that the discussion goes from the more concrete and obvious to the more abstract. In this sense, one will notice the rise away from many particular actions and ideas to fewer and more general concepts to account for these many actions and ideas. In this context, 'Patterns' emphasizes historical readings, primarily military, as the backdrop for its discussion while the final four sections draw away from this historical framework and increasingly emphasize theory spread over scientific backdrop as the medium for discussion.

Yet, the theme that weaves its way through this *Discourse on Winning and Losing* is not so much contained within each of the five sections, per se, that make up this *Discourse*, rather, it is the kind of thinking that both lies behind and makes-up its very essence. For the interested, a careful examination will reveal that the increasingly abstract discussion surfaces a process of reaching across many perspectives; pulling each and every one apart (analysis), all the while intuitively looking for those parts of the disassembled perspectives which naturally interconnect with one another to form a higher order, more general elaboration (synthesis) of what is taking place. As a result, the process not only creates the *Discourse* but it also represents the key to evolve the tactics, strategies, goals, unifying themes, etc., that permit us to actively shape and adapt to the unfolding world we are a part of, live-in, and feed-upon.

Destruction and Creation

Introduction

The foundation of *A Discourse* was laid in September 1976 with a concise, 16-page essay entitled *Destruction and Creation*. According to Hammond it is the culmination of a quest to find scientific, mathematical and logical verification for principles Boyd knew instinctively to be true. Thus tested and refined, it became the basis for most of his thoughts thereafter.[1] In this essay he combined concepts from the seemingly unrelated fields of mathematical logic, physics and thermodynamics, linking Gödel's Incompleteness Theorem, Heisenberg's uncertainty principle, and the Second Law of Thermodynamics.[2] But other concepts are either explicitly or implicitly incorporated in it as well, such as the arguments of Polanyi, Popper and Kuhn. The essay consists of an abstract and eight paragraphs. The essay is rendered in its entirety without commentary as it is self-explanatory (when read with the previous chapters as a conceptual background), contrary to the presentations that follow it. The only difference lies in the bibliography, which is included not at the end of the essay, but as Annex A of this study.

The heart of the essay is the discussion about the nature of knowledge. It is highly philosophical and obviously rooted in the epistemological debates that raged in the 1960s. Boyd associates these epistemological issues with struggles for survival. The fundamental, unavoidable and all-pervasive presence of uncertainty is the starting point. It leads to the requirement to learn, to develop adequate mental models, and to continually assess the adequacy of these models as the basis for survival for any organism. This process requires both analysis and synthesis, both induction and deduction. Boyd returned to the notions developed in this essay when developing his ideas about the character of a good command and control system and the essence of the strategic game. In 1996, he condensed his ideas in his final presentation, and in the five slides that make up this briefing again he returns to themes introduced in the essay. In the abstract of the essay he introduces the central theme. Then follows *the literal and entire text of the essay including Boyd's use of underlining.*

'Abstract'

To comprehend and cope with our environment we develop mental patterns or concepts of meaning. The purpose of this paper is to sketch out how we destroy and create these patterns to permit us to both shape and be shaped by a changing environment. In this sense, the discussion also literally shows why we cannot avoid this kind of activity if we intend to survive on our own terms. The activity is dialectic in nature, generating both disorder and order that emerges as a changing and expanding universe of mental concepts matched to a changing and expanding universe of observed reality.

Goal

Studies of human behavior reveal that the actions we undertake as individuals are closely related to survival, more importantly, survival on our own terms. Naturally, such a notion implies that we should be able to act relatively free or independent of any debilitating external influences – otherwise that very survival might be in jeopardy. In viewing the instinct for survival in this manner we imply that a basic aim or goal, as individuals, is to improve our capacity for independent action. The degree to which we cooperate, or compete, with others is driven by the need to satisfy this basic goal. If we believe that it is not possible to satisfy it alone, without help from others, history shows us that we will agree to constraints upon our independent action – in order to collectively pool skills and talents in the form of nations, corporations, labor unions, mafias, etc. – so that obstacles standing in the way of the basic goal can either be removed or overcome. On the other hand, if the group cannot or does not attempt to overcome obstacles deemed important to many (or possibly any) of its individual members, the group must risk losing these alienated members. Under these circumstances, the alienated members may dissolve their relationship and remain independent, form a group of their own, or join another collective body in order to improve their capacity for independent action.

Environment

In a real world of limited resources and skills, individuals and groups form, dissolve and reform their cooperative or competitive postures in a continuous struggle to remove or overcome physical and social environmental obstacles.[3] In a cooperative sense, where skills and talents are pooled, the removal or overcoming of obstacles represents an improved capacity for independent action for all concerned. In a competitive sense, where individuals and groups compete for scarce resources and skills, an improved capacity for independent action achieved by some individuals or groups constrains that capacity for other individuals or groups. Naturally, such a combination of real world scarcity and goal striving to overcome this scarcity intensifies the struggle of individuals and groups to cope with both their physical and social environments.[4]

Need for decisions

Against such a background, actions and decisions become critically important. Actions must be taken over and over again and in many different ways. Decisions must be rendered to monitor and determine the precise nature of the actions needed that will be compatible with the goal. To make these timely decisions implies that we must be able to form mental concepts of observed reality, as we perceive it, and be able to change these concepts as reality itself appears to change. The concepts can then be used as decision-models for improving our capacity for independent action. Such a demand for decisions that literally impact our survival causes one to wonder: How do we generate or create the mental concepts to support this decision-making activity?

Creating concepts

There are two ways in which we can develop and manipulate mental concepts to represent observed reality: We can start from a comprehensive whole and break it down to its particulars or we can start with the particulars and build towards a comprehensive whole.[5] Saying it another way, but in a related sense, we can go from the general-to-specific or from the specific-to-general. A little reflection here reveals that deduction is related to proceeding from the general-to-specific while induction is related to proceeding from the specific-to-general. In following this line of thought can we think of other activities that are related to these two opposing ideas? Is not analysis related to proceeding from the general-to-specific? Is not synthesis, the opposite of analysis, related to proceeding from the specific-to-general? Putting all this together: Can we not say that general-to-specific is related to both deduction and analysis, while specific-to-general is related to induction and synthesis? Now, can we think of some examples to fit with these two opposing ideas? We need not look far. The differential calculus proceeds from the general-to-specific – from a function to its derivative. Hence, is not the use or application of the differential calculus related to deduction and analysis? The integral calculus, on the other hand, proceeds in the opposite direction – from a derivative to a general function. Hence, is not the use or application of the integral calculus related to induction and synthesis? Summing up, we can see that: general-to-specific is related to deduction, analysis, and differentiation, while, specific-to-general is related to induction, synthesis, and integration.

Now keeping these two opposing idea chains in mind let us move on a somewhat different tack. Imagine, if you will, a domain (a comprehensive whole) and its constituent elements or parts. Now, imagine another domain and its constituent parts. Once again, imagine even another domain and its constituent parts. Repeating this idea over and over again we can imagine any number of domains and the parts corresponding to each. Naturally, as we go through life we develop concepts of meaning (with included constituents) to represent observed reality. Can we not liken these concepts and their related constituents to the domains and constituents that we have formed in our imagination? Naturally, we can. Keeping this relationship in mind, suppose we shatter the correspondence of each domain or concept with its constituent elements. In other words, we imagine the existence of the parts but pretend that the domains or concepts they were previously associated with do not exist. Result: We have many constituents, or particulars, swimming around in a sea of anarchy. We have uncertainty and disorder in place of meaning and order. Further, we can see that such an unstructuring or destruction of many domains – to break the correspondence of each with its respective constituents – is related to deduction, analysis, and differentiation. We call this kind of unstructuring a destructive deduction.

Faced with such disorder or chaos, how can we reconstruct order and meaning? Going back to the idea chain of specific-to-general, induction, synthesis, and integration the thought occurs that a new domain or concept can be formed if we can find some common qualities, attributes, or operations among some or many of these constituents swimming in this sea of anarchy. Through such connecting threads (that produce meaning) we synthesize constituents from, hence across, the domains we have just shattered.[6] Linking particulars together in this manner we can form a new domain or concept – providing, of course, we do not inadvertently use only those 'bits and pieces' in the same arrangement that we associated with one of the domains purged from our imagination. Clearly, such a synthesis would indicate we have generated something new and different from what previously existed. Going back to our idea chain, it follows that creativity is related to induction, synthesis, and integration since we proceeded from unstructured bits and pieces to a new general pattern or concept. We call such action a creative or constructive induction. It is important to note that the crucial or key step that permits this creative induction is the separation of the particulars from their previous domains by the destructive deduction. Without this unstructuring the creation of a new structure cannot proceed – since the bits and pieces are still tied together as meaning within unchallenged domains or concepts.

Recalling that we use concepts or mental patterns to represent reality, it follows that the unstructuring and restructuring just shown reveals a way of changing our perception of reality.[7] Naturally, such a notion implies that the emerging pattern of ideas and interactions must be internally consistent and match-up with reality.[8] To check or verify internal consistency we try to see if we can trace our way back to the original constituents that were used in the creative or constructive induction. If we cannot reverse directions the ideas and interactions do not go together in this way without contradiction. Hence, they are not internally consistent. However, this does not necessarily mean we reject and throw away the entire structure. Instead, we should attempt to identify those ideas (particulars) and interactions that seem to hold together in a coherent pattern of activity as distinguished from those ideas that do not seem to fit in. In performing this task we check for reversibility as well as check to see which ideas and interactions match-up with our observations of reality.[9] Using those ideas and interactions that pass this test together with any new ideas (from new destructive deductions) or other promising ideas that popped out of the original destructive deduction we again attempt to find some common qualities, attributes, or operations to re-create the concept – or create a new concept. Also, once again, we perform the check for reversibility and match-up with reality. Over and over again this cycle of Destruction and Creation is repeated until we demonstrate internal consistency and match-up with reality.[10]

Suspicion

When this orderly (and pleasant) state is reached the concept becomes a coherent pattern of ideas and interactions that can be used to describe some aspect of observed reality. As a consequence, there is little, or no, further appeal to alternative ideas and interactions in an effort to either expand, complete, or modify the concept.[11] Instead, the effort is turned inward towards fine-tuning the ideas and interactions in order to improve generality and produce a more precise match of the conceptual pattern with reality.[12] Toward this end, the concept – and its internal workings – is tested and compared against observed phenomena over and over again in many different and subtle ways.[13] Such a repeated and inward-oriented effort to explain increasingly more subtle aspects of reality suggests the disturbing idea that perhaps, at some point, ambiguities, uncertainties, anomalies, or apparent inconsistencies may emerge to stifle a more general and precise match-up of concept with observed reality.[14] Why do we suspect this?

On one hand, we realize that facts, perceptions, ideas, impressions, interactions, etc. separated from <u>previous</u> observations and thought patterns have been <u>linked</u> together to create a new conceptual pattern. On the other hand, we suspect that refined observations now underway will eventually exhibit either more or a different kind of precision and subtlety than the previous observations and thought patterns. Clearly, any anticipated difference, or differences, suggests we should expect a mismatch between the new observations and the anticipated concept description of these observations. To assume otherwise would be tantamount to admitting that previous constituents and interactions would produce the same synthesis as any newer constituents and interactions that exhibit either more or a different kind of precision and subtlety. This would be like admitting one equals two. To avoid such a discomforting position implies that we should anticipate a mismatch between phenomena observation and concept description of that observation. Such a notion is not new and is indicated by the discoveries of Kurt Gödel and Werner Heisenberg.

Incompleteness and consistency

In 1931 Kurt Gödel created a stir in the World of Mathematics and Logic when he revealed that it was impossible to embrace mathematics within a single system of logic.[15] He accomplished this by proving, first, that <u>any consistent system</u> – that includes the arithmetic of whole numbers – <u>is incomplete</u>. In other words, there are true statements or concepts within the system that cannot be deduced from the postulates that make-up the system. Next, he proved <u>even though such a system is consistent its consistency cannot be demonstrated within the system</u>.

Such a result does not imply that it is impossible to prove the consistency of a system. It only means that such a proof cannot be accomplished inside the system. As a matter of fact, since Gödel, Gerhard Gentzen and others have shown that a consistency proof of arithmetic can be found by appealing to systems outside that arithmetic. Thus, Gödel's Proof indirectly shows that in order to determine the consistency of any new system we must construct or uncover another system beyond it.[16] Over and over this cycle must be repeated to determine the consistency of more and more elaborate systems.[17]

Keeping this process in mind, let us see how Gödel's results impact the effort to improve the match-up of concept with observed reality. To do this we will consider two kinds of consistency: The consistency of the concept and the consistency of the match-up between observed reality and concept description of reality. In this sense, if we assume – as a result of previous destructive deduction and creative induction efforts – that we have a consistent concept and consistent match-up, we should see no differences between observation and concept description. Yet, as we have seen, on one hand, we use observations to shape or formulate a concept; while on the other hand, we use a concept to shape the nature of future inquiries or observations of reality. Back and forth, over and over again, we use observations to sharpen a concept and a concept to sharpen observations. Under these circumstances, a concept must be incomplete since we depend upon an ever-changing array of observations to shape or formulate it. Likewise, our observations of reality must be incomplete since we depend upon a changing concept to shape or formulate the nature of new inquiries and observations. Therefore, when we probe back and forth with more precision and subtlety, we must admit that we can have differences between observation and concept description; hence, we cannot determine the consistency of the system – in terms of its concept, and match-up with observed reality – within itself.

Furthermore, the consistency cannot be determined even when the precision and subtlety of observed phenomena approaches the precision and subtlety of the observer – who is employing the ideas and interactions that play together in the conceptual pattern. This aspect of consistency is accounted for not only by Gödel's Proof but also by the Heisenberg Uncertainty or Indeterminacy Principle.

Indeterminacy and uncertainty

The Indeterminacy Principle uncovered by Werner Heisenberg in 1927 showed that one could not simultaneously fix or determine precisely the velocity and position of a particle or body.[18] Specifically he showed, due to the presence and influence of an observer, that the product of the velocity and position uncertainties is equal to or greater than a small number (Planck's Constant) divided by the mass of the particle or body being investigated. In other words:

$$\Delta V \Delta Q \geq h/m$$

where ΔV is velocity uncertainty
ΔQ is position uncertainty and h/m is Planck's constant (h) divided by observed mass (m).

Examination of Heisenberg's Principle reveals that as mass becomes exceedingly small the uncertainty, or indeterminacy, becomes exceedingly large. Now

– in accordance with this relation – when the precision, or mass, of phenomena being observed is little, or no different than the precision, or mass, of the observing phenomena the uncertainty values become as large as, or larger than, the velocity and size frame-of-reference associated with the bodies being observed.[19] In other words, when the intended distinction between observer and observed begins to disappear,[20] the uncertainty values hide or mask phenomena behavior; or put another way, the observer perceives uncertain or erratic behavior that bounces all over in accordance with the indeterminacy relation. Under these circumstances, <u>the uncertainty values represent the inability to determine the character or nature (consistency) of a system within itself</u>. On the other hand, if the precision and subtlety of the observed phenomena is much less than the precision and subtlety of the observing phenomena uncertainty values become much smaller than the velocity and size values of the bodies being observed.[21] Under these circumstances, the character or nature of a system can be determined – although not exactly – since the uncertainty values do not hide or mask observed phenomena behavior nor indicate significant erratic behavior.

Keeping in mind that the Heisenberg Principle implicitly depends upon the indeterminate presence and influence of an observer,[22] we can now see – as revealed by the two examples just cited – that the magnitude of the uncertainty values represent the degree of intrusion by the observer upon the observed. When intrusion is total (that is, when the intended distinction between observer and observed essentially disappears)[23] the uncertainty values indicate erratic behavior. When intrusion is low the uncertainty values do not hide or mask observed phenomena behavior, nor indicate significant erratic behavior. In other words, the uncertainty values not only represent the degree of intrusion by the observer upon the observed but also the degree of confusion and disorder perceived by that observer.

Entropy and the Second Law of Thermodynamics

Confusion and disorder are also related to the notion of Entropy and the Second Law of Thermodynamics.[24] Entropy is a concept that represents the potential for doing work, the capacity for taking action or the degree of confusion and disorder associated with any physical or information activity. High entropy implies a low potential for doing work, a low capacity for taking action or a high degree of confusion and disorder. Low entropy implies just the opposite. Viewed in this context, the Second Law of Thermodynamics states that all observed natural processes generate entropy.[25] From this law it follows that entropy must increase in any closed system – or, for that matter, in any system that cannot communicate in an ordered fashion with other systems or environments external to itself.[26] Accordingly, whenever we attempt to do work or take action inside such a system – a concept and its match-up with reality – we should anticipate an increase in entropy hence an increase in confusion and disorder. Naturally, this means <u>we cannot determine the character or nature (consistency) of such a system within itself</u>, since the system is moving irreversibly toward a higher, yet unknown, state of confusion and disorder.

Destruction and creation

What an interesting outcome![27] According to Gödel we cannot – in general – determine the consistency, hence the character or nature, of an abstract system within itself. According to Heisenberg and the Second Law of Thermodynamics any attempt to do so in the real world will expose uncertainty and generate disorder. Taken together, these three notions support the idea that any inward-oriented and continued effort to improve the match-up of concept with observed reality will only increase the degree of mismatch. Naturally, in this environment, uncertainty and disorder will increase as previously indicated by the Heisenberg Indeterminacy Principle and the Second Law of Thermodynamics, respectively. Put another way, we can expect unexplained and disturbing ambiguities, uncertainties, anomalies, or apparent inconsistencies to emerge more and more often. Furthermore, unless some kind of relief is available, we can expect confusion to increase until disorder approaches chaos – death.

Fortunately, there is a way out. Remember, as previously shown, we can forge a new concept by applying the destructive deduction and creative induction mental operations. Also, remember, in order to perform these dialectic mental operations we must first shatter the rigid conceptual pattern, or patterns, firmly established in our mind. (This should not be too difficult since the rising confusion and disorder is already helping us to undermine any patterns). Next, we must find some common qualities, attributes, or operations to link isolated facts, perceptions, ideas, impressions, interactions, observations, etc. together as possible concepts to represent the real world. Finally, we must repeat this unstructuring and restructuring until we develop a concept that begins to match-up with reality. By doing this – in accordance with Gödel, Heisenberg and the Second Law of Thermodynamics – we find that the uncertainty and disorder generated by an inward-oriented system talking to itself can be offset by going outside and creating a new system. Simply stated, uncertainty and related disorder can be diminished by the direct artifice of creating a higher and broader more general concept to represent reality.

However, once again, when we begin to turn inward and use the new concept – within its own pattern of ideas and interactions – to produce a finer grain match with observed reality we note that the new concept and its match-up with observed reality begins to self-destruct just as before. Accordingly, the dialectic cycle of destruction and creation begins to repeat itself once again. In other words, as suggested by Gödel's Proof of Incompleteness, we imply that the process of Structure, Unstructure, Restructure, Unstructure, Restructure is repeated endlessly in moving to higher and broader levels of elaboration. In this unfolding drama, the alternating cycle of entropy increase toward more and more disorder and the entropy decrease toward more and more order appears to be one part of a control mechanism that literally seems to drive and regulate this alternating cycle of destruction and creation toward higher and broader levels of elaboration.

Now, in relating this deductive/inductive activity to the basic goal discussed in the beginning, I believe we have uncovered a Dialectic Engine that permits the construction of decision models needed by individuals and societies for determining and monitoring actions in an effort to improve their capacity for independent action. Furthermore, since this engine is directed toward satisfying this basic aim or goal, it follows that the goal seeking effort itself appears to be the other side of a control mechanism that seems also to drive and regulate the alternating cycle of destruction and creation toward higher and broader levels of elaboration. In this context, when acting within a rigid or essentially a closed system, the goal seeking effort of individuals and societies to improve their capacity for independent action tends to produce disorder towards randomness and death. On the other hand, as already shown, the increasing disorder generated by the increasing mismatch of the system concept with observed reality opens or unstructures the system. As the unstructuring or, as we'll call it, the destructive deduction unfolds it shifts toward a creative induction to stop the trend toward disorder and chaos to satisfy a goal-oriented need for increased order. Paradoxically, then, an entropy increase permits both the destruction or unstructuring of a closed system and the creation of a new system to nullify the march toward randomness and death.

Taken together, the entropy notion associated with the Second Law of Thermodynamics and the basic goal of individuals and societies seem to work in dialectic harmony driving and regulating the destructive/creative, or deductive/inductive, action – that we have described herein as a dialectic engine. The result is a changing and expanding universe of mental concepts matched to a changing and expanding universe of observed reality.[28] As indicated earlier, these mental concepts are employed as decision models by individuals and societies for determining and monitoring actions needed to cope with their environment – or to improve their capacity for independent action.

Patterns of Conflict

Introduction

Patterns of Conflict is a massive slide set of 193 pages. In one sense it can be read as an exercise to apply his arguments developed in *Destruction and Creation*. Indeed, the way Boyd constructs *Patterns of Conflict* is informed by the inductive–deductive approach. Here, as well as in subsequent presentations, Boyd offers an initial suggestion, argument or insight, which he then sets out to illustrate, to substantiate, to refute or to affirm, albeit then in modified form, taking into account the additional findings this exercise has generated.

In fact, *A Discourse* can be regarded in this light. The essay forms the inductive part, after which *Patterns of Conflict* seeks to affirm/refute these findings through a survey of military history and existing strategic theories. Having found sufficient grounds for accepting the validity of his initial arguments, he then proceeds to take the theory further into related questions – *Organic Design for Command and Control* – and to extrapolate the conceptual implications and possible generalizations – *Strategic Game of ? and ?*. On the other hand,

Patterns must be read as an argument in its own right, but one that is informed by and entirely consistent with the abstract argument from the essay. In *Patterns of Conflict* Boyd develops and substantiates his main arguments concerning warfighting – or rather operational art and strategy.

The first twelve pages contain the core of his theory, or what he calls 'an impression'. Taking off with some notes from 'A New Conception of Air-to-Air Combat', he sets out on a survey of military history in a series of historical snapshots. It proceeds in a generally chronological fashion and focuses on the evolution of war fighting. Gradually the 'impression' is expanded to become the key for grand strategy, but by then the concept of 'fast transients' has gained in dimensions and layers. From this broad survey he distills three distinct categories of conflict as well as a synthesis of the essence – the core elements – that characterizes these categories.

In the first half of the presentation Boyd takes his audience first through the exploits and ideas of Sun Tzu, Alexander, Hannibal, Belisarius, Genghis Khan and Tamerlane. He also discusses the eighteenth century French theoreticians Saxe, Bourcet, Guibert and Du Teil. His study of Napoleon and his interpreters brings him to the disastrous developments in the nineteenth century. This investigation then leads him to World War I and German infiltration techniques, T.E. Lawrence's theory of guerrilla warfare, the revolutionary warfare theories of Marx, Lenin and Mao, J.F.C. Fuller's work on maneuver warfare, the German Blitzkrieg doctrine, and modern guerrilla and finally to counter-guerrilla and counter-blitz methods, indicating his view on strategy as a dialectic interactive process. Boyd recognized a fundamental similarity among the processes that produced success at the tactical level and at the grand tactical level (what we would call the operational level) in guerrilla warfare, in the swarms of Genghis Khan that raided Europe, and in the Blitzkrieg concept. Regarding these concepts as superior he uses them as contrasts to the developments in the nineteenth century and World War I, the 'attritionist' era.

In the second half of the presentation he moves from the descriptive into the prescriptive/suggestive sphere and attempts to condense his thoughts in a more universal model. Altogether it is an interesting tour de force, a great survey of military history and strategic theory. On the other hand, it is also a biased approach to military history. Boyd wants to convey a message, an argument. This agenda becomes evident in the first pages of *Patterns* when he outlines the mission of the presentation.

Mission

The <u>mission</u> of *Patterns of Conflict* is fourfold:

- to make manifest the nature of <u>Moral-Mental-Physical Conflict</u>;
- to discern a <u>Pattern for successful operations</u>;
- to help <u>generalize Tactics and Strategy</u>;
- and to find a basis for <u>Grand strategy</u>.

And the <u>intent</u> is nothing less than 'to unveil the character of conflict, survival and conquest'.[29] He starts with presenting his audience with a number of impressions. First, he introduces his point of departure, which is the 'fast transients' of fighters as discussed in 'A New Conception of Air-to-Air Combat'. Next he introduces the OODA loop for the first time. The idea of 'fast transients', according to Boyd, suggests that

> In order to win we should operate at a <u>faster tempo or rhythm</u> or, better yet, operate inside adversary's Observation-Orientation-Decision-Action time cycle or loop.[30]

He then incorporates a section of the slide *a new conception* from this slightly older presentation. The goal is to have the adversary's system collapse into confusion and disorder by causing him to over- or under-react to activity that appears simultaneously menacing as well as ambiguous, chaotic or misleading. The mechanism for creating this situation is by creating a rapidly changing environment, thereby either effecting a compression of his available decision time or creating many mismatches in his normal decision cycle, thus inhibiting his capacity to adapt to such an environment. Figure 5.1 shows how Boyd made this point in graphic form.[31]

Human nature is the subsequent topic he introduces, which reveals his somewhat Darwinian (or Hobbesian) take on life, revealing the influence of both Heilbroner and Nicholas Georgescu-Roegen. The goal of organisms, according to Boyd, is:

- To survive, survive on own terms, or improve our capacity for independent action. The competition for limited resources to satisfy these desires may force one to:

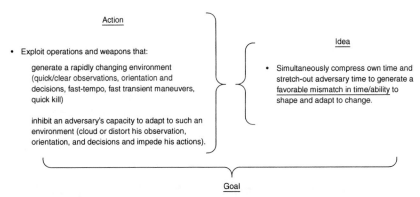

Figure 5.1 Boyd's starting idea.

- Diminish adversary's capacity for independent action, or deny him the opportunity to survive on his own terms, or make it impossible for him to survive at all.

The implication for Boyd is that *life is conflict, survival, and conquest.*[32] And this 'naturally' leads him to 'the Theory of Evolution by Natural Selection and The Conduct of War' (J.F.C. Fuller's book), since 'both treat conflict, survival and conquest in a very fundamental way'.[33] Boyd then offers the notion, not more than that, that

- It may be advantageous to possess a <u>variety</u> of responses that can be applied <u>rapidly</u> to gain sustenance, avoid danger and diminish an adversary's capacity for independent action.
- Organisms must also cooperate and <u>harmonize</u> their activities in their endeavors to survive as an organic synthesis.
- Furthermore to shape and adapt to change, one cannot be passive, but instead one must take the <u>initiative</u>.
- Thus <u>variety, rapidity, harmony and initiative</u> seem to be the key qualities that permit one to shape and adapt to an ever-changing environment.[34]

The entire presentation that follows is an elaboration of these ideas. He explains the working of the mechanism, the process and, using history as illustration and as a source for credibility, he applies it to several levels: the individual, the tactical, the operational (or grand tactical) on to the grand strategic level. So in a very few slides Boyd unfolds the basic contours of his entire strategic theory. And from here on he proceeds with a long section containing historical snapshots aimed at revealing patterns of winning and losing.

Historical snapshots

From Sun Tzu to Napoleon

The fundamental influence of several key theorists, most notably of Sun Tzu becomes evident right away. In Sun Tzu Boyd discovered an idiom and themes that reflected his own thoughts. Comparing the classical commanders Alexander, Hannibal to Tamerlane (all of whom he calls Eastern commanders) with the Western commanders, he states that the philosophy of the Eastern commanders seems more consistent with ideas of Sun Tzu in their attempts to shatter the adversary prior to battle. The approach advanced by Sun Tzu thus amounts to a distinct pattern in military history, and one which serves to contrast the pattern of attrition warfare. The following themes, taken from Sun Tzu, characterize this pattern:

- harmony   deception,
- swiftness of action   fluidity of action,
- dispersion/concentration   surprise
- shock

According to Boyd, Sun Tzu advocates a strategy with four key elements:

- Probe the enemy's organization and dispositions to unmask his strengths, weaknesses, patterns of movement and intentions.
- 'Shape' the enemy's perception of the world to manipulate his plans and actions.
- Attack enemy's plans as best policy. Next best disrupt his alliances. Next best attack his army. Attack cities only when there is no alternative
- Employ Cheng and Ch'i[35] maneuvers to quickly and unexpectedly hurl strengths against weaknesses.

And the desired outcome for Sun Tzu is, in Boyd's words, 'to subdue the enemy without fighting and avoid protracted war'. Western commanders by contrast, Boyd argues, have been more concerned with winning the battle. In order to make the argument that the approach of Sun Tzu has often been superior to this Western approach, he then explores several selected examples which not only bolster his argument but also illustrate in some detail what such an approach entails in terms of force structure, the employment of maneuver, movement, mass and shock. He described the battles of Marathon (490 BC) of the Greeks against the Persians, the Battle of Leuctra (371 BC) which saw combat between the Thebans and the Spartans, the Battle of Arbela (331 BC) in which the Persian King Darius was defeated by Alexander, and the Battle of Canae (216 BC).

The forces available to commanders such as Hannibal consisted of light troops, heavy troops and cavalry. The successful commanders combined these in patterns of maneuver with the light troops to 'unmask the enemy's disposition and hide one's own real strength and confuse the enemy'. Heavy troops in turn and in synergetic fashion would 'charge and smash thinned-out/scattered or disordered/bunched-up enemy formations generated by the interaction with light troops'. Alternatively, they would 'menace enemy formations to hold them in tight, or rigid, arrays thereby make them vulnerable to missiles of swirling light troops'. Thus, according to Boyd, 'light and heavy troops in appropriate combination pursue, envelop, and mop-up isolated remnants of enemy host'. The idea underlying this pattern for winning was to 'employ maneuver action by light troops with thrust action of heavy troops to confuse, break up, and smash enemy formations'.[36] An additional idea, also in line with Sun Tzu, was the deliberate employment of unequal distribution of forces, as the basis to achieve local superiority at the decisive point, and for decisive leverage to collapse adversary resistance.[37]

However, Boyd notes, these battle arrangements and maneuvers do not provide insight into how they play upon 'moral factors such as doubt, fear, anxiety'.[38] For this he turns to Genghis Khan's Mongol hordes and Napoleon's mass armies. Genghis Khan's established four 'key asymmetries':

- superior mobility
- superior communications

- superior intelligence
- superior leadership.

Guarding and exploiting these asymmetries to the fullest enabled the widely separated strategic maneuvers, the baited retreats, the hard-hitting thrusts and swirling envelopment he is remembered for. These movements uncovered and exploited an adversary's vulnerabilities and weaknesses. Rapid unexpected threatening movements in conjunction with propaganda and terror produced fear, anxiety and superstition. This in turn undermined an opponent's resolve and will to resist.[39] The outnumbered Mongols were capable of creating the impression of being everywhere and coming from nowhere. Mobility, swiftness and terror combined to produce collapse by draining the opponent's moral fiber.[40] Thus he makes the connection between physical movement and the moral factors:

- Subversive propaganda, clever stratagems, fast breaking maneuvers, and calculated terror not only created vulnerabilities and weaknesses, but also played upon moral factors that drain-away resolve, produce panic, and bring about collapse.

Indeed, he asserts, in doing so 'the Mongols operated inside adversary observation-orientation-decision-action loops'.[41]

The loss of flexibility: Napoleon and his interpreters

In contrast, Boyd finds fundamental faults in the nineteenth century style of warfare. It is the beginning of the costly and wasteful attrition style of warfare that characterized World War I and the strategic mindset ever since in the West, with some exceptions that he does not fail to highlight. Within the Napoleonic campaigns he discerns a shift in approach from the flexible to the rigid, from the unpredictable to the stereotype, from maneuver and focus on enemy weakness to set piece battles, which pit strength against strength. And this is remarkable in light of the fact that the French theoreticians, such as de Saxe, Bourcet, Guibert and Du Teil, who were of great influence on Napoleon, stressed flexible planning 'with several branches, mobility and fluidity of forces, cohesion, dispersion and concentration'. Furthermore, they stressed operating 'on a line that threatens alternative objectives'. At the tactical level these theorists prescribed 'to concentrate direct artillery fire on key points to be forced'.[42]

He explains that in the early campaigns Napoleon used the ideas of the theorists about variety (as in 'unexpected ways'), ambiguity, deception and rapidity in movement, to surprise and defeat fractions of superior forces. In addition, Boyd also recognized that these ideas are also at home with guerrilla warfare, for American colonists, Spanish and Russian guerrillas 'exploited variety and rapidity associated with environment background (terrain, weather, darkness, etc.) and mobility/fluidity of small bands with harmony of common cause against tyranny/injustice as basis to harass, confuse, and contribute toward the defeat of the British and the French under Napoleon'.[43] Here too he addresses the nexus of movement, ambiguity, rapidity, variety, mobility, fluidity on the one hand with their impact on the moral factor on the other.

Boyd shows how Napoleon was handed an inspired army with citizen-soldiers and new leaders generated by the revolution.[44] This army was organized along self-contained, but mutually supporting units (divisions) and could travel fast by living off the countryside without extensive baggage or supply trains. It could disperse and concentrate faster than opponents. The general features of Napoleon's way of employing these were:

- planning process which included variations and contingency plans;
- extensive information gathering operations which reduced uncertainty and simplified the planning process;
- the use of flexible and confusing configurations of units,
- that combined with screening operations masked his real intentions and movements thus ensuring security;
- the use of strategic dispersion and tactical contraction to create strategic confusion;
- which led to tactical dislocation of units,
- which by rapid concentration of one's own troops could be overwhelmed;
- and finally by a rapid succession and ever-shifting kaleidoscope of (strategic) moves and diversions which upset the enemy's actions, unsettle his plans and unbalance him psychologically which combined ensure a constant level of initiative.

Napoleon furthermore used unified lines of operations as the basis for mutual support between units. He threatened enemy communications to isolate the opponent. He forced the opponent to fight under unfavorable conditions through operations that held or diverted the enemy (feints, pinning maneuvers) and by attacks against exposed flanks or through weak fronts. All the while he maintained freedom of maneuver by setting up centers of operations and alternative lines of communications and keep these (at least some) open. As for command and control, Napoleon initially used a centralized concept with a low degree of tactical variety, which created strategic success to produce tactical success. So higher-level confusion within the enemy camp must make up for lower level uniformity of Napoleon's units and their operations.

In later campaigns Napoleon exchanged variety, rapidity and surprise for rigid uniformity and massed artillery fire, dense infantry columns and heavy artillery against regions of strong resistance. He de-emphasized loose, irregular methods at the tactical level. And in the end he thus failed.[45] Boyd sees in the early victories a substantiation of his own views, and in the latter of Napoleon's less victorious campaign he finds fault with the loss of variety and flexibility.

Next, he turns his critique on Clausewitz and Jomini, the premier analysts of Napoleon's art of war. In Boyd's view, Clausewitz proposed a strategy along the following lines:

- Exhaust the enemy by influencing him to increase his expenditure of effort.
- Seek out centers of gravity upon which all power/movement depend and, if possible, trace them back to a single one.
- Compress all effort, against those centers, into the fewest possible actions.
- Subordinate all minor or secondary actions as much as possible.
- Move at the utmost speed.
- Seek a major battle (with superiority of number and conditions) that will promise a decisive victory.

The aim for Clausewitz was to 'render the enemy powerless', which strongly implies 'the destruction of the opponent's armed forces'. And whereas Boyd, with Sun Tzu, regarded friction, uncertainty as fundamental and unavoidable but also a potential crucial tool, Clausewitz is thought to have considered uncertainty, fear, anxiety and other moral factors as an impediment.[46] These ideas were in obvious contradiction with Boyd's views, and he captures his critique on one slide, asserting that:[47]

- Clausewitz over-emphasized decisive battle and under-emphasized strategic maneuver.
- Clausewitz emphasized method and routine at the tactical level.
- Clausewitz was concerned with trying to overcome or reduce friction/ uncertainty and failed to address the idea of magnifying adversary's friction/uncertainty.
- Clausewitz was concerned with trying to exhaust adversary by influencing him to increase his expenditure of effort. He failed to address, or develop, the idea of trying to paralyze adversary by denying him the opportunity to expend effort.
- Clausewitz incorrectly stated: 'a center of gravity is always found where the mass is concentrated most densely' – then argued that this is the place where the blows must be aimed and where the decision should be reached. He failed to develop idea of generating many non-cooperative centers of gravity by striking at those vulnerable, yet critical, tendons, connections, and activities that permit a larger system's center of gravity to exist.

Boyd blames Clausewitz for not seeing 'that many non-cooperative, or conflicting, centers of gravity paralyze the adversary by denying him the opportunity to operate in a directed fashion, hence they impede vigorous activity and magnify friction'. And the likely result of the Clausewitzian approach, with its lack of variety, so he argues, would be operations that 'end in a bloodbath via the well regulated, stereotyped tactics and unimaginative battles of attrition suggested by Clausewitz'.[48]

Turning his attention to Baron Henri de Jomini, he discerns some interesting ideas. Jomini stresses free and rapid movements, which carry the bulk of the forces successively against fractions of the enemy. He advises to strike in the most decisive direction – that is to say against the center of one wing or the center and one wing simultaneously. If possible, one should seize the adversary's communications and force him to fight on a reverse front, by using the bulk of the forces to hit the flank and attack him in the rear. Detachments can be employed, if necessary, to block the arrival of reinforcements as well as for drawing the opponent's attention elsewhere. If the enemy's forces are too much extended, one should pierce his center to divide and crush his fractions separately.

However, Boyd parts ways with Jomini's 'preoccupation with the form of operations, spatial arrangement of bases, formal orders of battles and tactical formations while showing a lack of appreciation for the use of loose, irregular swarms of guerrillas and skirmishers for masking one's own operations and for confusing and disrupting the enemy's operations'. For Jomini also asserts that one should divide the theater of war and its subordinate components (zones, fronts, positions, etc.) into three subdivisions – a center and two wings – to facilitate envelopment of the opponent. In addition one should approach the opponent with one's forces aligned in an oblique order. Such an approach, like the one proposed by Clausewitz, could not but lead to stereotyped, predictable operations.[49]

Summarizing his critique on Napoleon, Clausewitz and Jomini, Boyd returns to the theme of adaptability. None of the three 'appreciated the importance of loose, irregular tactical arrangements and activities to mask or distort own presence and intentions as well as confuse and disorder adversary operations'. The main flaw according to Boyd was the fact that they 'viewed the conduct of war and related operations in essentially one direction – from the top down – emphasizing adaptability at the top and regularity at the bottom'.[50] And this set the scene for the slaughters of the nineteenth century and World War I.

The curse of the industrial revolution

Boyd lists six key military 'ingredients' of the nineteenth century that only served to reinforce tendencies of the Napoleonic era:

railroad	quick fire artillery
machine gun	repeating rifle
barbed wire	trenches

He observes an 'emphasis toward massed firepower and large armies supported by rail logistics; an increased emphasis on holding defense and flanking or wide turning maneuvers into the adversary's rear to gain a decision; and a trend of continued use of frontal assaults by large stereotyped infantry formations (e.g. regiments, battalions) supported by artillery barrages, against regions of strong resistance'. Not only were tactics now stereotyped. Strategy too had lost the elements of flexibility and surprise, and Boyd puts emphasis on this element of stereotyped operations at both levels in several slides. As he noted:

> huge armies, and massed firepower and other vast needs supported through a narrow fixed logistics network, together with tactical assaults by large stereotyped formations, suppressed <u>ambiguity, deception,</u> and <u>mobility</u> hence <u>surprise</u> of any operation.[51]

> The legacy of Napoleon, Clausewitz, and Jomini's tactical regularity and the continued use of large stereotyped formations for tactical assaults, together with the mobilization of large armies and massing of enormous supplies through a narrow logistics network, 'telegraphed' any punch hence minimized the possibility of exploiting <u>ambiguity,</u> deception, and mobility to generate surprise for a decisive edge.[52]

In this sense, technology was being used as a 'crude club' that generated frightful and debilitating casualties on all sides. Evolution of tactics did not keep pace with the increased weapons lethality developed and produced by nineteenth-century technology. The failure to evolve mentally and tactically in parallel with the technological (r)evolution, resulted in the massacres of the American Civil War (1861–65), the Austro-Prussian War (1866), the Franco-Prussian War (1870–71), the Boer War (1899–1902), the Russo-Japanese War (1904–05) and of World War I.[53]

For Boyd World War I is the highlight of the attritional style of warfare. Here he sees offensives conducted on wide frontages, emphasizing few (rather than many) harmonious yet independent thrusts. The advance was maintained in an even way to protect flanks and to provide artillery support as the advance made headway. Reserves were thrown in whenever an attack was held up, against regions or points of strong resistance. The defense was organized in response to this type of operation. It was organized in depth, consisting of successive belts of fortified terrain. Attackers would be stopped and pinned down by massed artillery and machine-gun fire. Any ground that would still be lost would be won back through counter-attacks. The predictable result was 'stagnation and enormous attrition since advances were generally made along expected paths of hardened resistance which in turn were dictated by both the dependence upon railroads and as well as the choice of tactics of trying to reduce strong points by massed firepower and infantry'.[54]

He thus gave his audience something to think about. First he introduced Sun Tzu and some other (Eastern) practitioners of strategy. These strategists all succeeded not by concentrating large numbers of forces in an attritional battle, but by movement, speed, surprise, variety and creating, and subsequently attacking, weaknesses instead of enemy strengths. Having described an ideal type he proceeded with criticizing the very masters of modern strategic thought and practice that had been taught about, and had been hailed, in most war colleges in the West, thus delivering a fundamental critique of the traditional Western style of warfare.[55]

Rediscovering flexibility

Boyd proceeds with the argument that during Western wars in the twentieth century there have been ideas and concepts that resembled the Eastern style of warfare, and which, an important point, had produced astounding success. He notes that the founding fathers of Communism such as Marx, Lenin and Stalin actually have some important lessons to teach, for they too think along the lines of Sun Tzu.

According to Boyd the solution to the enduring stalemate in the trench warfare during World War I came in the form of infiltration and guerrilla tactics. And in both methods the same processes seem to be at work. Infiltration tactics as practiced by the Germans under Ludendorff consisted of brief but intense artillery bombardment, that included gas and smoke shell, to disrupt and suppress defenses, to obscure the assault. Small, light teams of troops without any linear formation followed the barrage and spread out along the front in depth and in width. They did not attempt to maintain a uniform rate of advance or align formations. Instead, as many tiny, irregular swarms spaced in breadth and echeloned in depth, they seeped or flowed into any gaps or weaknesses they could find in order to drive deep into the adversary's rear. These small shock troops would be followed by small battle groups consisting of infantry, machine-gunners, mortar teams, artillery observers and field engineers. These groups were better equipped to deal with remaining exposed enemy flanks and to mop up isolated centers of resistance. Subsequently, reserves and stronger follow-on echelons moved through newly created breaches to maintain momentum and exploit success, as well as attack flanks and rear positions to widen the penetration and consolidate gains against the expected counter-attack.[56] The idea behind this was to:

> Hurl strength (echeloned in great depth) via an irruption of many thrusts, thru weaknesses along (many) paths of least resistance to gain the opportunity for breakthrough and development.

However, such a focus on maneuver did not sufficiently address how and why infiltration fire and movement schemes work. Again Boyd addresses the way physical movement, artillery fire, gas and smoke and size and mode of operation of the attack units affected enemy perception and psyche. The key points to note about infiltration tactics concern this relation between one's own actions and the enemy's mental processes:[57]

- Fire at all levels by artillery, mortars, and machine-guns is exploited to hold adversary attention and pin him down hence–
- Fire together with gas and smoke (as well as fog and mist) represent an immediate and ominous threat to capture adversary attention, force heads down and dramatically obscure view, thereby cloak infiltration movements.
- Dispersed and irregular character of moving swarms (as opposed to well defined line abreast formations) permit infiltrators to blend against irregular and changing terrain features as they push forward.

- Taken together, the captured attention, the obscured view, and the indistinct character of moving dispersed/irregular swarms deny adversary the opportunity to picture what is taking place.

The result of this dynamic is that

- Infiltration teams appear to suddenly loom-up out of nowhere to blow thru, around, and behind disoriented defenders.

In more abstract terms, Boyd defines the essence of infiltration tactics as:[58]

- Cloud/distort signature and improve mobility to avoid fire yet focus effort to penetrate, shatter, envelop, and mop-up disconnected or isolated debris of adversary system.

The intent of this is to:

- Exploit tactical dispersion in a focused way to gain tactical success and expand it into a grand tactical success.

This in turn implies, in yet more abstract terms that:

- Small units exploiting tactical dispersion in a focused way – rather than large formations abiding by the 'Principle of Concentration' – penetrate adversary to generate many non-cooperative (or isolated) centers of gravity as basis to magnify friction, paralyze effort, and bring about adversary collapse.

Up to the latter part of World War I, commanders had not been able to develop such a tactic due to various organizational and cultural obstacles. According to Boyd

> the aristocratic tradition, the top-down command and control system, the slavish addiction to the 'principle of concentration' and the drill regulation mind-set, all taken together, reveal an 'obsession for control' by high-level superiors over low-level subordinates to evolve the indistinct-irregular-mobile tactics that could counter the increase in weapons lethality.[59]

These ingrained features also prevented Ludendorff from capitalizing on the tactical successes of his platoon, company and battalion level infiltration units. Ludendorff violated his own novel concept by his tendency to use strategic reserves to reinforce against hardened resistance. Thus, at the strategic level, he seduced himself into supporting failure and not success. Moreover, the logistics set-up was not flexible enough to support rapid/fluid penetration and deeper exploitation of breakthroughs. Communication technology was still too immobile to allow command to quickly identify and reinforce successful advances. This caused infiltration units to end up operating beyond the reach of their own artillery support, exposing them to enemy artillery fire and flank attacks.[60] Boyd thus highlights the nexus between strategy and tactics on the one hand, and organization and culture on the other.

He nevertheless advances the idea that conceptually, 'infiltration tactics of fire and movement can be viewed as Napoleon's multi-thrust strategic penetration maneuvers being transformed into multi-thrust tactical penetration maneuvers to the lowest operational/organizational level – the squad'.[61] And infiltration tactics à la Ludendorff also seemed to be similar in nature to irregular or guerrilla tactics à la T.E. Lawrence, for both stress 'clouded/distorted signatures, mobility and cohesion of small units as basis to insert an amorphous yet focused effort into or thru adversary weaknesses'.[62] According to Boyd, Lawrence developed several key principles of guerrilla warfare that stood in stark contrast to the attritional style of warfare as taught and practiced during the nineteenth and early twentieth century:[63]

Action
- Gain support of population. Must 'arrange the minds' of friend, foe and neutral alike. Must 'get inside their minds'.
- Must 'be an idea or thing invulnerable, without front or back, drifting about like a gas' (inconspicuousness and fluidity-of-action). Must be an 'attack-in-depth'.
- Tactics 'should be tip-and-run, not pushes but strokes', with the 'use of the smallest force in the quickest time at the farthest place'.
- Should be war of detachment (avoiding contact and presenting a threat everywhere) using mobility/fluidity-of-action and environmental background (vast unknown desert) as basis for 'never affording a target' and never on the defensive except by accident and in error.

Idea
- Disintegrate existing regime's ability to govern.

Advances in the Interbellum: Lenin, Guderian and Mao

The themes of infiltration tactics and Lawrence's guerrilla warfare doctrine resurface in three major conceptual developments of the Interbellum: Soviet Revolutionary Strategy, Lightning War (or Blitzkrieg) and Maoist Guerrilla War. In introducing these three developments, he offers what for him are one or two key features of each concept.[64] Soviet Revolutionary Strategy, as developed by Lenin, and after him, Stalin, exploited the idea of crises and vanguard that arise out of Marxian contradictions within capitalism. This resulted in a scheme that emphasizes moral/psychological factors as a basis to destroy a regime from within. Lighting War (Blitzkrieg) arose from the mating of infiltration tactics of 1918 with technological advances in the tank, motorized artillery, tactical aircraft, motor transport and communications. It aims to generate a breakthrough by piercing a region with multiple narrow thrusts using armor, motorized infantry, and follow-up infantry divisions supported by tactical aircraft. Mao Tse-Tung, finally, synthesized Sun Tzu's ideas, classic guerrilla strategy and tactics, and Napoleonic style mobile operations under an umbrella of Soviet Revolutionary Ideas to create a powerful way for waging modern (guerrilla) war. This resulted in modern guerrilla warfare, which has become a comprehensive political, economic, social and military framework for 'total' war.[65] In all Boyd recognized similar elements such as a focus on disrupting enemy cohesiveness, use of small shock elements, the exploitation of surprise, the importance of timing and tempo and a focus on enemy weaknesses. And in all again he sees the direct logical connection between actions and the psychological dimension of war.

Boyd next provides a brief introduction on Blitzkrieg, and only briefly addresses Mao's version of guerrilla warfare, leaving a more detailed discussion for later when he describes modern guerrilla warfare developments. Before embarking on a twenty-page exposé on Blitzkrieg, Soviet Revolutionary Strategy is dealt with in only three pages. Boyd defined the communist task Lenin and Stalin had set as the destruction of capitalism, as well as its offspring imperialism, and its replacement with dictatorship of the proletariat. Then he lists the unique features marking their brand of strategic teaching, citing Lenin frequently.[66] This starts with a phase in which the public mood is the target and the aim is to create, magnify and exploit seams in the societal fabric:

- Employ agitation and propaganda in order to exploit opposing tendencies, internal tensions, etc. Object is to bring about a <u>crisis, to make revolution ripe</u> as well as convince masses that there is a way out. This is accomplished when the <u>vanguard</u> is able to:

  - Fan discontent/misery of working class and masses and focus it as hatred toward existing system.
  - Cause vacillation/indecision among authorities so that they cannot come to grips with existing instability.
  - 'Confuse other elements in society so that they don't know exactly what is happening or where the movement is going'.
  - Convince 'proletariat class they have a function – the function of promoting revolution in order to secure the promised ideal society'.

- Select 'the moment for the decisive blow, the moment for starting the insurrection, so timed as to coincide with the moment when the <u>crisis</u> has reached its climax, when the <u>vanguard</u> is prepared to fight to the end, the reserves are prepared to support the vanguard, and maximum consternation reigns in the ranks of the enemy'.

He refers to quotes from Lenin for describing when this moment – a 'tipping point' in modern parlance – has been reached:

- 'All the class forces hostile to us have become sufficiently entangled, are sufficiently at loggerheads, have sufficiently weakened themselves in a struggle which is beyond their strength';
- 'All the vacillating, wavering, unstable, intermediate elements – the petty bourgeoisie, the petty-bourgeois democrats as distinct from the bourgeois – have sufficiently exposed themselves in the eyes of the people, have sufficiently disgraced themselves through their practical bankruptcy';
- 'Among the proletariat a mass sentiment in favor of supporting the most determined, supremely bold, revolutionary action against the bourgeoisie has arisen and has begun to grow vigorously. Then revolution is indeed ripe. Then, indeed, if we have correctly gauged all the conditions indicated above . . . and if we have chosen the moment rightly, our victory is assured'.

When the revolution has already become ripe, perseverance is in order. And again Boyd quotes Lenin at length: 'Never play with insurrection, but, when beginning it, firmly realize that you must go to the end'. The decisive condition of success then is 'concentration of the main forces of the revolution at the enemy's most vulnerable spot at the decisive moment, when the offensive is going full-steam ahead, when insurrection is knocking at the door, and when bringing the reserves up to the vanguard'. Considering the limited resources you must try to 'take the enemy by surprise and seize the moment when his forces are scattered'. Such concentration and maintenance of the offensive is crucial, for the enemy 'has the advantage of better preparation and organization. The defensive is the death of an armed rising'. 'You must strive for daily successes even if small and at all costs retain the moral ascendancy'.

The Blitzkrieg concept

Discovering similarities

Boyd next makes the conceptual connection between guerrilla strategy and Blitzkrieg which, he states, lies in the mutual conceptual foundation in the ideas of Sun Tzu. Both Blitzers and guerrillas 'infiltrate a nation or regime at all levels to soften and shatter the moral fiber of the political, economic and social structure. Simultaneously, via diplomatic, psychological, and various sub-rosa or other activities, they strip-away potential allies thereby isolate intended victim(s) for forthcoming blows'. To carry out this program, à la Sun Tzu, Blitz and guerrillas:

- Probe and test adversary, and any allies that may rally to his side, in order to unmask strength, weaknesses, maneuvers, and intentions.
- Exploit critical differences of opinion, internal contradictions, frictions, obsessions, etc., in order to foment mistrust, sow discord and shape both adversary's and allies' perception of the world thereby:
- Create atmosphere of 'mental confusion, contradiction of feeling, indecisiveness, panic,' . . .

- Manipulate or undermine adversary's plans and actions.
- Make it difficult, if not impossible, for allies to aid adversary during his time of trial.

The purpose of this is either to 'force capitulation when combined with external political, economic, and military pressures, or to weaken the adversary to minimize his resistance against military blows that will follow'.[67]

Entering a long discussion on Blitzkrieg, he distills the elements that produce shock and confusion within the opponent and those that ensure that cohesion in one's own actions is maintained. The central idea behind actions designed according to guidelines of the Blitzkrieg concept is to:

- conquer an entire region or defeat an armed force in the quickest possible time by gaining <u>initial surprise</u> and exploiting the <u>fast tempo and fluidity of action</u> of armored teams combined with air support, as basis to repeatedly penetrate, splinter, envelop and roll-up/wipe-out disconnected remnants of an adversary's organism in order to confuse, disorder and finally shatter his will or capacity to resist.[68]

The mechanism that makes Blitzkrieg an effective method consists of four interdependent elements, and although Boyd does not list them as such, the elements of observation-orientation-decision-action can easily be discerned in his short description. Boyd also succeeds in pointing at the linkage with infiltration tactics.[69]

First is the novel idea (in the 1930s) of employing numerous air and ground reconnaissance actions, which together with other intelligence actions probe and test the adversary before and during combat operations both to uncover and to shape changing patterns of strengths, weaknesses, moves and intentions. The observed patterns of movement and actions, changes, etc., of the opponent are weighed against one's own situation to expose attractive, or appropriate, alternatives that exploit the adversary's vulnerabilities and weaknesses and thus help shape mission commitment and influence command intent.

The second element consists of deriving a mission from the correct assessment of the patterns in enemy behavior and, based on the mission and the observed patterns in enemy behavior, of selecting and nominating a 'Schwerpunkt' (center of gravity). This Schwerpunkt serves as the focus of the main effort. The Schwerpunkt can be shifted during actual operations to bypass the enemy's strength and strike at weaknesses. Related or supporting efforts are also established. As discussed above, Boyd labeled these 'Nebenpunkte'. These are threats, movements, combat actions, feints, etc. that tie up, focus or drain the attention of the enemy and his strength.

A plan having been formulated, the third element of the Blitzkrieg mechanism comes into play. From observation, orientation and decision, Boyd moves to action. Small teams are inserted into the enemy rear area from the air or through rapid ground infiltration. Aided by agents already present, these teams seize critical objects such as bridges, they destroy railroad crossings and communications, incapacitate or blow up power stations and generally generate confusion in the rear by their mere presence and by disseminating false messages and fake orders. Meanwhile, air power and artillery are used to impede (or channel) enemy movement, to disrupt communications, to suppress forward defensive fires, to mask one's own advance and to divert attention. Shock troops and leading armored columns advance rapidly from least expected regions and infiltrate the enemy's front to find the path of least resistance. Breaches are opened by fire and movement of air, armored and infantry-units. This will enforce a breakthrough, through which relatively independent mobile/armored units rush forward at high speed to penetrate the enemy's interior, in close coordination with air support, air reconnaissance and/or air transport. The object is to cut lines of communication, disrupt enemy movement, paralyze enemy command and control and envelop the enemy. Finally, follow-on infantry and armored units pour in to overwhelm isolated pockets of resistance, widen the breaches and secure the conquered territory.

Blitzkrieg disrupts the connections between and within units, thereby removing cohesion. The enemy system that relied on the combination of centers of gravity (constituting strengths, capabilities, objects or geographical features) and linkages between those centers of gravity is severely hurt by the disruption or destruction of these linkages. Or in Boyd's words,

> Blitzkrieg generates multiple non-cooperative centers of gravity, as well as undermines or seizes those that adversary depends upon, in order to impede vigorous activity and magnify friction, thereby paralyze adversary by denying him the opportunity to operate in a directed way.[70]

Operating philosophy

The obvious question is of course 'how do Blitzers simultaneously sustain rapid pace and abruptly adapt to changing circumstances without losing cohesion or coherence of their overall effort?' To avoid collapse itself, Blitzkrieg employs, as the last element of the mechanism, a concept for command and control in which each unit at the different levels of organization, from simple to complex, has its own specific OODA time cycle. The cycle time increases commensurate with an increase in the level of organization, as one tries to control more levels and issues. As the number of events increase, the longer it takes to observe, orient, decide and act. Thus

- the faster rhythm of the lower levels must work within the larger and slower rhythm of the higher levels so that overall system does not lose its cohesion or coherency.[71]

Considering this issue essential – referring to it as the first element of the 'Blitz Operating Philosophy' – he elaborates on it here, as well as in the subsequent presentation *Organic Design for Command and Control*. According to Boyd, the tension between the maintenance of control and cohesion on the one hand, and the demands of fluid tactical situations is resolved by giving the

- lower level commanders wide freedom 'within the overall Mind-Time-Space scheme', to shape/direct their own activities so that they can exploit faster tempo/rhythm at the tactical levels yet be in harmony with the larger pattern/slower rhythm associated with the more general aim and larger effort at the strategic level.

The 'Mission concept ensures subordinate commanders stay within the boundaries of acceptable initiative, it fixes responsibility and shapes commitment at all levels and through all parts of the organism'. Likewise, Boyd advocates the use of a 'Schwerpunkt concept through all levels to link differing rhythms/patterns so that each part or level of the organic whole can operate at its own natural rhythm – without pulling the organism apart – instead of the slower pace associated with a rigid centralized control'.[72]

Quoting the World War II Blitzkrieg practitioner General Gunther Blumentritt, this scheme, 'presupposes a common outlook based upon a body of professional officers who have received exactly the same training during the long years of peace and with the same tactical education, the same way of thinking, identical speech, hence a body of officers to whom all tactical conceptions were fully clear'. This in turn presupposes 'an officer training institution which allows the subordinate a very great measure of freedom of action and freedom in the manner of executing orders and which primarily calls for independent daring, initiative and sense of responsibility'.[73]

This goes some way in explaining Boyd's insistence on the primary role of a *common outlook* or orientation pattern and the element of 'previous experience' in the OODA loop graphic. Indeed he makes it a point that 'without a common outlook superiors cannot give subordinates freedom-of-action and maintain coherency of ongoing action'.[74] In this one page Boyd thus highlights the crucial relations between action and effectiveness during combat, command and control philosophy, organizational culture and peace time training and education and shows how the one is predicated upon the other. However, at this point, neither the Schwerpunkt concept nor the Mission concept have been sufficiently explained and Boyd therefore takes his audience deeper into the Blitzkrieg philosophy.

Mission, Schwerpunkt, and getting inside the OODA loop

The mission concept can be thought of as a contract, he argues,

hence an agreement, between the superior and subordinate. The subordinate agrees to make his actions serve his superior's intent in terms of <u>what</u> is to be accomplished, while the superior agrees to give his subordinate wide freedom to exercise his imagination and initiative in terms of <u>how</u> the intent is to be realized. As part of this concept, the subordinate is given the right to challenge or question the feasibility of his mission if he feels his superior's ideas on what can be achieved are not in accord with the existing situation or if he feels his superior has not given him adequate resources to carry it out'.[75]

While this explains one element required for maintaining cohesion at higher levels as well as adaptability at the lower level, it actually only gives form and expression to what is expected between an individual superior and subordinate. It does not suggest ways to coordinate or harmonize activities among many superiors and subordinates as a collective group. Here the Schwerpunkt concept comes in view. As Boyd explains it, the

- Schwerpunkt acts as a center, or axis or harmonizing agent that is used to help shape commitment and convey or carry-out intent, at all levels from theater to platoon, hence an image around which:
  - maneuver of all arms and supporting elements are focused to exploit opportunities and maintain tempo of operations, and
  - initiative of many subordinates is harmonized with superior intent.[76]

In this sense Schwerpunkt can be thought of as:

- a focusing agent that naturally produces an unequal distribution of effort as a basis to generate superiority in some sector by thinning out others, as well as
- a medium to realize superior intent without impeding initiative of many subordinates, hence a medium through which subordinate initiative is implicitly connected to superior intent.

Schwerpunkt thus represents

a <u>unifying concept</u> that provides a way to rapidly shape focus and direction of effort as well as harmonize support activities with combat operations, thereby permit a true decentralization of tactical command within centralized strategic guidance – without losing cohesion of overall effort. Or put in another way, it represents a <u>unifying medium</u> that provides a directed way to tie initiative of many subordinate actions with superior intent as a basis to diminish friction and compress time in order to generate a favorable mismatch in time and in the ability to shape and adapt to unfolding circumstances.[77]

Here Boyd introduces the effect of the Mission concept and the Schwerpunkt concept on the dimension of time. Before, these concepts were explored as essential elements for maintaining cohesion and harmonizing effort. Now they take on a different role, indeed, they become crucial advantages in themselves, for they allow swifter tempo of operations. Because the German operational philosophy was based upon a common outlook and freedom-of-action, which they realized through their concepts of Mission and Schwerpunkt, 'it emphasized implicit over explicit communication'. This suggests, according to Boyd, that 'the secret of the German Command and Control System lies in what's unstated or not communicated to one another – in order to exploit lower-level initiative yet realize higher level intent, thereby diminish friction and reduce time, hence gain both quickness and security'.[78] Again he quotes Blumentritt to make an important point flowing from this:

- The entire [German] operational and tactical leadership method hinged upon ... rapid concise assessment of situations, quick decision and quick execution, on the principle: 'each minute ahead of the enemy is an advantage'.

Boyd translated this in the more abstract but now well-known observation that they were able to 'repeatedly operate inside their adversary's observation-orientation-decision-action loops'.[79] Not surprisingly, Boyd's OODA loop graphic includes the elements of implicit guidance and control.

Towards the essence of Blitzkrieg

A final point concerning Blitzkrieg Boyd addresses, as in his discussion of the dynamics of infiltration tactics, is the connection between – the rationale for – the pattern of employing 'multiple thrusts, bundles of multiple thrusts or bundles of thrusts insides bundles of thrusts'. One can see how he draws his audience into a conversation with him, for he formulates this theme about the rationale as a question for the audience. Boyd provides the answer: multiple thrusts (etc.) 'present many (fast-breaking) simultaneous and sequential happenings to generate confusion and disorder – thereby stretch out time for [the] adversary to respond in a directed fashion'. Moreover, they must be regarded as 'multiple opportunities to uncover, create, and penetrate gaps, exposed flanks and vulnerable rears'. They also 'create and multiply opportunities to splinter [the] organism and envelop disconnected remnants thereby dismember [the] adversary thru the tactical, grand tactical, and strategic levels'.[80] This leads him to reveal the essence of Blitzkrieg:[81]

Employ a Nebenpunkte/Schwerpunkte maneuver philosophy to generate ambiguity, realize deception, exploit superior mobility and focus violence as the basis to quickly:

- Create many opportunities to penetrate weaknesses in the form of any moral or mental inadequacies as well as any gaps or exposed flanks that open into adversary's vulnerable rear and interior, hence –
- Create and exploit opportunities to repeatedly penetrate adversary

organism, at all levels (tactical, grand tactical, and strategic) and in many ways, in order to splinter, envelop, and roll-up/wipe-out isolated remnants, thereby generate confusion and disorder, hence –

- Create and exploit opportunities to disrupt his system for communication, command, and support, as well as undermine or seize those connections or centers that he depends upon, thus shake his will or capacity to decisively commit his back-up echelons, operational reserves, and/or strategic reserves, thereby magnify adversary's confusion and disorder and convince him to give up.

Note how he connects physical, spatial, temporal, informational, moral and mental dimensions into a logical causal chain and has moved slowly to a higher level of abstraction. This culminates in the formulation of the conceptual implication (which is of a yet higher level of abstraction) of this approach. He asserts that 'Blitzers, by being able to infiltrate or penetrate or get inside adversary's system, generate many moral-mental-physical non-cooperative (or isolated) centers of gravity, as well as undermine, or seize those centers of gravity adversary depends upon, in order to magnify friction, produce paralysis, and bring about adversary collapse'.[82]

To actually execute such an approach six interrelated conditions (all of which by now he already had addressed) must be met. While taking his inspiration from World War II he concludes this list with a slide, which mentions twelve successful Blitz campaigns versus five lost ones, so as to suggest that indeed, the keys to success he advances have proven their worth.[83] The process of OODA is constantly present at the background, and in particular the cognitive elements.

First, there must be an 'emphasis on a common outlook and freedom-of-action that are exploited by the Mission and Schwerpunkt concepts to fix responsibilities as well as to rapidly shape, focus and shift operations and support at all levels'. Second, there must be flexibility in command, 'based on a common outlook and freedom-of-action that are exploited by Mission and Schwerpunkt – that encourages lower-level combat leaders (forward) to exploit opportunities generated by rapid action within a broad loosely woven scheme laid down from central command'. The third condition also relates closely with the command (or better: the cognitive) function: 'intelligence, reconnaissance (air and ground) and stratagem emphasized before and during combat operations to unmask and shape patterns of adversary strengths, weaknesses, moves, and intentions'.

Only the fourth condition relates to physical movements in space and time, but even here he includes the idea that these are tied to the enemy's function of perception and his morale: 'Broad use of Schwerpunkt concept coupled with fast-tempo/fluidity-of-action of armored teams and air support permit Blitzers to repeatedly reshape strength and rapidly shift it against, or through, weaknesses thereby generate doubt and uncertainty which magnify into panic and chaos'.

These actions require (as a fifth condition) 'superior mobile communications to maintain cohesion of overall effort and to enable higher command levels to allocate reserves and support and to reshape as well as shift focus of main effort'. Again, the processes of observation and orientation take central place. The final condition is a small logistics tail (using airlift when appropriate and necessary) to support high-speed movement and rapid shift among routes of advance.[84] This section demonstrates that Boyd's OODA loop idea includes more elements than the notion of outpacing the opponent's decision cycle, which it is often equated with.

The modern guerrilla campaign

A similar dynamic

Boyd thus introduced infiltration tactics and Blitzkrieg warfare and has advanced the idea that in essence they 'work' because of similar dynamics at play. In his discussion of both he continuously emphasizes how actions work upon the enemy's processes of perception. He shows how the physical, the temporal and the mental dimensions interrelate, and that this connection actually provides the rationale for the physical actions. Already he has briefly suggested that in the revolutionary warfare concept developed in the Interbellum, such a dynamic could also be discerned. His next topic, which aims to further bolster his argument, is an exploration of modern guerrilla campaigns. Reaching back to his previous discussion of Lenin and Mao, he follows the by now familiar didactic structure. First he describes what in practical terms constitutes a guerrilla campaign, and the idea underlying it. From this he distills the essence and abstract intent, implications and the keys for success for his discussion concerning patterns of winning and losing.

The main idea, the logic behind the guerrilla warfare approach, is to

> Defeat the existing regime politically by showing they have neither the moral right, nor demonstrated ability to govern and militarily by continuously using stealth/fast-tempo/fluidity-of-action and cohesion of small bands and larger units in cooperation with political 'agitprop' (agitation/propaganda) teams as basis to harass, confuse and ultimately destroy the will or capacity to resist.[85]

According to Boyd, guerrillas capitalize on discontent and mistrust which is generated by corruption (real of imagined), exploitation, oppression, incompetence, and the unwanted presence of the existing regime. Thus they can evolve a common cause or a unifying theme as a basis to organize and maintain mass support through a militant political program. They build an administrative and military organization, create a sanctuary, and a communications network under the control of the political leadership of the guerrilla movement. They take care not to arouse the reigning regime's intelligence and security apparatus. A shadow government is created, with parallel hierarchies, in localities and regions that can be made ripe for insurrection/revolution by infiltration cadres (vanguards) who cannot only subvert the existing authority but also convert leaders and people to the cause and organizational way of the guerrillas. Based upon this structure, they attempt to subvert the government and convert people. This will create an alien atmosphere of security and intelligence in order to 'blind' the regime to the plans, operations and organization of the guerrilla movement, while at the same time the regime's strengths, weaknesses, moves and intentions become visible.

The next phase comes in the form of propaganda, inspiring civil disorder (such as rallies, demonstrations, strikes and riots). Selected acts of terrorism and sabotage will be conducted. The resulting misinformation can be exploited to expand mistrust and sow discord, which in turn magnifies the appearance of corruption, incompetence, etc., and the inability of the regime to govern. Tiny cohesive bands can then be employed for surprise hit-and-run raids against lines of communications to gain arms and supplies as well as to disrupt the communication, coordination and movement of the government. When superior government police and armed force do appear, these guerrilla bands should not engage in battle but instead retreat and melt into the environment. This scheme can be expanded. Such tiny bands can scatter across the country to arouse the people (and gain recruits) as well as to harass, wear out, and spread out government forces. When indeed government forces are thinly spread and operate not in superior force sizes but in small units, they can be engaged through ambushes and sneak attacks by larger bands, or mobile formations which concentrate to wipe out these dispersed, isolated and relatively weak fractions.

Meanwhile the effects of propaganda, re-education and selected military successes should be exploited. The grievances and obsessions of people should be played upon. The government must be encouraged to indiscriminately take harsh reprisal measures against the people in order to associate the government with the expanding climate of mistrust, discord and moral disintegration. Simultaneously and in stark contrast to the government, guerrillas should exhibit moral authority, offer competence, and provide desired benefits. This will assist in further eroding the government's influence, gaining more recruits and multiplying the base areas. Subsequently, the political infrastructure can expand, as well as the influence and control exerted by the guerrilla movement over the population and the countryside. This will culminate with the visible demonstration of the disintegration of the regime, which is effectuated by strikes of small fluid bands and ever-larger formations in a Cheng/Ch'i fashion, to split-up, envelop, and annihilate fractions of major enemy forces.[86]

The essence of the modern guerrilla campaign, according to Boyd, is thus to:[87]

- Capitalize on corruption, injustice, incompetence, etc., (or their appearances) as basis to generate atmosphere of mistrust and discord in order to sever moral bonds that bind people to existing regime
  Simultaneously
- Share existing burdens with people and work with them to root out and punish corruption, remove injustice, eliminate grievances, etc., as basis to form moral bonds between people and guerrillas in order to bind people to guerrilla philosophy and ideals.

The intent of guerrilla activities is to:

- Shape and exploit crises environment that permits guerrilla vanguards or cadres to pump-up guerrilla resolve, attract the uncommitted, and drain away adversary resolve as foundation to replace existing regime with guerrilla regime.

The conceptual implication of this is that:

- Guerrillas, by being able to penetrate the very essence of their adversary's moral-mental-physical being, generate many moral-mental-physical non-cooperative (or isolated) centers of gravity, as well as subvert or seize those centers of gravity that adversary regime must depend upon, in order to magnify friction, produce paralysis, and bring about collapse. Yet,
- Guerrillas shape or influence moral-mental-physical atmosphere so that potential adversaries, as well as the uncommitted, are drawn toward guerrilla philosophy and are empathetic toward guerrilla success.

Strategic philosophy

The strategic philosophy underlying modern guerrilla warfare, as well as Soviet Revolutionary Strategy and the impact of nineteenth-century capitalism on Insurrection/revolution can now be discerned. It is only a slightly different rendering of the short essence laid out above. According to Boyd, guerrilla vanguards employ a variety of means to play upon internal frictions within the regime, obsessions, etc., as well as stimulate discontent and mistrust of the people. In this way, vanguards sow discord that in turn magnifies the internal frictions within the regime. This paralyzes the regime's ability to come to grips with crises that further fan the atmosphere of mistrust and discord that feed the crises. This self-amplifying process pushes the regime out of control. The guerrilla vanguards on the other hand share the burden as well as help the people to cope with the turmoil – that the vanguards themselves keep fanning and enmesh people into – in order to demonstrate the ability to deal with surging crises as well as to shape the image that only guerrillas offer a way out of existing unpleasant circumstances.[88]

Now he slowly peels away more layers to get to the core dynamics of modern guerrilla warfare. The discussion above offers the insight, so Boyd suggests, that the 'insurrection/revolution becomes ripe when many perceive an illegitimate inequality – that is, when the people see themselves as being exploited and oppressed for the undeserved enrichment and betterment of an elite few. This means that the guerrillas not only need an illegitimate inequality but they also need support of the people, otherwise insurrection/revolution is impossible'.[89] The message to be derived from this insight is that:[90]

- Guerrillas must establish implicit connections or bonds with people and countryside.
  In other words
- Guerrillas must be able to blend into the emotional-cultural-intellectual environment of people until they become one with the people.
  In this sense
- People feelings and thoughts must be guerrilla feelings and thoughts while guerrilla feelings and thoughts become people feelings and thoughts; people aspirations must be guerrilla aspirations while guerrilla aspirations become people aspirations; people goals must be guerrilla goals while guerrilla goals become people goals.
  The result is that
- Guerrillas become indistinguishable from people while government is isolated from people.

A survey of twelve successful and five failed guerrilla campaigns of the past 200 years reveals, according to Boyd, the four keys to success, which again amount to a description of the dynamics of guerrilla warfare, from yet a slightly different angle and in more general terms: first, an ability to continuously demonstrate government weakness, to erode government influence and to cause the government to alienate itself from the people; second, the support of people (both psychological and physical) for intelligence, recruits, shelter, transportation, refuge, food, money and medical aid; third, access to (more of less permanent) safe sanctuaries or base areas and/or fluid bases that can be shifted from place to place, away from enemy forces – in order to rest, recuperate, repair materiel, etc., as well as to indoctrinate, train and equip recruits; and finally, the use of stealth/fast-tempo/fluidity-of-action coupled with cohesion of guerrilla bands as a basis for:

- dispersion, to arouse people, to avoid adversary strength, and to force government to thin-out, or disperse, its strength;
- concentration, to hit and wipe-out isolated fractions;
- shifting of effort (in these as well as other activities), in order to gain and keep initiative.[91]

The nucleus of victory: the themes of Blitzkrieg and guerrilla warfare

It is significant the way Boyd describes that guerrillas blend in with the environment just like infiltration units did, how he focuses on bonds and connections, as well as on the theme of the creation of isolation, which also appeared in his description of infiltration tactics and the Blitzkrieg concept. Also the choice of words for describing the keys to guerrilla warfare success is not coincidental. On the contrary, his particular formulation makes readily apparent the connection with other styles of warfare. Indeed, he claims that the elements that made Blitzkrieg successful can also be recognized in guerrilla warfare as theorized by

T.E. Lawrence, Soviet Revolutionary Strategy and Mao's guerrilla warfare concept, which combined ideas of Sun Tzu, Napoleon and Lenin. At an abstract level the processes and core concepts are similar, Boyd suggests. All revolve around maintaining cohesion among one's own units, creating confusion and disrupting cohesion in the enemy camp. By concentrating on processes and core concepts instead of other characteristics that give form to a particular style of warfare, such as technology, he uncovered similarities between these different styles.

Wrapping the essences of guerrilla warfare and Blitzkrieg together, he concludes that in both styles <u>battles are avoided</u>. Instead the essence of both is to:[92]

- penetrate an adversary to <u>subvert</u>, <u>disrupt</u> or <u>seize</u> those connections, centers, and activities that provide <u>cohesion</u> (e.g., psychological/moral bonds, communications, lines of communication, command and supply centers,...).
- exploit ambiguity, deception, superior mobility and sudden violence to generate initial <u>surprise</u> and <u>shock</u>, again and again and again.
- roll-up/wipe-out, the isolated units or remnants created by subversion, surprise, shock, disruption and seizure.

These actions aim to:

- exploit subversion, surprise, shock, disruption and seizure to generate <u>confusion</u>, <u>disorder</u>, <u>panic</u>, etc., thereby <u>shatter cohesion</u>, <u>paralyze effort</u> and <u>bring about adversary collapse.</u>

The reasons for the extraordinary level of success, or in Boyd's words, 'the message', lies in the fact that in both concepts:[93]

- one operates in a <u>directed</u> yet <u>more indistinct</u>, <u>more irregular</u> and <u>quicker manner</u> than one's adversaries.

This enables one to:

- Repeatedly concentrate or disperse more inconspicuously and/or more quickly from or to lower levels of distinction (operational, organizational and environmental) without losing internal harmony.

For the same reason one is able to:

- Repeatedly and unexpectedly <u>infiltrate</u> or <u>penetrate</u> adversaries' vulnerabilities and weaknesses in order to splinter, isolate or envelop and overwhelm disconnected remnants of adversary organism.

Or, put in another way, one can;

- operate inside the enemy's OODA loops or get inside their mind-time-space as a basis to penetrate the moral-mental-physical being of one's adversaries in order to pull them apart and bring about their collapse.

Such amorphous, lethal and unpredictable activity by Blitz and guerrillas make them appear awesome and unstoppable, which altogether produces uncertainty, doubt, mistrust, confusion, disorder, fear, panic and ultimately collapse. They affect the connections and centers that provide cohesion, as Boyd explains in yet another slide on the same theme.[94] This notion was already implied by Sun Tzu and more recently by the analysis J.F.C. Fuller had made of Ludendorff's infiltration tactics in 1918. Indeed, then, for Boyd there is continuity from Sun Tzu to the Vietnam War, from the early campaigns of Napoleon to the 1973 war in the Middle East.

Not surprisingly, he also attempts to uncover the counter to such successful stratagems: how can we defend against or counter the Blitz and the guerrilla movement? The answer follows directly from his analysis of the essence of both types of warfare. The difficulty with an enemy Blitz is to maintain cohesion while sustaining fast tempo when the enemy is forced to repeatedly and rapidly shift the concentration of strength against weaknesses. The counter to the Blitz thus lies in the same keys of success for Blitzkrieg, in addition to avoiding linear defense. Instead, defense should be in depth, with armored teams as mobile reserves in echelon behind reconnaissance parties, which try to locate the enemy thrusts. The defense should have better intelligence, operate faster, be more mobile, move even more inconspicuously, also with small combat teams operating according to the Schwerpunkt/mission concept, and maintain a higher level of cohesion to shatter the opponent's cohesion with counterstrokes on the enemy flanks and rear. It implies an acceptance of 'gaps' and 'risks'.[95] The idea is a mirror of the idea underlying the Blitz:

> Smash Blitz offensive by inconspicuously using fast-tempo/fluidity-of-action and cohesion of counter-Blitz combat teams as basis for shifting of forces and quick focus of air and ground effort to throttle momentum, shatter cohesion, and envelop Blitz in order to destroy adversary's capacity to resist.[96]

The Achilles heel for the guerrilla movement lies in its need for popular support. Guerrilla vanguards need a cause, the support of people and a crisis. The crisis and the vanguards represent the marriage of instability and initiative that create and expand guerrilla effort. Without support of people, the guerrillas have neither a vast hidden intelligence network nor an invisible security apparatus that permit them to see into the adversary's operations yet blind the adversary to their own operations. This automatically suggests that in order to dry up a guerrilla upsurge, one should strike at those root causes or illegitimate inequalities that generate and exacerbate crises as well as provide a favorable climate for vanguards to form and operate in. Thus the idea behind a counter-guerrilla campaign is to 'break guerrillas' moral-mental-physical hold over the population, destroy their cohesion, and bring about their collapse via political initiative that demonstrates <u>moral legitimacy</u> and <u>vitality</u> of government and by relentless military operations that emphasize <u>stealth/fast-tempo/fluidity-of-action</u> and cohesion of overall effort'.[97]

Categories of conflict

Three kinds of conflict

Based on his 'panorama' of military history, Boyd argues that one can imagine three kinds of human conflict:[98]

- <u>Attrition Warfare</u> – as practiced by the Emperor Napoleon, by all sides during the 19th Century and during World War I, by the Allies during World War II, and by present-day nuclear planners.
- <u>Maneuver Conflict</u> – as practiced by the Mongols, General Bonaparte, Confederate General Stonewall Jackson, Union General Ulysses S. Grant, Hitler's Generals (in particular Manstein, Guderian, Balck, Rommel) and the Americans under Generals Patton and MacArthur.
- <u>Moral Conflict</u> – as practiced by the Mongols, most Guerrilla Leaders, a very few Counter-Guerrillas (such as Magsaysay) and certain others from Sun Tzu to the present.

Boyd subsequently provides the essence of each kind of conflict. This synthesis offers novel aspects, for he often recombines and rephrases the terms or puts them in a different context. And in particular the category of moral conflict offers new material.

Attrition warfare

In just one slide (Figure 5.2) he captures the dynamics of attrition warfare, and this stands in marked contrast with his dealing with maneuver and moral conflict.[99] Firepower as a destructive force is king. Protection (trenches, armor, dispersion, etc.) is used to weaken or dilute effects of enemy firepower. Mobility is used to bring firepower to bear or to evade enemy fire. Measures of success are 'body count' and targets destroyed. Seize and hold terrain objectives replace Napoleon's dictum: destroy enemy army.[100]

Maneuver conflict

While covering just four slides, his summary of maneuver warfare offers new insights, describing it in new terms, allowing him to make a leap to a characteri-

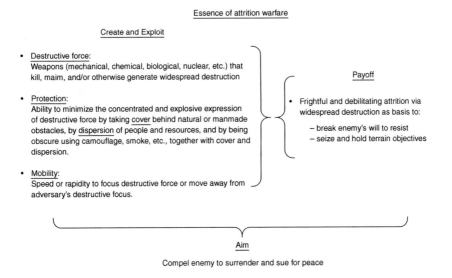

Figure 5.2 Dynamics of attrition warfare.

zation that transcends the historical connection to World War II Blitzkrieg. He deliberately raises the level of abstraction and inserts his theme of adaptability to recast maneuver warfare in yet another mold, giving new meaning to his previously discussed key elements. He offers three observations regarding maneuver.

First ambiguity, deception, novelty, and violence (or threat thereof) are used to generate surprise and shock. Second, fire and movement are used in combination, like Cheng/Ch'i or Nebenpunkte/Schwerpunkt, to tie-up, divert or drain-away the adversary's attention and strength in order to expose as well as menace and exploit vulnerabilities or weaknesses elsewhere. A final point is that indications of success tend to be qualitative and are related to the widespread onset of confusion and disorder, frequent envelopments, high prisoner counts or <u>any</u> other <u>phenomena that suggest inability to adapt to change</u>.[101]

Again in one slide (Figure 5.3) he paints an impression of the essence of maneuver conflict:[102] In light of his previous observation on the importance of adaptability, it is a noteworthy slide for it lists effects, which show an increasing level of erosion of the state of mental/moral coherence with the subsequent decreasing capability to cope and respond adequately. In addition, he returns to the theme of fast transients and the Darwinian perspective with which he started *Patterns of Conflict*.

In Figure 5.4 these terms have been arranged so as to depict the causal chain that is formed by the induced effects, according to Boyd's slide. The dotted boxes indicate the desired ultimate effects, the ultimate aim.

For Boyd, this still does not sufficiently capture the essence of maneuver

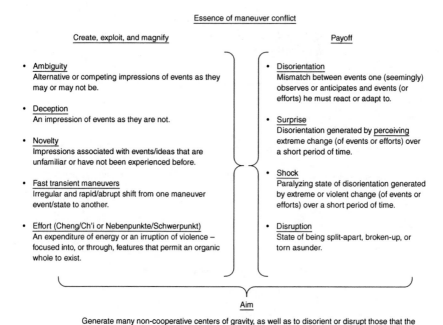

Figure 5.3 The essence of maneuver conflict (1).

conflict. He increases the emphasis on adaptability when he states next that 'shock and surprise can also be regarded as an overload caused by a welter of threatening events beyond one's mental or physical ability to respond and adapt or endure'. This results in a slightly amended version of the slide above. It contains two notable differences. It no longer regards disorientation as the only element affecting adaptability, but now also the element of overload due to 'a welter of threatening events'. So adaptability is affected not only by ambiguous information and uncertainty, but is also compounded by fear due to threatening events.

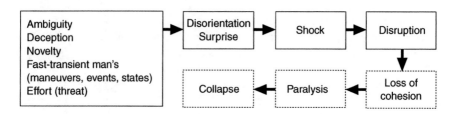

Figure 5.4 Causal chain of effects in maneuver conflict.

Moreover, Boyd modifies his aim. The employment of the various elements of maneuver conflict may not directly result in collapse, as one may have interpreted his statement on the 'aim of maneuver conflict'. Instead, he considers it equally valuable to aim for the creation of many isolated remnants of enemy forces that can later be mopped up. In light of the critique that Boyd, like Sun Tzu, expects victory through merely going through OODA cycles more rapidly, this is not a trivial transition. Thus the <u>essence of maneuver</u> conflict can also be viewed as depicted in Figure 5.5.[103]

Moral conflict

This category is novel for two reasons. Although it suggests that it equates with revolutionary war or guerrilla warfare, it includes but transcends those types. It is also novel in the discussion Boyd had up to this point with his audience. He had not alluded to it before. Therefore he starts his discussion with an examination of morale, aiming to uncover the nature of moral strength and the causes for

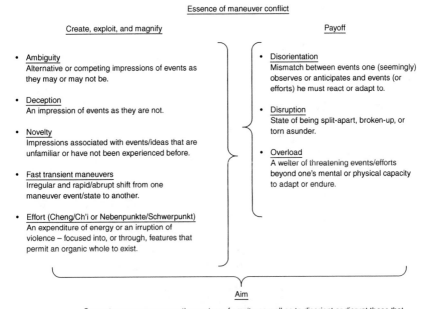

Figure 5.5 The essence of maneuver conflict (2).

losing it using the German Blitzer Hermann Balck and Cyril Fall's 1961 book *The Art of War from the Age of Napoleon to the Present Day* as examples.

Balck emphasized the importance of leadership in creating moral strength among troops. Leaders allowed subordinates freedom to exercise imagination and initiative, yet harmonize within the intent of superior commanders. Cohesion during combat relied more on moral superiority than on material superiority. Leaders must create this. This requires them to create a bond and breadth of experience based upon trust. They must also lead by example, demonstrating requisite physical energy, mental energy and moral authority to inspire subordinates to enthusiastically cooperate and take the initiative within the superior's intent. Leaders must be willing to share danger and discomfort with the troops at the front. They must show a willingness to support and even promote (unconventional or difficult) subordinates that accept danger, demonstrate initiative, take risks, and come-up with new ways towards mission accomplishment. Finally, they must manifest a dedication and resolve to face-up to and master uncomfortable circumstances that fly in the face of the traditional solution.

From Cyril Falls' book Boyd extracts insights concerning the reverse issue: when does moral strength evaporate? Boyd tells how during World War I in East End London air raids caused a tendency to panic in the latter part of 1917. Moreover, whether there was an air raid or not, some 300,000 people crowded each night into the underground railway stations and slept on the platforms. Although a single German airship did cause £1 million worth of damage in a raid, the success of airship attacks was mainly moral and measured in terms of absenteeism in factories and sensational drops in production of warlike material. A similar effect was noted by German Blitzers in their employment of dive-bombers, to which the German armies owed much in their victories in Poland, Belgium and France. Acting in close support to the armor and infantry, they often put hostile artillery out of action, not through destruction but by driving the detachment from their guns. Those successes were won for the most part by moral rather than material effect. To troops unused to them, these dive-bomber attacks proved extremely unsettling.[104]

Cyril Falls' comments suggest, according to Boyd, that moral effects are related to the menace posed by the Zeppelins and dive-bombers, and the uncertainty associated with not knowing what to expect or how to deal with this menace. Put simply, moral effects are related to menace and uncertainty. This also offers a preliminary suggestion that moral strength represents mental capacity to overcome menace and uncertainty.

One element is still missing, however: the element of trust. As was discussed above, guerrillas stress the use of propaganda, civil disorders, selected terrorism, etc., as the basis to generate mistrust and discord. Balck emphasized the importance of trust for cohesion. And as both guerrillas and Blitz commanders work in a hostile environment (of menace and uncertainty), which naturally breeds mistrust, it is clear that moral effects must include this factor. This suggests that moral strength represents mental capacity to overcome menace, uncertainty and mistrust.[105] From these insights Boyd develops five notions related to moral conflict:[106]

- <u>Moral strength</u>: mental capacity to overcome menace, uncertainty, and mistrust.
- <u>Moral victory</u>: triumph of courage, confidence, and esprit (de corps) over fear, anxiety, and alienation when confronted by menace, uncertainty, and mistrust.
- <u>Moral defeat</u>: triumph of fear, anxiety, and alienation over courage, confidence, and esprit when confronted by menace, uncertainty, and mistrust.
- <u>Moral values</u>: human values that permit one to carry on in the face of menace, uncertainty, and mistrust.
- <u>Moral authority</u>: person or body that can give one the courage, confidence, and esprit to overcome menace, uncertainty, and mistrust.

This leads to two wrap-up slides on the essence of moral conflict. The first (Figure 5.6) amounts to a 'what to do' summary. The second (Figure 5.7) improves upon the first, in similar fashion to the two slides on the essence of maneuver conflict.

So far it has become clear that courage, confidence and esprit the corps represent the positive counterweights to fear, anxiety and alienations. This does not reveal yet how to create, maintain and exploit moral strength among one's own troops. Positive counterweights to menace, uncertainty and mistrust still need to be developed. These are not very obvious. Boyd makes the suggestion, admittedly based in no small part on his own intuition, that the answer lies in the elements of harmony, adaptability and initiative, offering the following explanation:[107]

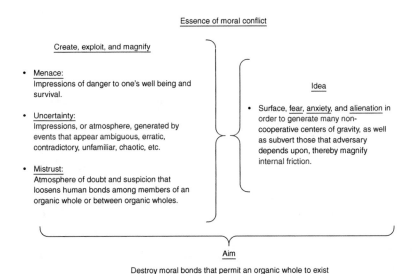

Figure 5.6 The essence of moral conflict (1).

- The presence of mistrust implies that there is a rupture or loosening of the human bonds or connections that permit individuals to work as an organic whole in <u>harmony</u> with one another. This suggests that harmony itself represents an appropriate counterweight to mistrust.
- In dealing with uncertainty, <u>adaptability</u> seems to be the right counterweight. Otherwise, how can one adjust to the unforeseen or unpredictable nature of uncertainty?
- Finally, with respect to menace one cannot be passive. Instead, <u>initiative</u> is needed otherwise menace may obliterate the benefits associated with harmony and adaptability. Intuitively, this suggests that initiative is the right counterweight here.

This then leads to the second wrap-up of the <u>essence of moral conflict</u> (Figure 5.7), which combines the negative and the positive factors, the offensive as well as the defensive side.[108]

Synthesis: pattern for successful operations

A short look back

By now Boyd is ready to come slowly to the abstract synthesis of the dynamics and patterns of winning and losing. In the first pages of *Patterns of Conflict* he has laid out the aim of this presentation and a number of key themes

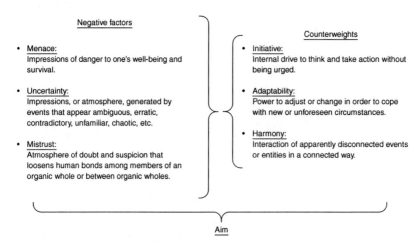

Negative factors

- Menace:
  Impressions of danger to one's well-being and survival.

- Uncertainty:
  Impressions, or atmosphere, generated by events that appear ambiguous, erratic, contradictory, unfamiliar, chaotic, etc.

- Mistrust:
  Atmosphere of doubt and suspicion that loosens human bonds among members of an organic whole or between organic wholes.

Counterweights

- Initiative:
  Internal drive to think and take action without being urged.

- Adaptability:
  Power to adjust or change in order to cope with new or unforeseen circumstances.

- Harmony:
  Interaction of apparently disconnected events or entities in a connected way.

Aim

- Pump-up friction via negative factors to breed fear, anxiety and alienation in order to generate many non-cooperative centers of gravity, as well as subvert those that adversary depends upon, thereby sever moral bonds that permit adversary to exist as an organic whole.

- Build-up and play counterweights against negative factors to diminish internal friction, as well as surface courage, confidence, and esprit, thereby make possible the human interactions needed to create moral bonds that permit us, as an organic whole to shape and adapt to change.

Figure 5.7 The essence of moral conflict (2).

and suggestions. He has taken his audience through detailed discussions of the style of warfare as practiced by Sun Tzu, Alexander, Genghis Khan and the early Bonaparte. He has argued that from the later Napoleonic battles to World War I bloody and wasteful attrition warfare was tragically in vogue. The solution to the costly loss of flexibility, to the stalemate of the trenches, was provided by infiltration tactics. Together with the development of the Blitzkrieg concept, Lawrence's version of guerrilla warfare and communist revolutionary warfare, this period manifested a de facto rediscovery of the teachings of Sun Tzu. Boyd then gradually shifts to higher levels of abstraction in his compression of the different styles of warfare to the key elements and fundamental dynamics of each. He now moves on to get to the most general and abstract formulation of the essence of strategy. In twenty pages he brings it all together, from the tactical to the grand strategic level, coming full circle to the ideas he bluntly put forward in his introduction. But by now he has taken his audience through 2,500 years of military history and strategic thought to argue his points.

Towards a new conceptualization of strategy

Restating his first ideas, propositions, findings and insights, including those of the essay, Boyd states that for any system the basic goal is to diminish the adversary's freedom of action, while improving our freedom of action so that we can cope with events while they unfold and he cannot.[109] This should also be the aim of any military commander. The plan for achieving this should incorporate the following eight steps (in which Sun Tzu and Liddell Hart can easily be recognized):

1 Probe and test the adversary to unmask strength, weaknesses, his maneuvers and intentions.
2 Employ a variety of measures that interweave menace, uncertainty and mistrust with tangles of ambiguity, deception and novelty as the basis to sever an adversary's moral ties and disorient or twist his mental images and thus mask, distort and magnify our presence and activities.
3 Select initiatives and responses that are least expected.
4 Planning should focus on a 'Schwerpunkt' with 'Nebenpunkte' and should have branches and sequels, and thus secure flexibility.
5 Threaten multiple and alternative objectives while,
6 Move along paths of least resistance to reinforce and exploit success.
7 Exploit, rather than disrupt or destroy those differences, frictions, obsessions, etc., of adversary organism that interfere with his ability to cope with unfolding circumstances.
8 Subvert, disorient, disrupt, overload or seize vulnerable and critical connections, centers and activities that provide cohesion and permit a coherent OODA cycle in order to dismember the organism and isolate remnants for absorption or mop-up.

When it comes to <u>action</u> the thing is to:

> 'OODA' <u>more inconspicuously</u>, <u>more quickly</u> and with <u>more irregularity</u> as basis to keep or gain initiative as well as shape or shift main effort; to repeatedly and unexpectedly penetrate vulnerabilities and weaknesses exposed by that effort or other effort(s) that tie up, divert, or drain-away adversary attention (and strength) elsewhere.

The whole operation should be supported by a superior mobile communications structure. Only essential logistics should be used. The command concept should be highly decentralized in a tactical sense to allow tactical commanders initiative. It should be centralized at the strategic level to establish aims, match ambitions with means, to sketch plans, allocate resources and shape the focus of overall effort.[110]

Up to this point Boyd's discussion has concerned the elements of setting goals, planning, action, support and command. Although abstract in the way he describes these elements, they still refer to the tactical level. He is still far removed from a general theory of winning and losing in which tactics (actions) are linked to strategy and the societal level. So, from this pattern of successful operations, Boyd proceeds to develop a set of hierarchically structured related definitions – or rather novel conceptualizations – of tactics, grand tactics (operational level in current parlance), strategy and grand strategy. Once more Boyd sets out to get to the essence of success in yet another higher level of abstraction to arrive first at the 'theme for disintegration and collapse' and then at the 'theme for vitality and growth'.

He first addresses the grand tactical level. The pattern he sketched out before suggests that the aim for any commander is to penetrate the adversary system and mask one's own system against any such attempts by the opponent. One wants to create a variety of impressions of what is occurring and what is about to occur. One aims to generate mismatches between what seems to be and what is and to push the adversary beyond his ability to adapt. The intention formulated in the plan requires the application of transients that make up the action part.[111] Here he emphasizes the element of uncertainty of combat and command, the relevance of mismatches and the value of creating a variety of impressions. These are enduring elements, indeed, vulnerabilities and weaknesses that commanders and subordinates alike must accept. To reinforce his point, Boyd returns to Napoleon, who asserted that:

> 'The art of land warfare is an art of genius, of inspiration ... A general never knows anything with certainty, never sees his enemy clearly, never knows positively where he is. When armies are face to face, the least accident in the ground, the smallest wood, may conceal part of the enemy army. The most experienced eye cannot be sure whether it sees the whole of the enemy's army or only three-fourths. It is by the mind's eye, by the integration of all reasoning, by a kind of inspiration, that the general sees, knows, and judges.'

'The first quality for a commander in chief is a cool head which receives a just impression of things; he should not allow himself to be confused by either good or bad news; the impressions which he receives successively or simultaneously in the course of a day should classify themselves in his mind in such a way as to occupy the place which they merit; because reason and judgment are the result of the comparison of various impressions taken into just consideration.'[112]

If the element of judgment in the face of uncertainty is of such prime importance for a commander such as Napoleon, this should indeed feature prominently in the conceptualization of grand tactics. Subsequently Boyd formulates a 'to do' definition of *grand tactics* which focuses in particular on the mind of the enemy commander, on the process of observation and orientation, while also containing familiar elements:

- Operate inside adversary's OODA-loops, or get inside his mind-time-space, to create a tangle of threatening and/or non-threatening events/efforts as well as repeatedly generate mismatches between those events/efforts adversary observes, or anticipates, and those he must react to, to survive;
  Thereby
- Enmesh adversary in an amorphous, menacing, and unpredictable world of uncertainty, doubt, mistrust, confusion, disorder, fear, panic, chaos,... and/or fold adversary back inside himself;
  Thereby
- Maneuver adversary beyond his moral-mental-physical capacity to adapt or endure so that he can neither divine our intentions nor focus his efforts to cope with the unfolding strategic design or related decisive strokes as they penetrate, splinter, isolate or envelop, and overwhelm him.[113]

He incorporated similar ideas in his advice for the strategic level, which to some extent he considers as comparable to the grand tactical level. However, the strategic level has a higher level of aggregation and complexity, it features more enemy elements and, importantly, a wider spectrum of options for compensation and adaptation, as well as a wider theater (in both time and space) with more options for manipulating, confusing and invalidating the strategic calculations and maneuvers of the adversary. Although Boyd in a sense merely seems to restate his previous arguments, at the strategic level he no longer sees the enemy as tactical units, but as an organic whole, as an adaptive system composed of a variety of subsystems. Another difference is that the cognitive element becomes more and more important at the strategic level. Figure 5.8 shows Boyd's list of methods for influencing the potential strategic behavior of the enemy.[114]

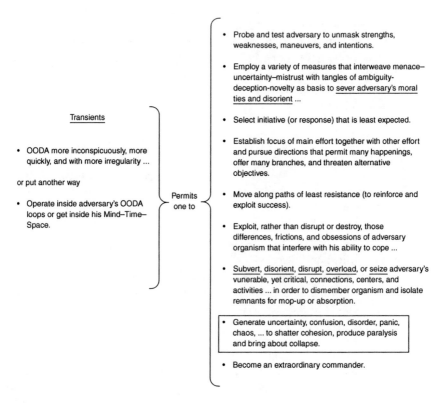

Figure 5.8 Influencing the enemy's strategic behavior.

This leads Boyd to the conclusion that in general terms the *strategic aim* is to:

> Penetrate moral-mental-physical being to dissolve his moral fiber, disorient his mental images, disrupt his operations, and overload his system, as well as subvert, shatter, seize or otherwise subdue those moral-mental-physical bastions, connections, or activities that he depends upon, in order to destroy internal harmony, produce paralysis, and collapse adversary's will to resist.[115]

This results in a synthesis of abstract formulations of prescriptions for actions and objectives of operations at the tactical, the grand tactical and strategic levels. It is in a sense a list of things 'to do'. However, it is not a check-list for commanders to follow, but a reconceptualization of what one should be trying to achieve vis à vis the opponent's level of cohesion, his capability to observe and orient correctly, and his ability to respond in a timely and relevant way. In other words, Boyd offers ideas for affecting the opponent's capability to adapt, arguing that any physical movement, as well as the hiding of movements, should relate directly to a cognitive effect one wants to achieve within the OODA process of the opponent:[116]

Tactics
- 'OODA' more inconspicuously, more quickly and with more irregularity as basis to keep or gain initiative as well as shape or shift main effort; to repeatedly and unexpectedly penetrate vulnerabilities and weaknesses exposed by that effort or other effort(s) that tie up, divert, or drain-away adversary attention (and strength) elsewhere.

Grand tactics
- Operate inside adversary's OODA-loops, or get inside his mind-time-space, to create a tangle of threatening and/or non-threatening events/efforts as well as repeatedly generate mismatches between those events/efforts adversary observes, or anticipates, and those he must react to, to survive;
  Thereby
- Enmesh adversary in an amorphous, menacing, and unpredictable world of uncertainty, doubt, mistrust, confusion, disorder, fear, panic, chaos, ... and/or fold adversary back inside himself;
  Thereby
- Maneuver adversary beyond his moral-mental-physical capacity to adapt or endure so that he can neither divine our intentions nor focus his efforts to cope with the unfolding strategic design or related decisive strokes as they penetrate, splinter, isolate or envelop, and overwhelm him.

Strategy
- Penetrate moral-mental-physical being to dissolve his moral fiber, disorient his mental images, disrupt his operations, and overload his system, as well as subvert, shatter, seize or otherwise subdue those moral-mental-physical bastions, connections, or activities that he depends upon, in order to destroy internal harmony, produce paralysis, and collapse adversary's will to resist.

Strategic aim
- Diminish adversary's capacity while improving our capacity to adapt as an organic whole, so that our adversary cannot cope while we can cope with events/efforts as they unfold.

Theme for disintegration and collapse

The name of the game

Boyd acknowledges that so far this exercise has not produced insights that are significantly different from the destructive attrition-maneuver-moral ideas played out in the synthesis of 'Categories of Conflict'. More is required to lay bare the essence of winning and losing. He subsequently recasts both 'Categories of Conflict' and the list of ideas above in the following schematic, once more showing the deeper meaning of the rapid OODA loop idea, dispelling the notion that mere information superiority or superior speed in command and control is the essence of that idea. In the schematic Boyd has captured and combined elements of maneuver and moral conflict, as well as an element of the description of grand tactics. By now he has worked his way towards a view on strategy, which focuses on those elements that allow complex social structures to exist and function in a purposeful way and to adapt to changes in the environment. Gradually his verbiage has become more abstract, general and conceptual in nature, and decreasingly recognizable as grounded in military history (Figure 5.9).[117]

His holistic approach, and his view of the adversary as a complex adaptive system, becomes even more manifest in the subsequent slides, which lead him to formulate nothing less than the *Theme for Vitality and Growth*. Boyd continues to strip down and recombine his ideas, focusing in particular on the element of cohesion. Not the manifestation of force but the cohesion that produces it should be the focus of planning, for the 'underlying insight' of the *Theme for Disintegration and Collapse*, is that:[118]

> unless one can <u>penetrate</u> adversary's moral-mental-physical being, and sever those interacting bonds that permit him to exist as an organic whole, by being able to subvert, shatter, seize, or otherwise subdue those moral-mental-physical bastions, connections, or activities that he depends upon, one will find it exceedingly difficult, if not impossible, to collapse adversary's will to resist.

Boyd then homes in on the meaning of the word 'penetrate'. Seen from a different angle, the observation above can be rephrased to produce the *name of the game* as:[119]

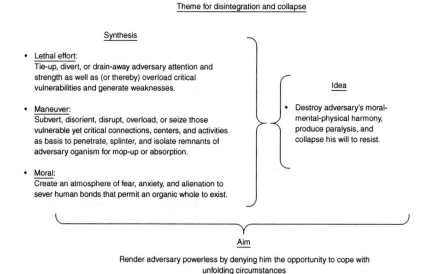

Figure 5.9 Theme for disintegration and collapse.

Morally-mentally-physically isolate adversary from allies or any outside support as well as isolate elements of adversary or adversaries from one another and overwhelm them by being able to penetrate and splinter their moral-mental-physical being at any and all levels.

From this perspective the nexus of military strategy and grand strategy comes into view, which involves other sources of power, national public support, ideology, etc. Or, put in the question Boyd asks his audience: 'How do we connect the tactical and strategic notions or the theme for disintegration and collapse with the national goal?' Again he provides the answer: 'via a sensible *grand strategy* that will':

- Support national goal.
- Pump-up our resolve, drain away adversary resolve, and attract the uncommitted.
- End conflict on favorable terms.
- Ensure that conflict and peace terms do not provide seeds for (unfavorable) future conflict.[120]

In his view, grand strategy first and foremost must be an appealing idea, or set of objectives and interests, which inspires and unites the populace as well as allies and the uncommitted. Grand strategy is directly related to, and should be a function of, the prime national goal, which Boyd earlier regarded as a Darwinian drive to improve the fitness of the nation to survive in the dynamic environment. The *essence of grand strategy* is to:

- Shape pursuit of national goal so that we not only amplify our spirit and strength (while undermining and isolating our adversaries) but also influence the uncommitted or potential adversaries so that they are drawn toward our philosophy and are empathetic toward our success.

Grand strategy should therefore be designed on the basis of:

- An appreciation for the underlying self-interests, critical differences of opinion, internal contradictions, frictions, obsessions, etc., that we as well as the uncommitted and any potential or real adversaries must contend with.[121]

Strategy as a mode of behavior

Boyd then presents the combined set of prescriptions concerning the modes of behavior that favor success and survival on the various levels in a hierarchical order.[122]

National goal
Improve fitness, as an organic whole, to shape and cope with an everchanging environment.

Grand strategy

Shape pursuit of national goal so that we not only amplify our spirit and strength (while undermining and isolating our adversaries) but also influence the uncommitted or potential adversaries so that they are drawn toward our philosophy and are empathetic toward our success.

Strategic aim

Diminish adversary's capacity while improving our capacity to adapt as an organic whole, so that our adversary cannot cope while we can cope with events/efforts as they unfold.

Strategy

Penetrate moral-mental-physical being to dissolve his moral fiber, disorient his mental images, disrupt his operations, and overload his system, as well as subvert, shatter, seize or otherwise subdue those moral-mental-physical bastions, connections, or activities that he depends upon, in order to destroy internal harmony, produce paralysis, and collapse adversary's will to resist.

Grand tactics

- Operate inside adversary's OODA-loops, or get inside his mind-time-space, to create a tangle of threatening and/or non-threatening events/efforts as well as repeatedly generate mismatches between those events/efforts adversary observes, or anticipates, and those he must react to, to survive;
  Thereby
- Enmesh adversary in an amorphous, menacing, and unpredictable world of uncertainty, doubt, mistrust, confusion, disorder, fear, panic, chaos,... and/ or fold adversary back inside himself;
  Thereby
- Maneuver adversary beyond his moral-mental-physical capacity to adapt or endure so that he can neither divine our intentions nor focus his efforts to cope with the unfolding strategic design or related decisive strokes as they penetrate, splinter, isolate or envelop, and overwhelm him.

Tactics

- 'OODA' more inconspicuously, more quickly and with more irregularity as basis to keep or gain initiative as well as shape or shift main effort; to repeatedly and unexpectedly penetrate vulnerabilities and weaknesses exposed by that effort or other effort(s) that tie up, divert, or drain-away adversary attention (and strength) elsewhere.

Boyd explains how the national goal and grand strategy, which tend to be *constructive* in nature, are directly related and in harmony with strategic aim, strategy, grand tactics and tactics, despite the fact that these four are *destructive* in nature. It is an important section, for it provides insight into his view of the main aim of warfare, and his close association with Sun Tzu, Fuller and Liddell Hart.

Following naturally from his discussion of the flaws of attrition warfare and his praise for the alternatives of moral and maneuver conflict, Boyd explains that:[123]

> ...application of these latter four strategic and tactical notions permit real leadership to *avoid high attrition, avoid widespread destruction, and gain a quick victory*. This, combined with shattered cohesion, paralysis, and rapid collapse demonstrated by the existing adversary regime, makes it appear corrupt, incompetent, and unfit to govern. Under these circumstances, leaders and statesmen offering generous terms can form the basis for a viable peace. In this sense, the first two and the latter four notions can be in harmony with one another.

Theme for vitality and growth

Boyd is still not satisfied because the destructive element is not sufficiently balanced by an awareness of the importance of a constructive element for national survival, asserting that

> up to this point – by repeatedly adding, stripping-away, and recombining many different, yet similar, ideas and thoughts – we have examined the nature of conflict, survival, and conquest in many different ways. A review and further manipulation of the ideas and thoughts that make-up these different ways suggest that, for success over the long whole and under the most difficult conditions, one needs some unifying vision that can be used to attract the uncommitted as well as pump-up friendly resolve and drive and drain-away or subvert adversary resolve and drive.
>
> In other words, what is needed is a vision rooted in human nature so noble, so attractive that it not only attracts the uncommitted and magnifies the spirit and strength of its adherents, but also undermines the dedication and determination of any competitors or adversaries. Moreover, such a unifying notion should be so compelling that it acts as a catalyst or beacon around which to evolve those qualities that permit a collective entity or organic whole to improve its stature in the scheme of things. Put another way, we are suggesting a need for a supra-orientation or center-of-gravity that permits leaders, and other authorities, to inspire their followers and members to enthusiastically take action toward confronting and conquering all obstacles that stand in the way.[124]

Enclosed in this section Boyd again, but now from yet another angle and now at the societal level, uncovers elements that foster initiative and harmony, two among four vital elements for survival he has already introduced on page 12 of the presentation. The themes he regards as vital for success are conceptually quite similar. For instance, Boyd sees a unifying vision as yet another way to achieve implicit control. Indeed, Boyd comes full circle in his formulation of the 'theme for vitality and growth' (Figure 5.10).

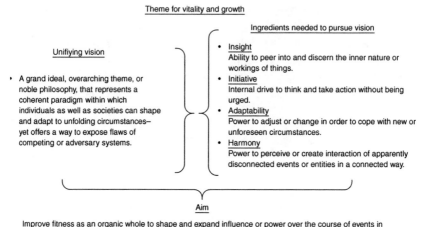

Figure 5.10 Theme for vitality and growth.

Application

Revisiting Sun Tzu, reinforcing key themes

In this section Boyd takes his audience on a tour through the early German military campaigns in Poland, the Low Countries and France and Russia. In that respect, this section resembles the previously discussed section titled 'Historical Snap-Shots'. The importance of this section, however, lies not so much in the historical analysis and illustrations. Instead, what makes this section relevant is the way he shows how military success is the result of a dialectic process of adaptation and counter-adaptation, of shaping and being shaped. He uses the Blitz–counter-Blitz dynamic to illustrate this. This seems merely an expansion of his earlier sections. However, now he ties the dynamics even more than before to the cognitive element of war. He returns to Sun Tzu to explain and re-emphasize this key argument to which he has already frequently alluded.

On the one hand, the discussion is thus a repetition of his earlier remarks on counter-Blitz but now with the following central theme: what matters at all levels of command is the cognitive impact of feints, maneuvers, attacks, retreats, threats, fire-engagements, etc. Collectively they constitute information, and this information, could reveal a pattern, and recognizing a pattern can lead the opponent to make predictions about the next steps. Consequently, the name of the game becomes one of consciously shaping the opponent's perception of the pattern of operations unfolding before him, while hiding the real picture.

Again Boyd stresses the connection between physical events and cognitive impact, and now he takes this to the logical conclusion that cognitive impact needs to be a core rationale for designing tactics, grand tactics and strategy.

Foreknowledge and judgment play central roles here. The influence of Sun Tzu is explicit not only because he includes Sun Tzu in the titles of slides 146–56, but also because he borrows heavily from Sun Tzu's *The Art of War*, with ideas such as *cheng/ch'i, the vacuous and substantial*, the idea of *formlessness and being unfathomable* echoing through.

The aim of Blitz and counter-Blitz, according to Boyd, is to 'blind side' the adversary regardless of the circumstances.[125] The 'human penchant for generating mental patterns' immediately suggests that it is important to shape the adversary's impression. Translated to the defense against a Blitz, shaping the opponent's impression is accomplished by arranging the elements of defense, as the basis to guide adversaries to form or project patterns on the environment they are facing. In other words, one should emphasize certain features so that the adversary's intelligence, recce, patrols, and other observation activity generate mental pictures of what we seem to be doing. In this sense, we cause the adversary to project a rhythm as well as a sense of or gestalt upon the environment. Naturally, Boyd tells his audience, this raises the question: How do we want our posture to appear to an adversary, i.e., what kind of mental picture do we want to generate in his mind?[126]

Designing one's defense on this basis is obviously quite a departure from the regular determinants of tactics and grand tactics, which were generally related to terrain and enemy position and strength. After literally repeating the 'things to do' for the counter-Blitz of slide 105,[127] Boyd reveals that at the strategic level the game of counter-Blitz is to:

- Shift from such an ambiguous or misleading posture into a gauntlet defense with alternative channels, sectors, or zones by thinning-out some sectors or zones in order to strengthen others.

The basic notion is to think in terms of channels, avenues and gauntlets (instead of just belts, bands and fronts) so that ambush gauntlets will naturally evolve or be set up to deal with forward as well as lateral (roll-out) thrusts of the adversary. In this way, ambush gauntlets can then be set up at any level from platoon to theater.[128]

At the tactical level one should use obstacles, delaying actions, hit-and-run attacks (note the inclusion of guerrilla tactics) and/or baited retreats in thinned-out sectors/zones together with 'shaping' and 'disruption' activities to disorient the adversary as well as to pile-up or stretch-out his maneuver. These actions should be accompanied with fire and movement (coming from one's own strengthened adjacent sectors/zones) into the flanks and/or rear of the adversary. This will slow the opponent's momentum and 'blow adversary away', or alternatively, channel the momentum. The thrust can then either be decapitated, or, in case of stretch-out, the cohesion of the thrust can be broken.[129]

The cognitive effects of these actions are what matter, and these cognitive effects will lead to an enemy response which is to some extent predictable, thus shaping the enemy's actions. As Boyd explains:

Mental picture

- Think of obstacles, delay, hit-and-run, and baited retreats together with shaping and disruption activities as Cheng or Nebenpunkte to create gaps, exposed flanks, and vulnerable rears by the pile-up/congestion or stretch-out of adversary maneuver.
- Think of Ch'i or Schwerpunkt maneuver (fire and movement) hitting unexpectedly thru gaps into adversary flank/rear, or blind-side, as a decisive stroke to pull enemy apart and roll-up his isolated remnants.[130]

A similar message lies in other related air and ground reconnaissance and offensive actions. They serve to harass and delay the enemy, to disorient him while at the same time providing information to one's own senior commanders to help them decide which sectors to thin out and which to strengthen.[131] Multiple counterstrokes, the interplay of Nebenpunkte and Schwerpunkte, disrupt the enemy offensive, force him to allow gaps and to stretch out his forces. Rapid shifts of forces can then reinforce a successful minor counter-attack into a 'super-Schwerpunkt'. Such maneuvers are effective not only because of the delay in the advance they cause but also by forcing the opponent to become 'preoccupied in overcoming the challenge posed by the Super Nebenpunkte'. Such counter-Blitz actions keep the pressure on the enemy, who now is continually forced to adapt to many abrupt and irregular changes.[132]

The general underlying idea of counter-Blitz, according to Boyd, is thus to:

> Pull adversary apart and bring about his collapse by causing him to generate or project mental images that agree neither with the faster tempo/rhythm nor with the hidden form of the transient maneuver patterns he must compete against.[133]

After a seventeen-page discussion of the German Blitz campaigns, and the successful Russian counter-Blitz, which serves to illustrate this underlying idea, Boyd arrives at the section of *Patterns of Conflict*, in which he ties the various key insights together in five pages and produces a conclusion of his view on the art of success.

Wrap Up, or coming full circle

The meaning of 'getting inside the OODA loop'

The wrap-up is a highly conceptual synthesis and reformulation of all of his previous arguments, ideas and themes. It includes direct reference to his earliest intuitive remarks as well as his last argument concerning the importance of shaping the opponent's perception. Here he abandons the division into tactical, grand tactical and strategic levels but combines them. He does not refer to attrition, maneuver or moral conflict anywhere, but merges the essence of the latter two. He attempts to strip away and recombine even further than before, to arrive at the most concise formula for explaining success and failure in conflict. In a sense the wrap-up is his way of proving he has validated the assertions he made in the first section of *Patterns of Conflict*. On slide 12 he had asserted that 'variety, rapidity, harmony and initiative seem to be the key qualities that permit one to shape and adapt to an ever-changing environment'. In the 'Wrap Up' he focuses on these four elements in particular to arrive at the most concise conceptualization of 'The Art of Success'. According to Boyd, the message thus far is that:[134]

- He who is willing and able to take the <u>initiative</u> to exploit <u>variety</u>, <u>rapidity</u>, and <u>harmony</u> – as basis to create as well as adapt to the more indistinct – more irregular – quicker changes of rhythm and pattern, yet shape focus and direction of effort – survives and dominates.
  or contrariwise
- He who is unwilling or unable to take the <u>initiative</u> to exploit <u>variety</u>, <u>rapidity</u>, and <u>harmony</u> . . . goes under or survives to be dominated.

The <u>Game</u> is to:

- Create tangles of threatening and/or non-threatening events/efforts as well as repeatedly generate mismatches between those events/efforts adversary observes or imagines (Cheng/Nebenpunkte) and those he must react to (Ch'i/Schwerpunkt)
  as basis to
- Penetrate adversary organism to sever his moral bonds, disorient his mental images, disrupt his operations, and overload his system, as well as subvert, shatter, seize or otherwise subdue those moral-mental-physical bastions, connections, or activities that he depends upon
  thereby
- Pull adversary apart, produce paralysis, and collapse his will to resist.

The way to accomplish this, the <u>how</u> to, in most abstract terms is to:

- Get inside adversary observation-orientation-decision-action loops (at all levels) by being more subtle, more indistinct, more irregular, and quicker – yet appear to be otherwise.[135]

Boyd then adds a short but new discussion on the implications of these observations, in particular how they relate to variety, rapidity, harmony and initiative. In this discussion he inserts Sun Tzu's idea of fluidity, an important theme from his essay *Destruction and Creation*, the element of organizational complexity as well as the discussion above on pattern recognition. Boyd asserts that:[136]

- In a <u>tactical sense</u>, these multidimensional interactions suggest a <u>spontaneous</u>, <u>synthetic/creative</u>, and <u>flowing</u> action/counteraction operation, rather than a <u>step-by-step</u>, <u>analytical/logical</u>, and <u>discrete</u> move/countermove game.

- in accepting this idea we must admit that increased unit complexity (with magnified mental and physical task loadings) <u>does not</u> enhance the spontaneous synthetic/creative operation. Rather, it constrains the opportunity for these <u>timely</u> actions/counteractions.
  or put in another way
- Complexity (technical, organizational, operational, etc.) causes commanders and subordinates alike to be captured by their own internal dynamics or interactions – hence they cannot adapt to rapidly changing external (or even internal) circumstances.

- In a <u>strategic sense</u>, these interactions suggest we need a <u>variety </u>of possibilities as well as the <u>rapidity</u> to implement and shift among them. Why?

  - Ability to <u>simultaneously</u> and <u>sequentially</u> generate <u>many different</u> possibilities as well as <u>rapidly</u> implement and shift among them permits one to repeatedly generate mismatches between events/efforts adversary observes or imagines and those he must respond to (to survive).
  - Without a <u>variety</u> of possibilities adversary is given the opportunity to read as well as adapt to events and efforts as they unfold.

Recombining these, in particular the comment on organizational complexity, and other comments and insights (including the Clausewitzian concept of friction) related to the four elements of variety/rapidity/harmony/initiative, Boyd shows what and how they contribute to victory by connecting them to the ability to adapt. He asserts that '<u>Variety </u>and <u>rapidity</u> allow one to magnify the adversary's friction, hence to stretch-out his time to respond. <u>Harmony</u> and <u>initiative</u> stand and work on the opposite side by diminishing one's own friction, hence compressing one's own time to exploit variety/rapidity in a directed way'. Altogether <u>variety/rapidity/harmony/initiative</u> enable one to:

> Operate inside adversary's observation-orientation-decision-action loops to enmesh adversary in a world of uncertainty, doubt, mistrust, confusion, disorder, fear, panic, chaos,... and/or fold adversary back inside himself so that he cannot cope with events/efforts as they unfold.

Simultaneously, so Boyd continues, 'by repeatedly rolling-thru OODA loops while appealing to and making use of the ideas embodied in 'Grand Strategy' and 'Theme for Vitality and Growth', we can evolve and exploit <u>variety/ rapidity/harmony/initiative</u> as a basis to:

> Shape or influence events so that we not only amplify our spirit and strength (while isolating our adversaries and undermining their resolve and drive) but also influence the uncommitted or potential adversaries so that they are drawn toward our philosophy and are empathetic toward our success.[137]

The Art of Success

Finally, Boyd arrives at his 'nutshell' formulation of what constitutes 'The Art of Success'. The two sentences that convey this view do not make a convincing assertion when read in isolation. Indeed, they may sound simplistic. However, when read in the context of the discourse he has had so far with his audience, the various exercises in abstraction, in stripping away and recombining, this final effort at getting to the essence of things contains a world of meaning, theories, theorists, schools of thought and concepts. Every word has been discussed before and has become a signifier of a train of thought. And in these few words Boyd both concludes and captures a discussion that spans 2,500 years of military history and strategic theory. In a few conceptually rich but very abstract words, he manages to combine in a logically connected way the 'things to do' at the tactical, grand tactical, the strategic and grand strategic levels, themes from moral and maneuver conflict and the themes for vitality and growth and for disintegration and collapse. Boyd's advice for success is to:[138]

The Art of Success
- Appear to be an unsolvable cryptogram while operating in a directed way to penetrate adversary vulnerabilities and weaknesses in order to isolate him from his allies, pull him apart, and collapse his will to resist;
yet
- Shape or influence events so that we not only magnify our spirit and strength but also influence potential adversaries as well as the uncommitted so that they are drawn toward our philosophy and are empathetic toward our success.

The first sentence is an advice to remain, in the words of Sun Tzu, unfathomable to the enemy, yet operate coherently in several levels of war and across different dimensions. While this part includes physical actions, the second sentence exclusively refers to the moral, ideological and political aspects of strategy.

In the Epilogue Boyd compares his arguments with the familiar principles of war. These principles suggest certainty and seem like a checklist for success. This makes them popular. To cater for those who favor a concise list of 'to do's', Boyd offers a list that captures in a sufficient way his thoughts, yet cannot be construed as 'principles'. They span the physical, temporal and the cognitive dimensions. They deal with adaptability and include the view of the enemy as an adaptive organism. Instead of principles, Boyd refers to them as:[139]

Appropriate Bits and Pieces
- Compress own time and stretch-out adversary time.
- Generate unequal distributions as basis to focus moral-mental-physical efforts for local superiority and decisive leverage.
- Diminish own friction (or entropy) and magnify adversary friction (or entropy).

- Operate inside adversary's observation-orientation-decision-action loops or get inside his mind-time-space.
- Penetrate adversary organisms and bring about his collapse.
- Amplify our spirit and strength, drain-away adversaries' and attract the uncommitted.

The 'Central Theme', Boyd concludes his massive search for the *Patterns of Conflict*, lies in these final words:

> Evolve and exploit insight/initiative/adaptability/harmony together with a unifying vision, via a grand ideal or an overarching theme or a noble philosophy, as basis to:
>
> - Shape or influence events so that we not only amplify our spirit and strength but also influence the uncommitted or potential adversaries so that they are drawn toward our philosophy and are empathetic toward our success,
>   Yet be able to
> - Operate inside adversary's observation-orientation-decision-action loops or get inside his mind-time-space as basis to:
> - Penetrate adversary's moral-mental-physical being in order to isolate him from his allies, pull him apart, and collapse his will to resist.

Concluding words

In *Patterns of Conflict* Boyd has thus offered his audience a new look at military history. With the conceptual lenses science offered him, with uncertainty as the key problem organisms and organizations have to surmount, he sheds new light on the dynamics of war. He has introduced familiar and some new case studies and theories. In particular, in the second half of the presentation Boyd makes a shift in level of abstraction. Applying the process of destruction and creation to his investigation, he uncovers underlying dynamics of each category of warfare and expresses these in an increasingly abstract and conceptual way. It implicitly manifests an increasing application of systems-theoretical perspectives. Expressed within the context of adaptation, he shows conceptual similarities between very distinct modes of warfare. Gradually he unfolds a novel conceptualization of tactics, grand tactics, strategy and grand strategy that revolves around the process of adaptation in which open, complex adaptive systems are constantly engaged in. The following presentations expand upon the arguments presented here.

6   Exploration and refinement

Introduction

This chapter presents Boyd's other five briefings. These can be considered an exercise in exploration and refinement of ideas presented in the essay and *Patterns of Conflict*. In the presentation titled *Organic Design for Command and Control* Boyd continues on the arguments he laid out in *Patterns*, but now focusing on the implicit arrangements that permit cooperation in complex, competitive, fast-moving situations. *The Strategic Game of ? and ?* emphasizes the mental twists and turns we undertake to surface appropriate schemes or designs for realizing our aims or purposes. It aims to uncover even more fundamental abstract dynamics than he has presented in *Patterns*. In *Revelation* Boyd makes visible the metaphorical message that flows from the *Discourse*. It is a restatement of the message of *Destruction and Creation*, which again he explores in detail and in less philosophical terms in *The Conceptual Spiral*. In the final presentation, *The Essence of Winning and Losing*, Boyd synthesizes for the last time in even more condensed form the core messages in a coherent comprehensive framework. In just a few pages and a graphic rendering of the OODA loop, he manages to merge Polanyi, Kuhn, Popper, Gell-Mann, Sun Tzu and Liddell Hart.

Organic Design for Command and Control

Introduction

Only open systems can adapt adequately to change, so an organism needs to maintain interaction with its environment if it is to survive, so Boyd had already argued. In military organizations this is the remit of the command and control system. In *Organic Design for Command and Control*, he develops the parameters for an adequate command and control concept. The briefing reflects insights of *Patterns of Conflict*, in particular from the sections on Blitzkrieg and maneuver conflict, and of several studies on leadership, command and small unit cohesion. The bibliography of *Patterns of Conflict* of December 1986 lists studies on generals Bonaparte, Grant, Lee, Patton, Genghis Khan, Guderian, the Prussian general staff system, German generalship during World War II, tactical genius, morale, several case studies on command and control and autobiographical works of generals Erwin Rommel and Heinz Guderian.[1]

His inspiration also came in part from some fiascos he had witnessed in the US armed forces exercises and operations, such as the failed evacuation operation Desert I in Iran. Reflecting the agenda of the Military Reform Movement, he notes in his introduction that normal 'institutional response to such failures is more and better sensors, more communications, more and better display devices, more satellites, more and better fusion centers, etc. – all tied into one giant fully informed, fully capable command and control system. This way of thinking emphasizes hardware as the solution'.[2] Boyd's approach is process oriented, or in his words, 'I think there is a different way, a way that emphasizes the implicit nature of human beings. In this sense, the following discussion will uncover what we mean by both implicit nature and organic design'.[3]

Criteria for command and control

He starts out with providing some guiding thoughts as the background for the rest of his argument, much as he had done in the first pages of *Patterns of Conflict*, effectively proposing a set of criteria around which a command and control philosophy must be designed. He asserts that we:

- Need <u>insight and vision</u> to unveil adversary plans and actions as well as 'foresee' own goals and appropriate plans and actions.
- Need <u>focus and direction</u> to achieve some goal or aim.
- Need <u>adaptability</u>, to cope with uncertain and ever-changing circumstances.
- Need <u>security</u>, to remain unpredictable.[4]

The rationale for these criteria is also offered and it is closely related to the two variants of the set of four elements he had introduced in *Patterns of Conflict*:

- variety/rapidity/harmony/initiative (*Patterns of Conflict*, p. 12);
- insight/initiative/adaptability/harmony (*Patterns of Conflict*, p. 185).

As Boyd explains,

> without insight and vision there can be no orientation to deal with both <u>present</u> and <u>future</u>. Without focus and direction, implied or explicit, there can be neither <u>harmony</u> of effort nor <u>initiative</u> for vigorous effort. Adaptability implies <u>variety</u> and <u>rapidity</u>. Without variety and rapidity one can neither be unpredictable nor cope with changing and unforeseen circumstances. Without security one becomes predictable, hence one loses the benefits of the above.[5]

From this basis, Boyd sets out to develop a normative view on a design for command and control. As in *Patterns of Conflict*, he starts with some 'samples from historical environment', offering nine citations from nine practitioners, including from himself (see Box 6.1):[6]

Sun Tzu (around 400 BC)
Probe enemy strength to unmask his strengths, weaknesses, patterns of movement and intentions. Shape enemy's perception of world to manipulate/undermine his plans and actions. Employ Cheng/Ch'I maneuvers to quickly and unexpectedly hurl strength against weaknesses.

Bourcet (1764–71)
A plan ought to have several branches ... One should ... mislead the enemy and make him imagine that the main effort is coming at some other part. And ... one must be ready to profit by a second or third branch of the plan without giving one's enemy time to consider it.

Napoleon (early 1800s)
Strategy is the art of making use of time and space. I am less chary of the latter than the former. Space we can recover, time never. I may lose a battle, but I shall never lose a minute. The whole art of war consists in a well-reasoned and circumspect defensive, followed by rapid and audacious attack.

Clausewitz (1832)
Friction (which includes the interaction of many factors, such as uncertainty, psychological/moral forces and effects, etc.) impedes activity. Friction is the only concept that more or less corresponds to the factors that distinguish

real war from war on paper. In this sense, friction represents the climate or atmosphere of war.

Jomini (1836)
By free and rapid movements carry bulk of the forces (successively) against fractions of the enemy.

N.B. Forrest (1860s)
Git thar the fustest with the mostest.

Blumentritt (1947)
The entire operational and tactical leadership method hinged upon ... rapid concise assessment of situations, ... and quick decision and quick execution, on the principle: each minute ahead of the enemy is an advantage.

Balck (1980)
Emphasis upon creation of implicit connections or bonds based upon trust, not mistrust, that permit wide freedom for subordinates to exercise imagination and initiative – yet harmonize within intent of superior commanders. Benefit: internal simplicity that permits rapid adaptability.

Yours truly
Operate inside adversary's observation-orientation-decision-action loops to enmesh adversary in a world of uncertainty, doubt, mistrust, confusion, disorder, fear, panic, chaos ... and/or fold adversary back inside himself so that he cannot cope with events/efforts as they unfold.

Box 6.1 Scene setter for command and control.

The <u>key points</u> Boyd derives from these quotations are that (1) the atmosphere of war is friction; (2) friction is generated and magnified by menace, ambiguity, deception, rapidity, uncertainty, mistrust, etc.; (3) friction is diminished by implicit understanding, trust, cooperation, simplicity, focus, etc.; and (4) in this sense, variety and rapidity tend to magnify friction, while harmony and initiative tend to diminish friction.[7] In other words, without harmony and initiative, variety and rapidity lead to confusion and disorder. Harmony and initiative without variety and rapidity lead to rigid uniformity and predictability and ultimately to non-adaptability. The problem for any command concept then becomes to find an answer to the question: How to generate harmony/initiative so that one can exploit variety/rapidity? Boyd comments on that question by suggesting that we must uncover those <u>interactions</u> that foster harmony and initiative yet do not destroy variety and rapidity.[8]

The big O: orientation

The ensuing discussion is quintessential for understanding Boyd, for it leads him to the key concept of Orientation. Although he does not explain it on paper explicitly, his focus on interactions lies in their function: interactions in various forms are the glue that binds the various nodes of a social system together. This becomes (albeit not self-) evident in the contrasting of positive and negative features of activities and linkages, which he apparently introduces for their emotive and associative effect. Positively valued activities for instance are radio transmission *and* reception, conversation, writing and teamwork. Positively valued features of linkages are common frequencies, common language, correlation among multiple sources and harmony of different efforts.[9] If this may not immediately appear to lead to a deeper understanding of, or to the rationale for focusing on interactions, the list of *negatively valued features* does (Box 6.2):[10]

This produces the insight that:

> interactions represent a <u>many-sided implicit cross-referencing process of projection, empathy, correlation, and rejection.</u>[11]

Activities	Linkages
• Compartmentation	• Disconnected bits and pieces
• Non-cooperative centers of gravity	• Islands of disconnected effort
• Alienation	• Disconnected from other humans
• Non-adaptive	• Disconnected from environment
• Fixed recipe	• Disconnected from environment, but connected to some formality

Box 6.2 Negatively valued features of linkages.

This is a deceptively simple description. The carefully chosen words, and the few examples which precede it, mask a spectrum of insights and theories. In the collision of ideas and hypothesis (projection) with reality contained within this description we find the Popperian process of conjecture and refutation. In its human elements, this description incorporates Polanyi's vision of knowing, while the aspect of the environment suggests systems-theoretical and neo-Darwinist roots, while it is tempting to see parallels with Lyotard and Derrida. All resurface in his next move.

This insight into the nature of interactions is the first step toward a definition of orientation. In his familiar way Boyd suggests to the audience that he suspects that this insight is in some way related to orientation, for:

> Orientation, <u>seen as a result</u>, represents images, views, or impressions of the world shaped by <u>genetic heritage</u>, <u>cultural tradition</u>, <u>previous experiences</u>, and <u>unfolding circumstances</u>.

Thus, in a few words, Boyd brings together synonyms for mental modules, schemata, memes, and tacit knowledge in a dynamic relation with the environment. He explains the sources of images, views or impressions, i.e. the conceptual lenses for observation. And the following step brings together interaction and this description of the result of orientation:[12]

> Orientation is <u>an interactive process</u> of <u>many sided implicit cross-referencing projections, empathies, correlations, and rejections</u> that is <u>shaped by</u> and <u>shapes</u> the interplay of <u>genetic heritage, cultural tradition, previous experiences</u> and <u>unfolding circumstances</u>.

Boyd would capture this dynamic in the OODA loop graphic. Again he is master of synthesis. He indicates that orientation is a dynamic process which results in views, images and impressions. This process is (and should be) continuous and is constituted by the development and maintenance of interactions of various kinds with the environment. The interactions are however also subject to modification, as much as the views, images and impressions. A long-term and rather immutable formative factor shaping this process is genetic heritage. A medium-term factor is culture, while a short term factor in shaping ideas and interactions is constituted by previous experiences. He offers his own <u>illumination</u>:[13]

> Orientation is the Schwerpunkt. It shapes the way we interact with the environment – hence orientation shapes the way we <u>observe</u>, the way we <u>decide</u>, the way we <u>act</u>.

In this sense

> Orientation shapes the character of <u>present</u> observation-orientation-decision-action loops – while these present loops shape the character of <u>future</u> orientation.

So from a discussion on the pervasive element of friction and the solution offered by harmony and initiative, from the stated need for adaptability, focus, direction, insight and vision, he has developed the argument that orientation is the center of gravity for command and control, the key factor – and variable – that enables or hinders generating harmony and initiative so that one can or cannot exploit variety/rapidity. From this point on, Boyd proceeds to explore the implications of this insight.

Implicit communication and organizational heat-death

The immediate implication of putting orientation center-stage for structuring one's own command set-up is quite obvious. As Boyd asserts, 'we need to create mental images, views, or impressions, hence patterns that match with activity of [the] world'. That this almost sounds like a truism, should not detract from the one new relevant element Boyd introduces: patterns (Boyd even suggests that patterns is equivalent to orientation). The reference to the essay is obvious, but his audience would most likely not be familiar with it. In this manner he managed to introduce an epistemological theme in a very pragmatic setting. Conversely, he continues, 'we need to deny [the] adversary the possibility of uncovering or discerning patterns that match our activity, or other aspects of reality in the world'.[14] For 'patterns (hence orientation), right or wrong or lack thereof, suggest ability or inability to conduct many-sided implicit cross-references'.

The next obvious issue is thus one of turning theory into practice: 'how do we set-up and take advantage of the many-sided implicit cross-referencing process of projection, empathy, correlation, rejection that make appropriate orientation possible?'[15] As alluded to before, it is tempting to suggest that the answer Boyd derived from the combination of Polanyi's *Knowing and Being*, Bronowski's *The Identity of Man* and various systems-theoretical works. Conceptually, Boyd asserts, it comes from ensuring variety in observation, i.e. variety in mental modules or schemata, within the organization, from conducting observation collectively and from communicating the perceptions. This will in turn lead to a shared, but enriched, understanding. Or in Boyd's words, the message is to

> expose individuals, with different skills and abilities, against a variety of situations – whereby each individual can observe and orient himself simultaneously to the others and to the variety of changing situations.

The reason is that 'in such an environment, a harmony, or focus and direction, in operations is created by the bonds of implicit communications and trust that evolve as a consequence of the similar mental images or impressions each individual creates and commits to memory by repeatedly sharing the same variety of experience in the same way'. The pay-off of implicit communications and trust which is created, lies in the temporal dimension; the command and control process will occur at an accelerated pace and, second, in an increase in the level of initiative that can be generated now that lower-level units can be given wide latitude. The pay-off is 'a command and control system, whose secret lies in what's unstated or not communicated to one another (in an explicit sense) – in order to exploit lower-level initiative yet realize higher-level intent, thereby diminish friction and compress time, hence gain both quickness and security'.[16]

To reinforce his point, Boyd addresses the consequences if one 'cannot establish these implicit connections or bonds – via similar mental images or impressions – as basis to cope with a many-sided uncertain and everchanging environment'.[17] For this exploration, Boyd explains that the previous discussion assumed interaction with both the <u>external</u> and <u>internal</u> environment. Rephrasing the question then becomes what would happen if a command and control system hinders interaction with the <u>external</u> world. According to Boyd, this implies a focus inward, rather than outward.[18] This brings him back to Darwin, Gödel, Heisenberg and the Second Law of Thermodynamics.

From Darwin, Boyd asserts once more, we observe that 'the environment selects', and this process is determined by the 'ability or inability to interact and adapt to exigencies of environment'. According to the Gödel Proof, the Heisenberg Uncertainty Principle and the Second Law of Thermodynamics, 'one cannot determine the character or nature of a system within itself, moreover, attempts to do so lead to confusion and disorder [. . .] because in the real world the environment intrudes'. Marrying these ideas to Clausewitz, Boyd suggests that:

> He who can generate many non-cooperative centers of gravity magnifies friction. Why? Many non-cooperative centers of gravity within a system restrict interaction and adaptability of system with its surroundings, thereby leading to a focus inward (i.e., within itself), which in turn generates confusion and disorder, which impedes vigorous or directed activity, hence, by definition, magnifies friction or entropy.[19]

In effect, Boyd argues that restricting interaction, and loss of subsystem cohesion will lead to the organizational equivalent of the Second Law of Thermodynamics. This key insight is reinforced in a sequence of statements:[20]

- Any command and control system that forces adherents to look inward, leads to dissolution/disintegration (i.e., system becomes unglued).
- <u>Without the implicit bonds or connections</u>, associated with similar images or impressions, there can be <u>neither harmony nor individual initiative</u> within a collective entity, therefore, <u>no way</u> that such an organic whole can stay together and cope with a many-sided uncertain and ever-changing environment.
- <u>Without implicit bonds or connections</u>, we magnify friction, produce paralysis and get system collapse.

Having shown what can happen to an enemy organization when it cannot recognize patterns, when it cannot interact with the environment, when units become isolated from their environment and unglued from each other, when they lack shared images, he returns to the meaning of all this for one's own organization. The first <u>insight</u> is that

> the key idea is to emphasize <u>implicit</u> over explicit in order to gain a favorable mismatch in <u>friction</u> and <u>time</u> (i.e., ours lower than any adversary) for superiority in shaping and adapting to circumstances.[21]

Second, Boyd asserts that one should suppress the tendency to build up explicit internal arrangements that hinder interaction with the external world. Instead, he argues for arranging a setting and the circumstances so that leaders and subordinates alike are given the opportunity to continuously interact with the external environment, and with each other, in order to more quickly make many-sided implicit cross-referencing projections, empathies, correlations and rejections as well as create the similar images or impressions, hence a similar implicit orientation, needed to form an organic whole.[22]

In effect, Boyd argues that all subsystems of an organization should be open systems, that is, systems with sufficient ability and authority to observe and interact with their respective environment, while at the same time having lateral and vertical linkages with other subsystems and higher directing entities. Such an arrangement is predicated upon the presence of a similar implicit orientation. The benefits of a similar implicit orientation for commander and subordinates alike, however, are obvious for Boyd as it will allow them to:

- Diminish their friction and reduce time, thereby permit them to:
- Exploit variety/rapidity while maintaining harmony/initiative, thereby permit them to:
- Get inside adversary's OODA loops, thereby:
- Magnify adversary's friction and stretch-out his time (for a favorable mismatch in friction and time), thereby:
- Deny adversary the opportunity to cope with events/efforts as they unfold.

Circling back to the beginning, to the set of criteria Boyd had stipulated for a 'first rate command and control system', Boyd concludes that it is <u>implicit orientation</u> which shapes the character of insight and vision, focus and direction, adaptability, and security. Therefore, a command and control system, any design or related operational methods should play to and expand, not play down and diminish, <u>implicit orientation</u>.[23] As he states, 'up to this point we have shown orientation as being a critical element in command and control – implying that without orientation there is no command and control worthy of the name. Very nice, but simply stated, what does this comment and everything else we've discussed so far tell us about command and control?'[24] He takes his audience by the hand by offering the following important <u>illumination</u>:[25]

- The process of observation-orientation-decision-action represents what takes place during the command and control process – which means that the OODA loop can be thought of as being the C&C loop.
- The second O, orientation – as the repository of our genetic heritage, cultural tradition, and previous experiences – is the most important part of the OODA loop since it shapes the way we observe, the way we decide, the way we act.
  Implication
- Operating inside adversary's OODA loop means the same things as operating inside adversary's C&C loop.

Redefining command and control

Thus far one could argue that Boyd has addressed the organic part of the title of the presentation. He has developed several ideas about the command and control process by taking a systems view, or rather a complex adaptive systems view. Although clear and persuasive, these ideas are still rather conceptual and general. So Boyd now makes his way toward the practical side of effective command and control, which will lead him to a redefinition of command and control and a focus on the essence of leadership.

His starting point, and the normative framework, is clearly the previous discussion on a first-rate command and control system. Indeed, his views on effective command and control aim to effectuate such a system. And again, he seeks inspiration, if not substantiation, in some historical snapshots he had already used in *Patterns of Conflict*. He refers among others to Napoleon's use of staff officers for personal reconnaissance, von Moltke's message directives of few words and the contrasting British approach of tight control during the Battle of the Somme in 1916.[26] But he leans in particular, and explicitly, on Martin van Creveld's study *Command in War* to gain a 'richer view'. Boyd includes an entire page from van Creveld's book that deals with the Israeli command set-up during the June 1967 War, an example which according to Boyd reveals 'our old friend – the many sided implicit cross-referencing process of projection, empathy, correlation, and rejection'.[27] In the June 1967 War, Boyd cites van Creveld,[28]

> General Yashayahu Gavish spent most of his time either 'accompanying' units down to brigade level – by which, according to his own definition, he meant staying at that unit's command post and observing developments at first hand – or else helicoptering from one unit to another; again, in his own words, 'there is no alternative to looking into a subordinate's eyes, listening to his tone of voice'. Other sources of information at his disposal included the usual reporting systems; a radio network linking him with three divisional commanders, which also served to link those commanders with each other; a signal staff whose task it was to listen in to the divisional communications networks, working around the clock and reporting to Gavish in

writing; messages passed from the rear, i.e., from General Headquarters in Tel Aviv, linked to Gavish by 'private' radiotelephone circuit; and the results of air reconnaissance forwarded by the Air Force and processed by Rear Headquarters. Gavish did not depend on these sources exclusively, however; not only did he spend some time personally listening in to the radio networks of subordinate units (on one occasion, Gavish says, he was thereby able to correct an entirely false impression of the battle being formed at Brigadier Gonen's headquarters) but he also had a 'directed tele-scope' in the form of elements of his staff, mounted on half tracks, follow-ing in the wake of the two northernmost divisions and constantly reporting on developments.

From this illustration, and from previous discussions here and in *Patterns of Conflict*, Boyd distills the <u>Epitome of Command and Control</u>, which is directly related to the theme of adaptability:[29]

<u>Nature</u>
- Command and control must permit one to direct and shape what is to be done as well as permit one to modify that direction and shaping by assess-ing what is being done.

<u>What does this mean?</u>
- Command must give direction in terms of what is to be done in a clear unambiguous way. In this sense, command must interact with system to shape the character or nature of that system in order to realize what is to be done;
  Whereas
- Control must provide assessment of what is being done also in a clear unambiguous way. In this sense, control must not interact nor interfere with system but must ascertain (not shape) the character/nature of what is being done.

<u>Implication</u>
- Direction and shaping, hence 'command', should be evident while assess-ment and ascertainment, hence 'control', should be invisible and should not interfere – otherwise 'command and control' does not exist as an effective means to improve our fitness to shape and cope with unfolding circum-stances.

This differs from traditional views on the meaning of command and control (C&C), and Boyd wants to emphasize just that (and here he is referring to his opening statements of the presentation on the reigning command and control philosophy and associated problems within the US armed forces at the time). In fact, he continues to reconceptualize C&C, exposing his audience to a subtle word game to arrive at a description of C&C with a much higher emotive and cognitive association.

The traditional definitions, Boyd explains, mean to direct, order, or compel while control means to regulate, restrain, or hold to a certain standard as well as to direct or command. Thus, the description offered above is different than the kind that is being applied. In this sense, the C&C he is speaking of seems, in his words, 'more closely aligned to leadership (rather than command) and to some kind of monitoring ability (rather than control) that permits leadership to be effective'. In other word, he continues,

> leadership with monitoring, rather than C&C, seems to be a better way to cope with the multi-faceted aspects of uncertainty, change, and stress. On the other hand, monitoring, per se, does not appear to be an adequate substitute for control. Instead, after some sorting and reflection, the idea of appreciation seems better. [. . .] First of all, appreciation includes the recognition of worth or value and the idea of clear perception as well as the ability to monitor. Moreover, next, it is difficult to believe that leadership can even exist without appreciation. Pulling these threads together suggests appreciation and leadership offer more appropriate and richer means than C&C for shaping and adapting to circumstances'.[30]

This discussion sheds another light on the epitome of C&C, laid out before. In a new set of definitions Boyd not only replaces command and control by appreciation and leadership, he also subtly inserts some words which emphasize the cognitive character of the process (those words are printed below in italics to show the differences clearly). These changes and additions are quite relevant for they lead to a description which is much less directive in nature and much more in line with Boyd's argument about the value of trust, implicit control, shared orientation, etc., he developed here and in *Patterns of Conflict*. Underlying this change is the idea that initiative will not be fostered by top–down, directive command and control system. Indeed, after the new conceptualization of C&C, Boyd states that C&C represents a top–down mentality applied in a rigid or mechanical (or electrical way) that ignores as well as stifles the implicit nature of human beings to deal with uncertainty, change and stress (examples: The Battle of the Somme, Evacuation of Saigon, Mayaguez Affair, Desert I, Nifty-Nugget [. . .]).[31]

Appreciation and Leadership:[32]
Nature
- *Appreciation and leadership* permit one to *discern*, direct and shape what is to be done as well as permit one to modify that direction and shaping by assessing what is being done *or about to be done (by friendlies as well as adversaries).*

What does this mean?
- *Leadership* must give direction in terms of what is to be done in a clear unambiguous way. In this sense, leadership must interact with system to shape the character or nature of that system in order to realize what is to be done.

whereas

- *Appreciation*, as part of leadership, must provide assessment of what is being done in a clear unambiguous way. In this sense, appreciation must not interact nor interfere with system but must *discern* (not shape) the character/nature of what is being done or about to be done;

Implication

- Assessment and discernment should be invisible and should not interfere with operations while direction and shaping should be evident to system – otherwise appreciation and leadership do not exist as an effective means to improve our fitness to shape and cope with unfolding circumstances.

To show the difference between C&C and Appreciation and Leadership once more and quite clearly, Boyd finalizes his presentation with a new set of definitions (Box 6.3).[33]

Subsequently Boyd concludes that the title 'organic design for command and control is not appropriate'. Instead, 'the following title more clearly reflects the spirit and content of this presentation: Appreciation and Leadership'.[34]

- Command
  Refers to the ability to direct, order, compel with or without authority or power.
- Control
  Means to have power or authority to regulate, restrain, verify (usually against some standard), direct or command. Comes from medieval Latin contrarotulus, a 'counter roll' or checklist (contra, against plus rotulus, list).

- Understanding
  Means to comprehend the import or meaning of something.
- Monitoring
  Refers to the process that permits one to oversee, listen, observe, or keep track of as well as to advise, warn, or admonish.
- Appreciation
  Refers to the recognition of worth or value, clear perception, understanding, comprehension, or discernment, etc.
- Leadership
  Implies the art of inspiring people to cooperate and enthusiastically take action toward the achievement of uncommon goals.

Box 6.3 Contrast of command and control, and appreciation and leadership.

The Strategic Game of ? and ?

Introduction

Although at places highly conceptual, *Patterns of Conflict* and *Organic Design for Command and Control* are in essence about military matters at the operational level. The historical examples he uses and the concepts he develops find their basis in operational art. He looks for patterns that produced success in military operations and he tries to distill some suggestions for future application. Boyd aims to develop and teach ideas with which a commander can improve his operational art. In particular in *Organic Design for Command and Control*, he stays close to German Blitz doctrine.

In his last briefing of *The Green Book – The Strategic Game of ? and ?* – he draws several of his findings of the other briefings together and applies it to the (grand-) strategic level, or rather, Boyd here develops a general strategic principle. He climbs one step higher in the level of decision making. But perhaps more importantly, he climbs to yet another higher level of abstraction. In this briefing he aims to formulate in even more general terms what lies at the heart of a strategic encounter with an opponent. What is the activity that one should be engaged in exactly? This briefing contains a search for what strategy is about, that is what the question marks stand for in the title.[35]

It is in a sense a similar exercise to the previous two presentations, and he develops quite similar arguments, but now coming from somewhat different angles with a focus on one specific question. Even more than the other two, this presentation bears the stamp of his widening frame of reference. Here we hardly see any military history, and all the more reference to brain research, complexity theory, anthropology and systems theory (in a way the entire presentation forms yet another exposé on the nature of open systems and the need for interaction with the environment). We find here an elaboration in particular on the set of definitions – or rather the list of 'to do's' he developed in *Patterns of Conflict* about tactics, grand tactics, strategy and grand strategy. He adds also several themes and arguments from *Organic Design* (and this makes it imperative to follow Boyd's order of the presentations). He also revisits a theme from the essay *Destruction and Creation*, highlighting again the importance of the combination of analysis and synthesis as a mode of thinking.

But this presentation is not merely a restatement of earlier arguments. Rather, it builds upon them – indeed, without the previous presentations, this one would be quite hard to understand – but then Boyd carries them to their logical abstract and general conclusion and makes previous themes and arguments more explicit. It highlights what Boyd really considers the essence of strategy and strategic behavior. Moreover, compared to *Patterns of Conflict*, this presentation sheds more light on the three components of war: the moral, the mental and the physical component.

It consists of fifty-nine pages divided in four sections. The first ten pages dwell on the importance of obtaining and applying multiple perspectives, and the powers of synthesis. This forms the argument that to understand strategy (as in military strategy, in which his prime audience is most interested) we need to look beyond familiar categorizations, theories, interpretations, and instead must look at strategic behavior in general. Boyd applies this in the second section, in which he addresses again the question of survival. The answer comes from a sixteen-page broad survey of insights from various sources, derived from studies of a variety of organisms. The survey leads to a short 'condensation to essential elements'. These generic elements are then put in a 'strategic context'. This constitutes a repeating rhetorical *pas de deux* of question and illumination, and climaxes after thirty pages in yet another formulation of 'the art of success', one that differs in some important ways from the formulation he offered in *Patterns of Conflict*. Not yet content, he applies the message he wants to get across in an example. He concludes with a slide which answers the four questions he offers as his outline at the beginning of *Strategic Game of ? and ?*.[36]

Approach, or building snowmobiles

The <u>outline</u> is as follows:[37]

- What is Strategy?
- What is the aim or purpose of strategy?
- What is the central theme and what are the key ideas that underlie strategy?
- How do we play to this theme and activate these ideas?

Boyd wants to reminds his audience of the importance of combining both analysis *and* synthesis and the relevance of continuously generating mental images. This has two reasons, one of which was discussed before in his essay. Here it also serves a different purpose. Without a conviction that this combination is indeed a useful approach for increasing knowledge, the following section – the broad survey – of this presentation does not make much sense. But if you *are* convinced, the broad survey will lead you to novel and valuable insights, and the argument he builds upon the broad survey will be considered valid, even when Boyd links the study of strategy to the study of Alzheimer's disease.

This time he asks his audience to join him in a mental exercise. As Boyd states,

> Imagine that you are on a ski slope with other skiers [. . .]. Imagine that you are in Florida riding in an outboard motorboat, maybe even towing water-skiers. Imagine that you are riding a bicycle on a nice spring day. Imagine that you are a parent taking your son to a department store and that you notice he is fascinated by the toy tractors or tanks with rubber caterpillar treads'.[38]
>
> Now imagine that you pull the ski's off but you are still on the ski slope. Imagine also that you remove the outboard motor from the motor boat, and you are not longer in Florida. And from the bicycle you remove the handle-

bar and discard the rest of the bike. Finally, you take off the rubber treads from the toy tractor or tanks. This leaves only the following separate pieces: skis, outboard motor, handlebars and rubber treads.

However, he challenges his audience, what emerges when you pull all this together?[39]

SNOWMOBILE

So he moves from Polanyi to snowmobiles. The message is obvious and a restatement of the one he also advanced in *Organic Design*: 'To discern what is going on we must interact in a variety of ways with our environment. We must be able to examine the world from a number of perspectives so that we can generate mental images or impressions that correspond to that world.' This serves as the introduction to the general survey, for Boyd 'will use this scheme of pulling things apart (analysis) and putting them back together (synthesis) in new combinations to find how apparently unrelated ideas and actions can be related to one another'.[40] And indeed, he does.

General survey

In this section his interest in science becomes readily apparent. According to Boyd, the answer about the nature of the question marks (i.e. the essence of strategy) comes from examining seven different disciplines or activities:[41]

- Mathematical Logic
- Physics
- Thermodynamics
- Biology
- Psychology
- Anthropology
- Conflict

To begin, he very briefly restates the point of departure with which he began *Patterns of Conflict*:[42]

Human Nature
Goal
- Survive, survive on own terms, or improve our capacity for independent action.

> The competition for limited
> resources to satisfy these
> desires may force one to

- Diminish adversary's capacity for independent action, or deny him the opportunity to survive on his terms, or make it impossible for him to survive at all.

A selection from newspaper articles, sections from books, his own presentations, a speech and a number of quotations follows to address the question he posits: 'in a most fundamental way, how do we realize this goal or make it difficult for others to realize this goal'?[43] Despite the fact that these quotations concern different types of organisms – animal, human, social, bio-chemical – they are all related, as he reveals thirteen pages later: all deal with the key issue he also addressed in *Organic Design*: *interaction*. But at first the audience must have been puzzled, for the first three quotations are clips from newspaper articles on recent brain research, while the fourth article deals with the loss of muscle tissue in rats during space flight, not quite familiar territory for most strategists or military practitioners:

'Nerve Cells Redo Wiring...' by Boyce Rensberger (from the *Washington Post*)
'Dale Purvis and Robert D. Hadley ... have discovered that a neuron's fibers can change significantly in a few days or weeks, presumably in response to changing demands on the nervous system ... research has shown neurons continually rewire their own circuitry, sprouting new fibers that reach out to make contact with new groups of other neurons and withdrawing old fibers from previous contacts.... This rewiring process may account for how the brain improves ones abilities such as becoming proficient in a sport or learning to play a musical instrument. Some scientists have suggested that the brain may use this method to store facts.... The research was on adult mice, but since all mammalian nervous systems appear to behave in similar ways, the researchers assume that the findings also apply to human beings.'

'The Soul of the Machine', by Richard M. Restak (Review of 'Neuronal Man', by Jean Pierre Changeux) (*The Washington Post Book World*)
'Changeux suggests that the complexity of the human brain is dependent upon the vast number of synapses (connections) between brain cells ... these synaptic connections are established or fall by the wayside according to how frequent they're used. Those synapses which are in frequent use tend to endure ("are stabilized") while others are eliminated.... In other words,... interactions with the environment' ... [exert] ... 'tremendous influence on the way the human brain works and how it has evolved.'[44]

'Brain Cells Try To Battle Alzheimer's...', by Jan Ziegler (*Washington Post*)
'A post mortem study of brains of Alzheimer's victims', (reported on by Dr. Carl Cotman and colleagues) 'showed that cells tried to repair connections destroyed by the disease by sprouting new branches,... A progressive, degenerative disease, it can cause memory loss, confusion, difficulty in speech and movement, inability to recognize even family members.... A characteristic of the disease is the death of neurons, or nerve cells, that connect to each other

by long fibers, which forces the brain to live with fewer and fewer connections. Analyzing cells from the hippocampus of six deceased Alzheimer's patients, Cotman and colleagues, found that axons – the output fibers of nerve cells, responsible for transmitting signals through the nervous systems – start to sprout, reforming the connections between remaining cells.... Ultimately however, the sprouting process cannot keep up with destruction. Either the sprouting stops, or too many nerve cells die...'

'Rats Lost Muscle, Bone Strength in Space Flight', by Paul Recer (*Erie Daily Times*)
'Space rats that spent seven days in orbit suffered massive losses of muscle and bone strength, suggesting that astronauts on long voyages must be protected from debilitating effects of zero gravity.... The young rats experienced a bone strength loss of up to 45 percent and a muscle tissue loss of up to 40 percent ... older rats ... suffered bone and muscle strength losses of about 15 percent.... Soviet space scientists reported a similar amount of muscle and bone loss in rats that were in space for more than 20 days...'[45]

Next he presents five sections from books. The first two concern the work on dissipative structures by Prigogine:[46]

'Order out of chaos', by Ilya Prigogine and Isabella Stengers
'Equilibrium thermodynamics provides a satisfactory explanation for a vast number of physicochemical phenomena. Yet it may be asked whether the concept of equilibrium structures encompasses the different structures we encounter in nature. Obviously the answer is no.'

'Equilibrium structures can be seen as the result of statistical compensation for the activity of microscopic elements (molecules or atoms). By definition they are inert at the global level.... Once they have been formed they may be isolated and maintained indefinitely without further interaction with their environment. When we examine a biological cell or a city, however, the situation is quite different: not only are these systems open, but also they exist only because they are open. They feed on the flux of matter and energy coming to them from the outside world. We can isolate a crystal, but cities and cells die when cut off from their environment. They form an integral part of the world from which they can draw sustenance, they cannot be separated from the fluxes that they incessantly transform.'

'Looking Glass Universe', by John P. Briggs and F. David Peat
'Prigogine called far-from-equilibrium forms like the vortex, "dissipative structures". The name comes from the fact that to keep their shape these structures must constantly dissipate entropy so it won't build up inside the entity and "kill" it with equilibrium.... [These dissipative structures] can survive only by remaining open to a flowing matter and energy exchange

with then environment. . . . The structure is stabilized by its flowing. It is stable but only relatively stable – relative to the constant energy flow required to maintain its shape. Its very stability is also paradoxically an instability because of its total dependence on its environment. The dissipative structure is autonomous (separate) but only relatively separate. It is a flow within a flow.'

And from here on he enters the social realm with a long piece on guerrilla warfare, on the relation between social order and strategy and one on the nature of culture (all of which re-emphasize the innate, tacit nature of culture and the importance of the moral dimension, in short, the glue of social structures) besides several quotations with an explicit military content:

'The War of the Flea', by Robert Taber
'Almost all modern governments are highly conscious of what journalism calls "world opinion". For sound reasons, mostly of an economic nature, they cannot afford to be condemned in the United Nations, they do not like to be visited by Human Rights Commissions or Freedom of the Press Committees; their need of foreign investment, foreign loans, foreign markets, satisfactory trade relationships, and so on, requires that they be members in more or less good standing of a larger community of interests. Often, too, they are members of military alliances. Consequently, they must maintain some appearance of stability, in order to assure the other members of the community or of the alliance that contracts will continue to be honored, that treaties will be upheld, that loans will be repaid with interest, that investments will continue to produce profits and be safe.'

'Protracted internal war threatens all of this . . . no ally wishes to treat with a government that is on the point of eviction.'

'It follows, that it must be the business of the guerrilla, and of his clandestine political organization in the cities, to destroy the stable image of the government, and so to deny its credits, to dry up its source of revenues, and to create dissension within the frightened owning classes, within the government bureaucracy (whose payrolls will be pinched), and within the military itself.'

'Isolation, military and political, is the great enemy of guerrilla movements. It is the task of the urban organization to prevent this isolation, to provide diversions and provocations when needed, to maintain contact, to keep the world aware of a revolution in progress even when there is no progress to report.'[47]

'Social Order and the General Theory of Strategy', Alexander Atkinson
'Moral fiber is the "great dam that denies the flood of social relations their natural route of decline towards violence and anarchy". . . . In this sense, "moral order at the center of social life literally saves society from itself".'

'Strategists must grasp this fact that social order is, at once, a moral order.... If the moral order on which rests a fabric of social and power relations is compromised, then the fabric (of social order) it upholds goes with it.'

In other words, 'the one great hurdle in the strategic combination (moral and social order) is the moral order. If this remains untouched the formation of new social relations and social ranking in status and power either never gets off the ground or faces the perennial specter of backsliding towards the moral attractions of established social and power relations.'

The strategic imperative, then, becomes one of trying to 'achieve relative security of social resources by subverting and reweaving those of the opponent into the fabric of one's own social order'.[48]

'Beyond Culture', by Edward T. Hall
'Everything man is and does is modified by learning and is therefore malleable. But once learned, these behavior patterns, these habitual responses, these ways of interacting gradually sink below the surface of the mind and, like the admiral of a submerged submarine fleet, control from the depths. The hidden controls are usually experienced as though they were innate simply because they are not only ubiquitous but habitual as well.'

'...The only time one is aware of the control system is when things don't follow the hidden program. This is most frequent in intercultural encounters. Therefore, the great gift that the members of the human race have for each other is not exotic experiences but an opportunity to achieve awareness of the structure of their own system, which can be accomplished only by interacting with others who do not share that system...'[49]

'Destruction and Creation', by Yours Truly (selection from an unpublished essay)
According to Gödel's Incompleteness Theorems, Heisenberg's Uncertainty Principle, and the Second Law of Thermodynamics one cannot determine the character or nature of a system within itself. Moreover, attempts to do so lead to confusion and disorder.[50]

'A Model of Soviet Mentality', by Dmitry Mikheyev (selection from a speech)
'Interaction between the individual and his environment starts with his perception of himself as a separate entity and the environment as everything outside of self. He learns his physical limits and desires, and how to fulfill them through interaction with the physical and social environment....

I maintain that the way the individual perceives the environment is crucial for his orientation and interaction with it.'

'Man's orientation will involve perceptions of self as both a physical and a psychological entity, as well as an understanding of the environment and of the possibilities for achieving his goals (Fromm, 1947). Society, meanwhile, has goals of its own – preservation of its physical integrity and spiritual identity. Pursuing these goals involves mobilizing and organizing its inner resources and interaction with the outside environment of other societies and nations. . . . An individual becomes a member of the society when he learns to act within its limits in a way that is beneficial to it'.[51]

Nearing the end of the sequence of illustrations, Boyd concludes with some short quotes. From Sun Tzu he borrows the famous lines 'know your enemy and know yourself; in one hundred battles you will never be in peril' as well as the one which forms the heart of the indirect approach: 'seize that which your adversary holds dear or values most highly; then he will conform to your desires'. Jomini's oft criticized emphasis on geographical disposition and logistics is brought along to support the importance of interactions: 'the great art, then, of properly directing lines of operations, is so to establish them in reference to the bases and to the marches of the army as to seize the communications of the enemy without imperiling one's own, and is the most important and most difficult problem in strategy'. Finally, he repeats his definition of leadership as yet another element in which interaction is key: 'the art of inspiring people to cooperate and enthusiastically take action toward the achievement of uncommon goals'.[52]

Condensation to essential elements

For Boyd there is a clear and united message in all of these illustrations that span also the previous presentations as well as the essay, and he captures the essential elements of the illustrations as follows:[53]

Compression

- Physical as well as electrical and chemical connections in the brain are shaped by interacting with the environment. Point: without these interactions we do not have the mental wherewithal to deal or cope with that environment.
- Gödel's Incompleteness Theorems, Heisenberg's Uncertainty Principle, and the Second Law of Thermodynamics, all taken together, show that we cannot determine the character or nature of a system within itself. Moreover, attempts to do so lead to confusion and disorder – mental as well as physical. Point: We need an external environment, or outside world, to define ourselves and maintain organic integrity, otherwise we experience dissolution/disintegration – i.e., we come unglued.

- Moral fibre or moral order is the glue that holds society together and makes social direction and interaction possible. Point: without the glue social order pulls apart towards anarchy and chaos leaving no possibility for social direction and interaction.
- Living systems are open systems; closed systems are non-living systems. Point: If we don't communicate with outside world – to gain information for knowledge and understanding as well as matter and energy for sustenance – we die out to become a non-discerning and uninteresting part of that world.

In one form or another, on various scales and in different realms, these illustrations reveal that 'as human beings, we cannot exist without an external or surrounding environment from which we can draw sustenance, nourishment, or support'. Reaching back to two themes from *Patterns of Conflict*, he recasts this insight as the message that '*interaction* permits vitality and growth while *isolation* leads to decay and disintegration'.[54] And with that, Boyd has come to the core, the barest essence, the shortest yet deepest principle of strategy, stating:

> '*The theme associated with the essay D&C and the presentations 'Patterns of Conflict' and 'Organic Design' is one of Interaction and Isolation'. While Organic Design emphasizes interaction, Patterns of Conflict emphasizes isolation. The essay Destruction and Creation is balanced between interaction and isolation.*[55]

Boyd has thus answered the question in the title:

> '*The Strategic Game is one of Interaction and Isolation'.*

That is what strategy is about. It is:

> '*a game in which we must be able to diminish an adversary's ability to communicate or interact with his environment while sustaining or improving ours'.*[56]

Strategic perspective

The obvious next question then concerns the pragmatic side of it: how does one do that? Again following J.F.C. Fuller's dimensions of control, he lists the three components – or here rather dimensions – he already introduced in *Patterns of Conflict*: the mental, moral and physical dimension, to analytically break up the enemy system and look for ways to apply the strategic principle and achieve isolation.[57] Although already employed before, also in their interrelationship, Boyd now thinks it appropriate to define the three dimensions and explain why we should use these:[58]

- Physical represents the world of matter-energy-information all of us are a part of, live in, and feed upon.
- Mental represents the emotional/intellectual activity we generate to adjust to, or cope with, that physical world.
- Moral represents the cultural codes of conduct or standards of behavior that constrain, as well as sustain and focus, our emotional/intellectual responses.

So Boyd discerns within the adversary system a physical, a mental and a moral dimension. Subsequently, isolation can occur – or be aimed for – in these different dimensions:

> Physical isolation occurs when we fail to gain support in the form of matter-energy-information from others outside ourselves. Mental isolation occurs when we fail to discern, perceive, or make sense out of what's going on around ourselves. Moral isolation occurs when we fail to abide by codes of conduct or standards of behavior in a manner deemed acceptable or essential by others outside ourselves.[59]

Interaction ensures the opposite:

> Physical interaction occurs when we freely exchange matter-energy-information with others outside ourselves. Mental interaction occurs when we generate images or impressions that match up with the events or happenings that unfold around ourselves. Moral interaction occurs when we live by the code of conduct or standards of behavior that we profess, and others expect us, to uphold.[60]

The question then becomes:

> How do we physically isolate our adversaries yet interact with others outside ourselves? How do we mentally isolate our adversaries yet keep in touch hence interact with unfolding events? How do we morally isolate our adversaries yet maintain the trust/confidence of others thereby interact with them?[61]

But before he arrives at these questions, let alone the answers, he pauses and plays the familiar game of question, illumination, suggestion and question again, connecting this discussion with several themes and insights from the previous presentations, even from the first pages of *Patterns of Conflict* that deal with air-to-air combat and the essay *Destruction and Creation*. This way the audience itself discovers the answers through applying the conceptual framework he has constructed up to this point, or at least internalizes the issues and way of thinking instead of merely listening to the solution. It is after all *A Discourse*. So Boyd asks:[62] 'how do we play to this theme and exploit these ideas?'

Hints
- Recall how we mentally constructed a snowmobile.
- Remember how we looked at ideas in mathematical logic, physics, thermo-dynamics, biology, psychology, anthropology, and conflict to surface a central theme.
- Remember our whole approach has been one of pulling things apart and putting them back together until something new and different is created.

Illuminating example[63]

? – What does the Second Law of Thermodynamics say – ?
All natural processes generate entropy.

? – What did Heisenberg say – ?
One cannot simultaneously fix or determine precisely
the momentum and position of a particle.

? – What did Gödel say – ?
One cannot determine the consistency of a system within itself.

The point of these questions is that 'as they appear, these statements and the ideas they embody seem unrelated to one another'. However, Boyd repeats, 'taken together Gödel, Heisenberg and the Second Law of Thermodynamics say that one cannot determine the character or nature of a system within itself. Moreover, attempts to do so lead to confusion and disorder.'

Then he asks another question: 'What do the tests of the YF-16 and the YF-17 say?' The message is that 'the ability to shift or transition from one maneuver to another more rapidly than an adversary enables one to win in air to air combat'. Again, this example does not seem related in any sense with the statements of Gödel *et al.*[64] However, taken together, the <u>overall message</u> is that:[65]

- The ability to operate at a faster tempo or rhythm than an adversary enables one to fold adversary back inside himself so that he can neither appreciate nor keep-up with what's going on. He will become disoriented or confused; which suggests that
- Unless such menacing pressure is relieved, adversary will experience various combinations of uncertainty, doubt, confusion, self-deception, inde-cision, fear, panic, discouragement, despair, etc., which will further:

Disorient or twist his mental images/impression of what's happening;
thereby
Disrupt his mental/physical maneuvers for dealing with such a menace;
thereby
Overload his mental/physical capacity to adapt or endure;
thereby
Collapse his ability to carry one.

These statements point to the idea he advanced also in *Destruction and Creation* that

> we can't just look at our own personal experiences or use the same mental recipes over and over again; we've got to look at other disciplines and activities and relate or connect them to what we know from our experiences and the strategic world we live in. If we can do this we will be able to surface new repertoires and (hopefully) develop a 'fingerspitzengefuhl' for folding our adversaries back inside themselves, morally-mentally-physically – so that they can neither appreciate nor cope with what's happening – without suffering the same fate ourselves.[66]

Again Boyd has touched a familiar theme. Superior orientation is key. In a way he has merely elaborated on the insights from slide 36. However, he has reminded the audience which path led to these insights. And in bringing several insights from different sources and different discussions from separate presentations together and succeeding in showing the conceptual linkages, he has also applied his own argument concerning the necessity of looking beyond one's familiar frames of reference. Moreover, slide 36 dealt with one's own side rather than the enemy's. And now he feels his audience is ready to tackle the issue how to fold the 'adversary back inside themselves, morally-mentally-physically, ... without suffering the same fate ourselves'.[67]

On isolation and interaction

Physically, Boyd argues,

> we can isolate our adversaries by severing their communications with the outside world as well as by severing their internal communications to one another. We can accomplish this by cutting them off from their allies and the uncommitted via diplomatic, psychological and other efforts. To cut them off from one another we should penetrate their system by being unpredictable, otherwise they can counter our efforts. Mentally we can isolate our adversaries by presenting them with ambiguous, deceptive or novel situations, as well as by operating at a tempo or rhythm they can neither make out nor keep up with. Operating inside their OODA loops will accomplish just this by disorienting or twisting their mental images so that they can neither appreciate nor cope with what's really going on. Morally our adversaries isolate themselves [!] when they visibly improve their well being to the detriment of others (allies, the uncommitted), by violating codes of conduct or behavior patterns that they profess to uphold or others expect them to uphold.[68]

The expected pay-off is

> disintegration and collapse, unless adversaries change their behavior patterns to conform to what is deemed acceptable by others outside themselves.[69]

While this is only a slight alteration by elaboration of slide 36, Boyd generates new clues concerning isolation. By exploring one side, he immediately sheds light – or as he calls it, 'illumination' – on the opposite. If the previous analysis of isolation is valid, the consequence for the analysis of interaction lies in the following new description:[70]

> <u>Physically</u> we <u>interact</u> by opening-up and maintaining many channels of communication with the outside world, hence with others out there, that we depend upon for sustenance, nourishment, or support. <u>Mentally</u> we <u>interact</u> by selecting information from a variety of sources or channels in order to generate mental images or impressions that match-up with the world of events or happenings that we are trying to understand and cope with. <u>Morally</u> we <u>interact</u> with others by avoiding mismatches between what we say we are, what we are, and the world we have to deal with, as well as by abiding by those other cultural codes or standards that we are expected to uphold.

Here the <u>expected pay-off</u> is:[71]

> vitality and growth, with the opportunity to shape and adapt to unfolding events thereby influence the ideas and actions of others.

Box 6.4 offers a comparison, showing that the latter discussion on isolation and interaction follows logically from the first one and forms a response to it.

So, far from seemingly similar and perhaps somewhat superfluous, the latter discussion on isolation and interaction puts into practice what the first take merely describes. The first take is 'a what', the second constitutes 'a how to', thus answering the questions he had set out for himself and the audience. Concluding the section ('Putting in Strategic Perspective'), Boyd pulls these discussions together to reveal another description of:[72]

<u>The Art of Success:</u>
- Shape or influence the moral-mental-physical atmosphere that we are part of, live in, and feed upon, so that we not only magnify our inner spirit and strength, but also influence potential adversaries and current adversaries as well as the uncommitted so that they are drawn toward our philosophy and are empathetic toward our success;

yet be able to

- Morally-mentally-physically isolate adversaries from their allies and outside support as well as isolate them from one another, in order to: magnify their internal friction, produce paralysis, bring about their collapse; and/or bring about a change in their political/economic/social philosophy so that they can no longer inhibit our vitality and growth.

Boyd's first take on isolation	Boyd's second view on isolation
Physical isolation occurs when we fail to gain support in the form of matter-energy-information from others outside ourselves.	Physically we can isolate our adversaries by severing their communications with the outside world as well as by severing their internal communications to one another. We can accomplish this by cutting them off from their allies and the uncommitted via diplomatic, psychological and other efforts. To cut them off from one another we should penetrate their system by being unpredictable, otherwise they can counter our efforts.
Mental isolation occurs when we fail to discern, perceive, or make sense out of what's going on around ourselves.	Mentally we can isolate our adversaries by presenting them with ambiguous, deceptive or novel situations, as well as by operating at a tempo or rhythm they can neither make out nor keep up with. Operating inside their OODA loops will accomplish just this by disorienting or twisting their mental images so that they can neither appreciate nor cope with what's really going on.
Moral isolation occurs when we fail to abide by codes of conduct or standards of behavior in a manner deemed acceptable or essential by others outside ourselves.	Morally our adversaries isolate themselves [!] when they visibly improve their well being to the detriment of others (allies, the uncommitted), by violating codes of conduct or behavior patterns that they profess to uphold or others expect them to uphold.

continued

Boyd's first take on interaction	Boyd's second view on interaction
Physical interaction occurs when we freely exchange matter-energy-information with others outside ourselves.	Physically we interact by opening-up and maintaining many channels of communication with the outside world, hence with others out there, that we depend upon for sustenance, nourishment, or support.
Mental interaction occurs when we generate images or impressions that match up with the events or happenings that unfold around ourselves.	Mentally we interact by selecting information from a variety of sources or channels in order to generate mental images or impressions that match-up with the world of events or happenings that we are trying to understand and cope with.
Moral interaction occurs when we live by the code of conduct or standards of behavior that we profess, and others expect us, to uphold.	Morally we interact with others by avoiding mismatches between what we say we are, what we are, and the world we have to deal with, as well as by abiding by those other cultural codes or standards that we are expected to uphold.

Box 6.4 Boyd's view on isolation and interaction.

Here too (Box 6.5), comparison with an earlier description of the art of success (from *Patterns of Conflict*, p. 178) shows the added value of the discussions in *The Strategic Game of ? and ?*.

It is interesting to note that he expands on this theme of moral isolation in the last few slides of the presentation. Here Boyd's concern with the moral high ground of our actions again emerges clearly, as it did in *Organic Design*. There it pertained to the operational or military strategic level leadership. This time he addresses the moral dimension at the nation-state or societal level, and 'the moral' should be read to signify national culture, ideology and/or political aspirations. He describes (or rather prescribes) the moral as a very functional and instrumental property, an observation reinforced by the following section in which Boyd implements his arguments in an example.

A moral design for grand strategy

If the previous argument is accepted, it follows that for designing grand strategy the name of the game is to 'use moral leverage to amplify our spirit and strength

The Art of Success (PoC)	The Art of Success (Strategic Game)
Appear to be an unsolvable cryptogram while operating in a directed way to penetrate adversary vulnerabilities and weaknesses in order to isolate him from his allies, pull him apart, and collapse his will to resist;	Shape or influence the moral-mental-physical atmosphere that we are part of, live in, and feed upon, so that we not only magnify our inner spirit and strength, but also influence potential adversaries and current adversaries as well as the uncommitted so that they are drawn toward our philosophy and are empathetic toward our success.
yet	yet be able to
Shape or influence events so that we not only magnify our spirit and strength but also influence potential adversaries as well as the uncommitted so that they are drawn toward our philosophy and are empathetic toward our success.	Morally-mentally-physically isolate adversaries from their allies and outside support as well as isolate them from one another, in order to: magnify their internal friction, produce paralysis, bring about their collapse; and/or bring about a change in their political/economic/social philosophy so that they can no longer inhibit our vitality and growth.

Box 6.5 The art of success.

as well as expose the flaws of competing or adversary systems, all the while influencing the uncommitted, potential adversaries and current adversaries so that they are drawn toward our success'. Put another way, 'one should preserve or build-up moral authority while compromising that of our adversaries in order to pump-up our resolve, drain away adversaries' resolve, and attract them as well as others to our cause and way of life'. If this is the challenge, the question is 'how do we evolve this moral leverage to realize the benefits cited above?'[73] The answer comes in two parts; one concerns our self, one concerns the adversary, and he prescribes both defensive as well as somewhat offensive measures for statecraft.

In a typical Boydian passage, he stresses that,

with respect to ourselves, we must surface, as well as find ways to overcome or *eliminate* those blemishes, flaws, or contradictions that generate mistrust and discord, so that these negative qualities either alienate us from one another or set us against one another, thereby destroy our internal harmony, paralyze us, and make it difficult to cope with an uncertain, ever-changing world at large. *In opposite fashion* we must *emphasize* those cultural traditions, previous experiences and unfolding events that build up harmony and trust, thereby create those implicit bonds that permit us as individuals and as a society, or as an organic whole, to shape as well as adapt to the course of events in the world.[74]

> <u>With respect to adversaries we should</u> reveal those harsh statements that adversaries make about us – particularly those that denigrate our culture, our achievements, our fitness to exist, etc. – as a basis to show that our survival and place in the scheme of things is not necessarily a birthright, but is always at risk.

This has an internally oriented focus evidently to avoid complacency among one's own people. But Boyd does not shun the offensive in the moral domain. As Boyd continues, 'we should reveal those mismatches in terms of what adversaries profess to be, what they are, and the world they have to deal with in order to surface to the world, to their citizens, and to ourselves the ineptness and corruption as well as the sub-rosa designs that they have upon their citizens, ourselves, and the world at large'.

At the same time one should engage in dialogue to convince the adversary of one's own benevolent nature and the benefits of cooperation: 'we should acquaint adversaries with our philosophy and way of life to show them that such destructive behavior works against, and is not in accord with, our (or any) social values based upon the dignity and needs of the individual as well as the security and well-being of society as a whole'.[75] We should 'respect their culture and achievements, show them we bear them no harm, and help them adjust to an unfolding world, as well as provide additional benefits and more favorable treatment for those who support our philosophy and way of doing things'. This accommodating attitude must be coupled to a show of resolve to guard one's interest if necessary. We should 'demonstrate that we neither tolerate nor support those ideas and interactions that undermine or work against our culture and our philosophy hence our interests and fitness to cope with a changing world'.[76]

The meaning of strategy and the art of success

Extrapolating from the previous set of propositions, Boyd develops a new notion of strategy at its most fundamental level, in its most abstract form, bringing to the fore again the theme of adaptation. Boyd answers the four questions he listed at the beginning of *Strategic Game of ? and ?*:[77]

? – What Is Strategy – ?

A mental tapestry of changing intentions for harmonizing and focusing our efforts,
as a basis for realizing some aim or purpose in an unfolding and often unforeseen world of many bewildering events and many contending interests.

<u>? – What Is the Aim or Purpose of Strategy – ?</u>
To improve our ability to shape and adapt to unfolding
circumstances, so that we (as individuals or as groups or as
a culture or as a nation-state) can survive on our own terms.

<u>? – What Is the Central Theme and What Are the Key Ideas that Underlie
Strategy – ?</u>
The central theme is one of interaction/isolation while the key ideas are the
moral-mental-physical means towards realizing this interaction/isolation.

<u>? – How Do We Play to this Theme and Activate these Ideas – ?</u>
By an instinctive see-saw of analysis and synthesis across a variety of
domains, or across competing independent channels of information, in order
to spontaneously generate new mental images or impressions that match-up
with an unfolding world of uncertainty and change.

In these propositions we can discern themes that have appeared in the essay and
the presentation: *adaptation, multiple perspectives, analysis/synthesis, inter-
action/isolation*. The definitions he offers here contain some elements of insights
he has developed in *Patterns of Conflict* and *Organic Design*, but with a slight
difference. Moreover, *Patterns of Conflict* culminated in a number of definitions
of strategy and tactics after a tour through military history, and those definitions
must to some extent still be understood within the context of the behavior of
armed forces. Here the definitions refer to organizations in general.

These definitions have no predecessors in military strategic theory. They are
unique, and at the time must have appeared definitely so. They are evidently
pregnant with influences of the scientific *Zeitgeist*. With this novel abstract conceptualization of the essence of strategy and strategic success, Boyd has come to
the climax of his presentation, and has almost arrived at the most condensed
essence of *A Discourse*.

Revelation

With only one slide following the slide with the title, this is the shortest of all
presentations. Referring back to 'the snowmobile', it cannot be understood
without the previous presentation, and must really be considered an epilogue to
it. Yet it reveals (hence the title) in emblematic form a core argument Boyd
wanted to get across:

- A <u>loser</u> is someone (individual or group) who <u>cannot</u> build snowmobiles
  when facing uncertainty and unpredictable change;
  whereas
- A <u>winner</u> is someone (individual or group) who <u>can</u> build snowmobiles, and
  employ them in appropriate fashion, when facing uncertainty and unpredictable change.

In stark language it argues for the requirement to have the capacity for both analysis *and* synthesis, destruction *and* creation, and creativity. In these very brief lines Boyd thus once more explains that this is the 'metaphorical message' of *Strategic Game*: It thus builds on, and reinforces the argument of *Strategic Game* as well as the essay. It also precedes the discussion contained in *Conceptual Spiral*, which is much longer, but in some ways also again an elaboration of the same argument, but now from yet again a different perspective.

The Conceptual Spiral

Introduction

Two statements of Michael Polanyi can nicely serve as an introduction for *The Conceptual Spiral:*

> A free society may be seen to be bent in its entirety on exploring self-improvement – every kind of self-improvement. This suggests a generalization of the principles governing the Republic of Science.[78]

> I have shown that all engineering and technology, comprising operational principles lies logically beyond the range of Laplacian knowledge and that the same is true for the operational principles established by physiology as the functions of living things.[79]

The Conceptual Spiral was completed in July/August 1992, sixteen years after the first versions of *Patterns of Conflict*. It consists of thirty-eight pages. It is the result of seven years of additional reading and distillation. Even more than the other presentations, it reflects Boyd's wide interest in subjects far beyond the traditional focus of military history or strategic studies. Boyd revisits his essay, reformulating the same argument, confirming the findings once more, but now employing illustrations from science, engineering and technology, all of which he conceptualizes as self-correcting mechanisms (or systems, or OODA loops indeed). These fields, and the illustrations Boyd derived from them, would be much more familiar to the general audience (although he expressly included sections to convince his audience they were actually quite ignorant) than the philosophical essay. Indeed, *The Conceptual Spiral* must be considered the equivalent of the essay, but now offered in a more easily accessible format, and in appearance less philosophical. The themes are familiar too:

- pervasive uncertainty as prime characteristic of life,
- the essence of combining analysis with synthesis, marrying induction and deduction,
- the importance of novelty, mismatches and creativity,
- and the requirement to combine multiple perspectives to form adequate orientation patterns.

The title itself hints at the core argument, which in part can be traced back to the work of Piaget: survival mandates reveling in a continuous conceptual spiral of induction and deduction, of creation and destruction.

Focus

Boyd starts with the familiar move. First he states the prime focus of the presentation:

> To make evident how science, engineering, and technology influence our ability to interact and cope with an unfolding reality that we are part of, live in, and feed upon.[80]

And the answer will come, he suggests, from revisiting and exploring the following key passage from the 'Abstract':[81]

> ...the theme that weaves its way through this 'Discourse on Winning and Losing' is not so much contained within each of the five sections, per se, that make up this 'Discourse', rather, it is the kind of thinking that both lies behind and makes-up its very essence. For the interested, a careful examination will reveal that the increasingly abstract discussion surfaces a process of reaching across many perspectives; pulling each and every one apart (analysis), all the while intuitively looking for those parts of the disassembled perspectives which naturally interconnect with one another to form a higher order, more general elaboration (synthesis) of what is taking place. As a result, the process not only creates the 'Discourse' but it also represents the key to evolve the tactics, strategies, goals, unifying themes, etc., that permit us to actively shape and adapt to the unfolding world we are a part of, live-in, and feed-upon.

The reason for including this section, Boyd says, is 'it suggests a general way by which we can deal with the world around us'. He subsequently asserts that he will show that:[82]

> By exploiting the theme contained within this passage and by examining the practice of science/engineering and the pursuit of technology we can evolve a conceptual spiral for comprehending, shaping, and adapting to that world.

Simple-minded message

The subsequent section aims to illustrate and substantiate this hunch. The first step is offering the audience a new view on the nature of science, engineering and technology. Boyd gives three preliminary definitions of the terms that make them conceptually comparable to each other:

- <u>Science</u> can be viewed as a self-correcting process of observation, hypothesis, and test.
- <u>Engineering</u> can be viewed as a self-correcting process of observation, design and test.
- <u>Technology</u> can be viewed as the wherewithal or state of the art produced by the practice of science and engineering.

Illustrations

This raises the question, according to Boyd, what the practice of science, engineering and the pursuit of technology has given us or done for us. The answer lies in a number of slides Boyd shows the audience, with a total of fifty-seven entries of persons, teams or companies and their specific contributions to science, engineering and technology (Boxes 6.6 through 6.8). Once more manifesting a

Some outstanding contributors	Contributions
Wright Brothers (1903)	Gasoline powered airplane
Christian Hulmeyer (1904)	Radar
V. Paulsen/R.A. Fessenden (1904/1906)	Wireless telephone
John A. Fleming/Lee de Forest (1904/1907)	Vacuum tube
Tri Ergon/Lee de Forest (1919/1923)	Sound motion picture
USA – Pittsburgh (1920)	Public radio broadcasting
American Car Locomotive (1925)	Diesel-electric locomotive
J.L. Baird (1926)	Television
Warner Brothers (1927)	Jazz singer/sound motion picture
Germany/USA (1932/1934)	Diesel-electric railway
Britain/USA/Germany (1935–39)	Operational radar
Germany/Britain/USA (1935/1936/1939)	Television broadcasting
Hans von Ohain/Germany (1939/1939)	Jet engine/jet airplane
Eckert and Mauchly (1946)	Electronic computer
Bardeen and Brattain and Shockley (1947)	Transistor
Ampex (1955)	Video recorder
J. Kilby/R. Noyce (1958/1959)	Integrated electric circuit
T.H. Maiman (1960)	Laser
Philips (1970)	Video cassette recorder
Sony (1980)	Video camcorder

Box 6.6 Examples from engineering (1).

Some outstanding contributors	Contributions
Savery/Newcomen/Watt (1698/1705/1769)	Steam engine
George Stephenson (1825)	Steam railway
H. Pixii/M.H. von Jacobi (1832/1838)	AC generator/AC motor
Samuel Morse (1837)	Telegraph
J.N. Nieqce/J.M. Daguerre/Fox Talbot (1839)	Photography
Gaston Plante (1859)	Rechargeable battery
Z. Gramme/H. Fontaine (1869/1873)	DC Generator/DC motor
Nicholas Otto (1876)	4-cycle gasoline engine
Alexander G. Bell (1876)	Telephone
Thomas A. Edison (1877)	Phonograph
Thomas A. Edison (1879)	Electric light bulb
Werner von Siemans (1879)	Electric locomotive
Germany (1881)	Electric metropolitan railway
Charles Parsons (1884)	Steam turbine
Benz/Daimler (1885/1886)	Gasoline automobile
T.A. Edison/J. LeRoy/T. Armat/*et al.* (1890–96)	Motion-picture camera/projector
N. Tesla/G. Marconi (1893/1895)	Wireless telegraph
Rudolf Diesel (1897)	Diesel locomotive
Italy (1902)	Electric railway

Box 6.7 Examples from engineering (2).

remarkable erudition, as well as substantiating the idea that Boyd was aware of the scientific changes of his time, the purpose of this list is to show how all are related through a most pervasive element that Piaget, Polanyi and deBono had discussed: *novelty through mismatches.*[83]

Grand message

This long list of past contributions by these people suggests a 'Grand Message' for now and for the future, Boyd continues.[84] And this grand message is an elaborate restatement of the ideas of Gödel and Heisenberg, first introduced in the essay, but now (almost) in layman's language. In the mathematical/logical sense, he asserts, the theorems associated with Gödel, Lowenheim and Skolem, Tarski, Church, Turing, Chaitin and others reveal that not only do the statements representing a theoretical system for explaining some aspect of reality explain that reality inadequately or incompletely but, like it or not, these statements spill out beyond any one system and do so in unpredictable ways. Or, conversely,

Some outstanding contributors	Contributions
Isaac Newton (1687)	'Exactness'/predictability via laws of motion/gravitation
Adam Smith (1776)	Foundation of modern capitalism
A.M. Ampere/C.F. Gauss (1820s/1830s)	Exactness/predictability via electric/magnetic laws
Carnot/Kelvin/Clausius/Bolzmann (1824/1852/1865/1870s)	Decay/disintegration via Second Law of Thermodynamics
Faraday/Maxwell/Herz (1831/1865/1888)	Union of electricity and magnetism via field theory
Darwin and Wallace (1838/1858)	Evolution via theory of natural selection
Marx and Engels (1848–95)	Basis for modern 'scientific socialism'
Gregory Mendel (1866)	Inherited traits via his laws of genetics
Henri Poincare (1890s)	Inexactness/unpredictability via gravitational influence of three bodies
Max Planck	Discreteness/discontinuity via his quantum theory
Albert Einstein	Exactness/predictability via his special and general relativity theories
Bohr/de Broglie/Heisenberg/ Schrodinger/Dirac/*et al.* (1913/1920s...)	Uncertainty/indeterminism in quantum physics
L. Lowenheim and T. Skolem (1915–33)	Unconfinement (non-categoricalness) in mathematics and logic
Claude Shannon (1948)	Information theory as basis for communication
Crick and Watson (1953)	DNA spiral helix as the genetically coded information of life
Lorenz/Prigogine/Mandelbrot/ Feigenbaum/*et al.* (1963/1970s)	Irregularity/unpredictability in non-linear dynamics
G. Chaitin/C. Bennett (1965/1985)	Incompleteness/incomprehensibility in information theory

Box 6.8 Examples from science.

these theorems reveal that we can neither predict the future migration and evolution of these statements nor just confine them to any one system nor suggest that they fully embrace any such system.

If we extend these ideas and build upon them in a scientific/engineering sense, we can say that any coherent intellectual or physical system we evolve to represent or deal with large portions of reality will at best represent or deal with that reality incompletely or imperfectly. Moreover, we neither have nor can we create beforehand a supersystem that can forecast or predict the kind of systems we will evolve in the future to represent or deal with that reality more completely or more perfectly. Furthermore, such a supersystem can neither forecast nor predict the consequences that flow from those systems that we create later on. Going even further, we cannot determine or discern the character or nature of such systems (super or otherwise) within themselves. These findings imply that:

> People using theories or systems evolved from a variety of information will find it increasingly difficult and ultimately impossible to interact with and comprehend phenomena or systems that move increasingly beyond and away from that variety – that is, they will become more and more isolated from that which they are trying to observe or deal with, unless they exploit the new variety to modify their theories/systems or create new theories/ systems.

This reveals that, 'while we can comprehend and predict some portions of the ever-changing world that unfolds before us, other portions seem forever indistinct and unpredictable'.[85]

Underlying dynamics

Obviously, here Boyd has reformulated one of his earliest statements, that we must constantly make sure we develop adequate mental models to make up for the ever-present and unavoidable level of uncertainty. For his present audience he keeps this insight hidden until later. Instead he raises the question 'what all this have to do with our ability to thrive and grow in such a world that is seemingly orderly and predictable yet disorderly and unpredictable?'[86]

To get at this question, he suggests to take a closer and more general look at what science, engineering, and the pursuit of technology produce and how this is accomplished. Furthermore, suspecting that these practices and pursuit are not wholly accidental, nor obvious and that they seem to change us in some ways, he also suggests to examine what keeps the whole enterprise going and how this enterprise affects us personally.[87] In other words, in order to gain a richer image of science, engineering, and technology, the following questions need to be addressed. What do science, engineering and technology produce? How is this accomplished? What is the driving mechanism that keeps the process alive and ongoing, or put another way, what phenomenon sustains or nourishes the whole enterprise? Finally, how does this enterprise of science, engineering, and technology affect us personally as individuals, as groups, or as societies?[88]

The answer he offers to the first question – what do science, engineering and technology produce – comes from a conceptual comparison of the three. The similarity lies not in anything tangible but in an intangible common element. As Boyd states, 'if we examine the contributions from the practice of science and engineering and generalize from these individual contributions what do we see? We see <u>new</u> ideas, <u>new</u> systems, <u>new</u> processes, <u>new</u> materials, <u>new</u> etc. In other words, science, engineering, and technology produce change via <u>novelty</u>'.[89]

The second question – how is novelty produced – also brings a familiar argument, but instead of arriving at it from the avenue of uncertainty, now he arrives at it from the avenue of novelty. To examine novelty, he explains, 'we speak of it in terms of those features that seem to be part of that novelty. In other words, we reduce a novel pattern down to some features that make up that pattern. Different people in examining such a pattern may see differing features that make it up. In other words, there are different ways by which a pattern can be reduced hence the possibility for differing features or parts. Regardless of how it comes out, we call this process of reduction: <u>analysis</u>.

Pushing this process even further we can reduce many different patterns (<u>analyses</u>) to parts that make up each pattern and use these parts, or variations thereof, to make a new pattern. This is done by finding some common features that interconnect some or many of these parts so that a new pattern – whether it be a new concept, new system, new process, new etc. – can be created. We call this process of connection: <u>synthesis</u>. Now if we test the result of this process with the world we're dealing with, we have an <u>analytical/synthetic</u> feedback loop for comprehending, shaping, and adapting to that world.[90] And pulling all this together we can say that:[91]

> Novelty is produced by a mental/physical feedback process of <u>analysis</u> and <u>synthesis</u> that permits us to interact with the world so that we can comprehend, cope with, and shape that world as well as be shaped by it.

This leads to the third question: what is the driving mechanism that keeps the process alive and ongoing.[92] What phenomena sustain or nourish the whole enterprise? One thing is clear, Boyd tells his audience, if our ideas and thoughts matched perfectly with what goes on in the world; and if the systems or processes we designed performed perfectly and matched with whatever we wanted them to do, what would be the basis for evolving or creating new ideas, new systems, new processes, new etc.? The answer: There wouldn't be any! In other words:

> The presence and production of mismatches are what sustain and nourish the enterprise of science, engineering, and technology, hence keep it alive and ongoing – otherwise there would be no basis for it to continue.

Boyd then sets out to explain how this enterprise of science, engineering and technology affects us personally as individuals, as groups, or as societies.[93] The previous discussion had shown that 'the practice of science/engineering and the pursuit of technology not only change the physical world we interact with – via new systems, new processes, new etc. – but they also change the mental/physical ways by which we think about and act upon that world. In this sense the practice of science/engineering and the pursuit of technology permit us to continually rematch our mental/physical orientation with that changing world so that we can continue to thrive and grow in it. Put simply:

> The enterprise of science, engineering, and technology affects us personally as individuals, as groups, or as societies by changing our orientation to match with a changing world that we in fact help shape.

The discussion up to this point has revealed that without the intuitive interplay of analysis and synthesis we have no basic process for generating novelty, no basic process for addressing mismatches between our mental images/impressions and the reality it is supposed to represent; and no basic process for reshaping our orientation toward that reality as it undergoes change. Put simply:

> Without the interplay of analysis and synthesis we have no basis for the practice of science/engineering and the pursuit of technology – since novelty, mismatches, and reorientation as the life blood ingredients that naturally arise out of such practice and pursuit can longer do so.[94]

These findings mandate a modification of the definitions of science and engineering offered earlier. The earlier definition of science regarded it as a 'self-correcting process of observation, hypothesis, and test'. Now, Boyd suggests, science is a 'self-correcting process of observation*s*, *analysis/synthesis*, hypothesis and test'. Note that he has changed observation into observations, to indicate the fact that it is a continuous process, and not merely a one-time event. The same holds true for engineering, which had been defined earlier as 'a self-correcting process of observation, design and test'. This now must be changed to read 'a self-correcting process of observation*s*, *analysis/synthesis*, design, and test'. The reason for this change of view is that 'without the interplay of analysis and synthesis one can evolve neither the hypothesis or design and follow-on test nor the original "simple-minded message" nor this presentation itself'.[95]

Final step: why novelty matters

Acknowledging that it is not obvious what bearing all this has on winning and losing,[96] he suggests that what applies to science and engineering also applies to life in general. Novelty, Boyd asserts, is not only produced by the practice of science/engineering and the pursuit of technology, it is also produced by the forces of nature, by our own thinking and doing as well as by others. Furthermore, novelty is produced continuously, if somewhat erratically or haphazardly. Now, in order to thrive and grow in such a world we must match our thinking and doing, hence our orientation, with that emerging novelty. Yet, any orientation constrained by experiences before that novelty emerges (as well as by the Grand Message discussed earlier) introduces mismatches that confuse or disorient us. However, the analytical/synthetic process, previously described, permits us to address these mismatches so that we can rematch thereby reorient our thinking and action with that novelty. Over and over this continuing whirl of <u>reorientation, mismatches, analysis/synthesis</u> enables us to comprehend, cope with, and shape as well as be shaped by novelty that literally flows around and over us.[97]

So, Boyd has established the link between the dynamics of science and engineering and life, which makes the foregoing discussion interesting also for its pragmatic insights. But he has not addressed yet how this relates to winning and losing. As he states: we still have a puzzle: why does our world continue to unfold in an irregular, disorderly, unpredictable manner even though some of our best minds try to represent it as being more regular, orderly, and predictable?[98] More pointedly, with so much effort over such a long period by so many people to comprehend, shape and adapt to a world that we depend upon for vitality and growth, why does such a world, although richer and more robust, continue to remain uncertain, everchanging and unpredictable?[99]

The answer, and the final piece of the argument, comes from connecting novelty with uncertainty. Very simply, he says, 'review of *Destruction and Creation,* this presentation, and our own experiences reveal that the various theories, systems, processes, etc. that we employ to make sense of that world contain features that generate mismatches that, in turn, keep such a world uncertain, everchanging, and unpredictable'.[100] Then he produces the list with entries drawn from a variety of scientific disciplines, all describing features that induce uncertainty (Box 6.9).[101]

Deeper message

This is the underlying message: There is no way out, unless we can eliminate the features just cited. Since we don't know how to do this we must continue the whirl of reorientation, mismatches, analysis/synthesis over and over again ad infinitum as a basis to comprehend, shape and adapt to an unfolding, evolving reality that remains uncertain, ever-changing, unpredictable.[102] And if we connect this continuing whirl of <u>reorientation, mismatches, analysis/synthesis</u> and the <u>novelty</u> that arises out of it with the previous

- <u>Uncertainty</u> associated with the unconfinement, undecidability, incompleteness theorems of mathematics and logic.
- <u>Numerical imprecision</u> associated with using the rational and irrational numbers in the calculation and measurement processes.
- <u>Quantum uncertainty</u> associated with Planck's Constant and Heisenberg's Uncertainty Principle.
- <u>Entropy increase</u> associated with the Second Law of Thermodynamics.
- <u>Irregular and erratic behavior</u> associated with far from equilibrium open non-linear processes or systems with feedback
- <u>Incomprehensibility</u> associated with the inability to completely screen, filter, or otherwise consider the spaghetti-like influences from a plethora of ever-changing, erratic, or unknown outside events.
- <u>Mutations</u> associated with environmental pressure, replication errors, or unknown influences in molecular and evolutionary biology.
- <u>Ambiguity</u> associated with natural languages as they are used and interact with one another.
- <u>Novelty</u> generated by the thinking and actions of unique individuals and their many-sided interactions with each other.

Box 6.9 Sources of uncertainty.

discussion, he tells his audience, we can see that we have 'a Conceptual Spiral for'[103]

•	Exploration	–	Discovery	–	Innovation
•	Thinking	–	Doing	–	Achieving
•	Learning	–	Unlearning	–	Relearning
•	Comprehending	–	Shaping	–	Adapting

Hence a Conceptual Spiral for Generating

•	Insight	–	Imagination	–	Initiative

Just to emphasize his point very clearly once more, Boyd asks the rhetorical question: Can we survive and grow without these abilities?[104] Of course the answer is a wholeheartedly ! NO ![105] This suggests then, that the conceptual spiral just formulated and derived from the previous explorations also represents:[106]

A
Paradigm
For Survival and Growth

The point of all this is that:

Since survival and growth are directly connected with the uncertain, ever-changing, unpredictable world of winning and losing, we will exploit this whirling (conceptual) spiral of <u>orientation, mismatches, analyses/synthesis, reorientation, mismatches, analyses/synthesis</u> ... so that we can comprehend, cope with, and shape, as well as be shaped by that world and the novelty that arises out of it.[107]

He has thus explained the essence of these somewhat cryptic slides once more, and now in unambiguous terms. He shows how the enterprise of science, engineering and the pursuit of technology is connected to the game of winning and losing, and how insight into the dynamics of science and engineering is useful for strategy. They are all self-correcting and evolving systems. He has shown a new parallel once more between dynamics in disparate fields, substantiating not only that the ideas developed in the essay and subsequent presentations are relevant for strategy, but also that strategic thinking should be infused with these ideas and these dynamics. The hidden message for his audience is that, if organizations want to survive in a highly dynamic environment, in peace-time as much as in war, they need to embrace uncertainty and novelty.

The Essence of Winning and Losing

Introduction

On 28 June 1995, two years before his death, Boyd finished the last addition to *A Discourse*. As the title suggests, it contains what Boyd considered at that moment the essence of his opus. It is extremely brief, covering only five slides, including the title slide which depicts a mounted knight. Yet it is also extremely important, for it contains the only graphic representation of the OODA loop, that up to this point he has only described in words in various sections of different presentations. And as Hammond concludes (referring to his own involvement in Boyd's 'big squeeze') it is a synthesis of all of Boyd's work, from *Aerial Attack Study* and OODA loops to his most recent interests in coevolution, sociobiology, genetic engineering, chaos theory, complexity, and non-linearity.[108] Boyd's simple model belies its sophistication, Robert Polk noted in his short but eloquent assessment.[109]

Indeed, in the five 'key statements' of this presentation, he manages to capture – and go back to – the arguments of some of the earliest literature he had studied in the early 1970s, such as Piaget, Popper, Polanyi, Monod, Bronowski and Conant, while directly marrying these once more to several of the key arguments and definitions he developed in *Patterns, Strategic Game* and *Organic Design*. He shows how the insights derived mainly from looking at military history, but inductively informed by the OODA loop idea and the themes from the essay, are conceptually related to the insights from *Strategic Game* and *Organic Design*, which find their basis much more in the sciences. These key statements also constitute both an explanation as well as a justification for the expanded OODA loop model that follows the statements:[110]

Key statements

- **Without our genetic heritage, cultural traditions, and previous experiences**, we do not possess an **implicit** repertoire of psychological skills shaped by environments and changes that have been previously experienced.
- Without **analysis and synthesis**, across a variety of domains or across a variety of competing/independent channels of information, we cannot evolve new repertoires to deal with unfamiliar phenomena or unforeseen change.
- **Without a many-sided implicit cross-referencing process of projection, empathy, correlation**, and **rejection** (across these many different domains or channels of information), we cannot even do **analysis** and **synthesis**.
- **Without OODA loops** we can neither sense, hence observe, thereby collect a variety of information for the above processes, nor decide as well as implement actions in accord with those processes.

Or put another way

- **Without OODA loops** embracing all the above and **without the ability to get inside other OODA loops** (or other environments), we will find it impossible to comprehend, shape, adapt to, and in turn be shaped by an unfolding, evolving reality that is uncertain, everchanging, unpredictable.

It is only a slight stretch of imagination to suggest that in the last statement Boyd connects grand tactics with epistemology. The next slide then offers the full graphic rendering of the cybernetic double-loop decision-making model. A comparison with the simplified but most frequently used model of the OODA loop and the picture below shows a much more complicated, more comprehensive, richer and deeper process, one which clearly suggests that there is more to Boyd's theory than the idea of rapid OODA looping. In Boyd's hands, the model (Figure 6.1) gains a much wider application and more profound meaning.[111]

Observation is the task that detects events within an individual's, or group's, environment. It is the method by which people identify change, or lack of change, in the world around them. While it is not the sole basis for Action, it is a primary source of new information in the behavioral process. Note, however, he stresses, 'how orientation shapes observation, shapes decision, shapes action, and in turn is shaped by the feedback and other phenomena coming into our sensing or observing window'. Without the context of Orientation, most Observations would be meaningless. Boyd is particularly detailed about Orientation. To survive and grow within a complex, ever changing world of conflict it is necessary to have insight and vision, focus and direction, he had stated earlier. To that end we must effectively and efficiently orient ourselves; that is, we must quickly and accurately develop mental images, or schema, to help comprehend and cope with the vast array of threatening and non-threatening events we face. This image construction, or orientation, is nothing more than the process of

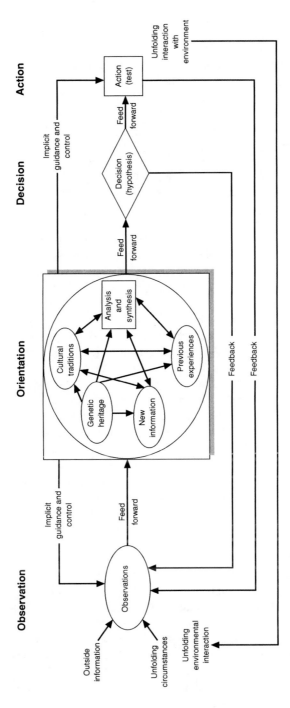

Figure 6.1 The real OODA loop.

destruction (analysis) and creation (synthesis) he discussed in his briefings. It is how we evolve.

'Also note how the entire "loop" (not just orientation) is an ongoing many-sided implicit cross-referencing process of projection, correlation, and rejection'. It is the process of examining the world from a number of perspectives so that we can generate mental images or impressions that correspond to that world. Done well, it is the key to winning instead of losing. Very illuminating is his expansion on the nature of Orientation. It shows why 'the big O' is indeed central and what elements constitute this filter and the dynamic at play. Indeed, in 'the big O', we find represented the first three of the five key statements. The mental images we construct are shaped by our personal experience, genetic heritage and cultural traditions, but they are also measured up against incoming new information to validate existing schemata. The entire OODA loop is a double-loop learning process, but the Orientation element itself thus also contains such a double-loop feature.

Observations that match up with certain mental schema call for certain decisions and actions. Significantly, whereas the D and A of the OODA loop generally are seen to stand for Decision and Action, in this model Boyd offers his own view on the meaning of both words by tying Decision to Hypothesis and Action to Test. Decision is the component in which actors decide among action alternatives that are generated in the Orientation phase. Boyd discusses Action more than the Decision component. Actions, according to Boyd, should be rapid, surprising, ambiguous, menacing and varied. Translated into action, decisions thus feed back into the systems as validity checks on the correctness and adequacy of the existing orientation patterns.

The OODA loop model as presented by Boyd therefore represents his view on the process of individual and organizational adaptation in general, rather than only the military-specific command and control decision-making process that it is generally understood to depict. It refers to the conceptual spiral as discussed in the previous presentation, to the process of learning, to doctrine development, to command and control processes and to the Popperian/Kuhnian ideas of scientific advance. The (neo-)Darwinists have their place, as do Piaget, Conant, Monod, Polanyi and Hall, while Prigogine and Goodwin are incorporated through Boyd's concluding statement in the final slide that follows the OODA loop picture:[112]

> The key statements of this presentation, the OODA Loop Sketch and related insights represent an evolving, open-ended, far from equilibrium process of self-organization, emergence and natural selection.

This relates the OODA loop clearly to Complex Adaptive Systems, the role of schemata and to the process of evolution and adaptation. Once again it shows that where the aim is 'to survive and prosper' in a non-linear world dominated by change, novelty and uncertainty, adaptation is the important overarching theme in Boyd's strategic theory.

Conclusion

Boyd's work is more comprehensive and subtle than the one thing with which Boyd is normally associated, namely the rapid OODA loop idea, and it contains various other very valuable insights. As these four presentations show, his work gives a novel interpretation of military history and strategic theory. Moreover, it deals with organizational culture and leadership and offers a new conceptualization of tactics, grand tactics, strategy and grand strategy, showing how systemic interaction and isolation is the name of the game of strategic behavior. In the final presentation he presents his own graphic model of the OODA loop, one which is much more comprehensive than the one Boyd is generally associated with. It shows that the common perception is incomplete, as the OODA loop contains more elements for success than only tempo and information. This integral rendition of his work thus indicates that the popular notion of the 'rapid OODA loop' idea does not adequately capture what Boyd meant by it, and that Boyd must be remembered for more than only the idea that one can gain military victory by more rapidly OODA looping than the opponent.

7   Completing the loop

The history of science demonstrates beyond a doubt that the really revolutionary and significant advances come not from empiricism.

James B. Conant[1]

To think theoretically one must be ready to appreciate and accept the need to sacrifice detailed descriptions for broad observations.

James N. Rosenau[2]

Beyond the rapid OODA idea

Summary

This study aimed to improve our understanding of Boyd's work as embodied in *A Discourse on Winning and Losing*. To that end Chapters 2, 3 and 4 discussed the formative factors of Boyd's work, offering insight into reasons why Boyd developed his theory, and the professional environment his ideas landed in, in response to which he in no small measure developed his ideas. In addition it showed a number of key themes, concepts and metaphors he derived from his background as fighter pilot, designer of fighter aircraft, his involvement in the Military Reform Movement, his reading of military history, and in particular from his study of scientific literature. Chapters 5 and 6 provided a comprehensive account of Boyd's work.

The essay highlighted that for Boyd uncertainty is the pervasive element of human endeavor, indeed, it is the prime characteristic of life, he repeated in *The Conceptual Spiral*, and it surfaces frequently across the presentations; so too his insistence that thinking strategically under such a condition requires a continuous combination of analysis and synthesis, induction and deduction, destruction and creation, and a multidisciplinary and multi-spectral approach. In *Patterns*, he develops the three categories of conflict, describing in detail the dynamics at play in each mode of warfare. He emphasizes the dynamic of move and counter-move, the cycle of alternating phases of dominance by either the offense or defense, the interplay of the physical, mental and the moral dimensions, as well as the importance of the set of four key traits – initiative, variety, harmony and rapidity.

While forming an argument against the attritionist mindset, Boyd moves on and beyond this argument, distilling in increasingly abstract form the essence of each warform, which in the end allows him to compare the different warforms and to formulate new definitions of strategy. He elaborates on several aspects of *Patterns*, disclosing what lies at the heart of the strategic game between open systems – interaction and isolation – and the features of the appropriate organizational structure and culture – flexibility, agility, network, autonomy, openness and trust – returning in the end to the message of the essay, translated in digestible form, showing that what lies at the heart of successful strategic behavior is similar to the dynamic at play in science, engineering and technology. Then, in a last exercise of synthesis, Boyd draws the comprehensive OODA loop graphic, accompanied by the five statements, showing what constitutes the OODA loop and what it means. In the words he used in the 1970s, it is a model of a 'meta-paradigm', a 'theory of intellectual evolution and growth'.

It has become evident that the common view that the OODA loop model, interpreted as an argument that victory goes to the side that can decide most efficiently, falls short of the mark in capturing the meaning and breadth of Boyd's work. *A Discourse* addresses the grand strategic, strategic, operational and the tactical levels, developing specific advise (or the name of the game) for action at each level, but all in logical relation to one another. Additionally it develops suggestions for command and control and organizational culture that are conceptually consistent with the overall thrust of his arguments on the nature of strategy and the essence of winning and losing.

Indeed, while his historical analysis is biased and occasionally flawed, while his presentations may lack clarity and academic rigor, the detailed discussion of *A Discourse* has demonstrated that Boyd's work constitutes a theory of considerable sophistication, consistency and persuasiveness, as well as originality. It is also more comprehensive, subtle and complex than the common rendering and the general perception of what Boyd argues. Finally it became evident that indeed the commonly held view on the meaning of the OODA loop is incomplete.

More than just rapid decision making

The comprehensive overview of Boyd's work shows that the OODA loop represents and means more than a decision process, and the model contains more elements for victory than information superiority and speed. The OODA loop is much less a model of decision-making than a model of individual and organizational learning and adaptation in which the element of orientation – made up of genetics, experience, culture – plays the dominant role in the game of hypothesis and test, of analysis and synthesis, of destruction and creation.

The first misconception about the OODA loop concerns the element of speed. The rapid OODA looping idea suggests a focus on speed of decision making, and 'out-looping' the opponent by going through consecutive OODA cycles faster. This is not incorrect, indeed, Boyd frequently suggested as much. However, Boyd also addressed the aspect of altering the tempo. Tempo makes it hard for the opponent to adequately adapt to the fast *changing* situation, including the element of speed. It is not absolute speed that counts; it is the relative tempo or a variety in rhythm that counts. Changing OODA speed becomes part of denying a pattern to be recognized.

Second, the emphasis on speed ignores the close interrelationship between physical action and the mental and moral component. One can have a distinct advantage in timely and accurate information, but if this cannot be translated into meaningful action, this 'information superiority' is useless. Boyd instead argues that the aim is to create and perpetuate a highly fluid and menacing state of affairs for the enemy, and to disrupt or incapacitate his ability to adapt to such an environment. Thus the psychological (mental/moral) and temporal mechanisms come into play only if and when the physical and spatial dimensions are also adequately manipulated.

Third, tempo is one dimension among a significant number of other control dimensions, and it is probably important in particular at the tactical level as a factor directly influencing chances of success. At the grand tactical level he is more concerned with 'operating inside adversary's mind-time-space', and with 'generating mismatches between those events he observes, or anticipates and those he must react to'. At this level, as well as at the strategic and the grand-strategic, other dimensions that can be manipulated span the spectrum of leverage points for manipulating a Complex Adaptive System that were described at the end of Chapter 4. Schwerpunkte, physical and non-physical, need to be attacked as well as Nebenpunkte. Physical as well as non-physical connections must be severed through the game of isolation and interaction. Conspicuous and varied actions are necessary and it is these, combined with the menacing aspect of those actions and impressions that produce paralysis, disintegration and non-cooperative centers of gravity, and that shatter cohesion. Indeed, a *variety* of factors need to combine with lack of time to induce a moral, mental and physical incapability to react.

The centrality of orientation

The narrow interpretation of the OODA loop also de-emphasizes another essential feature of Boyd's theory: *developing, maintaining and reshaping one's orientation*, the box around which the loop graphically revolves. Speed, brave decisions and heroic actions are pointless if the observation was inaccurate because of our inadequate orientation. Orientation shapes the way we interact with the environment. It is in a sense the 'genetic code' of an organism or organization.

In order to avoid predictability and ensuring adaptability to a variety of challenges, it is essential to have *a repertoire of orientation patterns* and *the ability to select the correct one* according to the situation at hand while denying the opponent the latter capability. Moreover, Boyd emphasizes the *capability to validate* the schemata before and during operations and *the capability to devise and incorporate new ones*, if one is to survive in a rapidly changing environment.

One may react very fast to unfolding events, but if one is constantly surprised nevertheless, apparently one has not been able to turn the findings of repeated observations and actions into a better appreciation of the opponent, i.e. one has not learned but instead has continued to operate on existing orientation patterns. Verifying existing beliefs and expectations, and if necessary modifying these in a timely manner, is crucial. The way to play the game of interaction and isolation is to spontaneously generate new mental images that match up with an unfolding world of uncertainty and change, Boyd asserted in *The Strategic Game*.

The larger theme: organizational adaptability

So, the abstract aim of Boyd's method is to render the enemy powerless by denying him the time to mentally cope with the rapidly unfolding, and naturally uncertain, circumstances of war, and only in the most simplified way, or at the tactical level, can this be equated with the narrow, rapid OODA loop idea. Indeed, it is only at the tactical level that Boyd actually refers to 'OODA more inconspicuously, more quickly and with more irregularity'. So, the view that the rapid OODA loop idea captures Boyd's work is valid only if one confines oneself to the tactical level, but it leaves unaddressed the fact that Boyd also dealt with the other levels of war, that he dealt with other subjects such as organizational culture, as well as the fact that at the other levels of war Boyd focused on other factors relevant for adaptability.

This points to the major overarching theme throughout Boyd's work: *the capability to evolve, to adapt, to learn, and deny such capability to the enemy*. Indeed, rapid OODA looping is merely one aspect of the process of adaptation. In the comprehensive OODA loop model Boyd's attention to this broader theme comes most clearly to the fore. While the early presentations are clearly aimed at a military audience and pertain to operational art, by shifting his focus to a number of processes that in abstract are similar for a variety of organisms and social systems, Boyd steers *A Discourse* beyond military history and warfare. In particular during his later period Boyd approached and explained patterns for winning and losing from this more abstract point of view, suggesting patterns in the behavior of organisms and organizations when confronted with threats and challenges of an even more general nature.

Boyd regards the contestants, the armies, their headquarters and societies in terms of living systems, as organisms, that aim to survive and prosper. To that end they – individuals, platoons, brigades, divisions, army corps, nations and any other type of social system – observe, learn and adapt. Adaptation naturally follows from Boyd's view of war as being about survival. The strategic aim, he asserts in 'Patterns', is 'to diminish adversary's capacity to adapt while improving our capacity to adapt as an organic whole, so that our adversary cannot cope while we can cope with events/efforts as they unfold'.

Adaptation occurs across various timescales and he develops a view on what adaptability means and requires at each level. Each level knows its specific 'name of the game'. At the *tactical level and operational level* actions, movements, attacks, feints, threats, etc., disrupt the enemy's organizational processes, confuse commanders and personnel, attrit his forces and dislocate his units. Confusion, fear and lack of information or the ability to react upon correct perception of the threats degrade trust, cohesion and courage, and thus the ability to cohere and respond collectively and to take the initiative, i.e. to adapt adequately as an organization. Adaptation is rather direct.

At the *strategic level* adaptation is more indirect and takes longer time intervals. It revolves around adjusting doctrines and force structures and disorienting the opponent's orientation patterns, or mental images. At the *grand-strategic level* it revolves around shaping the political and societal environment, including an attractive ideology, and selecting a form of warfare. The theme for vitality and growth lists as the aim improving fitness as an organic whole to shape and expand influence or power over the course of events in the world. This also surfaces as the national goal where the emphasis is on the effective combination of isolation and preservation strategies in all the dimensions, the mental, moral and the physical. Here is no emphasis on the temporal aspect because success here is not (only) overloading the opponent's OODA system but derives from the interplay of leveraging across multiple dimensions. Success is the result of playing the game of interaction and isolation well.

Mental and organizational agility

Boyd's advice for organizational culture and structure is consistent with his emphasis on adaptability. Boyd advocates an agile cellular organization – networked through ideology, experience, trust, aim and orientation pattern – that thrives in uncertainty and fosters innovation, creativity and initiative. Boyd's command philosophy is essential for the Boydian operational art to succeed. Warning against the dangers of relying on explicit communication and control mechanisms, he advocates a command arrangement with some explicit control mechanism and feedback loops, but one that is in particular reliant on implicit ones, formed by common frames of reference, shared ideas, shared experiences, trust, etc.

If everyone understands clearly, and is attuned to, the organization's purpose and/or the commander's intent, explicit communication beyond the objective is superfluous. Because of the shared outlook one knows what to do and what one can expect of others, be it supporting units, higher commands, etc. Implicit communication will suffice. Self-organization will be the result. At the strategic and grand strategic levels an equivalent dynamic is argued. Leaders should develop attractive and inspiring national goals and philosophies that unite and guide the nation as well as attract the uncommitted.

Command, Boyd indicates, is therefore a wrong term, as is control. Echoing the mode of operation of Polanyi's 'Republic of Science', Boyd advocates lateral relations and continuous, open, two-way communication between hierarchies. Higher command levels must restrain themselves in their desire to know all that is going on at lower levels and to interfere. Higher commands must shape the 'decision space' of subordinate commanders. They must trust and coach. They must encourage cooperation and consultation among lower levels. They must accept bad news and be open for suggestions, lower-level initiatives and critique. It is thus more a question of leadership and appreciation of what is going on and comparing this to what is expected.

Moreover, success of such open systems is self-reinforcing. The strategic and operational levels set the overall direction and make sure there is variety of action and rapidity and keep the opponent guessing. This will translate into tactical advantage for lower levels, for the tactical units of the opponent will be misguided by their confused higher command level. Strategic mismatches create tactical mismatches that in turn, in the next OODA loop of the opponent, will lead to another strategic mismatch on his part.

According to Boyd the command and control philosophy, as well as his advice for the grand-strategic level, ensures that units at all levels can maintain a sufficient degree of interaction with their environment, while the opponent is denied such ability to interact. In the abstract sense, it is a self-correcting mechanism, much as the way science, technology and engineering are driven by self-correcting mechanisms.

Thus, *A Discourse* not only contains suggestions for winning battles, but also for maintaining organizational fitness, learning and change. Boyd examined organizational and species evolution, growth and survival, highlighting the essential similarity of the processes and factors that are at play when such complex adaptive systems face challenges to their existence. He extends it to economies, societies and to science and technology, showing how in these fields, too, self-correcting processes, the discovery of novelties, mismatches and anomalies, the continuous creative interplay of destruction and creation and the dialectic of analysis and synthesis keep the process going. Therefore one could perhaps better describe *A Discourse* not as a general theory of war but as a general theory of the strategic behavior of complex adaptive systems in adversarial conditions.

A novel strategic theory

On the face of the first 100 pages of *Patterns of Conflict*, it can be asserted that Boyd merely 'repackaged' familiar ideas and arguments and offered a biased overview of military history. Indeed, there are some remarkable shortfalls in his dealing with history (nuclear warfare, naval- and air-power theory for instance). And indeed, his work followed closely the ideas, and sometimes biased views, advanced by Sun Tzu, Julian Corbett, Basil Liddell Hart, J.F.C. Fuller and T.E. Lawrence. Much like Fuller and Liddell Hart, Boyd wrote to convince people that the military doctrine and practice of the day was fundamentally flawed, opposing attrition type warfare and favoring paralysis through maneuver. Instead of using military history as contrast, Boyd used these strategists to provide empirical validation for patterns he observed in air-to-air combat and in other arenas, for illustration, and for providing his presentations a necessary sense of credibility.

The view of Boyd as a 'great synthesizer', however, fails to acknowledge genuine novel elements he added to this synthesis. First, Boyd did make an important contribution by rediscovering, translating and updating the concepts of Sun Tzu and the other strategists to suit the era he found himself in. To some extent one could also consider his rediscovery of operational art a novelty in his day.

Second, he transcends the classical theorists of the maneuvrist school of strategic thought in a number of ways. Although *Patterns of Conflict* initially does suggest that Boyd had been merely looking for confirmation of his hunch about the general validity of the rapid OODA loop idea, his study was not so selective, nor preconceived. And although Boyd did favor the maneuvrist style of combat when he discusses conventional warfare (a preference which is understandable in light of his environment), when he shifts his attention to the essence of strategy, he sees the maneuvrist style of warfare just as one of three possible 'categories of conflict'.

It is when Boyd leaves his historical overview – the snapshots – behind that Boyd starts to move beyond the work of the authors he leaned upon. First of all he delves deep to get to the essence of various modes of strategic behavior, showing what mental, moral and physical factors are at play in each pattern of conflict. Second, in this effort to get to the essence, his work integrates different strategic theories. In particular, after his general overview of military history the synthetic character of his work becomes prevalent. Boyd's genius lies in uncovering and recognizing the similarity in the principal factors and processes that produced success in the different categories of conflict. This integrative feature of Boyd's work is a remarkable performance and strength of his work.

In an abstract sense, Boyd regards these schools of thought as alternative modes of behavior, and the theories as orientation patterns. He regards strategic theories and strategic concepts, like doctrines, as part of the repertoire of a strategist's orientation pattern, integrating them in the cognitive dimension and in the discovery of fundamental similarities when he strips the theories to their bare essentials and expresses them in systems-theoretical/neo-Darwinist terms.

Even when Boyd acknowledges his preference, he still is much less dogmatic than, for instance, Liddell Hart.[3] Where Liddell Hart asserted that all victories could in the end be attributed to the application of the indirect approach, Boyd included an elaborate discussion of cases and causes in which the indirect approach (or Blitzkrieg concept) succeeded or failed. Indeed, each mode of warfare is joined by a discussion of the counter-move to that mode. His eye was trained upon the dialectic, the paradoxical and evolutionary character of strategy. Where Liddell Hart saw victory always accruing from the application of the indirect approach, Boyd saw the process of action–reaction, of learning, anticipation, invention and counter-movements. Boyd searched not for one particular optimum, but instead acknowledged the contingent nature of war, and focused on the universal processes and features that characterize war, strategy, and the game of winning and losing. Thus Boyd took his audience to insights that he considered more important: a balanced, broad and critical view instead of the doctrinaire.

Finally, of course, both in its simplified and in its comprehensive form, the OODA loop is a valuable novel feature in strategic theory, pointing to the fundamental processes ongoing in any strategic encounter.

Science and strategic theory

An important novelty in Boyd's work lies in his approach to the study of military history, operational art and strategic theory. He was the first strategist to introduce the epistemological debates of the 1960s and 1970s into strategic thought and to see the value and consequences of these debates for strategy. He married military history with science, building his theory upon Gödel, Heisenberg, Popper, Kuhn, Piaget and Polanyi, who highlighted the unavoidable feature of uncertainty in any system of thought (as well as the limits of the Newtonian paradigm). Cybernetics and systems theory offered him the concept of feedback, the combination of analysis–synthesis as well as the Second Law of Thermodynamics and entropy, the distinction between open and closed systems, the importance of interactions and relations, and the need for a holistic approach. The cognitive revolution, combined with neo-Darwinist studies, showed him the role of schemata formed by genetics, culture and experience. Chaos theory highlighted non-linear behavior. These ideas returned in various guises in complexity theory, emphasizing the general theme of adaptation. Thus he introduced into strategic theory the concept of open complex adaptive systems struggling to survive in a contested, dynamic, non-linear world pregnant with uncertainty, constantly attempting to improve and update its schemata and repertoire of actions and its position in the ecology of the organization.

Such an eclectic holistic approach became an argument in itself: he considered it a prerequisite for sound strategic thinking. He wanted to inculcate his audience not so much with a doctrine as with an understanding of the dynamics of war and strategy and a style of thinking about that dynamic that differed from the deterministic mindset that prevailed in the strategic discourse of the 1960s and 1970s. Applying his argument in practice – constantly showing the dynamic of move and countermove, stripping bare, analyzing, the essence of certain strategies, and then recombining them with new insights and hypotheses – allowed him to expand and go 'deeper' into the essence of strategy and war than previous strategists. It showed him similarities and parallels between, as well as distinct features unique to different modes of warfare, or categories of conflict

Science also helped him explain and connect in a novel way and lead him to new perspectives, hypotheses and insights. It gave him new metaphors to conceptualize strategy and war. It also allowed him to make connections between strategic behavior of different kinds of organisms and see the similarities, suggesting that what applied in war often applied in other arenas of competition as well, and vice versa.

While many before him recognized that war and strategy revolve around the mind,[4] no contemporary strategist developed a theory based on the scientific concepts Boyd discovered in his deliberate and broad study of scientific literature during a time that saw the paradigm shift that has since been heralded as the postmodern era. It resulted in a unique set of terms and concepts, a new language, leading him to distinctly novel conceptualization of strategic behavior and insights into the essence of the game of winning and losing.

The first postmodern strategist

Indeed, building upon the previous observation, in light of his eclectic approach, the specific sources he drew inspiration and insight from, and because of the close resemblance of both his method and his arguments to leading contemporary postmodern theorists, it is fruitful and warranted to regard Boyd as the first postmodern strategist.

He called his work *A Discourse* because it was through interaction with his public that understanding and meaning would be generated. He also had a discourse with history and science, using various lenses to analyze events, to derive meaning and understanding of a complex phenomenon called war, and the non-linear way people acted, and attempted to control events in it through a dialectic process, a constant process of analysis and synthesis, based on experience, culture, genetics, one's relationships with others, etc.

Moreover, his approach and his views on combat and strategy implicitly are pregnant with postmodern epistemological principles. As is the case with postmodernism, at the heart of Boyd's view on war and strategy resides the fundamental issue of epistemology and the view of knowledge as unfolding, evolving, as a dialectic process and uncertain. His first step in developing *A Discourse* is an attempt to discover how we develop knowledge, how we learn. His very starting premise is that the world is fundamentally uncertain, truth is an arena of combat, knowledge is a weapon, as is the capability to evolve one's knowledge base. He warns against monochromatic views and argues that command organizations should consist of people with different frames of reference, thereby ensuring a variety of interpretations of one observation. Truth is dialogical, in postmodern terms; it arises from people in discourse. Assigning meaning to events, phenomena or objects is not just an individual process. The OODA loop itself indeed is an epistemological statement. It is an abstract and theoretical model of the way we derive knowledge from our environment. Although he would feel more acquaintance with Kuhn than with Lyotard, Bourdieu, Derrida or Giddens, their ideas echo through in *A Discourse*.

As a model for postmodern strategy, the value of the OODA loop, and the arguments Boyd makes using it, lies in pointing towards the non-traditional tools for creating combat power and non-traditional targets in an enemy system. Language, doctrine, belief systems, experience, culture, symbols, schemata, dataflows, knowledge about itself and its opponent, perception, organizational ability for learning, the capability to change practices, all positioned in the temporal dimension, are at least as valuable as technology, weapons, numbers of soldiers in defining combat effectiveness.

Lawrence Freedman acknowledged that 'the practical strategist is (perhaps unwittingly) something of a constructivist'.[5] In light of the above analysis, concluding that Boyd may be considered the first postmodern strategist is as warranted as it is beneficial in understanding his work.

The continuing relevance of *A Discourse*

Postmodern war

Boyd's legacy continued to exert an influence on military thought throughout the 1990s. His ideas surface in literature on so-called 'Postmodern war' and 'the postmodern military', as well as in studies on the Revolution in Military Affairs and Network Centric Warfare. Moreover, 'asymmetric warfare', a theme of many studies in the aftermath of 9/11 and the wars in Afghanistan and Iraq in its wake, has also been approached and explained from a Boydian perspective in articles that introduce the concept of Fourth Generation Warfare. First a note on postmodern war.

The discourse on the shape of warfare in the post-Cold War era reflects his arguments. Indeed, a new mode of warfare coined postmodern war revolves around the importance of knowledge, situational awareness, exploiting information superiority and adopting network structures because of the inherent flexibility of such arrangements. Its project is a way of warfare distinctly not resembling modern-era industrial-style attrition-type warfare.

The postmodern school of thought in military studies points at new modes of economic production (from the industrial age to the information age), associated new sources of power (information), new modes of representation (virtual reality), and new forms of organization (cross-border commercial firms, borderless internet, erosion of the status of the nation-state due to globalization). These studies highlight the sweeping sociological changes affecting the militaries of the West after the end of the Cold War.[6]

We are in a period of transition away from the 'modern' mass army, characteristic of the age of nationalism, to a 'postmodern' military with large-scale conscription giving way to fully professional armed forces of smaller scale. At the same time threats are not defined by the Cold War superpower conflict. Instead there is 'threat-complexity' – a very wide range of security risks which are difficult to prioritize – and a corresponding mixture of missions, ranging from high intensity war fighting to low intensity conflicts and peace keeping operations.[7] Meanwhile, in an era in which the West was no longer faced with 'wars of necessity' but only 'wars of choice', there is an avoidance of full-fledged war and prolonged combat. In 'wars of choice' vital interests were not at stake, and subsequently casualties among own and even enemy military units needed to be minimized and public and politicians alike manifest abhorrence towards 'collateral damage'. This loss of belligerency produced 'post-heroic warfare'. If wars are fought, the West would play by its strengths – economic power and technological supremacy – to achieve its objectives at minimal cost and bloodshed and in minimum time. These developments occurred against a backdrop of a societal trend in which military force as an instrument had gained questionable legitimacy. Avoiding casualties and destruction is a humanizing trend and the only way to maintain legitimacy for conducting combat operations.[8] As Coker asserts, 'to be just, wars have to be humane. Western societies can now only fight wars which minimize human suffering, that of their enemies as well as their own. Western societies are trying to humanize war. It is the great project for the twenty-first century'.[9]

Information, or rather, knowledge, is a pervading theme in these studies. Gray contends that: 'As a weapon, as a myth, as a metaphor, or as a force multiplier, as an edge, as a trope, as a factor, as an asset, information (and its handmaidens – computers to process it, multimedia to spread it, systems to represent it) has become the central sign of postmodernity. In war information has always been important. Now it is the single most significant military factor',[10] not only for controlling the battlespace: controlling information at home is just as important.[11] Information is the organizing principle of war and postmodernity, hence postmodern war.[12]

For nihilist or subversive postmodernists such as Braudillard, the essence of postmodern war lies in the new methods of representation and experience of reality offered by new tools of information and communication. In a series of articles on the Gulf War he questions the very reality of the event itself. Our understanding of that war was constructed and mediated by a continuous series of symbolic images and virtual media events – simulacra that are not real, but instead 'stand in for the real'. Braudillard thus prompts us to question whether modern conceptions of military conflict and the central role warfare has played in geopolitics during the modern era have any credibility in a security environment characterized by deterrence, culturally imposed restraint, instantaneous media transmission, and adversaries with profound disparities in their military capabilities.[13] It was a virtual event which is less a representation of real war than a spectacle, a theme picked up by Michael Ignatieff and Colin McInnes to comment on NATO's war in Kosovo – 'a virtual war' – and the way such 'humanitarian' wars have been experienced by the western publics – 'spectator sport warfare'.[14]

For Booth *et al.*, several (and Boydian) developments arise from this postmodern phenomenon. The first is that 'the transmission of real-time media from the battlefield creates a continuous feedback loop in post-Cold War military operations in which the public can be directly influenced in a more or less predictable fashion depending on the content selected for transmission [. . .] the role of the soldier-statesman will become crucial in courting the media for the purpose of retaining some element of that control'. Additionally they note that 'it becomes possible to employ the media directly as a conduit for disinformation' and a 'marriage of military strategy with the real time transmission capabilities of an ostensibly independent global mass media that invites comparison with the postmodern'.[15]

War in the information age

Others focused more on the new forms of warfare emanating from the changes in the economy, discerning a transition from the industrial age to the 'Information Age'. Alvin and Heidi Toffler for instance noted in their bestseller *War and Anti-War, Survival at the Dawn of the Information Age*, that the West today makes wealth through the information-age – or 'third wave' – economy, inevitably resulting in 'third wave warfare' in which information would be the critical component.[16] In the modern era, armed forces were based on nineteenth-century-style mass armies, consisting of conscripts operating mechanized military systems produced by industrial-age heavy industries. These forces adhered to an attrition-type doctrine of war in which victory depended on out-producing an opponent while eliminating its armed forces. In contrast, postmodern militaries consisting of professional armed forces of highly skilled personnel that operated not weapons but a conglomerate of increasingly capable precision sensors and long-range stand-off precision munitions, aimed to paralyze the opponent through system-wide parallel attacks on numerous centers of gravity.[17]

The transition to the Information Age implied, and was manifested in, the awareness that information was becoming the driving factor in warfare.[18] Information and communication technology improved the quality of sensor systems, it increased transparency of the battlefield, it enhanced precision of weapons systems and, finally, it enhanced speed of command and shortened the 'sensor-to-shooter time'. In short, as many noted, information-age technologies improved the capabilities for observation, orientation and decision, they allowed for compressing the time to complete an OODA cycle.

These features were the very subject of the discourse on the 'Revolution in Military Affairs', a revolution people became aware of after the Gulf War.[19] The RMA literature argues for various doctrinal and organizational changes which are fully in line with Boyd's work, and which are considered to 'point to a qualitative break with the patterns of warfare characteristic of the Modern Era'.[20] The RMA promised (and proved) to reduce the exposure of troops to danger, in minimizing the risks of war more generally, and in reducing collateral damage. It fitted the pattern of war the West hoped to fight.[21]

One of the early and influential definitions of this discourse[22] stated that: 'a revolution in military affairs occurs when technological change makes possible material, which when combined with organizational and operational change, results in a transformation in the conduct of warfare'.[23] The RMA is the product of a confluence of three streams of technological change combined with organizational changes. First, surveillance capabilities improved. It became possible to detect, observe and track things and people of military concern in all weather and during day and night time. This translated into improved ability to track potential or actual targets, no matter what their speed. The second technological stream concerned advances in information processing and presentation. The rapid increase in computing power and transmission capabilities of modern communication systems offered the opportunity to analyze, disseminate and access unprecedented quantities of information in ever-shortening time. Commanders and tactical operators gained direct access to sensors, dramatically improving their situational awareness. And this translated into the third technical stream; the ability to hit targets precisely and quickly. Eliot Cohen described it as 'anything that moves on the battlefield can be seen and what can be seen can be hit'.[24]

On the organizational and doctrinal level, this implied an empowerment of small units and the ability of armed forces to cover larger distances quicker, to influence events over larger swaths of territory, and to do more things in a given period of time. Combat intensity would go up, risk would go down. Massing of forces would become a thing of the past. Instead, fires would be massed, coming from stand-off weapons launched from ships, aircraft or ground-based rocket launchers. Finally, it would become harder for an opponent to find sanctuary anywhere. Indeed, the cumulative effects of the technological and organizational changes stimulated by the information revolution would be revolutionary.

Thus, Eliot Cohen claimed that 'a revolution in military affairs is under way'.[25] Others asserted that the RMA offered a transition from attrition warfare to precision warfare or knowledge-intensive warfare.[26] Capturing the widely shared vision of future war employing RMA capabilities, one author summarized several studies as:

> The battlefield of the 21st Century will be dominated, not by massed troops and armor, but by long-range smart munitions able to strike with precision over great distances, stealthy and unpiloted weapon platforms with stand-off capabilities; air and space-based sensors that can effectively eliminate the 'fog and friction' of war and provide 'dominant battlespace awareness'; and advanced battle management and communication systems able to integrate, process and distribute information so that commanders can apply dominant forces in just the right place and at just the right time.
>
> [Instead of] attrition and the conduct of set piece battles along a continuous front such operations will give way to 'non-linear operations' [...] involving high-tempo attacks conducted simultaneously against key tactical, operational and strategic targets throughout the length, depth and breadth of the battlespace.[27]

Cyberwar and swarming

To illustrate the essence of this discourse and to show the parallels with Boyd's work (such as an emphasis on tempo, situational awareness, network structures and agility), some quotes from a notable article by John Arquilla and David Ronfeldt, two leading authors on information war, will suffice. *Cyberwar is coming*, sported the article they published in 1993, in which they argued how the information revolution would affect warfare, showing many features favored by Boyd:

warfare is no longer primarily a function of who puts the most capital, labor, and technology on the battlefield, but of who has the best information about the battlefield. What distinguishes the victors is their grasp of information, not only from the mundane standpoint of knowing to find the enemy while keeping it in the dark, but also in doctrinal and organizational terms [...] information is becoming a strategic resource that may prove as valuable and influential in the post-industrial era as capital and labor have been in the industrial age.[28]

They posited that in the future war must be waged according to 'information related principles'.[29] Additionally conflict may have to be interpreted in a different light, away from the industrial-age conception of armed conflict. They distinguish Netwar and Cyberwar, where Netwar surpasses the military dimension and includes economic, political and virtual dimensions. It refers to ideational conflicts, waged in part through internetted modes of communication. Cyberwar refers to conducting and preparing to conduct military operations according to information-related principles. Although information and communication matters, what the authors consider the real significance is that these are forms of war about 'knowledge' – about who knows what, when, where and why, and about how secure a society or military is regarding its knowledge of itself and its adversaries.

It is exactly this knowledge that they suggest should be shaped. Pregnant with Boydian notions, postmodern – reflexivist – references and Braudillard's fears, they suggest that conflict in the Information Age means:

> trying to disrupt, damage, or modify what a target population knows or thinks it knows about itself and the world around it. A Netwar may focus on public or elite opinion, or both. It may involve public diplomacy measures, propaganda and psychological campaigns, political and cultural subversion, deception of or interference with local media, infiltration of computer networks and databases, and efforts to promote dissident or opposition movement across computer networks.[30]

With information the key weapons and target of the Information Age, strategy in Cyberwars is equally in tune with Boyd, for the focus during a conflict must lie on disrupting, if not destroying information and communication systems on which the adversary relies in order to know itself: who it is, where it is, what it can do when, why it is fighting, which threats to counter first, etc. It means turning the balance of information and knowledge in one's favor. It means using knowledge so that less capital and labor may have to be expended.[31]

The close parallels with Boydian military thinking also come to the fore in the consequences for organization and command-and-control philosophy. Noting that Cyberwar is as much about organization as technology, they assert that the information revolution:

disrupts and erodes the hierarchies around which institutions are normally designed. It diffuses and redistributes power, often to the benefit of what may be considered weaker, smaller actors. It crosses borders, and redraws the boundaries of offices and responsibilities. It expands the spatial and temporal horizons that actors should take into account.[32]

Thus the advice to adaptive organization is that they:

evolve from traditional hierarchical forms to new, flexible, network-like models of organization. Success will depend on learning to interlace hierarchical and network principles. . . . Indeed, the information revolution favors the growth of such networks by making it possible for diverse, dispersed actors to communicate, consult, coordinate, and operate together across greater distances, and on the basis of more and better information than ever before.[33]

Adopting a network structure is not an option but an imperative, for case studies strongly suggest that 'institutions can be defeated by networks and it may take networks to counter networks'.[34] Command and organization for future warfare:

may require major innovations in organizational design, in particular a shift from hierarchies to networks. The traditional reliance on hierarchical designs may have to be adapted to network-oriented models to allow greater flexibility, lethal connectivity, and teamwork across institutional boundaries. The traditional emphasis on command and control may have to give way to an emphasis on consultation and coordination, the crucial building blocks of network designs.[35]

Several years after this article, Arquilla and Ronfeldt explored in more detail the possible optimal organizational concept for information-age warfare. The idea that small units now had access to unprecedented levels of situational awareness, and could call in stand-off precision firepower offered new possibilities. They offered the 'Swarming concept' as the logical emerging paradigm in warfare, following three earlier paradigms in military history: the melée, massing, maneuver. The central idea is that information technology offers the potential for small networked units to operate as a swarm in a

seemingly amorphous but deliberately structured, coordinated strategic way to strike from all direction, by means of a sustainable pulsing of force and/or fire, close in as well as from stand-off positions. It works best if it is designed mainly around the deployment of myriad, small, dispersed maneuver units that are tightly internetted and capable to communicate and coordinate with each other at will and are expected to do so.[36]

A swarm force must not only engage in strike operations, but also form part of a 'sensory organization', providing the surveillance and synoptic-level observations necessary to the creation and maintenance of 'topsight'.[37] A Boydian concept indeed.

Network Centric Warfare

These studies did not remain confined to the academic world. On the contrary, they came to define the US way of war and the vision of the future for the Pentagon. In 1997 then US Defense Secretary William Cohen asserted that:

> the information revolution is creating a Revolution in Military Affairs that will fundamentally change the way US forces fight. We must exploit these and other technologies to dominate in battle. Our template for seizing on these technologies and ensuring dominance is Joint Vision 2010, the plan set forth by the Chairman of the Joint Chiefs of Staff for military operations in the future.[38]

Joint Vision 2010 condensed both some core Boydian ideas, the tenets of information-age – or postmodern – warfare and the US defense aspirations in the following lines:

> By 2010, we should be able to change how we conduct the most intense joint operations. Instead of relying on massed forces and sequential operations, we will achieve massed effects in other ways. Information superiority and advances in technology will enable us to achieve the desired effects through the tailored application of joint combat power. Higher lethality weapons will allow us to conduct attacks currently that formerly required massed assets applied in a sequential manner. With precision targetting and longer range systems commanders can achieve the necessary destruction or suppression of enemy forces with fewer systems, thereby reducing the need for time consuming and risky massing of people and equipment. Improved command and control, based on fused, all-source real-time intelligence will reduce the need to assemble maneuver formations days and hours in advance of attacks. Providing improved targetting information directly to the most effective weapon system will potentially reduce the traditional force requirements at the point of main effort. All of this suggests that we will be increasingly able to accomplish the effects of mass – the necessary concentration of combat power at the decisive time and place – with less need to mass forces physically than in the past.[39]

In similar vein, in 1998 the US Army stated in one of its visionary publications that

> knowledge is paramount ... the unprecedented level of battle space awareness that is expected to be available will significantly reduce both fog and friction. Knowledge will shape the battle space and create conditions for success. It will permit ... distributed, decentralized, noncontiguous operations...[40]

The Marine Corps explored a 'biological systems inspiration', asserting that, instead of the Newtonian, mechanical and ordered model of warfare, a more likely model is 'a complex system that is open ended, parallel and very sensitive to initial conditions and continued inputs'. To be successful in such an environment, structures and tactics should have the following operational characteristics:

- Dispersed
- Autonomous
- Adaptable
- Small.[41]

In the latter part of the 1990s, an overarching concept – Network Centric Warfare (NCW) – was proposed, that incorporated many of the concepts developed in various studies on the impact of the Information Age on warfare, including swarming and the network structure. NCW, according to its advocates, is the emerging theory of war in the Information Age, a paradigm shift, and the military embodiment of information-age concepts and technologies.[42] It became the concept for US armed forces in the first decade of the twenty-first century, and with the agreement by NATO in 2002 to create the NATO Response Force and embark on 'military transformation', it has also entered the debates among European militaries.

NCW is a 'set of warfighting concepts designed to create and leverage information'.[43] The essence of NCW is captured in the following description:

> the US is poised to harness key information technologies – microelectronics, data networking, and software programming – to create a networked force, using weapons capable of pinpoint accuracy, launched from platforms beyond range of enemy weapons, utilizing the integrated data from all-seeing sensors, managed by intelligent command nodes. By distributing its forces, while still being able to concentrate fires, the US military is improving its mobility, speed, potency, and invulnerability to enemy attack.[44]

The network structure is essential, not a specific weapon or support system: 'In NCW no single platform or sensor is the heart of the system', the NCW Report to Congress states.[45] NCW derives its power from the strong networking of a well-informed but geographically dispersed force.[46] And networking stretches beyond technological connectivity, for NCW proponents maintain that reaping the maximum benefit of information-age tools, organization, command and control philosophy and doctrine, along with tactics and procedures, should also be radically adjusted.[47]

With explicit reference to Boyd's OODA loop it is noted that the advantage for forces that implement NCW lies in gaining and exploiting an information advantage. 'NCW allows the force to achieve an asymmetrical information advantage. NCW capabilities allow a force to attain an improved information position that can partially 'lift the fog of war' and enable commanders to improve their decision making and fight in ways that were not previously possible'. This will be achieved if the following is accomplished in three domains of armed forces.[48] In the 'Physical domain', 'all elements of the force are robustly networked', which will enable 'achieving secure and seamless connectivity'. In the 'Information domain' the force must have the 'capability to collect, share, access, and protect information', as well as 'the capability to collaborate in the information domain, which enables a force to improve its information position through processes of correlation, fusion, and analysis'. This will allow a force to 'achieve information advantage over an adversary in the information domain'. Importantly, in the 'Cognitive domain' the force must have 'the capability to develop and share high quality situational awareness' and the 'capability to develop a shared knowledge of commander's intent'. This will enable 'the capability to self-synchronize its operations'. A force with these attributes and capabilities will be able to increase combat power by

- Better synchronizing effects in the battlespace
- Achieving greater speed of command
- Increasing lethality, survivability, and responsiveness.[49]

Thus Steven Metz concludes that 'the US military will be the first postmodern state combatant, attaining greatly amplified speed and precision by the integration of information technology and development of a system of systems which link together methods for target acquisition, strikes, maneuver, planning, communication, and supply'.[50] And in postmodern war, 'time will be the key element. Postmodern militaries will attempt to use speed and knowledge to bring the conflict to quick resolution'.[51]

At the same time, alongside and in support of these conceptual developments, the US Department of Defense published a series of books highlighting the characteristics, benefit and need for agile innovative organizations. Agility referred to resilience and robustness. Agile – or 'edge' – organizations were characterized by the ability to combine information in new ways, the ability to apply a variety of perspectives and the ability to change the employment of assets commensurate with the changing situation.[52]

Although the OODA loop appears frequently in these studies, it is unwarranted to see too much of Boyd's ghost at work here. On the other hand, while Boyd would not care much about those who emphasize the technological aspect of postmodern war, he certainly would agree with this emphasis on continuous innovation and agility, as well as with the doctrinal and organizational tenets and the operational and strategic benefits accruing from the new model of warfare encapsulated in the term Information Age Warfare.

Fourth-generation warfare

Boyd would, however, also have agreed with those who argue that, precisely because the West has unsurpassed conventional military power, future opponents will revert to unconventional – asymmetrical – methods. At the same time that analysts described the contours of the RMA and the value of NCW, others put emphasis on this emerging phenomenon of asymmetric warfare.

On the one hand this referred to the character of warfare in the third world,[53] and the fact that for some peoples and cultures war may have different purposes (symbolic, ritual or existential instead of instrumental) and follow different rules, and may not be so linked and constrained by politics.[54] Kalevi Holsti, for instance, points at the fundamentally different political processes in a large number of wars of the 'Third Kind': 'most fundamentally, the assumption that the problem of war is primarily a problem of the relations between states has to be seriously questioned', because 'security between states in the Third World has become increasingly dependent upon security within those states. The problem of- contemporary and future international politics is essentially a problem of domestic politics. The source of the problem is found in the nature of new states'.[55] Also the reasons for fighting cannot be understood within the nation-state framework: 'more fundamental is the clash over different conceptions of community and how these conceptions should be reflected in political arrangements and organizations'.[56]

What Holsti labeled 'Wars of the Third Kind', Mary Kaldor considers 'New Wars'.[57] She agrees with Holsti that 'identity politics' is central: 'the exclusive claim to power on the basis of tribe, nation, clan or religious community. These identities are politically constituted.' Interestingly, war is not something that needs to be finished. These wars rage 'in regions where local production has declined and state revenues are very low, owing to widespread corruption'. In this context the warring states seek finance from external sources, diaspora support, taxation of humanitarian aid and through negative redistribution of resources – local looting, pillaging, enforcing unequal terms of trade through checkpoints and other restrictions, exhorting money, etc.[58] Moreover, all of these sources of finance depend on continued violence. The consequence is a set of predatory social relations that have a tendency to spread.[59] Because the various warring parties share the aim of sowing fear and hatred, they operate in a way that is mutually re-inforcing, helping each other to create a climate of insecurity and suspicion.[60]

This echoes van Creveld's statement that 'there exists a sense in which war, more than any other human activity, can make sense only to the extent that it is experienced not as a means but as an end'.[61] Indeed, both agree with van Creveld that modern war is of intrastate nature in which the Western rules and conventions guiding and constraining the conduct of war do not apply at all. The distinction between combatant and non-combatant is irrelevant. Deliberately ignoring and destroying this distinction is an explicit part of strategy in these conflicts.[62] There are no fronts, no campaigns, no bases, no uniforms, no publicly displayed honors, and no respect for the territorial limits of states. In wars between communities as opposed to armies, everyone is automatically labeled a combatant merely by virtue of their identity. In wars of the third kind, the deadly game is played in every home, church, government office, school, highway and village.[63]

Military victory is not decisive, nor aimed at. Instead, territorial gains are aimed at through acquisition of political power, not through military force. Weapons and methods to gain political power include ethnic cleansing, rape, assassination of key figures of the opponent, and terror.[64] Instead of conventional armies, the participants are irregular militant factions, terrorist groups and criminal organizations. 'This is a new age of warlordism', maintains Ralph Peters: 'paramilitary warriors-thugs whose talent for violence blossoms in civil war, defy legitimate governments and increasingly end up leading governments they have overturned'.[65]

These wars are difficult to approach from the Clausewitzian paradigm, according to van Creveld: 'war as a continuation of politics by other means' no longer applies 'when the stakes are highest and a community strains every sinew in a life and death struggle that the ordinary strategic terminology fails [...] to say that war is "an instrument" serving the "policy" of the community that "wages" it is to stretch all three terms to the point of meaninglessness. Where the distinction between ends and means breaks down, even the idea of war fought "for" something is only barely applicable. [...] war of this type [...] merges with policy, becomes policy, is policy.'[66] Subsequently, van Creveld warns, 'much of present day military power is simply irrelevant as an instrument for extending or defending political interest over much of the globe'.[67]

Whereas this phenomenon occurs within these regions, and may not be the result of a counter to the western concept of war and warfare, others point out that precisely because the West has been highly successful in a certain style of warfare, other countries or groups will not abide by those rules. War, so the argument goes, is a contest of ideas, and the highly visible Western pattern of operations makes the West predictable. A deliberate response can be expected. Not only would trusted tactics such as camouflage and dispersion be vigorously employed to negate the advantage of precision stand-off weapons, but opponents were expected to turn the Western conceptualization of war – its orientation pattern – against itself. If civilian casualties are to be avoided by Western militaries, opponents will aim to cause the West to inflict massive and highly visible civilian casualties. The use of human shields and using schools, mosques, cultural objects and hospitals as hiding places for military equipment are examples of this mode of thinking that have been witnessed during Desert Storm, Allied Force, Enduring Freedom, Iraqi Freedom and the ensuing stabilization operations. Additionally, adversaries can employ non-military forms of combat such as information war, extortion, bribery, etc.[68]

Thus, the current Western mode of thinking and waging war, which is founded on Clausewitzian principles, is giving rise to non-Clausewitzian styles of warfare, with obvious consequences for the state of strategic theory. Instead of countering the West in the military dimension, nations – but in particular non-governmental actors – respond in the moral dimension.

To illustrate this line of thinking, two serving senior officers of the Chinese armed forces unveiled their view on how to counter the Western style of warfare in their book *Unrestricted Warfare*.[69] Based on a thorough examination of the way the West, and in particular the US, has fought wars in the past decade, they formulate a strategic response that is multidimensional and deliberately not confined to the military dimension. Box 7.1 lists the domains in which war can be waged, according to the authors.

They advocate non-military means such as Information Warfare-related concepts, such as the use of hackers, the mass media and financial information terrorism. Rules and conventions, such as the Laws of Armed Conflict, are not adhered to, while the West's political, moral and military restraints that fighting according to these rules implies, are fully exploited.

More philosophically, the authors turn the West's perception concerning the nature, the meaning and purpose of war against itself. War is not identical with violent military clashes, instead it must be understood as constant contest or struggle. The authors deliberately redefine the meaning of war and stretch it far beyond what most western societies consider the current meaning of war. Thus, academically they open the possibility of being engaged in a war, employing non-military methods to achieve their aim, while the West would not recognize that it was engaged in one.

While sometimes too extreme, it is hard to disagree when van Creveld concludes in *The Transformation of War* that 'The nature of the entities by which war is made, the conventions by which it is surrounded, and the ends for which it is fought may change.' Thus, in reaction to the terrorist attacks of September 11, 2001 on New York and Washington, authors such as Phillip Bobbit, John Lynn and Christopher Coker indeed make the argument that the West needs to reconceptualize war, for the West's instrumental view of war is severely challenged by the clash with groups who experience war as existential.[70] The attacks of September 11, 2001 were so shocking in part because they broke the pattern

Military war	Beyond military war	Non-military war
Nuclear	Diplomatic	Financial
Conventional	Internet	Trade
Bio-Chemical	Information Ops	Natural Resource
Ecological	Psychological	Economic Aid
Space	High Tech	Law and Regulations
Electronic	Smuggling	Sanctions
Guerrilla	Drug	Media War
Terrorism	Deterrence	Ideological

Box 7.1 Domains of *Unrestricted Warfare*.

of Western-style warfare, they shattered the framework of war and warfare that Western society had become accustomed to.

Interestingly, this line of reasoning was the essence of an article published as early as 1989 by Boyd's close associate, Bill Lind, and a group of officers.[71] They argued that maneuver warfare – '3rd Generation Warfare' – would be followed by '4th Generation Warfare (4GW)'. Recognizing that the West has only ever been beaten in unconventional wars, bound by a common ideology, practitioners of 4GW wage protracted asymmetric war. Non-state actors would freely roam through the open societies of the West and could strike with non-military means. Regarding war not as a military but as a political struggle, they focus on the political will of western politicians and polities; exploit their impatience and casualty-sensitivity. This idea-driven fourth-generation warfare would be a war fought at the ideological and moral level by small cells operating in decentralized fashion. Terrorism would be one visible manifestation of it.

In the aftermath of 11 September 2001, the article was rediscovered, and with the costly and prolonged stabilization operations in Iraq after the 'end of hostilities' in May 2003, and the subsequent apparent rise of the global Islamist insurgency, 4GW attracted an increasing following. Not surprisingly, the authors of 4GW articles frequently cite from Boyd's work, for instance from Boyd's section on moral war and from the *Strategic Game*, to explain how US policies and military actions isolated the US from the Iraqi population;[72] another testimony to the merits of Boyd's mode of thinking, as well as his continuing influence.

Analysis/synthesis

John Boyd is dead but he has left a sophisticated, multi-layered and multidimensional legacy and a new set of terms and concepts to study conflict that is useful, if at places abstract, biased, cryptic, and difficult to fathom. Boyd's ideas involve much more than exclusively the idea of 'rapid OODA looping' or a theory for maneuver warfare. Contradicting those who categorically dismiss the validity of the OODA concept, the idea was found to be deep and rich in ideas, explanations, hypotheses, propositions, concepts and suggestions concerning conflict in general. These concepts are firmly based on a thorough study of military history and informed by insights on learning and the behavior of social systems derived from various disciplines.

The narrow interpretation of Boyd's work is inaccurate and incomplete. Not only has Boyd addressed a multitude of topics, besides the rapid OODA loop idea, offering new conceptualizations of strategy, and introducing new concepts for thinking about the interactions at the different levels of war, it is moreover only either in the most abstract and short-hand rendering, or at the tactical level, that the rapid OODA-looping idea in its narrow interpretation mirrors Boyd's work to some extent. And even at the tactical level Boyd argues for a more comprehensive approach, focusing on the interplay of actions and threats as they manifest themselves in the physical, moral and mental dimensions.

Instead of a focus on information, he displays a focus on the myriad factors that produce the internal cohesion required for a system to survive, and the multidimensional connections a system needs to maintain with the outside environment. Whereas rapid OODA looping is often equated with superior speed in decision making, Boyd employs the OODA loop model to show how organisms evolve and adapt. It has become evident that, in addition to the common, narrow interpretation of the OODA loop idea, Boyd's work is infused with the larger theme of equal or even surpassing importance of multidimensional organizational adaptation in a dynamic non-linear environment. While rapid OODA looping – as in rapid decision making – is quite relevant for success at the tactical level, and to some extent also at the operational level, Boyd regards the OODA loop schematic in general as a model for organizational learning, or even more general, the way organisms adapt and thus evolve.

Boyd's work conceptually follows, clearly, closely in the footsteps of Sun Tzu, Julian Corbett, J.F.C. Fuller, T.E. Lawrence and Basil Liddell Hart. His work is rooted in an impressive, if sometimes biased, study of military history. But in his synthesis and deep analysis his work contains novel insights. An important and often-overlooked element lies in Boyd's approach to studying strategy and operational art, and conflict in general, in his holistic approach, and in particular in his use of contemporary scientific insights from a variety of disciplines to study conflict. An overview of the scientific *Zeitgeist* which Boyd deliberately followed, provided metaphors and concepts that helped explain and understand his arguments, and demonstrated that the scientific *Zeitgeist*, which has since then been labeled as the postmodernist era, offered Boyd new modes of conceptualizing strategy and war. The value of his work lies of course in the concepts he develops, but at least to an equal extent it lies in the novel approach for thinking about strategy, making strategic theory and making strategy, and in introducing current scientific developments into strategic theory.

Although Boyd would probably have disapproved of this label, in this aspect of his work also lies the justification for regarding him as the first postmodern strategist, both in content and in his approach to making strategy and strategic theory, in light of the similarities of his work and his sources with moderate postmodern social theorists, postmodern security and strategic studies, and because of his lasting shadow on postmodern war and 4GW.

Boyd infected a generation of senior military and political leaders with the virus of novelty and led them to think in different ways about the conduct of war. It inspired AirLand Battle and US Marines doctrine. Today his ideas inform emerging war-fighting concepts such as Network-Centric Warfare. His language and logic, his ideas, terms and concepts are part and parcel now of the military conceptual frame of reference. Western military organizations have to a large extent internalized Boyd's concepts, and perhaps even learned Boyd's way of thinking.

Boyd's work also offers important insights for understanding the threats of the 'post-9/11' world. So-called asymmetric responses to western modes of warfare become a natural feature, only to be expected from adversaries. The attacks of '9/11' and the insurgency wars being waged in their wake, introduced the contours of a new warform, and the West has been challenged to understand the nature of this new game of survival.

This pertains to the value of his work for the field of strategic theory. Because a theory can be both commendably sound and disappointingly banal, it must be evaluated not only in terms of its epistemological virtues, but also by the value of the increment in knowledge it seeks to provide. This is determined by the scope of the phenomena it accounts for and the significance of the phenomena it addresses. A theory of great scope is one from whose premises many implications may be drawn. Theories that correctly account for many phenomena that had previously been poorly understood, or that adumbrate new paths to explanation, are obviously better than those that illuminate a very narrow range of questions, or questions to which we already have satisfactory answers.[73] In that respect, Colin Gray was right in stating that Boyd's OODA loop is a grand theory in the sense that the model has an elegant simplicity, an extensive domain of application, and contains a high quality of insight about strategic essentials.[74]

Perhaps, in due course Boyd's work may be looked upon as not very remarkable nor distinctive. Yet even then this remark by Richard Dawkins will apply to the relevance of John Boyd:

> Often the most important contribution a scientist can make is to discover a new way of seeing old theories or facts. A change of vision can usher in a whole climate of thinking in which many exciting and testable theories are born, and unimagined facts laid bare.[75]

He developed a rich, comprehensive, novel theory that has proven strong, valuable and influential, even if he deliberately left it incomplete.

Annexes

Annex A: bibliography of *Destruction and Creation*

1 Beveridge, W.I.B., *The Art of Scientific Investigation*, Vintage Books, 3rd edn, 1957.
2 Boyd, John R., *Destruction and Creation*, 23 March 1976.
3 Brown, G. Spencer, *Laws of Form*, Julian Press, Inc., 1972.
4 Conant, James Bryant, *Two Modes of Thought*, Credo Perspectives, Simon and Schuster, 1970.
5 DeBono, Edward, *New Think*, Avon Books, 1971.
6 DeBono, Edward, *Lateral Thinking: Creativity Step by Step*, Harper Colophon Books, 1973.
7 Foster, David, *The Intelligent Universe*, Putnam, 1975.
8 Fromm, Erich, *The Crisis of Psychoanalysis*, Fawcett Premier Books, 1971.
9 Gamow, George, *Thirty Years That Shook Physics*, Anchor Books, 1966.
10 Gardner, Howard, *The Quest for Mind*, Vintage Books, 1974.
11 Georgescu-Roegen, Nicholas, *The Entropy Law and the Economic Process*, Harvard University Press, 1971.
12 Gödel, Kurt, *On Formally Undecidable Propositions of the Principia Mathematica and Related Systems*, pp. 3–38, 'The Undecidable', Raven Press, 1965.
13 Heilbroner, Robert L., *An Inquiry into the Human Prospect*, Norton and Co., 1974.
14 Heisenberg, Werner, *Physics and Philosophy*, Harper Torchbooks, 1962.
15 Heisenberg, Werner, *Across the Frontiers*, World Perspectives, Harper and Row, 1974.
16 Hoyle, Fred, *Encounter with the Future*, Credo Perspectives, Simon and Schuster, 1968.
17 Hoyle, Fred, *The New Face of Science*, Perspectives in Humanism, World Publishing Co., 1971.
18 Kramer, Edna E., *The Nature and Growth of Modern Mathematics*, Fawcett Premier Books, 1974.
19 Kuhn, Thomas S., *The Structure of Scientific Revolutions*, University of Chicago Press, 1970.
20 Layzer, David, 'The Arrow of Time', *Scientific American*, December 1975.
21 Levinson, Harry, *The Exceptional Executive*, Mentor Books, 1971.
22 Maltz, Maxwell, *Psycho-Cybernetics*, Wilshire Book Co., 1971.
23 Nagel, Ernest and Newman, James R., *Gödel's Proof*, New York University Press, 1958.
24 Osborne, Alex F., *Applied Imagination*, Scribners and Sons, 1963.

25 Pearce, Joseph Chilton, *The Crack in the Cosmic Egg*, Pocket Book, 1975.
26 Pearce, Joseph Chilton, *Exploring the Crack in the Cosmic Egg*, Pocket Book, 1975.
27 Piaget, Jean, *Structuralism*, Harper Torchbooks, 1971.
28 Polanyi, Michael, *Knowing and Being*, University of Chicago Press, 1969.
29 Singh, Jagjit, *Great Ideas of Modern Mathematics: Their Nature and Use*, Dover, 1959.
30 Skinner, B.F., *Beyond Freedom and Dignity*, Bantam/Vintage Books, 1972.
31 Thompson, William Irwin, *At the Edge of History*, Harper Colophon Books, 1972.
32 Thompson, William Irwin, *Evil and World Order*, World Perspectives, Harper and Row, 1976.
33 Tse-Tung, Mao, *Four Essays on China and World Communism*, Lancer Books, 1972.
34 Waismann, Friedrich, *Introduction to Mathematical Thinking*, Harper Torchbooks, 1959.
35 Watts, Alan, *The Book*, Vintage Books, 1972.
36 Yukawa, Bideki, *Creativity and Intuition*, Kodansha International LTD, 1973.

Annex B: bibliography of the works of John Boyd

Aerial Attack Study, 1960 (monograph, 147 pages)
A New Conception of Air to Air Combat, August 1976 (presentation, 24 slides)
Destruction and Creation, September 1976 (essay, 16 pages)
Patterns of Conflict, September 1976–December 1986 (presentation, 93 slides)
Organic Design for Command and Control, first draft 1982, release May 1987 (presentation, 37 slides)
The Strategic Game of ? & ?, first draft 1986, release June 1987 (presentation, 59 slides)
Revelation (presentation, 2 slides)
A Discourse on Winning and Losing, August 1987 (essay *Destruction and Creation* and presentation *Patterns of Conflict*, *Organic Design*, *The Strategic Game*, *Revelation*)
The Conceptual Spiral, July 1992 (presentation, 38 slides), added to *A Discourse*
The Essence of Winning and Losing, January 1995 (presentation, 5 slides)

Notes

1 Introduction

1 Robert Coram, *Boyd, The Fighter Pilot Who Changed the Art of War*, Boston: Little Brown & Company, 2002, p. 451.
2 John Boyd, 'Abstract', in *A Discourse*, p. 1.
3 Ibid.
4 Coram, op. cit., p. 445.
5 James Burton, *The Pentagon Wars: Reformers Challenge the Old Guard*, Annapolis, MD: Naval Institute Press, 1993, p. 10.
6 Colin Gray, *Modern Strategy*, Oxford: Oxford University Press, 1999, pp. 90–1.
7 In Chapter 2 Boyd's involvement with the development of AirLandBattle will be elaborated upon.
8 *British Defence Doctrine, Joint Warfare Publication 0-01*, London: Her Majesty's Stationery Office, 1997, pp. 4.8–4.9.
9 See for Boyd's role for instance Richard Hallion, *Storm over Iraq, Air Power and the Gulf War*, Washington, D.C.: Smithsonian Institution Press, 1992, pp. 38–42, and pp. 278–81.
10 Coram, op. cit., pp. 425, 444. The other two were Mike Wyly and Huba Wass de Czege, who were closely involved in the doctrinal shifts of the US Marines and US Army respectively. Chapter 31 of Coram's book describes Boyd's role in Desert Storm.
11 Ibid., pp. 446–7.
12 See the interview with general Tommy Franks in P. Boyer, 'The New War Machine', *The New Yorker*, 30 June 2003, p. 70. In the article the author also introduces the military reform movement and Boyd's role in it, asserting that current US Secretary of Defense Donald Rumsfeld had been influenced in the seventies and eighties and had become a supporter for military reform and innovation in strategy. Franks repeated this in his biography *An American Soldier*, New York: Regan Press, 2004, on p. 466. However, for a balancing view see William Lind's reaction to various commentators 'The Three Levels of War, Don't Take John Boyd's Name in Vain', *Counterpunch*, 3 May 2003. Online. Available at: www.counterpunch.org/lind05032003.html (accessed 16 December 2003).
13 Grant Hammond, *The Mind of War, John Boyd and American Security*, Washington, D.C.: Smithsonian Institution Press, 2001, p. 56.
14 Ibid., p. 11.
15 See George Stalk, Jr. and Thomas M. Hout, *Competing Against Time, How Time-Based Competition Is Reshaping Global Markets*, New York, The Free Press, 1990, pp. 180–4. The copy of this book in Boyd's possession includes a note of appreciation to Boyd by the authors.
16 Coram, op. cit., p. 429.

17 General C.C. Krulak, Commandant of the Marine Corps, *Inside the Pentagon*, 13 March 1997, p. 5.

18 See Gray, op. cit., p. 91. See for similar interpretation David Fadok, who wrote one the earliest studies on Boyd, stating that for Boyd the crux of winning becomes the relational movement of opponents through their respective OODA loops; David S. Fadok: *John Boyd and John Warden: Air Power's Quest for Strategic Paralysis*, in Col. Phillip Meilinger (ed.), *The Paths to Heaven*, Maxwell AFB: Air University Press, 1997, p. 366. Fadok distills the gist from Boyd's slides and presents them clearly in a chapter in which he compares and contrasts Boyd and Warden. As such it is an excellent primer on Boyd's ideas.

19 Chairman of Joint Chiefs of Staff, *Joint Vision 2010*, Washington, D.C.: US Department of Defense, 1996, cited in Lonnie D. Henley, 'The RMA After Next', *Parameters*, Winter 1999–2000, p. 46. For other examples see for instance Phillip S. Meilinger, 'Air Targetting Strategies: An Overview', in Richard Hallion, *Air Power Confronts An Unstable World*, London: Brassey's, 1997, pp. 60–1; Phillip S. Meilinger, *Ten Propositions Regarding Air Power*, Washingon, D.C.: Air Force History and Museums Program, 1995, pp. 31–2; Gary Vincent's two articles 'In the Loop, Superiority in Command and Control', *Airpower Journal*, Vol. VI, Summer 1992, pp. 15–25, and 'A New Approach to Command and Control, the Cybernetic Design', *Airpower Journal*, Vol. VII, Summer 1993, pp. 24–38. See also Gordon R. Sullivan and James M. Dublik, 'War in the Information Age', *Military Review*, April 1994, p. 47, where the authors lay out a vision of war in the information age, incorporating the same pictogram of the OODA loop as used above. Remarkably, Boyd is not listed as the intellectual father of the OODA loop, suggesting that the OODA construct had already become very commonplace..

20 Such as Shimon Naveh, *In Pursuit of Excellence: The Evolution of Operational Theory*, London: Frank Cass, 1997.

21 See David R. Mets, 'Boydmania', *Air & Spacepower Journal*, Fall 2004, Vol. XVIII, no. 3, pp. 98–107.

22 See examples in note 19. In addition, see Paolo Bartolomasi, 'The Realities and Challenges for Concepts and Capabilities in Joint Manoeuvre', *RUSI Journal*, August 2000, pp. 8, 9.

23 Thomas Hughes, 'The Cult of the Quick', *Airpower Journal*, Vol. XV, no. 4, Winter 2001, pp. 57–68. Only in the endnotes does Hughes acknowledge that Boyd's ideas are more complex than this interpretation.

24 See for a recent informed but still unsatisfactory discussion on the merits of the OODA loop in this respect, for instance, Tim Grant and Bas Kooter, 'Comparing OODA & other models as Operational View C2 Architecture', paper delivered at the 10th International Command and Control Symposium. Online. Available at: www.ccrp.osd.dod.mil (accessed 15 December 2005).

25 See Jim Storr, 'Neither Art Nor Science – Towards a Discipline of Warfare', *RUSI Journal*, April 2001, p. 39. Emphasis is mine. Referring to Karl Popper, Storr states that 'induction is unsafe' and 'to generalize about formation-level C2 from aircraft design is tenuous'.

26 Hammond, op. cit., p. 13.

27 Coram, op. cit., p. 329. In recent years an attempt has been made to make his work accessible through the maintenance of a website dedicated to his work. See www.belisarius.com.

28 Fadok's study has been mentioned already. In addition see Anthoni Rinaldi, 'Complexity Theory and Air Power; a new paradigm for air power in the 21st century', in *Complexity, Global Politics and National Security*, Washington, D.C.: NDU Press. Online. Available at: www.ndu.edu/ndu/inss/books/complexity/ch10a.html (accessed 11 February 1999), and Michael T. Plehn, '*Control Warfare: Inside The OODA Loop*', Maxwell AFB: Air University Press, June 2000.

29 Robert Coram's work focuses in particular on Boyd's life and less on Boyd's strategic theory. Grant Hammond's study surpasses Coram in his rendering of Boyd's strategic theory, but while touching upon Boyd's wide array of sources underlying his work, space restrictions prevented a proper discussion of the intellectual background of Boyd's work.

30 See also Hammond, op. cit., p. 15.

31 John Boyd, *The Strategic Game of ? and ?*, p. 58.

32 The description of military theory and doctrine are derived from Antulio J. Echevarria, *After Clausewitz, German Military Thinkers Before the Great War*, Lawrence: University Press of Kansas, 2000, pp. 7–8.

33 J. Mohan Malik, 'The Evolution of Strategic Thought', in Graig Snyder (ed.), *Contemporary Security and Strategy*, London: Macmillan, 1999, p. 13.

34 Carl von Clausewitz, *On War*, trans. Michael Howard and Peter Paret, Princeton, NJ: Princeton University Press, 1976, p. 128.

35 Gray, op. cit., p. 17.

36 J.C. Wylie, *Military Strategy: A General Theory of Power Control*, New Brunswick: Rutgers University Press, p. 13.

37 André Beaufre, *An Introduction to Strategy*, New York: Praeger, 1963, p. 22.

38 Williamson Murray and Mark Grimsley, 'Introduction: On Strategy', in Murray, MacGregor Knox and Alvin Bernstein (eds), *The Making of Strategy: Rulers, States, and War*, Cambridge: Cambridge University Press, 1994, p. 1.

39 Malik, op. cit., p. 14.

40 Henk W. Volberda and Tom Elfring, *Rethinking Strategy*, London: Sage Publications, 2001, op. cit., p. 1.

41 Adopted from Henry Minzberg *et al.*, *Strategy Safari*, New York: Free Press, 1998, p. 16.

42 Gray, op. cit., p. 47.

43 Gray, ibid., p. 44.

44 Richard K. Betts, 'Is Strategy an Illusion?', *International Security*, Vol. 25, No. 2, Fall 2000, p. 5.

45 Williamson Murray and MacGregor Knox, 'Conclusion, the future behind us', in MacGregor Knox and Williamson Murray, *The Dynamics of Military Revolution, 1300–2050*, Cambridge: Cambridge University Press, 2001, p. 180.

46 Gray, op. cit., p. 50.

47 Ibid., p. 124.

48 Gary King *et al.*, p. 20.

49 Bruce Russett and Harvey Starr, *World Politics, A Menu for Choice*, San Francisco, 1981, p. 32. Laws are hypotheses that are confirmed in virtually all of the classes of phenomena to which they are applied.

50 Clausewitz, op. cit., p. 140.

51 Ibid., p. 141.

52 Ibid., p. 136. This critique was directed against Jomini and Bulow.

53 John C. Garnett, *Commonsense and the Theory of International Politics*, London: Macmillan, 1984, p. 46.

54 Alexander George, *Bridging the Gap, Theory and Practice in Foreign Policy*, Washington, D.C.: United States Institute of Peace Press, 1993, p. 117.

55 Gray, op. cit., pp. 125–6.

56 Ibid., p. 128.

57 In fact, most strategic theorists argue that a specific method will most likely under all circumstances provide victory. Famous authors such as Jomini, Douhet and Liddell Hart were not above that.

58 Gray, op. cit., p. 36.

59 See John Tetsuro Sumida, *Inventing Grand Strategy and Teaching Command*, Washington, D.C.: The Woodrow Wilson Center Press, Washington, D.C., 1997, p. xix.

60 Stephen M. Walt, 'The Search for a Science of Strategy', *International Security*, Summer 1987, Vol. 12, no. 1, p. 141.

61 See Alexander George, *Bridging the Gap, Theory and Practice in Foreign Policy*, Washington, D.C.: United States Institute of Peace Press, 1993, for a discussion on the value of theory for foreign policy making which is quite relevant for understanding the value of strategic theory.

62 Ibid., p. xviii.

63 Gray, op. cit., pp. 35–6.

64 Ibid., p. 123.

65 Ibid., p. 134.

66 Ibid., p. 4.

67 Ibid., pp. 24–6.

68 Bernard Brodie, *War and Politics*, New York: Macmillan, 1973, p. 452.

69 See for instance Ken Booth, 'The Evolution of Strategic Thinking', in John Baylis, Ken Booth, John Garnett and Phil Williams, *Contemporary Strategy*, Volume I, second edition, New York: Holmes & Meier, 1987.

70 Avi Kober, 'Nomology vs Historicism: Formative Factors in Modern Military Thought', *Defense Analysis*, Vol. 10, No. 3, 1994, p. 268.

71 This is similar to Anthony Giddens' notion of 'reflexivity', as will be discussed in Chapter 4.

72 Luttwak, *Strategy, the Logic of War and Peace*, Cambridge, MA: Harvard University Press, 1987.

73 See Chapter 7 for a brief discussion on asymmetric warfare.

74 Todd Stillman, 'Introduction: Metatheorizing Contemporary Social Theorists', in George Ritzer, *The Blackwell Companion to Major Contemporary Social Theorists*, Oxford: Blackwell Publishing, 2003, p. 3.

75 Mintzberg *et al.*, op. cit., pp. 8–9. See also Volberda, op. cit., p. 7.

76 Quincy Wright, *The Study of International Relations*, New York: The University of Chicago Press, 1955, p. 149.

77 Kober, op. cit., p. 268. Actually he also states that the way lessons are learned affects military theory. However, Kober fails to show to what extent it is markedly different in its effect on theory making, as compared to the more thoroughly discussed factor of the nature of war.

78 Ibid., pp. 272–3.

79 Ibid., p. 276.

80 Azar Gat, *Fascist and Liberal Visions of War*, Oxford: Clarendon Press, 1998, p. 175.

81 Ibid., pp. vii, viii.

82 Azar Gat, *The Origins of Military Thought*, Oxford: Clarendon Press, 1989, p. 25.

83 Azar Gat, *The Development of Military Thought: The Nineteenth Century*, Oxford: Clarendon Press, Oxford, 1992, p. 1. See also Gat, *A History of Military Thought, From the Enlightenment to the Cold War*, Oxford: Oxford University Press, 2001, Book I, pp. 141–51 for a short discussion of the shifting intellectual *Zeitgeist* that occurred around 1800.

84 Amos Perlmutter, 'Carl von Clausewitz, Enlightenment Philosopher: A Comparative Analysis', *The Journal of Strategic Studies*, Volume 11, March 1988, number 12, p. 16.

85 Ibid., p. 12.

86 See also Peter Paret, who argues that Clausewitz, both in method and in terminology, was influenced by the philosophers of the Enlightenment and of German idealism, such as Kant, Herder and Fichte, who inspired him not only directly through their works but also through the filter of German historical writings that was influenced by them. See Peter Paret, *Clausewitz and the State*, Princeton, NJ: Princeton University Press, 1976, p. 84.

87 Robert P. Pellegrini, *The Links Between Science and Philosophy and Military Theory*,

Understanding the Past; Implications for the Future, Maxwell A.F.B., AL: Air University Press, June 1995, p. 33.

88 Barry Watts, *The Foundations of US Air Doctrine, the Problem of Friction in War*, Maxwell A.F.B., AL: Air University Press, 1984, p. 106. Laplace established that the solar system was stable and completely determined by physical laws, hence entirely predictable.

89 Ibid., p. 108.

90 Ibid., p. 116.

91 Ibid., pp. 119, 121.

92 This is not incidentally similar to Boyd's use of these scientists. As Watts explained to the author, he was thoroughly familiar with Boyd's maturing work, and had frequent detailed and long discussions with him about Boyd's ideas as well as on scientific ideas in general.

93 Ibid., p. 109.

94 Ibid., p. iii.

95 Ibid., p. 8.

2 The seeds of a theory and the fertile soil

1 Karl Popper, *The Logic of Scientific Discovery*, New York: Routledge, 1968, p. 32.

2 This list is based on Jeffrey Cowan (2000), *From Fighter Pilot to Marine Corps Warfighting*. Online. Available at: www.defence-and-society.org/FCS_Folder/Boyd_thesis.htm (accessed 14 August 2002), pp. 29–30; and Grant T. Hammond, *The Mind of War, John Boyd and American Security*, Washington, D.C.: Smithsonian Institution Press, 2001, p. 155.

3 Hammond, op. cit., p. 35.

4 Ibid., p. 39.

5 Ibid., pp. 44, 46–7; Cowan, op. cit., pp. 11–12.

6 See Robert Coram, *Boyd, The Fighter Pilot Who Changed the Art of War*, Boston: Little Brown & Company, 2002, pp. 127–34, for an anecdotal account of the way Boyd gained this insight and made the analogy to air combat.

7 Ibid., p. 127. Both Hammond and Coram rightfully discuss the importance of Tom Christie in the development of EM Theory.

8 See Hammond, op. cit., pp. 52–61 and Cowan, op. cit., pp. 12–13.

9 Coram deals extensively with Boyd's involvement in the design of the F-15 and the F-16 in Part II.

10 Richard P. Hallion, *Storm over Iraq, Air Power and the Gulf War*, Washington, D.C.: Smithsonian Institution Press, 1992, p. 38. See also Cowan, op. cit., pp. 13–15, and Hammond, op. cit., pp. 67–100. All attest to Boyd's considerable influence.

11 This section benefited from some corrective suggestions by Barry Watts.

12 See Hammond and Hallion as well as James Burton, *The Pentagon Wars: Reformers Challenge the Old Guard*, Annapolis, MD: Naval Institute Press, 1993.

13 Hammond, op. cit., pp. 121–3.

14 James Burton, op. cit., pp. 46, 49.

15 John Boyd, 'A New conception for Air-to-Air Combat', slides 6, 18, underlining in original.

16 Ibid., p. 19.

17 Ibid., p. 21.

18 Ibid., p. 22.

19 Ibid., p. 23.

20 According to Barry Watts, as communicated to the author, those views were reinforced if not preceded by the strong opinion of Pierre Sprey, one of Boyd's close associates.

21 Julian S. Corbett, *Some Principles of Maritime Strategy*, Annapolis, MD: Naval Institute Press, 1988 (originally published in 1911).

22 T.E. Lawrence, *The Seven Pillars of Wisdom*, Ware, Hertfordshire: Wordsworth Editions, 1997, p. 177.

23 Ibid., p. 178.

24 Ibid., p. 179.

25 Ibid., pp. 185–6.

26 Ibid., pp. 182–4.

27 Ibid., pp. 188–90.

28 Ibid., p. 185.

29 Azar Gat, *Fascist and Liberal Visions of War, Fuller, Liddell Hart, Douhet and other Modernists*, Oxford: Clarendon Press, 1998, p. 33.

30 Ibid. Gat cites from Guderian's work.

31 J.F.C. Fuller, *The Conduct of War, 1789–1961: A Study of the Impact of the French, Industrial and Russian Revolutions on War and Its Conduct*, New Brunswick, NJ: Da Capo Press, 1992, pp. 242–3.

32 Ibid.

33 Gat, op. cit., p. 40.

34 Ibid., p. 39.

35 For the evidence of Liddell Hart's plagiarism see Gat, op. cit., pp. 146–50.

36 The bibliography attached to *Patterns of Conflict* shows Boyd studied the following works by Liddell Hart: *A Science of Infantry Tactics Simplified* (1926); *The Future of Infantry* (1933); *The Ghost of Napoleon* (1934); *The German Generals Talk* (1948); and *Strategy* (1967).

37 For this study I used the second revised edition of 1967, the one Boyd also read and which he heavily annotated.

38 Liddell Hart has been thoroughly criticized for his methods, his sloppy history and his misinterpretation of Clausewitz and the actions of senior military figures in World War I. However, recently several authors acknowledge that Liddell Hart's later work is more sophisticated and original, that indeed the *Blitzkrieg* practitioners were inspired by Fuller and Liddell Hart, and that his interpretation of Clausewitz is not too wide off the mark altogether. See for instance Alex Dachev, 'Liddell Hart's Big Idea', *Review of International Studies* (1999), 25, pp. 29–48.

39 Gat, op. cit., pp. 150–3.

40 Ibid.

41 Jay Luvaas, 'Clausewitz: Fuller and Liddell Hart', *Journal of Strategic Studies*, 9 (1986), p. 209.

42 Liddell Hart, *Strategy*, p. 212.

43 Ibid.

44 Ibid., pp. 321–2.

45 Ibid., p. 323.

46 Ibid., p. 324.

47 Ibid., my emphasis partly.

48 Here Boyd actually noted in the margins that this equates to 'getting inside the adversary's OODA or mind-space-time framework'.

49 Ibid., p. 327. Emphasis in original. Here we see Liddell Hart outlining an idea similar to the concept of *ch'i* and *cheng*; the unorthodox and the orthodox and the idea of shaping the opponent, as will be explained in more detail below.

50 Ibid.

51 Ibid., p. 329. Emphasis is mine.

52 Ibid.

53 Ibid., p. 330.

54 Ibid. Emphasis is mine.

55 Ibid., pp. 335–6.

56 In Hammond, op. cit., p. 105.

57 It also helps to explain some of the terms Boyd put in his slides without much explanation. The following is based on my chapter titled 'Asymmetric Warfare: Rediscovering the Essence of Strategy', in John Olson, *Asymmetric Warfare*, Oslo: Royal Norwegian Air Force Academy Press, 2002.

58 For some additional meanings see Roger Ames (transl.), *Sun Tzu, The Art of Warfare*, New York: Ballantine Books, 1993, p. 73.

59 Taken from Ralph D. Sawyer (transl.), *Sun Tzu: The Art of War*, New York: Barnes and Noble, 1994.

60 Ibid., p. 191.

61 Ibid., p. 178.

62 Ibid., p. 179.

63 Ibid., p. 177.

64 Ibid., p. 224.

65 Ames, op. cit., p. 84.

66 See Sawyer, op. cit., p. 193: 'The army's disposition if force (*hsing*) is like water. Water's configuration avoids heights and races downward. The army's disposition of force avoids the substantial and strikes the vacuous. Water configures its flow in accord with the terrain; the army controls its victory in accord with the enemy. Thus the army does not maintain any constant strategic configuration of power (*shih*), water has no constant shape. One who is able to change and transform in accord with the enemy and wrest victory is termed spiritual.'

67 Ames, op. cit., p. 84.

68 Sawyer, op. cit., p. 224.

69 Ibid., p. 178.

70 Ibid., p. 199.

71 Sun Tzu's military thought has frequently been erroneously identified solely with deceit and deception. These two terms, however, connect ideas that ultimately need to produce surprise. Only twice do deception and deceit appear explicitly in the book.

72 Ibid., p. 188.

73 Ibid., p. 220.

74 Ibid., p. 193.

75 See Sawyer, op. cit., p. 187: 'In general in battle one engages with the orthodox and gains victory through the unorthodox [. . .] the changes of the unorthodox and orthodox can never be completely exhausted. The unorthodox and the orthodox mutually produce each other, just like an endless cycle. Who can exhaust them?'

76 Ibid., pp. 147–50.

77 The source for this section is O'Dowd and Waldron, 'Sun Tzu for Strategists', *Comparative Strategy*, Volume 10, 1991, pp. 31–2.

78 See Coram, op. cit., Chapter 19, for Boyd's command experience in Thailand.

79 See for instance Edward Luttwak, 'The Operational Level of War', *International Security*, Winter 1980/81 (Vol. 5, No. 3), pp. 61–79.

80 Or almost unpaid: he did receive symbolic payment in order to retain access to the Pentagon. I am endebted to Chet Richards for this remark.

81 See Hammond, op. cit., pp. 101–17 for a full discussion of Boyd's role and the activities of the reform movement, as well as Coram, Chapters 25 to 31, in particular Chapter 25. See also Lieutenant Colonel Mark Hamilton, 'Maneuver Warfare and All That', *Military Review*, January 1987, p. 3; William Lind, 'Defining Maneuver Warfare for the Marine Corps', *Marine Corps Gazette*, March 1980, p. 56; and William Lind, Colonel Keith Nightengale, Captain John Schmitt, Colonel Joseph Sutton, Lieutenant Colonel G.I. Wilson, 'The Changing Face of War, Into the Fourth Generation', *Military Review*, October 1989, p. 4.

82 For two balanced and thorough critical discussions see John J. Mearsheimer,

'Maneuver, Mobile Defense, and the NATO Central Front', *International Security*, Winter 1981/82 (Vol. 6, No. 3), pp. 104–22, and Richard K. Betts, 'Conventional Strategy, New Critics, Old Choices', *International Security*, Spring 1983 (Vol. 7, No. 4), pp. 140–63, from which this assessment was gleaned.

83 Bernard Brodie, *War and Politics*, New York: Macmillan, 1973, p. 473.

84 See Colin Gray, 'Strategy in the Nuclear Age', in Williamson Murray, MacGregor Knox and Alvin Bernstein, *The Making of Strategy, Rulers, States, and War*, Cambridge: Cambridge University Press, 1994, pp. 587–93.

85 Larry H. Addington, *The Patterns of War Since the Eighteenth Century*, Bloomingdale: Indiana University Press, second edition, 1994, p. 290. For a critical view on this see for instance Richard K. Betts, 'Should Strategic Studies Survive?', *World Politics*, Vol. 50, No. 1, 1997.

86 Benjamin Lambeth, *The Transformation of American Air Power*, Santa Monica: RAND, 2000, p. 35.

87 Russell F. Weighly, *The American Way of War, A History of United States Military Strategy and Policy*, New York: Macmillan Publishing Co., 1973, p. 476. In Europe US units were stationed to share risk and signal commitment, as well as to act as a trigger. They were not expected to hold off a large scale Soviet invasion with conventional fighting for long, and defense plans in the 1960s did not exceed ninety days of conventional fighting. See Phil Williams, 'United States Defence Policy', in John Baylis, *et al.*, *Contemporary Strategy, Theories and Policies*, New York: Holmes and Meter, 1975, pp. 196–206.

88 See for instance Andrew Krepinevich, *The Army and Vietnam*, Baltimore: Johns Hopkins University Press, 1986, Chapter 2; Stephen Peter Rosen, *Winning the Next War*, Ithaca: Cornell University Press, 1991, Chapter 1; Deborak Avant, *Political Institutions and Military Change*, Ithaca: Cornell University Press, 1994, Chapter 3; and M.L.R. Smith, 'Strategy in an Age of "Low Intensity" Warfare', in Isabelle Duyvesteyn and Jan Angstrom (eds), *Rethinking the Nature of War*, Abingdon: Frank Cass, 2005.

89 Hallion, op. cit., p. 48.

90 Hammond, op. cit., p. 106.

91 Hallion, op. cit., p. 18.

92 Lambeth, op. cit., p. 69; Shimon Naveh, *In Pursuit of Excellence, The Evolution of Operational Theory*, London: Frank Cass, 1997, p. 254.

93 Lambeth, op. cit., pp. 54–5.

94 Ibid., pp. 55–6.

95 See James Fallows, *National Defense*, New York: Random House, 1981, pp. 15–17.

96 Burton, op. cit., p. 43.

97 Brodie, op. cit., p. 458.

98 See Paul Johnston, 'Doctrine is not Enough: the Effect of Doctrine on the Behavior of Armies', *Parameters*, Autumn 2000, pp. 30–9, for a short if somewhat too rosy account of this change in atmosphere.

99 See Lambeth, op. cit., pp. 59–81.

100 Weighley (1973), pp. 475–7.

101 Andrew Latham, 'A Braudelian Perspective on the Revolution in Military Affairs', *European Journal of International Relations*, Vol. 8 (2), June 2002, p. 238.

102 Peter Faber, 'The Evolution of Airpower Theory in the United States', in John Olson (ed.), *Asymmetric Warfare*, Oslo: Royal Norwegian Air Force Academy Press, 2002, p. 109.

103 Coram, op. cit., p. 322.

104 Hammond, op. cit., p. 154.

105 Ibid., p. 17. See also Coram, op. cit., p. 309; and Cowan, op. cit., p. 17.

106 Cowan, op. cit., p. 19.

107 Ibid., pp. 23–8; Hammond, op. cit., pp. 195–6; Coram, op. cit., Chapters 27–8.

108 *Marine Corps Doctrinal Publication 1, Warfighting*, Washington, D.C.: Department of Defense, 1997, p. 74.

109 Ibid., p. 77.

110 John Schmitt, 'Command and (Out of) Control: The Military Implications of Complexity Theory', in David Alberts and Thomas Czerwinski, *Complexity, Global Politics and National Security*, Washington, D.C.: National Defense University Press, 1998, Chapter 9.

111 Ibid., preface, p. 2.

112 See General Donn A. Starry, 'Tactical Evolution – FM 100–5', *Military Review*, August 1978, pp. 2–11, for an account by one of the leading senior officers of this reorientation process.

113 Richard Lock-Pullan, '"An Inward Looking Time": The United States Army, 1973–1976', *The Journal of Military History*, 67, April 2003, p. 485.

114 Ibid., pp. 486–90. See for a contemporary feeling of the mood, for instance Major Marc B. Powe, 'The US Army After The Fall of Vietnam', *Military Review*, February 1976, pp. 3–17.

115 See for instance William (Bill) Lind, 'Some Doctrinal Questions for the United States Army', *Military Review*, March 1977, pp. 54–65; Archer Jones, 'The New FM 100–5: A View From the Ivory Tower', *Military Review*, February 1977, pp. 27–36; Major John M. Oseth, 'FM 100–5 Revisited: A Need for Better "Foundations Concepts"?', *Military Review*, March 1980, pp. 13–19; Lieutenant Colonel Huba Wass de Czege and Lieutenant Colonel L.D. Holder, 'The New FM 100–5', *Military Review*, July 1982, pp. 24–35.

116 Conrad C. Crane, *Avoiding Vietnam: The US Army's Response to Defeat in Southeast Asia*, US Army Carlisle Barracks: Strategic Studies Institute, September 2002, pp. v, 4. Donn Starry too saw this as one of the merits of the 1976 version of FM 100–5.

117 Captain Anthony Coroalles, 'Maneuver to Win: A Realistic Alternative', *Military Review*, September 1981, p. 35.

118 Ibid. Coroalles for instance refers to an article in *The Marine Corps Gazette* of December 1979 titled 'Winning Through Maneuver' by Captain Miller.

119 See, for instance, Colonel Wayne A. Downing, 'Firepower, Attrition, Maneuver, US Army Doctrine: A Challenge for the 1980s and Beyond', *Military Review*, January 1981, pp. 64–73; Roger Beaumont, 'On the Wehrmacht Mystique', *Military Review*, January 1981, pp. 44–56; Archer Jones, 'FM 100–5: A view from the Ivory Tower', *Military Review*, May 1984, pp. 17–22; Major General John Woodmansee, 'Blitzkrieg and the AirLand Battle', *Military Review*, August 1984, pp. 21–39; Colonel Huba Wass de Czege, 'How to Change an Army', *Military Review*, November 1984, pp. 32–49; Captain Antulio J. Echevarria II, 'Auftragstaktik: in its Proper Perspective', *Military Review*, October 1986, pp. 50–6; Daniel Hughes, 'Abuses of German Military History', *Military Review*, December 1986, pp. 66–76; Major General Edward Atkeson, 'The Operational Level of War', *Military Review*, March 1987, pp. 28–36.

120 Coroalles, op. cit., pp. 37–8. See for reference to Boyd and the OODA loop in the development of US Army doctrine also Naveh, op. cit., pp. 256–62, 297, 301.

121 Ibid., p. 38.

122 Good short descriptions are provided by Hallion, op. cit., pp. 72–82; Lambeth, op. cit., pp. 83–91; and Richard M. Swain, 'Filling the Void: The Operational Art and the US Army', in B.J.C. McKercher and Michael A. Hennessy, *The Operational Art, Developments in the Theories of War*, Westport: Preager, 1996. For a very detailed account see Naveh, op. cit., Chapters 7 and 8.

123 Lambeth, op. cit., p. 91; and General William Richardson, 'FM 100–5, The AirLand Battle in 1986', *Military Review*, March 1986, pp. 4–11 (Richardson was the commander of the organization responsible for the publication of the new doctrine).

124 Naveh, op. cit., pp. 252–6.
125 Burton, op. cit., pp. 43–4.
126 Ibid., p. 51.
127 Department of Defense, *Field Manual 100–5, Operations*, Washington, D.C.: Department of the Army, 1982, Section 2–1. Boyd, however, never accepted the principle of synchronization.
128 Hallion, op. cit., pp. 77–8.
129 Naveh, op. cit., p. 252.
130 Steven Metz, 'The Next Twist of the RMA', *Parameters*, Autumn 2000, p. 40.
131 Burton, op. cit., p. 44.

3 Science: Boyd's fountain

1 Grant T. Hammond, *The Mind of War, John Boyd and American Security*, Washington, D.C.: Smithsonian Institution Press, 2001, p. 118.
2 Robert Coram, *Boyd, The Fighter Pilot Who Changed the Art of War*, Boston: Little Brown & Company, 2002, p. 271.
3 Hammond, Burton and Corum make frequent references to Boyd's obsessive study and his frequent late-night phone calls. See for instance Coram, op. cit., pp. 319–20 and Hammond, op. cit., pp. 180–6, and James Burton, *The Pentagon Wars: Reformers Challenge the Old Guard*, Annapolis, MD: Naval Institute Press, 1993, p. 44.
4 Peter Faber, in John Olson, *Asymmetric Warfare*, Oslo: Royal Norwegian Air Force Academy Press, 2002, p. 58.
5 Peter Watson, *A Terrible Beauty, The People and Ideas that Shaped the Modern Mind*, London: Phoenix Press, 2000, Chapter 33.
6 Francis Fukuyama, *The Great Disruption, Human Nature and the Reconstitution of Social Order*, New York: The Free Press, 1999. See also Eric Hobsbawm, *The Age of Extremes, A History of the World, 1914–1991*, New York, Vintage Books, 1994, Chapter 14 in particular.
7 Watson, op. cit., pp. 595–6.
8 His list of personal papers includes, for instance, Donella Meadows *et al.*, *The Limits to Growth: A Report to the Club of Rome's Report on the Predicament of Mankind*, New York: Signet, 1972; as well as Mihajlo Mesarovic and Eduard Pestel, *Mankind at the Turning Point: The Second Report to the Club of Rome*, New York: E.P. Dutton & Co., 1974; and Jan Tinbergen, *Rio: Reshaping the International Order: A Report to the Club of Rome*, New York: Signet, 1977.
9 Robert Heilbroner, *An Inquiry into The Human Prospect*, New York: W.W. Norton & Company, 1974, p. 13. Heilbroner also touches upon the Rome Report. Jeremy Rifkin's work, *Entropy, A New World View*, New York: The Viking Press, 1980, is another book in this vein and also appears in Boyd's list of personal papers. This book popularized Nicholas Georgescu-Roegen's book *The Entropy Laws and the Economic Process*, Cambridge, MA: Harvard University Press, 1971, a book central to Boyd's essay.
10 This influence should not be underestimated. Robert Persig's book was a bestseller in Boyd's time and a manifestation of the sense of crisis of the rational (western) mode of thinking. The character, Phaedrus, sees the social crisis of the 'most tumultuous decade of this century' as the result of western reductionist and analytical mindset which has lost sight of the elements of quality and wholeness. It contains extensive sections of dialogue and critique on western philosophers from Aristotle, to Hume, Kant and Hegel up to Henry Poincaré, who noted already in the nineteenth century the relevance of the act of observation and selecting facts for observation in the scientific enterprise, thus negating the existence of objectivity. The book that offers the way out for Phaedrus is the ancient Chinese book the *Tao I Ching* of Lao Tzu, a book also on Boyd's list of personal papers.

11 Watson, op. cit., p. 618.

12 Ibid.

13 Monod's book too is on Boyd's list. Interestingly, Monod's book includes the idea that living things, as isolated, self-contained energetic systems, seem to operate against entropy, an idea included in Boyd's work.

14 Steven Pinker, *How the Mind Works*, New York: Norton & Company, 1997, pp. 43–7.

15 See Fred Hoyle's, *Encounter with the Future*, New York: Simon and Schuster, 1968; and his *The New Face of Science*, New York: The World Publishing Company, 1971.

16 Derek Gjertsen, *Science and Philosophy, Past and Present*, London, Penguin Books, 1989, p. 6.

17 Paul Lyotard, *The Postmodern Condition*, Minneapolis: University of Minnesota Press, 11th printing, 1997, p. 3.

18 In his copy of *Exploring the Crack in the Cosmic Egg*, that deals with split brains, Boyd recognizes his own brain at work in a section dealing with the working of the minds of geniuses such as Einstein and Mozart.

19 See for instance, Boyd's notes in Conant's *Two Modes of Thought*, on p. 78; in Joseph Chilton Pearce's *The Crack in the Cosmic Egg*, on p. 95; in Piaget's *Structuralism*, on p. 143.

20 See Boyd's notes in Kuhn's *The Structure of Scientific Revolutions*, on pp. 64, 66, 86, 162; and in Polanyi's *Knowing and Being*, on p. 155.

21 John Horgan, *The End of Science*, New York: Broadway Books, 1997, p. 34.

22 Watson, op. cit., pp. 380, 488.

23 Alan Chalmers, *What is this thing called Science?*, Cambridge: Hackett, 3rd edition, 1999, pp. 59–60.

24 John Boyd, *The Conceptual Spiral*, p. 7.

25 For an excerpt of Popper's 1975 lecture on evolutionary epistemology see David Miller, *A Pocket Popper*, Oxford: Fontana, 1983, pp. 78–86.

26 David Deutsch, *The Fabric of Reality*, London: Penguin Books, 1998, p. 69. See Chapter 3 in particular on the relevance of Popper. For an assessment of the current value of Popper see Chapter 13.

27 Richard Dawkins, *The Selfish Gene*, Oxford: Oxford University Press, paperback edition, 1989, p. 190. See Chapter 11 for a full explanation of the idea of meme.

28 Marjorie Green, 'Introduction', in Michael Polanyi, *Knowing and Being*, London: Routledge and Kegan Paul, 1969, p. xi.

29 See 'The Structure of Consciousness', in Polanyi, op. cit., pp. 211–24.

30 Boyd, *Destruction and Creation*, p. 3.

31 In the 1990s his work has come to be seen by many philosophers as part of the shift to a postmodern context for philosophical thought.

32 Watson, op. cit., p. 472.

33 Polanyi, op. cit., p. 117.

34 Ibid.

35 This is taken from Joseph Chilton Pearce, *The Crack in the Cosmic Egg, Challenging Constructs of Mind and Reality*, New York: Pocket Books, 1974, p. 94.

36 Polanyi, op. cit., p. 118.

37 Ibid., p. 79.

38 Ibid., p. 119.

39 Ibid., p. 68.

40 Ibid., p. 49.

41 Ibid., p. 54.

42 Ibid., p. 66.

43 Ibid., pp. 55–6.

44 Ibid., p. 70.

45 Ibid., p. 31.

46 Ibid., p. 36.

47 As did Imre Lakatos. Lakatos will not be discussed here as available sources do not indicate specifically that Boyd read any of his material. For a general overview of recent history of the philosophy of science see, for instance, the essays of Peter Machamer, John Worrall and Jim Woodward, in Peter Machamer and Michael Silberstein, *The Blackwell Guide to the Philosophy of Science*, Oxford: Blackwell Publishers, 2002. For more technical and more polemic studies see, for instance, Adam Morton, 'The Theory of Knowledge: Saving Epistemology from the Epistemologists' and Noretta Koertge, 'New Age Philosophies of Science: Constructivism, Feminism and Postmodernism', all in Peter Clark and Katherina Hawley, *Philosophy of Science Today*, Oxford: Clarendon Press, 2000; and Steve Fuller, 'Being There with Thomas Kuhn: A Parable for Postmodern Times', *History and Theory*, October 1992, Vol. 31, Issue 3, pp. 241–75. In this article the influence of Polanyi is also addressed. For a concise critique of Kuhn see Deutsch, op. cit., in particular Chapter 13.

48 Chalmers, op. cit., p. 91.

49 Fritjof Capra, *The Web of Life, A New Scientific Understanding of Living Systems*, New York, Anchor Books, 1997, p. 5.

50 John Steinbrunner, *The Cybernetic Theory of Decision*, Princeton, NJ: Princeton University Press, 1974, p. 10.

51 Chalmers, op. cit., p. 118.

52 Ibid., pp. 108, 112.

53 Capra, op. cit., 1997, p. 5.

54 Ilya Prigogine and Isabella Stengers, *Order Out Of Chaos, Man's New Dialogue With Nature*, London: Flamingo, 1984, p. 308.

55 Ludwig von Bertalanffy, *General Systems Theory*, New York: George Brazilier, 1968, p. 18.

56 Chalmers, op. cit., pp. 115, 121.

57 Ibid., p. 118, emphasis is mine to highlight the connection with Boyd's use of wording.

58 Boyd, *Destruction and Creation*, p. 7.

59 Boyd, *The Conceptual Spiral*, p. 22. All underlining in original.

60 Ibid., p. 23.

61 Ibid., p. 24.

62 Ibid., p. 31. Although it is likely that Boyd followed Kuhn in this idea of creative destruction, it cannot be ruled out that Boyd was also influenced by Joseph Schumpeter, whose work *Capitalism, Socialism and Democracy* Boyd had read. Schumpeter is credited with the idea of the merits of creative destruction as an engine for economic growth.

63 Ibid., pp. 37–8. Italics are mine.

64 Watson, op. cit., pp. 740, 757.

65 Fritjof Capra, *The Turning Point*, New York: Bantam Books, 1991 [1975], pp. 56–7. I deliberately refer directly to this book as it is one read by Boyd in the early stages of his research but the issue of determinism is also discussed at length in other books Boyd read.

66 Steven Best and Douglas Kellner, *The Postmodern Turn*, New York: The Guilford Press, 1997, p. 203.

67 Ibid., p. 202.

68 See Rifkin, op. cit., p. 224; Prigogine and Stengers, op. cit., p. 309; and Murray Gell-Mann, *The Quark and the Jaguar, Adventures in the Simple and the Complex*, New York: Freeman & Company, 1994, p. 136.

69 Fritjof Capra, *The Tao of Physics* (Boston: Shambala, 3rd edition, 1991 [1975] [1982], p. 101.

70 At Georgia Tech Boyd had studied James B. Jones and George A. Hawkins, *Engineering Thermodynamics* (1960), but later works, such as Rifkin's, take the concept far beyond the realm of engineering.
71 Fritjof Capra, *The Turning Point*, New York, Bantam Books, 1982, pp. 72–4.
72 Ibid.
73 Capra (1975), op. cit., pp. 61–2.
74 Ibid., p. 81 (note that this work was on Boyd's early reading lists).
75 Gary Zukav's, *The Dancing Wu Li Masters: An Overview of the New Physics*, New York: Bantam, 1979, is one of the books Boyd read that described these developments in detail.
76 Ibid., p. 125.
77 Cited in Capra (1997), op. cit., p. 40.
78 Prigogine and Stengers (1984), op. cit., pp. 222–5.
79 Boyd, *Destruction and Creation*, p. 10.
80 Jean Piaget, *Structuralism*, London: Routledge and Kegan Paul, 1971, pp. 32–3.
81 Watson, op. cit., pp. 270–2.
82 Boyd, *Destruction and Creation*, pp. 8–9.
83 Rifkin mentions Heisenberg and the Second Law in one chapter, but not in all three.
84 Besides the already mentioned early works of Capra, Prigogine, etc., that are listed in the bibliographies of his first papers, his personal papers include a large number of other books on the history of science. Early works include, for instance, George Gamow *Thirty Years That Shook Physics, The Story of Quantum Physics* (1966) and Werner Heisenberg's *Physics and Philosophy: The Revolution in Modern Science* (1962).
85 Fritjof Capra, *The Tao of Physics*, Boston: Shambala, 3rd edition, 1991, p. 54. The first edition of 1975 already included this passage.
86 Jean Piaget, *Structuralism*, London: Routledge and Kegan Paul, 1971, p. 44.
87 Ibid., p. 140.
88 Another study on structuralism Boyd had read, Howard Gardner's *The Quest for Mind, Piaget, Levi-Strauss and the Structuralism Movement*, Chicago: University of Chicago Press, 1972, actually regards structuralism as the 'worldview' that took hold during the 1960s.
89 Capra (1982), op. cit., pp. 77–8.
90 Ludwig von Bertalanffy, op. cit., p. 186.
91 Prigogine and Stengers (1984), op. cit., p. xxix.
92 Uri Merry, *Coping With Uncertainty, Insights from the New Sciences of Chaos, Self-Organization, and Complexity*, Westport, CT: Preager, 1995, p. 100.
93 Watson, op. cit., p. 757.
94 Capra (1997), op. cit., p. 5; Prigogine and Stengers (1984), op. cit., p. xxvii.
95 Ibid., p. 309.
96 Capra (1997), op. cit., p. 31. A similar discussion can be read in Piaget's *Structuralism*.
97 Ibid., pp. 29–35.
98 Bertalanffy, op. cit., p. 19.
99 James Bryant Conant, *Two Modes of Thought*, New York: Trident Press, 1964, p. 31. This short book includes several examples of scientific breakthroughs in the nineteenth century.
100 Ibid., p. 91.
101 *Destruction and Creation*; pp. 5–6.
102 *The Strategic Game of ? and ?*, p. 10.
103 In the bibliography of *Destruction and Creation* he lists also Maxwell Maltz, *Psycho-Cybernetics* (1971). The personal papers include U.S. Anderson; *Success-Cybernetics: the Practical Application of Human-Cybernetics* (1970), F.H. George, *Cybernetics* (1971) and Y. Sabarina, *Cybernetics Within Us* (1969), and Marvin

Karlins and Lewis Andrews, *Biofeedback: Turning on the Power of Your Mind* (1973) and Norbert Wiener's *The Human Use of Human Beings: Cybernetics and Society* (1967). Chilton Pearce's works, too, include many references to cybernetics.

104 After Capra (1996), p. 59.

105 Joseph O'Connor and Ian McDermott, *The Art of Systems Thinking*, San Francisco: Thorsons, 1997, p. 236.

106 Capra (1997), op. cit., pp. 56–64.

107 Ibid., p. 43.

108 Bartallanffy, op. cit., p. 94.

109 Ibid., p. 39.

110 Ibid., p. 141.

111 W. Ross Ashby, *An Introduction to Cybernetics*, New York: John Wiley & Sons, 1956, pp. 127–31.

112 Bertalanffy, op. cit., p. 150. In popular systems thinking, this feature is enclosed in the notion of feedforward, actions which are the result of expectation and anticipation. See O'Connor and McDermott, op. cit., pp. 48–52.

113 Capra (1997), op. cit., pp. 46–50.

114 Watson, op. cit., pp. 495–6.

115 Ibid., p. 551.

116 Boyd, *Patterns of Conflict*, p. 128. On p. 159 in Chilton Pearce's *The Crack in the Cosmic Egg* Boyd noted that a passage reminded him of his idea of 'survival on our own terms – capacity for independent action'.

117 Dennis Coon, *Essential of Psychology*, Pacific Grove, CA: Brookes/Cole, 7th edition, p. 17.

118 Machamer, op. cit., p. 10; and Rick Grush, 'Cognitive Science', in Machamer and Silberstein, op. cit., Chapter 13.

119 Adapted from Peter H. Lindsay and Donald A. Norman, *Human Information Processing*, New York: Academic Press, 1977, p. 689. Similar ones can be found in books Boyd read, such as Daniel Goleman's *Vital Lies, Simple Truths* (1985), on pp. 58, 63, 64.

120 O'Connor and McDermott, op. cit., p. 118, and Coon, op. cit., p. 279. See also Gareth Morgan, *Images of Organizations*, Beverly Hills, CA: Sage, 1986, Chapter 4, in particular pp. 84–97.

121 Ibid., op. cit., p. 119.

122 One very readable account Boyd studied was, for instance, Howard Gardner, *The Mind's New Science, A History of the Cognitive Revolution*, New York: Basic Books, 1985. Other works he read that are considered part of the cognitive revolution include John von Neumann, *The Computer and the Brain* (1958), Norbert Wiener, *The Human Use of Human Beings, Cybernetics and Society* (1967) and Gilbert Ryle, *The Concept of Mind* (1966); Richard Restak, *The Brain, The Last Frontier* (1979); Marvin Minsky, *The Society of Mind* (1986).

123 Gregory Bateson, *Mind and Nature, A Necessary Unity*, Cresskill, NJ: Hampton Press, 2002.

124 Sergio Manghi, 'Foreword', in Bateson, op. cit., p. xi.

125 Monod, op. cit., p. 149.

126 Ibid., p. 154.

127 See for instance Gardner, op. cit.

128 Rick Grush, 'Cognitive Science', in Machamer and Silberstein, op. cit., pp. 273–7.

129 In *Structuralism*, Piaget advanced the idea that there are 'mental structures' that exist midway between genes and behavior. Mental structures build up as the organism develops and encounters the world. Structures are theoretic, deductive, a process. Interestingly, Piaget was influenced by, e.g., Ludwig von Bertalanffy. See Watson, op. cit., pp. 629–30.

130 Ibid., p. 674. Bronowski, another author Boyd studied, meanwhile highlighted the

power of for instance literature and poetry to provide meaning and to develop new insights, thus allowing for a large measure of subjectivism. See Jacob Bronowski, *The Identity of Man*, New York: Prometheus Books, [1964] 2002.

131 This is an important quotation from Hall's work (to be found on p. 42). It is (with Clifford Geertz' work) one of the few works in the bibliography of *Patterns of Conflict* that has culture as its main subject. A very brief summary of Hall's view of culture is as follows: culture = models/templates. Culture is innate but learned (i.e. we are born with the physical necessity and capacity to specialize our bodies, brains, hearts in line with cultural patterns). Culture is living, interlocking system(s) – touch one part, the rest moves. Culture is shared; it is created and maintained through *relationship*. It is also a highly selective screen between man and the outside world. Culture designates what we pay attention to and what we ignore. Hall discusses 'monochromatic' organizations and argues that, as they grow larger, they turn inward, becoming blind to their own structure; they grow rigid and are even apt to lose sight of their original purpose (p. 24). Another topic frequently advanced is the fact that 'we have been taught to think linearly rather than comprehensively' (p. 11), a 'compartmentalized way of thinking' (p. 12). Interestingly, Hall also included a quote from J. Bronowski that was close to Boyd's heart: 'There is no absolute knowledge, and those who claim it, whether they are scientists or dogmatists, open the door to tragedy' (p. 71).

132 Grush, op. cit., p. 275.

133 Piaget, op. cit., p. 51.

134 Capra (1996), op. cit., pp. 51–68.

135 O'Connor and McDermott, op. cit., pp. 63–5.

136 Edward Borodzicz and Kees van Haperen, 'Individual and Group Learning in Crisis Simulations', in *Journal of Contingencies and Crisis Management*, Vol. 10, No. 3, September 2002, p. 141. The authors have copied the model from D. Kolb, *Experiential Learning: Experience as the Source of Learning and Development*, which was published in 1984. Later studies and concepts such as Recognition Primed Decision making explore the influence of training and experience in similar loop models, affirming Boyd's model (see for instance Gary Klein, 'Strategies of Decision Making', *Military Review*, May 1989; and *Sources of Power, How People Make Decisions*, Cambridge, MA: MIT Press, 1999). Interestingly though, Boyd's reading list does not include any of the well-known works on crisis decision-making theory emerging from political science during the 1970s and 1980s, such as Graham Allison's 1971 landmark study *Essence of Decision*, Robert Jervis' *Perception and Misperception in International Politics* (1976) and Irvin Janis' *Groupthink* (1982).

137 Piaget (1971), op. cit., p. 133.

138 O'Connor and McDermott, op. cit., pp. 140–1.

139 Peter Senge, *The Fifth Discipline, The Art and Practice of The Learning Organization*, London: Doubleday, 1992, p. 150. This book is a highly popular systems-theory based work on organizational learning.

140 Boyd would underline several citations of Senge in other books such as John Briggs and F. David Peat, *Turbulent Mirror, An Illustrated Guide to Chaos Theory and the Science of Wholeness*, New York: Harper & Row, 1989, pp. 176–80, 200.

141 *Destruction and Creation*, p. 5.

142 Coon, op. cit., pp. 386–9.

143 See Morgan, op. cit., p. 44. Chapters 3, 4 and 8 are based on evolution theory, systems theory and complexity theory and provide an early synthesis of these developments and apply them to organization theory.

144 See, of the books on management in his bibliography, in particular Masaaki Imai, *Kaizen, The Key to Japan's Competitive Success* (1986), and also William Ouchi, *Theory Z* (1981), Rafael Aguayo, *Dr. Deming* (1990) and Richard Tanner Pascale and Anthony Athos, *The Art of Japanse Management* (1981).

145 This is adapted from David A. Garwin, *Learning in Action*, Boston: Harvard Business School Press, 2000, p. 10.
146 Henry Mintzberg, Joseph Lampel and Bruce Ahlstrand, *Strategy Safari*, New York: The Free Press, 1998, p. 229.
147 Garwin, op. cit., p. 9.
148 Chris Argyris and Donald Schon, *Organizational Learning: A Theory of Action Perspective*, Reading, MAs: Addison-Wesley, 1978, pp. 38–9, 143, 145.
149 Garwin, op. cit., pp. 28–43.
150 Adapted from J. Edward Russo & Paul J.H. Schoemaker, *Winning Decisions*, New York: Doubleday, 2002, pp. 227–8.
151 Capra (1991), op. cit., pp. 328–33.
152 Piaget (1971), op. cit., p. 34.
153 Boyd, *Patterns of Conflict*, p. 144.
154 Boyd, 'Strategic Game of ? & ?', p. 28.
155 Boyd, *Organic Design*, p. 20. See also 'Strategic Game of ? & ?', p. 41.
156 Boyd, *Patterns of Conflict*, p. 184. Note how Boyd uses the Clausewitzian concept of friction not in the mechanical sense, as Clausewitz did, but in the thermodynamical sense, indicating that for Boyd friction refers to disorder.
157 Ibid., pp. 12–13.
158 *Destruction and Creation*, p. 3.
159 'Organic Design for Command and Control', p. 13.
160 Ibid., p. 16. Underlining in original.
161 Ibid., p. 15.
162 Ibid., p. 18.
163 'Strategic Game of ? & ?', p. 10.
164 Ibid., p. 45.
165 Ibid., p. 58.

4 Completing the shift

1 James Gleick, *Chaos: Making a New Science*, New York: Viking Penguin, 1987, p. 304.
2 Jeremy Rifkin, *Time Wars, The Primary Conflict in Human History*, New York: Henry Holt & Co, 1987, p. 185.
3 'Organic Design for Command and Control', p. 20.
4 This list was provided by Hammond.
5 Adapted from Eric B. Dent, 'Complexity Science: A Worldview Shift', *Emergence*, Vol. 1, issue 4 (1999), p. 8.
6 Fritjof Capra, *The Web of Life, A New Understanding of Living Systems*, New York: Doubleday, 1997, p. 85.
7 Ibid., pp. 86–9.
8 Ilya Prigogine and Isabella Stengers, *Order Out of Chaos*, London: Bantam, 1984, p. 287.
9 Capra, op. cit., p. 180.
10 Boyd, *Strategic Game*, p. 18. On page 19 Boyd included a section from *Looking Glass Universe* by John Briggs and David Peat which once more describes Prigogine's concept of dissipative structures.
11 John Horgan, *The End of Science*, New York: Broadway Books, 1996, p. 182.
12 See Glenn E. James, *Chaos Theory: The Essentials for Military Applications*, Newport, RI: Naval War College Press, 1995, for a good concise description.
13 Capra, op. cit., p. 123.
14 Murray Gell-Mann, *The Quark and the Jaguar, Adventures in the Simple and the Complex*, New York: Freeman & Company, 1994, p. 26.
15 This description is based primarily on Prigogine and Stengers, op. cit., Chapter V.

16 Several of the books Boyd read use this illustration. See for instance Coveney and Highfield (1991), p. 166; John Briggs and F. David Peat, *Turbulent Mirror, An Illustrated Guide to Chaos Theory and the Science of Wholeness*, New York: Harper & Row, 1989, p. 143; and Ian Stewart, *Does God Play Dice?*, Oxford: Basil Blackwell, 1989, p. 200.

17 Jong Heon Byeon, 'Non-Equilibrium Thermodynamic Approach to the Change in Political Systems', *Systems Research and Behavioral Science*, 16, (1999), pp. 286–90. See also Kenyon B. Green, 'Field Theoretic Framework for the Interpretation of the Evolution, Instability, Structural Change, and Management of Complex Systems', in L. Douglas Kiel and Euel Eliot (eds), *Chaos Theory in the Social Sciences*, Ann Arbor: University of Michigan Press, 1997.

18 Capra, op. cit., p. 183.

19 G. Nicolis, *Introduction to Non-linear Science*, Cambridge: Cambridge University Press, 1995, p. 96.

20 Capra, op. cit., p. 95.

21 Ibid., p. 98.

22 Ibid., p. 267.

23 Ibid., pp. 218–19.

24 Ibid., p. 266.

25 Ibid., p. 220.

26 Gareth Morgan, *Images of Organizations*, New York: Sage, 1986, pp. 235–40, in particular pp. 239–40. See also Stuart Kauffman, *The Origins of Order, Self-Organization and Selection in Evolution*, Oxford: Oxford University Press, 1993, in particular Chapter 1.

27 Capra, op. cit., pp. 265–70.

28 Boyd, *Organic Design*, p. 16. Note the title of this presentation, which once more indicates Boyd's frame of reference.

29 In Briggs and Peat, op. cit., Maturana's ideas are discussed in some length.

30 See *Strategic Game*, pp. 16–17.

31 Ibid., both on p. 16.

32 Ibid., p. 28.

33 Peter Watson, *A Terrible Beauty, The People and Ideas that Shaped the Modern Mind*, London: Phoenix Press, p. 747. Watson refers to James Gleick's *Chaos, Making a New Science*. See Mitchell Waldrop, *Complexity: The Emerging Science at the Edge of Order and Chaos*, London: Viking, 1993.

34 See for a brief discussion of what complexity science is, also Kurt Richardson and Paul Cilliers, 'What is Complexity Science? A View from Different Directions', *Emergence*, Vol. 3, No. 1 (2001), 5–22.

35 Jacco van Uden, Kurt Richardson and Paul Cilliers, 'Postmodernism Revisited? Complexity Science and the Study of Organizations', *Tamara*, Vol. 1, No. 3 (2001), 53–67. See also Michael Lissack, 'Complexity: the Science, its Vocabulary, and its Relation to Organizations', *Emergence*, Vol. 1, No. 1 (1999), p. 112.

36 Waldrop, op. cit., pp. 11–13.

37 See Waldrop, op. cit., pp. 225–35.

38 Capra, op. cit., citing Stuart Kauffman, p. 204.

39 Gell-Mann, op. cit., p. 17; Waldrop citing Holland, op. cit., p. 145.

40 Richard Pascale, 'Surfing the Edge of Chaos', *Sloan Management Review*, Spring 1999, p. 85.

41 Most of these are derived from John Holland, *Hidden Order, How Adaptation Builds Complexity*, Reading, Mass: Perseus Books, 1995. In addition see Russ Marion and Josh Bacon, 'Organizational Extinction and Complex Systems', *Emergence*, Vol. 1, No. 4 (2000), p. 76; and Gell-Mann, op. cit., p. 235.

42 See John Holland, op. cit., pp. 31–4 and Gell-Mann, op. cit., pp. 17–25.

43 Gell-Mann, interestingly, makes the comparison between schemata and scientific

theories, noting how Popper's falsification principle acts as a selection mechanism. However, he also notes that science does not progress this neatly and that theories are selected for other reasons as well, referring to Kuhn. See in particular Chapter 7.

44 Gell-Mann, op. cit., pp. 303–4.
45 Boyd, *The Conceptual Spiral*, p. 14.
46 Gell-Mann, op. cit., p. 25. In fact, similar to Boyd, Gell-Mann includes language, traditions, customs, laws and myths, all of which can be regarded as 'cultural DNA'. All encapsulate the shared experience of many generations and comprise the schemata for the society which itself functions as a complex adaptive system.
47 Gell-Mann, op. cit., pp. 292–4.
48 Gell-Mann actually includes a military illustration here. See p. 293.
49 Fritjof Capra, *The Turning Point*, New York: Bantam Books, 1982, pp. 273–4. Capra also discusses Gell-Mann's first three modes of adaptation.
50 Boyd, *Patterns of Conflict*, p. 141.
51 Ibid., p. 143.
52 Ibid., p. 144.
53 Ibid., p. 143.
54 Ibid., p. 141.
55 Ibid.
56 Ibid.
57 Capra (1996), op. cit., pp. 301–3.
58 Ilya Progogine, *The End of Certainty*, New York: The Free Press, 1996, p. 73.
59 Holland in Waldrop, op. cit., p. 147.
60 For instance: Richard K. Betts, *Surprise Attack* (1982), Anthony Cave Brown, *Bodyguard of Lies* (1975); Charles Cruickshank, *Deception in World War II* (1979); Donald Daniel and Katherine Herbig, *Strategic Military Deception* (1982); Michael Handel, 'The Yom Kippur War and the Inevitability of Surprise', *International Studies Quarterly* (September 1977); David Kahn, *The Codebreakers* (1967); R.V. Jones, *Intelligence and Deception* (1979); Ronald Lewin, *Ultra Goes to War* (1978); Amnon Sella, 'Surprise Attack and Communication', *Journal of Contemporary History* (1978).
61 Boyd, *The Conceptual Spiral*, p. 32.
62 Ibid., p. 22.
63 Ibid., p. 23.
64 Ibid., p. 24.
65 Ibid., p. 28.
66 Ibid., p. 38.
67 Ibid., p. 125.
68 See Steven Best and Douglas Kellner, *Postmodern Theory*, New York: The Guilford Press, 1991, Chapter 1, for a good archeology of postmodernism.
69 Steven Best and Douglas Kellner, *The Postmodern Turn*, New York: The Guilford Press, 1997, pp. 195–6. Interestingly, they find the historical foundation for postmodern ideas in Kierkegaard, Marx, and in particular Nietsche. Boyd read Marx, but also Nietsche's works *Beyond Good and Evil, Thus Spoke Zarathustra* and *Twilight of the Idols*. See also Damian Popolo, 'French Philosophy, Complexity, and Scientific Epistemology: Moving Beyond the Modern Episteme', *Emergence*, Vol. 5, No. 1, 2003, pp. 77–98, for the link between Foucault, Deleuze, Popper, Bergson and Prigonine.
70 Christopher Coker, 'Post-modernity and the end of the Cold War: has war been disinvented?', *Review of International Studies*, 1992, Vol. 18, p. 189. See also Bradford Booth, Meyer Kestnbaum, and David R. Segal, 'Are Post-Cold War Militaries Postmodern?', *Armed Forces & Society*, Vol. 27, No. 3 (Spring 2001), pp. 319, where they assert that 'the theoretical perspective of postmodernism has become commonplace in sociology'. See for an introduction into modernity and postmodernity also

Kenneth Thompson, 'Social Pluralism and Post-Modernity', and Gregor McLennan, 'The Enlightenment Project Revisited', both in Stuart Hall, David Held and Tony McGrew, *Modernity and its Futures*, Oxford: Polity Press, 1992.

71 Pauline Rosenau, *Post-Modernism and the Social Sciences*, Princeton, NJ: Princeton University Press, 1992, p. 15. The first chapter provides a concise overview of both various interpretations and meanings of postmodernism as its intellectual lineage and history.

72 Darryl Jarvis, 'Postmodernism: A Critical Typology', *Politics and Society*, Vol. 26, No. 1 (March 1998), p. 98.

73 Alvin and Heidi Toffler, *War and Anti War, Survival at the Dawn of the Information Age*, London: Little Brown, 1993. See for a landmark text also Daniel Bell, *The Coming of the Post-Industrial Society*, New York: Basic Books, 1973. See for instance Charles Jencks, *Post-Modernism, the New Classicism in Art and Architecture*, London: Academy Editions, 1987 for a discussion of cultural aspects of postmodernism.

74 Jarvis, op. cit., p. 126.

75 Ibid., pp. 108, 114–15.

76 See for instance Jean-Paul Lyotard, *The Postmodern Condition: A Report on Knowledge*, Manchester: Manchester University Press, 1984 [1979]; K.R. Dark, *The Waves of Time*, London: Pinter, 1998; and Paul Cilliers, *Complexity and Postmodernism*, London: Routledge, 1998, for similar observations.

77 Watson, op. cit., p. 668.

78 Lyotard, op. cit., p. xxiii. See also Gregor McLennan, 'The Enlightenment Project Revisited', in Hall, Held and McGrew, op. cit., pp. 328–30. Writers Boyd was familiar with, such as Geertz, Bronowski, Rifkin and Capra, shared these views.

79 McLennan, op. cit., pp. 332–3.

80 David Harvey, *The Condition of Postmodernity*, cited in Kenneth Thompson, 'Social Pluralism and Post-Modernity', in Hall, Held and McGrew, op. cit., p. 261.

81 McLennan, op. cit., p. 333.

82 Cilliers, op. cit., p. 118.

83 For an introduction to Giddens, see McLennan, op. cit., pp. 342–7. McLennan positions Giddens as a happy compromise between Enlightenment and (the more extreme and nihilistic versions of) postmodernism.

84 Stefano Guzzini, 'A Reconstruction of Conservativism in International Relations', *European Journal of International Relations*, Vol. 6(2) (2000), p. 152.

85 Andreas Bieler and Adam David Morton, 'The Gordion Knot of Agency-Structure in International Relations: a neo-Gramscian Perspective', *European Journal of International Relations*, Vol. 7(1) (March 2001), p. 22.

86 Ibid., p. 27.

87 Giddens employs the terms reflexive modernization, radical-modernity, high-modernity and post-traditional society.

88 Anthony Giddens, 'Living in a Post-Traditional Society', in Ulrich Beck, Anthony Giddens, Scott Lash, *Reflexive Modernization*, Stanford: Sage, 1994, p. 87.

89 Ibid., pp. 86–8.

90 Ibid., p. 184.

91 Giddens, *The Consequences of Modernity*, Stanford: Stanford University Press, 1990, p. 38.

92 Ibid., pp. 53–4.

93 See Anthony Giddens, *The Constitution of Society*, Cambridge: Polity Press, 1984, p. 284.

94 Guzzini, op. cit., p. 162.

95 See Kurt A. Richardson, Graham Mathieson and Paul Cilliers, 'The Theory and Practice of Complexity Science: Epistemological Considerations for Military Operational Analysis', *SysteMexico*, 1 (2000), pp. 19–20, and Cilliers, op. cit., p. 22, and Chapters 3 and 7.

96 Boyd, *Strategic Game of ? and ?*, p. 58.

97 Richardson, Mathieson and Cilliers, op. cit., p. 22.

98 Jarvis, op. cit., p. 105.

99 This is based on Steve Smith, 'The Increasing Insecurity of Security Studies: Conceptualizing Security in the Last Twenty Years', in Stuart Croft and Terry Terriff (eds), *Critical Reflections on Security and Change*, London: Frank Cass, 2000; John Mearsheimer, 'Back to the Future: Instability in Europe after the Cold War', *International Security*, Vol. 15, No. 1 (1990); and David Mutimer, 'Beyond Strategy: Critical Thinking and the New Security Studies', in Craig Snyder, *Contemporary Security and Strategy*, London: Macmillan, 1999.

100 Theo Farrell, 'Constructivist Security Studies: Portrait of a Research Program', *International Studies Review*, 4/1 (2002), p. 49. See also Alexander Wendt, 'Constructing International Politics', *International Security*, 20, No. 1 (1995); and Alexander Wendt, 'Anarchy is what states make of it: The social construction of power politics', *International Organization*, 46/2, 1992, pp. 391–425. For a elaborate argument about the constructed nature, and the role of language and discourse, of US deterrence policy, see also Bradley Klein, *Strategic Studies and World Order: The Global Politics of Deterrence*, Cambridge: Cambridge University Press, 1994. See also Ted Hopf, 'The Promise of Constructivism in International Relations Theory', *International Security*, Vol. 23, No. 1 (Summer 1998), pp. 172–3.

101 Keith Krause and Michael Williams (eds), *Critical Security Studies, Concepts and Cases*, Minneapolis, MN: University of Minnesota Press, 1997, p. 49.

102 After Wendt, *Social Theory of International Politics*, Cambridge: Cambridge University Press, 1999, p. 372. For a critical account see Dale C. Copeland, 'The Constructivist Challenge to Structural Realism', *International Security*, Vol. 25, No. 2 (Fall 2000), pp. 187–212.

103 Hopf, p. 177.

104 Wendt (1999), pp. 92–138.

105 Farrell, op. cit., p. 50.

106 Michael C. Desch, 'Culture Clash, Assessing the Importance of Ideas in Security Studies', *International Security*, Vol. 23, No. 1 (Summer 1998), pp. 142–3.

107 Ibid., p. 313.

108 Horgan, op. cit., p. 192.

109 Jay Forrester in L. Douglas Kiel and Euel Elliott (eds), *Chaos Theory in the Social Sciences, Foundations and Applications*, Ann Arbor: The University of Michigan Press, 1996, p. 2. See for other examples of investigations on the relevance of chaos/complexity theory and social sciences for instance David Byrne, *Complexity Theory and the Social Sciences, An Introduction*, London: Routledge, 1998, and Paul Cilliers, *Complexity and Postmodernity*, London: Routledge, 1998; and Raymond Eve, Sara Horsfall and Mary Lee (eds), *Chaos, Complexity and Sociology, Myths, Models and Theories*, Thousand Oaks, CA: Sage, 1997.

110 Brian Arthur, 'Positive Feedback in the Economy', *Scientific American* (February, 1990), 131–40.

111 See for instance William McNeil, 'History and the Scientific Worldview', *History and Theory*, Feb. 1998, Vol. 37, No. 1 (Feb. 1998), pp. 1–13; and 'The Changing Shape of World History', *History and Theory*, Vol. 34, No. 2 (May 1995), pp. 8–26. Coveney and Highfield (1995), op. cit., p. 338; James Rosenau, *Turbulence in World Politics*, New York: Harvester Wheatsheaf, 1990, pp. 47, 58. Chapter 3 deals entirely with chaos and complexity theory. He likens the transformation of the interstate system to a Prigoginian bifurcation point, for instance. See also James Rosenau, 'Many Damn Things Simultaneously: Complexity Theory and World Affairs', in Davids and Czerwinski (1997), Chapter 4.

112 Charles Perrow, *Normal Accidents*, Princeton: Princeton University Press, 1999, p. 90.

113 For an in-depth account of the working of tightly coupled and non-linear effects see in particular Robert Jervis, *System Effects, Complexity in Political and Social Life*, Princeton: Princeton University Press, 1997.

114 Perrow, op. cit., pp. 93–4. See also Perrow, *Complex Organizations; A Critical Essay* (Glenview, IL: Scott, Foresman, 1972; and Jos A. Rijpma, 'Complexity, Tight coupling and Reliability: Connecting Normal Accidents Theory and High Reliability Theory', *Journal of Contingencies and Crisis Management*, Vol. 5, No. 1 (March 1997), pp. 15–23.

115 Perrow, op. cit., pp. 331–4.

116 See Michael Lissack, 'Complexity: the Science, its Vocabulary, and its Relation to Organizations', *Emergence*, Vol. 1, No. 1 (1999), pp. 110–26.

117 Russ Marion and Josh Bacon, 'Organizational Extinction and Complex Systems', *Emergence*, 1(4) (1999), p. 76.

118 Ibid.

119 Susanne Kelly and May Ann Allison, *The Complexity Advantage, How the Sciences Can Help Your Business Achieve Peak Performance*, New York: McGraw-Hill, 1999, p. 5.

120 Henry Coleman, 'What Enables Self-Organizing Behavior in Businesses', *Emergence*, Vol. 1, No. 1 (1999), p. 37.

121 Ibid., p. 40.

122 The literature on complexity theory and its relevance for the humanities, social sciences, and management theory is burgeoning. See for instance: Shona L. Brown and Kathleen M. Eisenhardt, *Competing on the Edge, Strategy as Structured Chaos*, Boston: Harvard Business School Press, 1998; Uri Merry, *Coping With Uncertainty, Insights from the New Sciences of Chaos, Self Organization, and Complexity*, Westport, CT: Praeger, 1995; Raymond A. Eve *et al.*, *Chaos, Complexity, and Sociology*, London: Sage, 1997; Kathleen Eisenhardt and Donald N. Sull, 'Strategy as Simple Rules', *Harvard Business Review*, January 2001, pp. 107–16; Eric D. Beinhocker, 'Robust Adaptive Strategies', *Sloan Management Review*, Spring 1999, pp. 95–106; Michael Church, 'Organizing Simply for Complexity: Beyond Metaphor Towards Theory', *Long Range Planning*, Vol. 32, No. 4 (1999), pp. 425–40.

123 See for instance Alvin Saperstein, 'Chaos – A Model for the Outbreak of War', *Nature* 309, pp. 303–5. See also 'The Prediction of Unpredictability: Applications of the New Paradigm of Chaos in Dynamical Systems to the Old Problem of the Stability of a System of Hostile Nations', in L. Douglas Kiel and Euel Elliott, pp. 139–64; and Roger Beaumont, *War, Chaos, and History*, Westport, CT: Praeger, 1994.

124 Robert Jervis, 'Complexity and the analysis of Political and Social Life', *Political Science Quarterly*, Vol. 112, No. 4 (1997–98), p. 593; and 'Complex Systems: The Role of Interactions', Chapter 3, in Paul Davis and Thomas Czerwinski, *Complexity, Global Politics and National Security*, Annapolis: NDU Press, 1997.

125 Jervis (1997), op. cit., p. 10.

126 Ibid., p. 17.

127 Ibid., p. 18.

128 Jervis includes the example of the Allied Combined Bomber Offensive during World War II. When the Allied Bombers attacked the German railroad system industry was able to divert rail traffic along the widely developed rail system. But doing so after a period of bombing created bottlenecks in response to which individual industries began to take individual measures, which took away the flexibility of the system and subsequently paralyzed it.

129 Ibid., p. 261.

130 Ibid.

131 Ibid.

132 Ibid., p. 194.

133 Steven Mann, 'Chaos Theory and Strategic Thought', *Parameters*, Vol. XXII, No. 2 (Autumn 1992), pp. 54–68.

134 Alan Beyerchen, 'Clausewitz, Nonlinearity, and the Unpredictability of War', *International Security*, Vol. 17, No. 3 (Winter 1992), pp. 55–90. This section is a very concise summary.

135 Pat Pentland, *Center of Gravity Analysis and Chaos Theory*, Maxwell Air Force Base, AL: Air University Press, April 1993. Interestingly, he also incorporates Boyd's OODA loop, acknowledging that this model and the essay, although developed in the 1970s, anticipated many of tenets of chaos theory, and is consistent with it.

136 Ibid., p. 25.

137 Ibid., p. 17.

138 Ibid., p. 31.

139 Ibid., pp. 11–12.

140 Ibid., pp. 34–6.

141 The literature on military applications of chaos and complexity theory has burgeoned in the 1990s. To illustrate this, an inventory of articles dealing with non-linearity and military affairs drawn up by the US National Defense University in 1999 listed 144 entries. Available at: www.clausewitz.com (accessed 10 July 1999). For some accessible papers see for instance Glenn E. James, *Chaos Theory, The Essentials for Military Applications*, Newport: Naval War College Press, 1996; Linda Beckerman, 'The Non-linear Dynamics of War', online. Available at: www.belisarius.com/modern_business_strategy/beckerman/non_linear.htm (accessed 27 April 1999). This article, though technical, is often referred to. She regards attrition style warfare as a linear process and, interestingly, refers to Boyd's OODA loop as a model which captures the dynamics of non-linear systems; and Jason B. Tanner, Walter E. Lavrinovich and Scott R. Hall: 'Looking at Warfare Through a New Lens', *Marine Corps Gazette*, Vol. 82, No.. 9 (September 1998), pp. 59–61; David S. Alberts and Thomas Czerwinski, *Complexity, Global Politics, and National Security*, Washington, D.C.: National Defence University Press, 1998; and Thomas J. Czerwinski, *Coping with the Bounds, Speculations on Nonlinearity in Military Affairs*, Washington, D.C.: National Defence University Press, 1999. For a recent study relating Clausewitz to chaos see Stephen J. Cimbala, *Clausewitz and Chaos, Friction in War and Military Policy*, Westport, CT: Praeger, 2001, in particular Chapters 1 and 7.

142 Ibid., pp. 12–13.

143 James Burton, *The Pentagon Wars: Reformers Challenge the Old Guard*, Annapolis, MD: Naval Institute Press, 1993, pp. 46–7.

144 Boyd, *Strategic Game of ? and ?*, p. 12.

145 Hammond, op. cit., p. 15.

146 Boyd, *A Discourse*, Abstract, p. 2.

147 Alberts and Czerwinski (1998), op. cit., Preface, p. 1.

148 Boyd, *The Essence of Winning and Losing*, p. 5;

149 Hammond, op. cit., p. 12; Coram, op. cit., p. 330.

150 On the merit of metaphors see for instance Morgan, op. cit., Chapter 11. The first three metaphors I mention here are directly from this book, Chapters 3, 4 and 8.

5 Core arguments

1 Grant T. Hammond, *The Mind of War*, Washington, D.C.: Smithsonian Institution Press, 2001, p. 118.

2 Grant T. Hammond, 'The Essential Boyd', unpublished paper. Online. Available at: www.belisarius.com (Accessed 4 June 2000), p. 8.

3 In the essay Boyd frequently inserts a number that refers to the number of a book listed in the bibliography attached to *Destruction and Creation*, and indicates the

source for a particular insight. For clarity, here both the number and the works referred to are given. The entire bibliography can be found in Annex A. The sources Boyd refers to here are books number 11: Nicholas Georgescu-Roegen, *The Entropy Law and the Economic Process*; and 13: Robert Heilbronner, *An Inquiry into the Human Prospect*.

4   Ibid.

5   Here Boyd refers to sources 28: Michael Polanyi, *Knowing and Being;* and 24: Alex F. Osborne, *Applied Imagination.*

6   Boyd refers to Osborne again.

7   Again Boyd refers to Polanyi.

8   Here Boyd refers to sources 14 and 15: two works of Werner Heisenberg: *Physics and Philosophy*, and *Across the Frontiers.*

9   Boyd refers to source 27: Jean Piaget, *Structuralism*; as well as to both works of Heisenberg listed above.

10 Besides the two works of Heisenberg, Boyd here refers to source 19: Thomas Kuhn, *The Structure of Scientific Revolutions.*

11 This description of the dynamics of normal science Boyd derived from Kuhn.

12 Ibid.

13 Ibid.

14 Ibid.

15 Boyd refers to sources 12: Kurt Gödel, *On Formally Undecidable Propositions of the Principia Mathematica and Related Systems*, pages 3–38, 'The Undecidable'; and 23: Ernest Nagel and James Newman, *Gödel's Proof.*

16 Boyd derived this insight from sources 29: Jagjit Singh, *Great Ideas of Modern Mathematics*; and 27: Jean Piaget, *Structuralism.*

17 Ibid.

18 Boyd refers to source 14 again (Heisenberg (1962)); and source 9: George Gamow, *Thirty Years That Shook Physics.*

19 Gamow is referred to again.

20 Here Boyd refers to source 3: Spencer Brown: *Laws of Form.*

21 Gamow.

22 Heisenberg (1962).

23 Brown.

24 For this introduction to thermodynamics Boyd consulted Georgescu-Roegen and source 20: David Layzer, 'The Arrow of Time', an article in *Scientific American* of December 1975.

25 Layzer is referred to as the source.

26 Ibid.

27 As before, these are Boyd's own words.

28 Here Boyd refers to sources 27: Jean Piaget, *Structuralism*; and 28: Michael Polanyi, *Knowing and Being.*

29 *Patterns of Conflict*, p. 2, underlining as in original. Where used in the following chapters, underlining directly follows Boyd's text.

30 Ibid., p. 5.

31 Ibid., p. 7.

32 Ibid., p. 10. In the essay Boyd shows an awareness that various other survival strategies exist. Cooperation as the optimal mode for long-term survival often overrides the short-term strategy of direct conflict. Interestingly, Darwin actually stated that 'it's not the strongest who survive, but those most responsive to change', a message Boyd would strongly agree with. Survival is the consequence of differences in fitness, resulting in greater reproduction, along with persistent variation in heritable traits that make for fitness differences. See Robert Brandon and Alex Rosenberg, 'Philosophy of Biology', in Peter Clark and Katherine Hawley, *Philosophy of Science Today*, Oxford: Oxford University Press, 2003, in particular pp. 167–75.

33 Ibid., p. 11.

34 Ibid., p. 12.

35 This refers to the use of 'the orthodox and the unorthodox' methods of employing troops, as discussed in Chapter 3.

36 Ibid., p. 16.

37 Ibid., pp. 19, 24.

38 Ibid., p. 24.

39 Ibid., p. 25.

40 Ibid., pp. 27–8.

41 Ibid., p. 28.

42 Ibid., p. 31.

43 Ibid., pp. 30–1.

44 Ibid., pp. 33–4 for the following section.

45 Ibid., p. 31. Here he obviously followed the contentious views of Liddell Hart, Lawrence and Fuller. As Azar Gat makes clear, Liddell Hart too made the mistake of missing the points that (1) the allied forces learned during the protracted wars against Napoleon and (2) that the blatant aggression led to their adoption of several tactical and stragical methods of Napoleon, including mass mobilization. So Napoleon's failure cannot be attributed to his tactical concepts. See Azar Gat, *Fascist and Liberal Visions of War, Fuller, Liddell Hart, and other Modernists*, Oxford: Clarendon Press, 1998, p. 165.

46 Ibid., p. 40.

47 Ibid., p. 41. Clausewitz actually mentions several other centers of gravity as well. It can be an alliance, a capital, a political leader, and other 'focal' points of power. See for a detailed recent corrective Antulio Echevarria II, *Clausewitz's Center of Gravity: Changing Our Warfighting Doctrine-Again*, Carlisle Barracks, PA: Strategic Studies Institute, 2002.

48 Ibid., p. 42.

49 Ibid., pp. 44–5.

50 Ibid., p. 46.

51 Ibid., p. 48.

52 Ibid., p. 49.

53 Ibid. Like Fuller in *The Conduct of War*, after this slide Boyd makes a brief excursion to Marxist revolutionary thought, noticing, however, that at this point in his presentation it is not clear how revolutionary strategy and guerrilla tactics fit in his argument, and he tells his audience that this will become evident after his discussion of World War I.

54 Ibid., p. 55.

55 As Azar Gat has recently convincingly argued, and as Michael Howard did before him, there certainly were genuine efforts to counter the increased lethality of the battlefield. See Azar Gat, *The Development of Military Thought: The Nineteenth Century*, Oxford: Clarendon Press, 1992, in particular Chapter 3, and Michael Howard, 'The Influence of Clausewitz', in Karl von Clausewitz, *On War*, (transl.), Princeton: Princeton University Press, 1976. For the German efforts in this vein, and a similar corrective message, see Antulio J. Echevarria II, *After Clausewitz, German Military Thinkers Before the Great War*, Lawrence: University Press of Kansas, 2000.

56 Ibid., p. 57.

57 Ibid., p. 59.

58 Ibid., p. 60.

59 Ibid., p. 62.

60 Ibid., p. 63.

61 Ibid., p. 62.

62 Ibid., p. 65.

63 Ibid., p. 64.
64 Interestingly, in selecting these concepts Boyd ignored developments some consider also of prime importance such as the development of (strategic) air power theory (with well known names such as Guilio Douhet and Billy Mitchell) or the introduction of carriers which transformed the face of sea power.
65 Ibid., p. 66.
66 Ibid., pp. 67–8.
67 Ibid., p. 69.
68 Ibid., p. 70.
69 Ibid.
70 Ibid., p. 71.
71 Ibid., p. 72.
72 Ibid. Note the use of the term 'organism'.
73 Ibid., p. 74.
74 Ibid.
75 Ibid., p. 76.
76 Ibid., p. 78.
77 Ibid. Note how Boyd quietly moves to a higher level of abstraction when he asserts that the Schwerpunkt helps in establishing an advantage in adaptability.
78 Ibid., p. 79.
79 Ibid.
80 Ibid., p. 86.
81 Ibid., p. 87.
82 Ibid.
83 See p. 89.
84 Ibid., p. 88.
85 Ibid., p. 90.
86 Ibid.
87 Ibid., p. 91.
88 Ibid., p. 93.
89 Ibid., p. 94.
90 Ibid., p. 95.
91 Ibid., p. 96.
92 Ibid., p. 98.
93 Ibid., p. 101.
94 Ibid., p. 99.
95 Ibid., pp. 104–6.
96 Ibid., p. 105.
97 Ibid., pp. 107–8.
98 Ibid., p. 111.
99 Ibid., p. 113.
100 Ibid., p. 112. Notice the specific Cold War and post-Vietnam era elements.
101 Ibid., p. 114.
102 Ibid., p. 115.
103 Ibid., p. 117.
104 Ibid., p. 119.
105 Ibid., p. 120.
106 Ibid., p. 121.
107 Ibid., p. 124.
108 Ibid., p. 125.
109 Ibid., p. 128.
110 Ibid., p. 128.
111 Ibid., p. 129.
112 Ibid., p. 130.

113 Ibid., p. 131.
114 Ibid., p. 132.
115 Ibid., p. 133.
116 Ibid., p. 134.
117 Ibid., pp. 135–6.
118 Ibid., p. 137.
119 Ibid.
120 Ibid., pp. 138–9.
121 Ibid., p. 140.
122 Ibid., p. 141.
123 Ibid., p. 142.
124 Ibid., p. 143.
125 Ibid., p. 148.
126 Ibid.
127 Ibid., p. 149.
128 Ibid., p. 150.
129 Ibid., p. 151. This strongly suggests there is more than only 'OODA looping faster' than the opponent.
130 Ibid.
131 Ibid., p. 152.
132 Ibid., pp. 152–3.
133 Ibid., p. 156.
134 Ibid., p. 174.
135 Ibid., p. 175.
136 Ibid., p. 176.
137 Ibid., p. 177.
138 Ibid., p. 178.
139 Ibid., p. 184.

6 Exploration and refinement

1 Various sources have already been mentioned in footnotes in the previous chapter. Here it is worthwhile to note the following works that appear in Boyd's bibliography: David Downing, *The Devil's Virtuosos: German Generals at War 1940–1945* (1977); T.N. Dupuy, *The Military Life of Genghis, Khan of Khans* (1969) and *A Genius for War* (1977); J.F.C. Fuller, *Grant ands Lee*, (1932); Richard Gabriel and Paul Savage, *Crisis in Command* (1978); Richard Gabriel and Reuven Gal, 'The IDF Officer: Linchpin in Unit Cohesion', *Army* (January 1984); John Gardner, *Morale* (1978); Simon Goodenough and Len Deighton, *Tactical Genius in Battle* (1979); Heinz Guderian, *Panzer Leader* (1952); Richard Humble, *Hitler's Generals* (1974); Albert Kesselring, *Manual for Command and Combat Employment of Smaller Units* (1952); Harold Lamb, *Genghis Khan* (1927); Kenneth Macksey, *Guderian, Creator of the Blitzkrieg* (1976); S.L.A. Marshall, *Men Against Fire* (1947); Erwin Rommel, *Infantry Attacks* (1937); Charles Whiting, *Patton* (1970); and importantly, Martin van Creveld, *Command in War* (1982). Boyd's C2 concept is one among many but he does not dwell on alternatives. See for a discussion of six different command arrangements for instance Chapter 6 of David Alberts and Richard E. Heyes, *Command Arrangements for Peace Operations*, Washington, D.C.: US Department of Defense, CCRP publications, 1995.
2 'Organic design for Command and Control', p. 2.
3 Ibid. It is not difficult to see the influence of *The Tacit Dimension* in this.
4 Ibid., p. 3.
5 Ibid., p. 4.
6 Ibid., pp. 7–8.

7 Ibid., p. 8.
8 Ibid., p. 9.
9 Ibid., p. 10.
10 Ibid.
11 Ibid., p. 11.
12 Ibid., p. 15.
13 Ibid., p. 16.
14 Ibid.
15 Ibid., p. 17.
16 Ibid., p. 18.
17 Ibid., p. 19.
18 Ibid., p. 20.
19 Ibid.
20 Ibid., p. 21.
21 Ibid., p. 22.
22 Ibid., p. 23.
23 Ibid., p. 24.
24 Ibid., p. 25.
25 Ibid., p. 26.
26 Ibid., p. 28.
27 Ibid., p. 30.
28 Ibid., p. 29.
29 Ibid., p. 31.
30 Ibid., p. 32.
31 Ibid., p. 35.
32 Ibid., p. 34.
33 Ibid., p. 37. The definitions of command and control are here contrasted deliberately against those of understanding, monitoring, appreciation and leadership. Boyd actually listed them together in one sequence.
34 Ibid., p. 36.
35 *Strategic Game of ? and ?*, p. 1.
36 The 'approach' Boyd takes in this presentation and described here is on p. 4.
37 Ibid., p. 3.
38 Ibid., p. 6.
39 Ibid., pp. 7–9.
40 Ibid., p. 10.
41 Ibid., p. 12.
42 Ibid., p. 14.
43 Ibid., p. 15.
44 Ibid., p. 16. Quotations are presented here as in the presentation.
45 Ibid., p. 17. Erie was Boyd's former hometown.
46 Ibid., pp. 18–19.
47 Ibid., p. 20.
48 Ibid., p. 21.
49 Ibid., p. 22.
50 Ibid., p. 23.
51 Ibid., p. 24.
52 Ibid., p. 25.
53 Ibid., p. 28.
54 Ibid., p. 29. Italics are mine.
55 Ibid., p. 30.
56 Ibid., p. 33. Italics are mine.
57 Ibid., p. 34.
58 Ibid., p. 35.

59 Ibid., p. 36.
60 Ibid., p. 37.
61 Ibid., p. 46.
62 Ibid., p. 38.
63 Ibid., p. 39.
64 Ibid., pp. 40–3.
65 Ibid., p. 44.
66 Ibid., p. 45.
67 Ibid., p. 46.
68 Ibid., p. 47.
69 Ibid., p. 48.
70 Ibid., p. 49.
71 Ibid., p. 50.
72 Ibid., p. 51.
73 Ibid., p. 54.
74 Ibid., p. 55.
75 Ibid., p. 56.
76 Ibid., p. 57.
77 Ibid., p. 58.
78 Michael Polanyi, *Knowing and Being*, London: Routledge and Kegan Paul, p. 70.
79 Ibid., p. 177.
80 Boyd, *The Conceptual Spiral*, p. 2.
81 Ibid., p. 4.
82 Ibid., p. 5.
83 Ibid., pp. 9–12.
84 Ibid., p. 14. The next section almost literally follows Boyd's text on p. 14.
85 Ibid., p. 16.
86 Ibid., p. 17.
87 Ibid., p. 18.
88 Ibid., p. 19.
89 Ibid., p. 20.
90 Ibid., p. 21.
91 Ibid., p. 22.
92 Ibid., p. 23.
93 Ibid., p. 24.
94 Ibid., p. 25.
95 Ibid., p. 26, italics are mine.
96 Ibid., p. 27.
97 Ibid., p. 28.
98 Ibid., p. 29.
99 Ibid., p. 30.
100 Ibid., p. 31.
101 Ibid., p. 32.
102 Ibid., p. 33.
103 Ibid., p. 34.
104 Ibid., p. 35.
105 Ibid., p. 36.
106 Ibid., p. 37.
107 Ibid., p. 38.
108 Grant T. Hammond, *The Mind of War, John Boyd and American Security*, Washington, D.C.: Smithsonian Institution Press, 2001, p. 188.
109 Robert Polk, 'A Critique of the Boyd Theory – Is it Relevant to the Army?', *Defense Analysis*, Vol. 16, No. 3, 2000, p. 259.
110 Grant T. Hammond, *The Essence of Winning and Losing*, op. cit., p. 2.

111 Ibid., p. 4.
112 Ibid., p. 5.

7 Completing the loop

1 Cited in Abraham Kaplan, *The Conduct of Scientific Inquiry*, San Francisco: Chandler Publishing, 1964, p. 303.
2 James N. Rosenau, *The Scientific Study of Foreign Policy*, New York: The Free Press, 2nd edition, 1980, p. 26.
3 Jay Luvaas, 'Clausewitz: Fuller and Liddell Hart', *Journal of Strategic Studies*, 9 (1986), p. 207.
4 In *Introduction to Strategy*, London: Preager, 1965, on p. 45 and p. 136 Beaufre for instance states that 'strategy must be a continuous process of original thinking, based upon hypotheses which must be proved true or false as action proceeds'. Furthermore Beaufre recognizes that initiative and freedom of action are essential (p. 36).
5 John Baylis, James Wirtz, Eliot Cohen, Colin Gray, *Strategy in the Contemporary World*, Oxford: Oxford University Press, 2002, p. 338.
6 See for instance Charles C. Moskos and James Burk, 'The Postmodern Military', in James Burk, *The Military in New Times*, Boulder, CO: Westview Press, 1994, pp. 142–4. Christopher Dandeker notes similar changes, but prefers the term 'late-modernity'.
7 Christopher Dandeker, 'A Farewell to Arms? The Military and the Nation-State in a Changing World', in Moskos and Burk, op. cit., pp. 128.
8 See for instance Andrew Latham, 'Warfare Transformed: A Braudelian Perspective on the "Revolution in Military Affairs"', *European Journal of International Relations*, Vol. 8 (2) (June 2002), pp. 231–66; Colin McInnes, *Spectator-Sport Warfare, The West and Contemporary Conflict*, Boulder, CO: Lynne Rienner, 2002; Zeev Maoz and Azar Gat (eds), *War in a Changing World*, Ann Arbor: The University of Michigan Press, 2001, in particular Edward Luttwak, 'Blood and Computers: The Crisis of Classic Military Power in Advanced Postindustrialist Societies and the Scope of Technological Remedies', and Azar Gat, 'Isolationism, Appeasement, Containment, and Limited War: Western Strategic Policy from the Modern to the "Postmodern" Era'.
9 Christopher Coker, *Humane Warfare*, London: Routledge, 2001, pp. 2–5. See also Martin Shaw, 'The Development of "Common-Risk" Society: A Theoretical View', in Jurgen Kulman and Jean Callaghan (eds), *Military and Society in 21st Century Europe*, Garmisch-Partenkirchen: George C. Marshall Center for Security Studies, 2000, especially pp. 15–19. He liberally refers to postmodern theorists such as Giddens and Bauman. See also Robert Cooper, *The Post-Modern State*, London: Demos, The Foreign Policy Centre, 1996 for use of similar typology.
10 Chris Hables Gray, *Postmodern War, the New Politics of Conflict*, London: Routledge, 1997, pp. 21–2. For a critique see Errol A. Henderson and J. David Singer, '"New Wars" and rumours of "New War"', *International Interactions*, 28: 2002, p. 165.
11 Ibid., pp. 38–40
12 Ibid., p. 81.
13 Ken Booth, Meyer Kestnbaum and David Segal, 'Are Post-Cold War Militaries Postmodern?', *Armed Forces & Society*, Vol. 27, No. 3 (Spring 2001), pp. 333–4.
14 Michael Ignatieff, *Virtual War: Kosovo and Beyond*, London: Penguin, 2000; Colin McInnes (2002), op. cit.
15 Booth, Kestnbaum and Segal, op. cit., p. 335. Emphasis is mine.
16 Alvin and Heidi Toffler, *War and Anti-War, Survival at the Dawn of the 21st Century* (New York: Little Brown & Company, 1993, p. 81.
17 See for instance John Warden, 'The Enemy as a System', *Airpower Journal*, No. 9 (Spring 1995), pp. 40–55.

18 Zalmay M. Khalizad and John P. White (eds), *Strategic Appraisal: The Changing Role of Information in Warfare*, Santa Monica: RAND, 1999.

19 This section is derived from Frans Osinga and Rob de Wijk, 'The Emergence of the Post-Modern Warform: Assessing a Decade of Changes in Military Affairs', in Alfred van Staden, Jan Rood and Hans Labohm (eds), *Cannon and Canons, Clingendael Views of Global and Regional Politics*, Assen: Royal van Gorcum, 2003; and from a series of articles on Network Centric Warfare, see Frans Osinga: 'Netwerkend de oorlog in? Network Centric Warfare en de Europese militaire transformatie', Deel I, *Militaire Spectator*, JRG 172, 7/8–2003, pp. 386–99; and Frans Osinga, 'Netwerkend de oorlog in? NCW als product van de revolutie', Deel II, *Militaire Spectator*, JRG 172, 9–2003, pp. 433–45.

20 Charles C. Moskos, John Allen Williams and David R. Segal (eds), *The Postmodern Military, Armed Forces after the Cold War*, Oxford: Oxford University Press, 2000, p. 5.

21 McInnes (2002), op. cit., p. 139.

22 This is not the place to discuss the merits of the RMA thesis. Several critical studies have been published that argue that there either is no RMA, it is irrelevant because it is only due to technical developments, or its effects are only very temporary in light of the enduring complexity of war. See for instance MacGregor Knox and Williamson Murray, *The Dynamics of Military Revolution 1300–2050*, Cambridge: 2001; and Colin S. Gray, *Strategy for Chaos: Revolutions in Military Affairs and the Evidence of History*, Portland: Frank Cass, 2002.

23 Andrew Marshall, Testimony before the senate Armed Services Committee, subcommittee on Acquisition and Technology, 5 May 1995. See for an early study also Andrew Krepinevich, 'From Cavalry to Computer', *The National Interest*, No. 37 (Fall 1994), pp. 30–42.

24 Eliot Cohen, 'A Revolution in Warfare', *Foreign Affairs*, Vol. 75, No. 2 (1996), p. 54.

25 Ibid., p. 37.

26 Andrew Latham, 'Re-Imagining Warfare', in Craig Snyder, op. cit., p. 219.

27 Ibid., p. 239.

28 John Arquilla and David Ronfeldt, 'Cyberwar is Coming', *Comparative Strategy*, Vol. 12, No. 2 (1993), p. 141. They elaborated on these ideas in an edited volume of studies on information war. See John Arquilla and David Ronfledt (eds), *In Athena's Camp, Preparing for Conflict in the Information Age*, Santa Monica: RAND, 1997. This volume includes the article 'Cyberwar is Coming'.

29 Ibid., p. 146.

30 Ibid., p. 144.

31 Ibid.

32 Ibid., p. 143.

33 Ibid., p. 144.

34 Ibid., p. 152.

35 John Arquilla and David Ronfeldt, 'Emerging Modes of Conflict', *Comparative Strategy*, Vol. 12, No. 4 (1993), p. 158.

36 John Arquilla and David Ronfeldt, *Swarming and the Future of Conflict*, Santa Monica: RAND, 2000, pp. 21–3.

37 Ibid.

38 William S. Cohen, *Report of the Quadrennial Defense Review*, Washington, D.C.: U.S. Department of Defense, 1997, p. iv.

39 Joint Chiefs of Staff, *Joint Vision 2010*, Washington, D.C.: U.S. Department of Defense, 1997, p. 17. For a short description of *JV2010* see Major-General Charles Link, '21st Century Armed Forces – Joint Vision 2010', *Joint Forces Quarterly*, Autumn 1996, pp. 69–73.

40 Second Annual Report of the Army After Next Project, Headquarters US Army Training and Doctrine Command, Fort Monroe, Virginia, 7 December, 1998, pp. 11–13.

41 Cited in Christopher Coker, *The Future of War*, Oxford: Blackwell Publishing, 2004, p. 41.
42 David Alberts, *Information Age Transformation, Getting to a 21st Century Military*, Washington, D.C.: Department of Defence, CCRP publications, June 2002, p. 18.
43 Ibid., p. 7.
44 David Gompert, Richard Kugler and Martin Libicki, *Mind the Gap, Promoting a Transatlantic Revolution in Military Affairs*, Washington, D.C.: National Defence University Press, 1997, p. 4.
45 *DoD Report to Congress on NCW*, Washington, D.C.: Department of Defense, CCRP publications, July 2001, p. vii.
46 David S. Alberts, John J. Gartska, and Frederick P. Stein, *Network Centric Warfare*, Washington, D.C.: U.S. Department of Defense, CCRP publications, 1999, p. 90.
47 *DoD Report to Congress on NCW*, pp. 3–5 and 3–1.
48 Ibid., pp. 3–9 and 3–10.
49 These 'tenets' appear in several NCW publications. See *DOD Report to Congress*, p. i, v, or 3–10.
50 Steven Metz, *Armed Conflict in the 21st Century: The Information Revolution and Post-Modern Warfare*, Carlisle Barracks: US Army Strategic Studies Institute, April 2000, p. 24.
51 Ibid., p. 87.
52 See for instance David Alberts and Richard E. Hayes, *Command Arrangements for Peace Operations*, Washington, D.C.: U.S. Department of Defense, CCRP publications, 1995; David Alberts, John J. Gartska, Richard E. Hayes and David T. Signori, *Understanding Information Age Warfare*, Washington, D.C.: U.S. Department of Defense, CCRP publications, 2001; David Alberts and Richard E. Hayes, *Power to the Edge, Command and Control in the Information Age*, Washington, D.C.: U.S. Department of Defense, CCRP publications, 2003; and Simon R. Atkinson and James Moffat, *The Agile Organization*, Washington, D.C.: U.S. Department of Defense, CCRP publications, 2005.
53 See for a good empirical survey, for instance, Robert E. Harkavy and Stephanie G. Neuman, *Warfare in the Third World*, New York: Palgrave, 2001.
54 This is the contested but nevertheless pertinent argument that historians John Keegan, Martin van Creveld and some others make. See for a concise discussion and refutation Christopher Bassford, 'John Keegan and the Grand Tradition of Trashing Clausewitz', *War and History*, Vol. 1, No. 3 (November 1994). For a recent study in military cultures which highlights the alternatives to the western instrumentalist view of war, see for instance Christopher Coker, *Waging War Without Warriors, The Changing Culture of Military Conflict*, Boulder, CO: Lynne Rienner, 2003.
55 Kalevi J. Holsti, *The State, War, and the State of War*, Cambridge University Press, Cambridge, 1996, pp. 14, 15. Others too have described this type of conflict. See for instance Michael Ignatieff, *Blood and Belonging*, London: Vintage, 1994; and *The Warrior's Honor*, London: Vintage, 1999; or Robert D. Kaplan, *The Coming Anarchy*, New York: Vintage, 2001.
56 Holst, op. cit., p. 18.
57 Mary Kaldor, *New & Old Wars, Organized violence in a Global Era*, Cambridge: Polity, 1999.
58 Mary Kaldor, 'Introduction', in Mary Kaldor (ed.), *Global Insecurity*, London: Cassell/Pinter, 2000, pp. 5–6.
59 Ibid.
60 Kaldor, (1999), op. cit., p. 9.
61 Martin van Creveld, *The Transformation of War*, New York: The Free Press, 1991, p. 221.
62 Ibid., p. 202.
63 Holsti, op. cit., pp. 36–9.

64 Kaldor (2000), op. cit., p. 6.
65 Ralph Peters, 'The New Warrior Class', *Parameters*, Summer 1994, p. 16. See also his book *Fighting for the Future*, Mechanicsburg, PA: Stackpole Books, 1999.
66 Van Creveld, op. cit., pp. 142–3.
67 Ibid., p. 27.
68 See for instance Barry Posen, 'The War for Kosovo; Serbia's Political–Military Strategy', *International Security*, Vol. 24, No. 4 (2000), pp. 39–84; I. Arreguin-Toft, 'How the Weak Win; A Theory of Asymmetric Conflict', *International Security*, Vol. 26, No. 1 (2001), pp. 93–128; R.H. Robert Scales, 'Adaptive Enemies: Dealing With the Strategic Threat after 2010', *Strategic Review*, Vol. 27, No. 1 (1999), pp. 5–14; Steven Metz, 'Strategic Asymmetry', *Military Review*, July–August 2001, pp. 23–31, Stephen Biddle, 'The Past as Prologue: Assessing Theories of Future Warfare', *Security Studies*, 8, No. 1 (1998), pp. 1–74; Charles Dunlap, 'Technology: Recomplicating Moral Life for the Nation's Defenders', *Parameters*, Autumn 1999, pp. 24–53.
69 Qiao Liang and Wang Xiangsui, *Unrestricted Warfare*, Beijing: 1999, p. 156. For an overview of the debate on this topic and some notable studies, see also my chapter titled 'Asymmetric Warfare; Rediscovering the Essence of Strategy', in John Olson (ed.), *Asymmetric Warfare*, Oslo: 2002.
70 See John Lynn, *Battle, A History of Combat and Culture*, Boulder, CO: 2003, Westview Press, in particular the Epilogue; Christopher Coker, *Waging War Without Warriors*, London: IISS, 2002; and Phillip Bobbit, *The Shield of Achilles*, London: Penguin, 2002, in particular Prologue and Chapters 10–13; and any of the articles by Ralph Peters, for instance 'The New Warrior Class', *Parameters*, Summer 1994, pp. 16–26. For a lengthy rebuttal and an argument for continuity, see Colin Gray, 'Clausewitz, History, and the Future Strategic World', paper for a National Intelligence Council Workshop on 'The Changing Nature of Warfare', Washington, D.C., 25 May 2004. Online. Available at: www.cia.gov/NKIC_2020 (accessed 3 March 2005).
71 See William Lind, Keith Nightengale, John Schmitt, Joseph Sutton, Gary Wilson, 'The Changing Face of War: Into the Fourth Generation', *Marine Corps Gazette*, Oct. 1989, pp. 22–6. See for a restatement in 1994 of this idea Thomas X. Hammes, 'The Evolution of War: The Fourth Generation', *Marine Corps Gazette*, September 1994. This is a much simplified rendering of the argument.
72 See for instance Grant T. Hammond, 'The Paradoxes of War', *Joint Forces Quarterly*, Spring 1994, pp. 7–16; Thomas X. Hammes, *The Sling and the Stone*, St Paul, MN: Zenith Press, 2004; Gary Wilson, Greg Wilcox and Chet Richards, *Fourth Generation Warfare & OODA Loop Implications of the Iraqi Insurgency*, presentation, www.belisarius.com, site (accessed 5 January 2005); or Myke Cole, 'Confronting the 4th Generation Enemy', *Journal of Counterterrorism & Homeland Security*, Vol. 11, No. 4, pp. 22–4; or Tony Corn, 'World War IV As Fourth Generation Warfare', *Policy Review*, January 2006, for a small sampling of this strand of thought. For a timely balanced critical review of the 4GW school of thought, see the August 2005 issue of *Contemporary Security Policy*, Vol. 26, No. 2, dedicated to this topic.
73 See Miroslav Nincic and Joseph Lepgold (ed.), *Being Useful, Policy Relevance and International Relations Theory*, Ann Arbor: University of Michigan Press, 1998, pp. 25–6.
74 Colin S. Gray, *Modern Strategy*, Oxford: Oxford University Press, 1999, p. 91.
75 Richard Dawkins, *The Selfish Gene*, Oxford: Oxford University Press, 1999 [1976], p. xi.

Select bibliography

Adams, T.K., 'The Real Military Revolution', *Parameters*, Vol. 30, Autumn 2000, 54–65.

Addington, L.H., *The Patterns of War Since the Eighteenth Century*, Bloomington: Indiana University Press, 2nd edn, 1994.

Aguayo, R., *Dr. Deming, The American Who Taught the Japanese About Quality*, New York: Simon and Schuster, 1990.

Alberts, D.S., *Information Age Transformation, Getting to a 21st Century Military*, Washington, D.C.: Department of Defense, CCRP Publication Series, 2002.

Alberts, D.S. and Czerwinski, T.J., *Complexity, Global Politics, and National Security*, Washington, D.C: National Defense University Press, 1998.

Alberts, D.S. and Hayes, R.E., *Command Arrangements for Peace Operations*, Washington, D.C.: U.S. Department of Defense, CCRP publications, 1995.

Alberts, D.S. and Hayes, R.E., *Power to the Edge, Command and Control in the Information Age*, Washington, D.C.: US Department of Defense, CCRP Publication Series, 2003.

Alberts, D.S., Gartska, J.J., Hayes, R.E. and David A. Signori, *Understanding Information Age Warfare*, Washington, D.C.: US Department of Defense, CCRP Publication Series, 2001.

Alberts, D.S., Gartska, J.J. and Stein, F.P., *Network Centric Warfare, Developing and Leveraging Information Superiority*, Washington, D.C.: US Department of Defense, CCRP Publication Series, 2nd rev. edn, 2002.

Allardice, R.R., *One Half a Revolution in Orientation, implications for Decision Making*, Maxwell AFB, AL: Air University Press, 1998.

Ames, R. (transl), *Sun Tzu, The Art of Warfare*, New York: Ballantine Books, 1993.

Argyris, C. and Schon, D., *Organizational Learning: A Theory of Action Perspective*, Reading, MA: Addison-Wesley, 1978.

Arquilla, J. and Ronfeldt, D., 'Cyberwar is Coming', *Comparative Strategy*, Vol. 12, No. 2 (1993), 141–56.

Arquilla, J. and Ronfeldt, D., 'Emerging Modes of Conflict', *Comparative Strategy*, Vol. 12, No. 4 (1993).

Arquilla, J. and Ronfeldt, D. (eds), *In Athena's Camp, Preparing for Conflict in the Information Age*, Santa Monica: RAND, 1997.

Arquilla, J. and Ronfeldt, D., *Swarming and the Future of Conflict*, Santa Monica: RAND, 2000.

Arreguin-Toft, I., 'How the Weak Win: A Theory of Asymmetric Conflict', *International Security*, Vol. 26, No. 1 (2001), 93–128.

Ashby, W.R., *An Introduction to Cybernetics*, New York: John Wiley & Sons, 1956.

Atkeson, E., 'The Operational Level of War', *Military Review*, March 1987, 28–36.

Atkinson, S.R. and Moffat, J., *The Agile Organization*, Washington, D.C.: US Department of Defense, CCRP publications, 2005.

Avant, D., *Political Institutions and Military Change*, Ithaca: Cornell University Press, 1994.

Bartolomasi, P., 'The Realities and Challenges for Concepts and Capabilities in Joint Manoeuvre', *RUSI Journal*, August 2000, 8–14.

Bassford, C., 'John Keegan and the Grand Tradition of Trashing Clausewitz', *War and History*, Vol. 1, No. 3 (November 1994).

Bateson, G., *Mind and Nature, A Necessary Unity*, Cresskill, NJ: Hampton Press, 2002.

Baucom, D., 'Military Reform: An Idea Whose Time Has Come, *Air University Review*, January–March 1987. Online. Available at: www.airpower.maxwell.af.mil/airchronicles/aureview/1987/jan-mar87.html (accessed 27 May 2005).

Baylis, J., Booth, K., Garnett, J. and Williams, P., *Contemporary Strategy, Theories and Policies*, New York: Holmes and Meter, 1975.

Baylis, J., Wirtz, J., Cohen, E. and Gray, C.S., *Strategy in the Contemporary World*, Oxford: Oxford University Press, 2002.

Beaufre, A., *An Introduction to Strategy*, London: Praeger, 1963.

Beaumont, R., 'On the Wehrmacht Mystique', *Military Review*, January 1981, 44–56.

Beaumont, R., *War, Chaos and History*, Westport, CT: Praeger, 1994.

Beck, U., Giddens, A. and Lash, S., *Reflexive Modernization*, Stanford: Sage Publications, 1994.

Beckerman, L.P., *The Non-Linear Dynamics of War*, SAIC, 1999. Online. Available at: www.belisarius.com/modern_business_strategy/beckerman/non_linear.htm (accessed 27 April 1999).

Beinhocker, E.D., 'Robust Adaptive Strategies', *Sloan Management Review*, Spring 1999, 95–106.

Bernstein, S., Lebow, R.N., Stein, J.G. and Weber, S., 'God Gave Physics the Easy Problems: Adapting Social Science to an Unpredictable World', *European Journal of International Relations*, Vol. 6, No. 1 (2000), 43–76.

Bertalanffy, L. von, *General Systems Theory*, New York: George Braziller, 2nd edn, 1968.

Best, S. and Kellner, D., *Postmodern Theory*, New York: The Guilford Press, 1991.

Best, S. and Kellner, D., *The Postmodern Turn*, New York: The Guilford Press, 1997.

Betts, R.K., 'Conventional Strategy, New Critics, Old Choices', *International Security*, Vol. 7, No. 4 (Spring 1983), 140–62.

Betts, R.K., 'Should Strategic Studies Survive?', *World Politics*, Vol. 50, No. 1 (1997), 7–33.

Betts, R.K., 'Is Strategy an Illusion?', *International Security*, Vol. 25, No. 2 (Fall 2000), 5–50.

Beyerchen, A.D., 'Clausewitz, Nonlinearity and the Unpredictability of War', *International Security*, Vol. 17, No. 3 (Winter 1992), 59–90.

Biddle, S., 'The Past as Prologue: Assessing Theories of Future Warfare', *Security Studies*, Vol. 8, No. 1 (1998), 1–74.

Bieler, A. and David Morton, A., 'The Gordian Knot of Agency-Structure in International Relations: a Neo-Gramscian Perspective', *European Journal of International Relations*, Vol. 7, No. 1 (March 2001), 5–35.

Bobbit, P, *The Shield of Achilles*, London: Penguin, 2002.

Booth, B., Kestnbaum, M. and Segal, D.R., 'Are Post-Cold War Militaries Postmodern?', *Armed Forces & Society*, Vol. 27, No. 3 (Spring 2001), 319–342.

Borodzicz, E. and Haperen, K., van, 'Individual and Group Learning in Crisis Simulations', *Journal of Contingencies and Crisis Management*, Vol. 10, No. 3 (September 2002), 139–47.

Boyer, P.J., 'The New War Machine', *The New Yorker*, 30 June 2003, 55–71.

Briggs, J. and Peat, F.D., *Turbulent Mirror, An Illustrated Guide to Chaos Theory and the Science of Wholeness*, New York: Harper and Row, 1989.

British Defence Doctrine, Joint Warfare Publication 0-01, London: Her Majesty's Stationery Office, 1997.

Brodie, B., *War and Politics*, New York: Macmillan, 1973.

Brodie, B., 'Strategy as an Art and a Science', *Naval War College Review*, Vol. 51, No. 1 (Winter 1998), 26–38.

Bronowski, J., *The Identity of Man*, New York: Prometheus Books edition, 2002 [1964].

Bronowski, J., *The Ascent of Man*, Boston: Little Brown & Company, 1973.

Brown, S.L. and Eisenhardt, K.M., *Competing on the Edge, Strategy as Structured Chaos*, Boston, Harvard Business School Press, 1998.

Burk, J., *The Military in New Times*, Boulder, CO: Westview Press, 1994.

Burton, J., *The Pentagon Wars: Reformers Challenge the Old Guard*, Annapolis, MD: Naval Institute Press, 1993.

Byrne, D., *Complexity Theory and the Social Sciences, An Introduction*, London: Routledge, 1998.

Capra, F., *The Turning Point*, New York: Bantam Books, 1982.

Capra, F., *The Tao of Physics: An Exploration of the Parallels Between Modern Physics and Eastern Mysticism*, Boston: Shambala, 3rd edn, 1991.

Capra, F., *The Web of Life, A New Understanding of Living Systems*, New York: Anchor Books, 1996.

Cebrowksi, A. and Gartska, J.J., 'Network Centric Warfare: Its Origin and Future', *Proceedings of the Naval Institute*, Vol. 124, No. 1 (January 1998), 28–35.

Cebrowski, A., 'President's notes', *Naval War College Review*, Vol. 52, No. 4 (Autumn, 1999).

Chalmers, A., *What is this thing called Science?*, Cambridge: Hackett, 3rd edn, 1999.

Chandler, D., *The Campaigns of Napoleon*, New York: Scribner, 1966.

Church, M., 'Organizing Simply for Complexity: Beyond Metaphor Towards Theory', *Long Range Planning*, Vol. 32, No. 4 (1999), 425–40.

Cilliers, P., *Complexity and Postmodernism*, London: Routledge, 1998.

Clausewitz, K. von, *On War* (trans. Michael Howard and Peter Paret), Princeton, NJ: Princeton University Press, 1976.

Cohen, E., 'A Revolution in Warfare', *Foreign Affairs*, Vol. 75, No. 2 (1996), 37–54.

Cohen, W.S., *Report of the Quadrennial Defense Review*, Washington, D.C.: US Department of Defense, 1997.

Coker, C., 'Post-modernity and the end of the Cold War: has war been disinvented?', *Review of International Studies*, Vol. 18 (1992), 189–98.

Coker, C., *Humane Warfare*, London: Routledge, 2001.

Coker, C., *Waging War Without Warriors, The Changing Culture of Military Conflict*, IISS, London: Oxford University Press, 2002.

Coker, C., *The Future of War*, Oxford: Blackwell Publishing, 2004.

Coleman, H., 'What Enables Self-Organizing Behavior in Businesses', *Emergence*, Vol. 1, No. 1 (1999), 33–48.

Conant, J.B., *Two Modes of Thought*, New York: Trident Press, 1964.

Coon, D., *Essentials of Psychology*, Pacific Grove, CA: Brookes/Cole, 7th edn, 1997.

Copeland, D.C., 'The Constructivist Challenge to Structural Realism', *International Security*, Vol. 25, No. 2 (Fall 2000), 187–212.

Coram, R., *Boyd, The Fighter Pilot Who Changed the Art of War*, Boston: Little Brown & Company, 2002.

Corbett, J.S., *Some Principles of Maritime Strategy*, Annapolis, MD: Naval Institute Press, 1988 [1911].

Coroalles, A., 'Maneuver to Win: A Realistic Alternative', *Military Review*, September 1981, 35–46.

Coveney, P. and Highfield, R., *The Arrow of Time*, London: Flamingo, 1991.

Coveney, P. and Highfield, R., *Frontiers of Complexity, The Search for Order in a Chaotic World*, New York: Ballantine Books, 1996.

Cowan, J., *From Fighter Pilot to Marine Corps Warfighting*. Online. Available at: www. defence-and-society.org/FCS_Folder/boyd_thesis.htm (accessed 14 August 2002).

Crane, C.C., *Avoiding Vietnam: The US Army's Response to Defeat in Southeast Asia*, US Army Carlisle Barracks: Strategic Studies Institute, 2002.

Creveld, M. van, *Command in War*, Boston: Harvard University Press, 1986.

Creveld, M. van, *The Transformation of War*, New York: The Free Press, 1991.

Croft, S. and Terriff, T. (eds), *Critical Reflections on Security and Change*, London: Frank Cass, 2000.

Czerwinski, T.J., 'Command and Control at the Crossroads', *Parameters*, Autumn 1996, 121–32.

Czerwinski, T.J., *Coping with the Bounds, Speculations on Nonlinearity in Military Affairs*, Washington, D.C.: National Defense University Press, 1999.

Danchev, A., 'Liddell Hart's Big Idea', *Review of International Studies*, Vol. 25, No. 1 (1999), 29–48.

Dark, K.R., *The Waves of Time*, London: Pinter, 1998.

Davies, P., *God and the New Physics*, London: Penguin Books, 1990.

Dawkins, R., *The Selfish Gene*, Oxford: Oxford University Press, 1989.

Dent, E.B., 'Complexity Science: A Worldview Shift', *Emergence*, Vol. 1, No. 4 (1999), 5–19.

Desch, M.C., 'Culture Clash, Assessing the Importance of Ideas in Security Studies', *International Security*, Vol. 23, No. 1 (Summer 1998), 141–70.

Deutsch, D., *The Fabric of Reality*, London: Penguin Books, 1998.

Downing, W.A., 'Firepower, Attrition, Maneuver, US Army Doctrine: A Challenge for the 1980s and Beyond', *Military Review*, January 1981, 64–73.

Dunlap, C., 'Technology: Recomplicating Moral Life for the Nation's Defenders, *Parameters*, Autumn 1999, 24–53.

Durham, S.E., *Chaos Theory For The Practical Military Mind*, Maxwell AFB, AL: Air University Press, 1997.

Duyvesteyn, I. and Angstrom, J. (eds), *Rethinking the Nature of War*, Abingdon: Frank Cass, 2005.

Echevarria, A.J., II, 'Auftragstaktik: in its Proper Perspective', *Military Review*, October 1986, 50–6.

Echevarria, A.J., II, *After Clausewitz, German Military Thinkers Before the First World War*, Lawrence: University Press of Kansas, 2000.

Echevarria, A.J., II, '"Reining in" the Center of Gravity Concept', *Air & Space Power Journal*, Vol. 17, No. 2 (Summer 2003), 87–96.

Echevarria, A.J., II, 'Deconstructing the Theory of Fourth Generation War', *Contemporary Security Policy*, Vol. 26, No. 2 (August 2005), 233–41.

Eve, R. Horsfall, S. and Lee, M. (eds), *Chaos, Complexity and Sociology, Myths, Models and Theories*, Thousand Oaks, CA: Sage Publications, 1997.

Faber, P., 'The Evolution of Airpower Theory in the United States', in John Olson (ed.), *Asymmetric Warfare*, Oslo: Royal Norwegian Air Force Academy, 2002.

Fadok, D.S., 'John Boyd and John Warden: Air Power's Quest for Strategic Paralysis', in Meilinger, P. (ed.), *The Paths to Heaven*, Maxwell AFB, AL: Air University Press, 1997.

Fallows, J., *National Defense*, New York: Random House, 1981.

Farrell, T., 'Constructivist Security Studies: Portrait of a Research Program', *International Studies Review*, Vol. 4, No. 1 (2002): 49–72.

Felker, E.J., *Airpower, Chaos and Infrastructure, Lords of the Rings*, Maxwell AFB, AL: Air University Press, 1998.

Franks, T., *American Soldier*, New York: Harper Collins, 2004.

Freedman, L., 'The First Two Generations of Nuclear Strategists', in Paret, P. (ed.), *Makers of Modern Strategy*, Princeton, NJ: Princeton University Press, 1986.

Freedman, L., 'The Third World War?', *Survival*, Vol. 43, No. 4 (Winter 2001–02), 61–88.

Freedman, L., 'War Evolves into the Fourth Generation: A Comment on Thomas X. Hammes', *Contemporary Security Policy*, Vol. 26, No. 2 (August 2005), 254–63.

Fromm, E., *The Crisis of Psychoanalysis*, Greenwich, CT: Fawcett Publications, 1970.

Fukuyama, F., *The Great Disruption, Human Nature and the Reconstitution of Social Order*, New York: Free Press, 1999.

Fuller, J.F.C., *The Foundations of the Science of War*, London: Hutchinson and Company, 1925.

Fuller, J.F.C, *The Conduct of War, 1789–1961*, New Brunswick, NJ: Da Capo Press edition 1992 [1961].

Fuller, S., 'Being There with Thomas Kuhn: A Parable for Postmodern Times', *History and Theory*, Vol. 31, No. 3 (October 1992), 241–75.

Gardner, H., *The Quest for Mind, Piaget, Lévi-Strauss and the Structuralism Movement*, Chicago: University of Chicago Press, 2nd edn, 1981 [1972]).

Gardner, H., *The Mind's New Science, A History of the Cognitive Revolution*, New York: Basic Books, 1985.

Garwin, D.A., *Learning in Action*, Boston, MA: Harvard Business School Press, 2000.

Gat, A., *The Origins of Military Thought*, Oxford: Clarendon Press, 1989.

Gat, A., *The Development of Military Thought: The Nineteenth Century*, Oxford: Clarendon Press, 1992.

Gat, A., *Fascist and Liberal Visions of War, Fuller, Liddell Hart, Douhet, and other Modernists*, Oxford: Clarendon Press, 1998.

Gat, A., *A History of Military Thought, From the Enlightenment to the Cold War*, Oxford: Oxford University Press, 2001.

Gat, A., 'Isolationism, Appeasement, Containment, and Limited War: Western Strategic Policy from the Modern to the "Postmodern" Era', in Maoz, Z. and Gat, A. (eds), *War in a Changing World*, Ann Arbor: The University of Michigan Press, 2001.

Geertz, C., *The Interpretation of Cultures*, New York: Basic Books, 1973.

Gell-Mann, M., *The Quark and the Jaguar, Adventures in the Simple and the Complex*, New York: Freeman & Company, 1994.

Ghysczy, T. von, Oetinger, B. von and Bassford, C., *Clausewitz on Strategy*, New York: John Wiley & Sons, 2001.

Giddens, A., *The Constitution of Society*, Cambridge: Polity, 1984.

Giddens, A., *The Consequences of Modernity*, Stanford: Stanford University Press, 1990.

Gjertsen, D., *Science and Philosophy, Past and Present*, London: Penguin Books, 1989.

Gleick, J., *Chaos, Making a New Science*, New York: Penguin Books, 1987.

Goleman, D., *Vital Lies, Simple Truths*, New York: Simon and Schuster, 1985.

Gompert, D., Kugler, R. and Libicki, M., *Mind the Gap, Promoting a Transatlantic Revolution in Military Affairs*, Washington, D.C: National Defense University Press, 1997.

Goodwin, B., *How the Leopard Changed Its Spots, The Evolution of Complexity*, New York: Charles Scribner's Sons, 1994.

Gray, C.H., *Postmodern War, the New Politics of Conflict*, London: Routledge, 1997.

Gray, C.S., *Explorations in Strategy*, Westport, CT: Greenwood Press, 1996.

Gray, C.S., *Modern Strategy*, Oxford: Oxford University Press, 1999.

Gray, C.S., *Strategy for Chaos, Revolutions in Military Affairs and the Evidence of History*, Portland: Frank Cass, 2002.

Guzzini, S., 'A Reconstruction of Constructivism in International Relations', *European Journal of International Relations*, Vol. 6, No. 2 (2000), 147–82.

Hall, E.T., *Beyond Culture*, New York: Anchor Books, 1977.

Hall, S., Held, D. and McGrew, T., *Modernity and its Futures*, Oxford: Polity Press, 1992.

Hallion, R., *Storm over Iraq, Air Power and the Gulf War*, Washington, D.C.: Smithsonian Institution Press, 1992.

Hallion, R., *Air Power Confronts An Unstable World*, London: Brassey's, 1997.

Ham, P. van, *European Integration and the Postmodern Condition*, London: Routledge, 2001.

Hamilton, M., 'Maneuver Warfare and All That', *Military Review*, January 1987, 3–10.

Hammes, T.X., *The Sling and the Stone*, St. Paul, MN: Zenith Press, 2004.

Hammond, G.T., 'The Paradoxes of War', *Joint Forces Quarterly*, Spring 1994, 7–16.

Hammond, G.T., *The Mind of War, John Boyd and American Security*, Washington, D.C.: Smithsonian Institution Press, 2001.

Harkavy, R.E. and Neuman, S.G., *Warfare in the Third World*, New York: Palgrave, 2001.

Heilbroner, R., *An Inquiry into The Human Prospect*, New York: W.W. Norton & Company, 1974.

Heisenberg, W., *Physics and Philosophy: The Revolution in Modern Science*, London: Penguin, 1990 [1960].

Henderson, E.A. and Singer, J.D., '"New Wars" and Rumors of "New War"', *International Interactions*, 28 (2002), 165–90.

Henley, L.D., 'The RMA After Next', *Parameters*, Winter 1999–2000, 46–57.

Herbert, N., *Quantum Reality, Beyond the New Physics*, New York: Anchor Books, 1987.

Holland, J., *Hidden Order, How Adaptation Builds Complexity*, Reading, MA: Perseus Books, 1995.

Holsti, K.J., *The State, War, and the State of War*, Cambridge: Cambridge University Press, 1996.

Hopf, T., 'The Promise of Constructivism in International Relations Theory', *International Security*, Vol. 23, No. 1 (Summer 1998), 171–200.

Horgan, J., *The End of Science*, New York: Broadway Books, 1996.

Hoyle, F., *Encounter with the Future*, New York: Simon and Schuster, 1965.

Hoyle, F., *The New Face of Science*, New York: World Publishing, 1971.

Hughes, D., 'Abuses of German Military History', *Military Review*, December 1986, 66–76.

Hughes, T., 'The Cult of the Quick', *Airpower Journal*, Vol. 15, No. 4 (Winter 2001), 57–68.

Ignatieff, M., *Virtual War: Kosovo and Beyond*, London: Penguin, 2000.

Imai, M., *Kaizen, the Key to Japan's Competitive Success*, New York: McGraw-Hill, 1986.

Jablonsky, D., *Roots of Strategy, Book 4*, Mechanicsburg, PA: Stackpole Books, 1999.

James, G.E., *Chaos Theory: The Essentials for Military Applications*, Newport RI: Naval War College Press, 1995.

Jantsch, E., *The Self-Organizing Universe, Scientific and Human Implications of the Emerging Paradigm of Evolution*, Oxford: Pergamon Press, 1980.

Jarvis, D., 'Postmodernism: A Critical Typology', *Politics and Society*, Vol. 26, No. 1 (March 1998), 95–142.

Jencks, C., *Post-Modernism, the New Classicism in Art and Architecture*, London: Academy Editions, 1987.

Jervis, R., 'Complexity and the analysis of Political and Social Life', *Political Science Quarterly*, Vol. 112, No. 4 (1997–98), 569–603.

Jervis, R., *System Effects, Complexity in Political and Social life*, Princeton, NJ: Princeton University Press, 1997.

Johnston, P., 'Doctrine is not Enough: the Effect of Doctrine on the Behavior of Armies', *Parameters*, Autumn 2000, 30–9.

Jones, A., 'The New FM 100–5: A View From the Ivory Tower', *Military Review*, February 1977, 27–36.

Jones, A., 'FM 100–5: A View From the Ivory Tower', *Military Review*, May 1984, 17–22.

Kaldor, M., *New & Old Wars, Organized Violence in a Global Era*, Cambridge: Polity Press, 1999.

Kaldor, M., (ed.), *Global Insecurity*, London: Cassell/Pinter, 2000.

Kaplan, R.D., *The Coming Anarchy*, New York: Vintage Books, 2000.

Katzenstein, P. (ed.), *The Culture of National Security, Norms and Identity in World Politics*, New York: Columbia University Press, 1996.

Katzenstein, P.J. and Okawara, N., 'Japan, Asian-Pacific Security, and the Case for Analytic Eclecticism', *International Security*, Vol. 26, No. 3 (Winter 2001/02), 153–85.

Kauffman, S., *The Origins of Order, Self-Organization and Selection in Evolution*, Oxford: Oxford University Press, 1993.

Kauffman, S., *At Home in the Universe, The Search for the Laws of Complexity*, London: Penguin Books, 1995.

Kelly, S. and Allison, M.A., *The Complexity Advantage, How the Sciences Can Help Your Business Achieve Peak Performance*, New York: McGraw-Hill, 1999.

Khalizad, Z.M. and White, J.P. (eds), *Strategic Appraisal: The Changing Role of Information in Warfare*, Santa Monica: RAND, 1999.

Kiel, L.D. and Elliott, E. (eds), *Chaos Theory in the Social Sciences, Foundations and Applications*, Ann Arbor: The University of Michigan Press, 1996.

Klein, B., *Strategic Studies and World Order: The Global Politics of Deterrence*, Cambridge: Cambridge University Press, 1994.

Kline, M., *Mathematics, The Loss of Certainty*, Oxford: Oxford University Press, 1980.

Knox, M. and Murray, W., *The Dynamics of Military Revolution 1300–2050*, Cambridge: Cambridge University Press, 2001.

Kober, A., 'Nomology vs Historicism: Formative Factors in Modern Military Thought', *Defense Analysis*, Vol. 10, No. 3 (1994), 267–84.

Krause, K. and Williams, M. (eds), *Critical Security Studies, Concepts and Cases*, London: University of Minnesota Press, 1997.

Krepinevich, A., *The Army and Vietnam*, Baltimore: Johns Hopkins University Press, 1986.

Krepinevich, A., 'From Cavalry to Computer', *The National Interest*, No 37 (Fall 1994), 30–42.

Krulak, C.C., 'Obituary', *Inside the Pentagon*, 13 March 1997.

Kuhn, T., *The Structure of Scientific Revolutions*, Chicago: University of Chicago Press, 1970.

Kulman, J. and Callaghan, J. (eds), *Military and Society in 21st Century Europe*, Garmisch-Partenkirchen: George C. Marshall Center for Security Studies, 2000.

Lambeth, B., *The Transformation of American Air Power*, Santa Monica: RAND, 2000.

Laqueur, W., 'Postmodern Terrorism', *Foreign Affairs*, September/October 1996, 24–36.

Laszlo, E., 'The Contribution of the System Sciences to the Humanities', *Systems Research and Behavioral Sciences*, Vol. 14, No. 1 (1997).

Latham, A., 'A Braudelian Perspective on the Revolution in Military Affairs', *European Journal of International Relations*, Vol. 8, No. 2 (June 2002), 231–66.

Lawrence, T.E., *The Seven Pillars of Wisdom*, Ware, Hertfordshire: Wordsworth Editions, 1997 [1927].

Lewin, R. and Regine, B., 'An Organic Approach to Management', *Perspective on Business Innovation*, Ernst & Young's *Perspectives in Business Innovation*, Issue 4 (January 2000), 19–26.

Liang, Q. and Xiangsui, W., *Unrestricted Warfare*, Bejing: PLA Literature and Arts Publishing House, 1999.

Liddell Hart, B., *Strategy: The Indirect Approach*, London: Faber & Faber Ltd, 1967.

Lind, W., 'Some Doctrinal Questions for the United States Army', *Military Review*, March 1977, 54–65.

Lind, W., 'Defining Maneuver Warfare for the Marine Corps', *Marine Corps Gazette*, March 1980, 55–8.

Lind, W., *Maneuver Warfare Handbook*, Boulder, CO: Westview Press, 1985.

Lind, W., 'The Three Levels of War, Don't Take John Boyd's Name in Vain', *Counterpunch*, 3 May 2003, Online at: www.counterpunch.org/lind05032003.html (accessed 16 December 2003).

Lind, W., Nightengale, K., Schmitt, J., Sutton, J. and Wilson, G.I., 'The Changing Face of War, Into the Fourth Generation', *Marine Corps Gazette*, October 1989, 22–6.

Link, C., '21st Century Armed Forces – Joint Vision 2010', *Joint Forces Quarterly*, Autumn 1996, 69–73.

Liotta, P.H., 'Chaos as Strategy', *Parameters*, Summer 2002, 47–56.

Lissack, M., 'Complexity: the Science, its Vocabulary, and its Relation to Organizations', *Emergence*, Vol. 1, No. 1 (1999), 110–26.

Lock-Pullan, R., '"An Inward Looking Time": The United States Army, 1973–1976', *The Journal of Military History*, Vol. 67, No. 2 (April 2003), 483–511.

Luttwak, E., 'The Operational Level of War', *International Security*, Vol. 5, No. 3 (Winter 1980/81), 61–79.

Luttwak, E., *Strategy, the Logic of War and Peace*, Cambridge, MA: Harvard University Press, 1987.

Luvaas, J., 'Military History: Is It Still Practicable?', *Parameters*, March 1982, 2–24.

Luvaas, J., 'Clausewitz: Fuller and Liddell Hart', *Journal of Strategic Studies*, 9 (1986), 197–212.

Lynne, J., *Battle, A History of Combat and Culture*, Boulder, CO: Westview Press, 2003.

Lyotard, J., *The Postmodern Condition*, Minneapolis: University of Minnesota Press, 11th printing, 1997 [1979, 1984].

Machamer, P. and Silberstein, M., *The Blackwell Guide to the Philosophy of Science*, Oxford: Blackwell Publishers, 2002.

Malik, J.M., 'The Evolution of Strategic Thought', in Snyder, G. (ed.), *Contemporary Security and Strategy*, London: Macmillan, 1999.

Maltz, M., *Psycho-Cybernetics*, Hollywood: Wilshire Book Company, 1971.

Mann, S.R., 'Chaos Theory and Strategic Thought', *Parameters*, Autumn 1992, 54–68.

Manwaring, M.G., *Internal Wars: Rethinking Problem and Response*, US Army Carlisle Barracks: Strategic Studies Institute, September 2001.

Maoz, Z. and Gat, A. (eds): *War in a Changing World*, Ann Arbor: The University of Michigan Press, 2001.

March, J.G. and Olson, J.P., 'The Uncertainty of the Past: Organizational Learning Under Ambiguity', *European Journal of Political Research*, Vol. 3 (1975), 147–71.

Mayr, E., *The Growth of Biological Thought*, Cambridge, MA: Harvard University Press, 1982.

McInnes, C., *Spectator-Sport Warfare, The West and Contemporary Conflict*, Boulder, CO: Lynne Rienner, 2002.

McKercher, B.J.C. and Henness, M.A., *The Operational Art, Developments in the Theories of War*, Westport, CT: Praeger, 1996.

McNeil, W., 'The Changing Shape of World History', *History and Theory*, Vol. 34, No. 2 (May 1995), 8–26.

McNeil, W., 'History and the Scientific Worldview', *History and Theory*, Vol. 37, No. 1 (February 1998), 1–13.

Mearsheimer, J., 'Maneuver, Mobile Defense, and the NATO Central Front', *International Security*, Vol. 6, No. 3 (Winter 1981/82), 104–22.

Mearsheimer, J., *Liddell Hart and the Weight of History*, New York: Ithaca, 1988.

Meilinger, P.S., *Ten Propositions Regarding Air Power*, Washington, D.C.: Air Force History and Museums Program, 1995.

Meilinger, P.S. (ed.), *The Paths to Heaven*, Maxwell AFB, AL: Air University Press, 1997.

Merry, U., *Coping with Uncertainty, Insights from the New Sciences of Chaos, Self-organization and Complexity*, Westport, CT: Praeger, 1995.

Mets, D.R., 'Boydmania, Review Essay', *Air & Space Power Journal*, September 2004, 98–108.

Metz, S., *Armed Conflict in the 21st Century: The Information Revolution and Post-Modern Warfare*, US Army Carlisle Barracks: Strategic Studies Institute, April 2000.

Metz, S., 'The Next Twist of the RMA', *Parameters*, Autumn 2000, 40–53.

Metz, S., 'Strategic Asymmetry', *Military Review*, July–August 2001, 23–31.

Miller, D., *A Pocket Popper*, Oxford: Fontana, 1983.

Minsky, M., *The Society of Mind*, New York: Simon and Schuster, 1986.

Mintzberg, H., Ahlstrand, B. and Lampel, J., *Strategy Safari, A Guided Tour Through the Wilds of Strategic Management*, New York: The Free Press, 1998.

Monod, J., *Chance and Necessity*, New York: Alfred A. Knopf, 1971.

Morgan, G., *Images of Organization*, New York: Sage, 1986.

Moskos, C.C., Williams, J.A. and Segal, D.R (eds), *The Postmodern Military, Armed Forces after the Cold War*, Oxford: Oxford University Press, 2000.

Murdock, P., 'Principles of War on the Network-Centric Battlefield: Mass and Economy of Force', *Parameters*, Spring 2002, 86–95.

Murray, W., Knox, M. and Bernstein, A., *The Making of Strategy, Rulers, States, and War*, Cambridge: Cambridge University Press, 1994.

Murray, W. and Millett, A.R., *Military Innovation in the Interwar Period*, Cambridge: Cambridge University Press, 1996.

Nagel, E. and Newman, J.R., *Gödel's Proof*, New York: New York University Press, 1974.

Naveh, S., *In Pursuit of Excellence, The Evolution of Operational Theory*, London: Frank Cass, 1997.

Nicholls, D. and Tagarev, T., 'What Does Chaos Theory Mean for Warfare?', *Aerospace Power Journal*, Fall 1994, 48–58.

Nicolis, G., *Introduction to Non-linear Science*, Cambridge: Cambridge University Press, 1995.

O'Connor, J. and McDermott, I., *The Art of Systems Thinking*, San Francisco, Thorsons Press, 1997.

O'Dowd, E. and Waldron, A., 'Sun Tzu for Strategists', *Comparative Strategy*, Vol. 10 (1991), 25–36.

Olson, J., *Asymmetric Warfare*, Oslo: Royal Norwegian Air Force Academy, 2002.

Oseth, J.M., 'FM 100–5 Revisited: A Need for Better "Foundations Concepts"?', *Military Review*, March 1980, 13–18.

Pagels, H., *The Cosmic Code, Quantum Physics as the Language of Nature*, New York: Simon and Schuster, 1982.

Paret, P. (ed.), *Makers of Modern Strategy*, Princeton, NJ: Princeton University Press, 1986.

Pascale, R., 'Surfing the Edge of Chaos', *Sloan Management Review*, Vol. 40, No. 3 (Spring 1999), 83–94.

Pearce, J.C., *The Crack in the Cosmic Egg: Challenging Constructs of Mind and Reality*, New York: Pocket Books, 1974.

Pearce, J.C., *Exploring the Crack in the Cosmic Egg: Split Minds and Meta-Realities*, New York: Pocket Books, 1975.

Pellegrini, R.P., *The Links Between Science and Philosophy and Military Theory, Understanding the Past; Implications for the Future*, Maxwell AFB, AL: Air University Press, 1997.

Pentland, P.A., *Center of Gravity Analysis and Chaos Theory*, Maxwell AFB, AL: Air University Press, 1993.

Perlmutter, A., 'Carl von Clausewitz, Enlightenment Philosopher: A Comparative Analysis', *The Journal of Strategic Studies*, Vol. 11, No. 12 (March 1988), 8–19.

Perrow, C., *Complex Organizations*, Glenview, IL: Scott, Foresman, 1972.

Perrow, C., *Normal Accidents*, Princeton: Princeton University Press, 1999 [1984].

Peters, R., 'The New Warrior Class', *Parameters*, Summer 1994, 16–26.

Peters, R., 'The Culture of Future Conflict', *Parameters*, Winter 1995–96, 59–69.

Peters, R., *Fighting for the Future*, Mechanicsburg, PA: Stackpole Books, 1999.

Pfaff, C.A., Chaos, 'Complexity and the Battlefield', *Military Review*, July–August 2000, 82–6.

Piaget, J., *Structuralism*, London: Routledge and Kegan Paul, 1971.

Pinker, S., *How the Mind Works*, New York: Norton & Company, 1997.

Plehn, M.T., '*Control Warfare: Inside The OODA Loop*', Maxwell AFB, AL: Air University Press, 2000.

Polanyi, M., *Knowing and Being*, London: Routledge and Kegan Paul, 1969.

Polk, Robert: 'A Critique of the Boyd Theory – Is it Relevant to the Army', *Defence Analysis*, Vol. 16, No. 3 (2000), 257–76.

Popper, K., *The Logic of Scientific Discovery*, New York: Routledge, 2000 [1968].

Popper, K., *Objective Knowledge*, Oxford: Oxford University Press, 1972.

Posen, B.R., *The Sources of Military Doctrine, France, Britain, and Germany Between the World Wars*, Ithaca: Cornell University Press, 1984.

Powe, M.B., 'The US Army After The Fall of Vietnam', *Military Review*, February 1976, 3–17.

Prigogine, I. and Stengers, I., *Order out of Chaos*, London: Bantam, 1984.

Prigogine, I., *The End of Certainty*, New York: The Free Press, 1996.

Richardson, K.A., Mathieson, G. and Cilliers, P., 'The Theory and Practice of Complexity Science: Epistemological Considerations for Military Operational Analysis', *Syste-Mexico*, 1 (2000), 25–66.

Richardson, K.A. and Cilliers, P., 'What is Complexity Science? A View from Different Directions', *Emergence*, Vol. 3, No. 1 (2001), 5–22.

Richardson, W., 'FM 100–5, The AirLand Battle in 1986', *Military Review*, March 1986, 4–11.

Rifkin, J., *Entropy, A New World View*, New York: The Viking Press, 1980.

Rifkin, J., *Time Wars, The Primary Conflict in Human History*, New York: Henry Holt & Co., 1987.

Rijpma, J., 'Complexity, Tight coupling, and Reliability Theory', *Journal of Contingencies and Crisis Management*, Vol. 5, No. 1 (March 1997), 15–23.

Rinaldi, S.M., *Beyond the Industrial Web, Economic Synergies and Targeting Methodologies*, Maxwell AFB, AL: Air University Press, 1995.

Rosen, S.P., *Winning the Next War, Innovation and the Modern Military*, Ithaca: Cornell University Press, 1991.

Rosenau, J.N., *Turbulence in World Politics*, New York: Harvester Wheatsheaf, 1990.

Rosenau, P., *Post-Modernism and the Social Sciences*, Princeton: Princeton University Press, 1992.

Russ, M. and Bacon, J., 'Organizational Extinction and Complex Systems', *Emergence*, Vol. 1, No. 4 (2000), 71–95.

Russo, J.E. and Schoemaker, P.J.H., *Winning Decisions*, New York: Doubleday, 2002.

Sanders, I., *Strategic Thinking and the New Science*, New York: The Free Press, 1998.

Saperstein, A., 'Chaos – A Model for the Outbreak of War', *Nature* 309, 303–5.

Sawyer, R.D. (trans.), *The Seven Military Classics of Ancient China*, Boulder, CO: Westview Press, 1993.

Sawyer, R.D. (trans.), *Sun Tzu, the Art of War*, New York: Barnes and Nobles, 1994.

Scales, R.H., 'Adaptive Enemies: Dealing With the Strategic Threat after 2010', *Strategic Review*, Vol. 27, No. 1 (1999), 5–14.

Senge, P., *The Fifth Discipline, The Art and Practice of The Learning Organization*, London: Doubleday, 1992.

Shermer, M., 'Exorcising Laplace's Demon: Chaos and Antichaos, History and Metahistory', *History and Theory*, Vol. 34, No. 1 (February 1995), 59–83.

Skinner, B.F., *Beyond Freedom and Dignity*, London: Jonathan Cape, 1972.

Smith, H., 'The womb of war: Clausewitz and international politics', *Review of International Studies*, 16 (1990), 39–58.

Snyder, G., (ed.), *Contemporary Security and Strategy*, London: Macmillan, 1999.

Stalk, G. and Hout, T.M., *Competing Against Time*, New York: The Free Press, 1990.

Starry, D.A., 'Tactical Evolution – FM 100–5', *Military Review*, August 1978, 2–11.

Stein, G., 'Information Warfare', *Airpower Journal*, No. 1 (Spring 1995), 30–9.

Steinbrunner, J.D., *The Cybernetic Theory of Decision*, Princeton, NJ: Princeton University Press, 1974.

Stewart, I., *Does God Play Dice, The Mathematics of Chaos*, Oxford: Basil Blackwell, 1989.

Storr, J., 'Neither Art Nor Science – Towards a Discipline of Warfare', *RUSI Journal*, April 2001, 39–45.

Sullivan, G.R. and Dublik, J.M., 'War in the Information Age', *Military Review*, April 1994, 46–62.

Sumida, J.T., *Inventing Grand Strategy and Teaching Command*, Washington, D.C.: The Woodrow Wilson Center Press, 1997.

Tanner, J.B., Lavrinovich, W.E. and Hall, S.R., 'Looking at Warfare Through a New Lens', *Marine Corps Gazette*, Vol. 82, No. 9 (September 1998), 59–61.

Toffler, A. and Toffler, H., *War and Anti-War, Survival at the Dawn of the 21st Century*, New York: Little Brown, 1993.

Uden, J. van, Richardson, K.A. and Cilliers, P., 'Postmodernism Revisited? Complexity Science and the Study of Organizations', *Tamara*, Vol. 1, No. 3 (2001), 53–7.

US Department of Defense, *Field Manual 100–5, Operations*, Washington, D.C., 1982.

US Department of Defense, *Joint Vision 2010*, Washington, D.C., 1996.

US Department of Defense, *Marine Corps Doctrinal Publication 1, Warfighting*, Washington, D.C., 1997.

US Department of Defense, *Report to Congress on NCW*, Washington, D.C., July 2001.

Vincent, G.A., 'In the Loop, Superiority in Command and Control', *Airpower Journal*, Summer 1992, 15–25.

Vincent, G.A., 'A New Approach to Command and Control, the Cybernetic Design', *Airpower Journal*, Summer 1993, 24–38.

Volberda, H.W. and Elfring, T., *Rethinking Strategy*, London: Sage Publications, 2001.

Waldrop, M., *Complexity: The Emerging Science at the Edge of Order and Chaos*, London: Viking, 1993.

Walt, S.M., 'The Search for a Science of Strategy', *International Security*, Vol. 12, No. 1 (Summer 1987), 140–65.

Walton, C.D., 'The Strategist in Context: Culture, the Development of Strategic Thought, and the Pursuit of Timeless Truth', *Comparative Strategy*, Vol. 23, No. 1 (2004), 93–9.

Warden, J.A., 'The Enemy as a System', *Airpower Journal*, Spring 1995, 40–55.

Wass de Czege, H. and Holder, L.D., 'The New FM 100–5', *Military Review*, July 1982, 24–35.

Wass de Czege, H., 'How to Change an Army', *Military Review*, November 1984, 32–49.

Watson, P., *A Terrible Beauty, The People and Ideas that Shaped the Modern Mind*, London: Phoenix Press, 2000.

Watts, B., *The Foundations of US Air Doctrine, the Problem of Friction in War*, Maxwell AFB, AL: Air University Press, 1984.

Watts, B., *Clausewitzian Friction and Future War*, Washington, D.C.: revised edition, National Defense University Press, 2000.

Weighley, R.F., *The American Way of War, A History of United States Military Strategy and Policy*, New York: Macmillan Publishing Co., 1973.

Wendt, A., 'Constructing International Politics', *International Security*, Vol. 20, No. 1 (1995), 71–81.

Wendt, A., 'Anarchy is what states make of it: The social construction of power politics', *International Organization*, Vol. 46, No. 2 (1992), 391–425.

Wendt, A., *Social Theory of International Politics*, Cambridge: Cambridge University Press, 1999.

Woodmansee, J., 'Blitzkrieg and the Airland Battle', *Military Review*, August 1984, 21–39.

Wylie, J.C., *Military Strategy: A General Theory of Power Control*, New Brunswick, NJ: Rutgers University Press, 1967.

Index

Boid's Slides

(T) SLIDE 20: STRATEGIC AIM, STRATEGY, TACTICS

(A) SLIDE 17: PATTERN FOR SUCCESSFUL OPERATIONS BY DOING SLIDE 18, 19

(E) OUR ENEMY, LIKE US, UNDERGOES A NATURAL PROCESS FOR

SURVIVAL — A PROCESS OF COMMUNICATION, INTERACTION, SYNTHESIS
AND ACTION